HIGH COURTS IN GLOBAL PERSPECTIVE

Constitutionalism and Democracy

GREGG IVERS AND KEVIN T. McGUIRE, EDITORS

High Courts in Global Perspective

Evidence, Methodologies, and Findings

Edited by Nuno Garoupa,
Rebecca D. Gill, and Lydia B. Tiede

University of Virginia Press
CHARLOTTESVILLE AND LONDON
University of Virginia Press

© 2021 by the Rector and Visitors of the University of Virginia
All rights reserved
Printed in the United States of America on acid-free paper

First published 2021

9 8 7 6 5 4 3 2 1

Library of Congress Cataloging-in-Publication Data

Names: Garoupa, Nuno, editor. | Gill, Rebecca D., editor. | Tiede, Lydia Brashear, editor.
Title: High courts in global perspective : evidence, methodologies, and findings / edited by Nuno Garoupa, Rebecca D. Gill, and Lydia B. Tiede.
Description: Charlottesville : University of Virginia Press, 2021. | Series: Constitutionalism and democracy | Includes bibliographical references and index.
Identifiers: LCCN 2021005716 (print) | LCCN 2021005717 (ebook) | ISBN 9780813946153 (hardcover) | ISBN 9780813946160 (epub)
Subjects: LCSH: Courts of last resort—Congresses. | Constitutional courts—Congresses. | Judicial process—Congresses. | Political questions and judicial power—Congresses.
Classification: LCC K2123 .F33 2018 (print) | LCC K2123 (ebook) | DDC 347/.035—dc23
LC record available at https://lccn.loc.gov/2021005716
LC ebook record available at https://lccn.loc.gov/2021005717

Cover art: World map, 1942. (P. J. Mode collection of persuasive cartography, #8548, Division of Rare and Manuscript Collections, Cornell University Library; Geographicus Rare Antique Maps, http://www.geographicus.com)

CONTENTS

ACKNOWLEDGMENTS

THIS PROJECT has benefited greatly from both individual and group efforts. The volume was originally conceived from draft papers, conversations, and commentary at the Workshop: Facilitating Empirical Studies of Judicial Behavior on Constitutional Courts from a Comparative Perspective (National Science Foundation Grant SES #1744299) held at the Texas A&M University School of Law, in Dallas from May 11–12, 2018. Over the two-day conference, authors presented their papers, which were followed by in-depth commentary and discussion by workshop participants. This volume benefited greatly from those scholars who participated in the conference and the lively debates that ensued regarding how best to approach the study of comparative high court behavior from an empirical perspective.

We would like to acknowledge and thank the following conference participants, without whom this volume would not have been possible: Susan Achury, Carolina Arlotta, Aylin Aydin-Cakir, Christine Bird, Tanya Bagashka, Bethany Blackstone, Dan Brinks, Clifford Carrubba, Chien-Chih Lin, Amanda Driscoll, Tao Dumas, Arthur Dyevre, Rhonda Evans, Joshua Fischman, Tom Ginsburg, Melinda Gann Hall, Chris Hanretty, Lori Hausegger, Alexander Hudson, Mark Hurwitz, Devon Jones, Vivian Kalu, Diana Kapiszewski, Lewis Kornhauser, Haimo Li, Dominique H. Lewis, Monica Lineberger, Felipe Lopes, Pedro Magalhães, Alison Merrill, Sunita Parikh, Rebecca Reid, Kristen Renberg, Julio Ríos-Figueroa, Russell Smyth, Jeff Staton, Maryam Stevenson, Jason Todd, Lee Walker, and Christopher Zorn. We also thank the authors of this volume, who put in countless hours writing their essays, which we believe form a substantial contribution to the field.

Finally, the project benefited greatly from comments received from anonymous reviewers and the support of Nadine Zimmerli, our editor at University of Virginia Press.

HIGH COURTS IN GLOBAL PERSPECTIVE

INTRODUCTION

SPECIALIZED CONSTITUTIONAL courts play a large and growing role in the review of both proposed and enacted laws. In recent years they have made decisions upholding or striking down some of the most controversial laws enacted in their jurisdictions. For example, the Portuguese Constitutional Court in 2012 invalidated many budget cuts previously negotiated with the International Money Fund. In 2017, the Spanish Constitutional Court found illegal a law that would allow a referendum for Catalonian independence, and the Supreme Court of the United Kingdom weighed in on Parliament's procedure for Brexit. In 2019, the Italian Constitutional Court ruled that assisted suicide is not always a crime, and the following year the German Constitutional Court challenged the European Central Bank's policies.

Similar developments abound outside the European context. The Colombian Constitutional Court upheld a constitutional amendment for President Uribe to be reelected to a subsequent term in 2005 but in 2010 found unconstitutional a law that convoked a referendum allowing him a third term in office. The Turkish Constitutional Court decided to ban one political party close to Kurdish movements in 2009. Chile's Constitutional Tribunal approved a law decriminalizing abortion when the pregnancy endangered a woman's life or was due to rape or an extreme fetal pathology. Taiwan's Supreme Court legalized same-sex marriage, while the Kenyan Supreme Court upheld colonial-era laws that criminalized homosexual acts. As these examples show, high courts around the world have been engaged in nearly all conceivable policy areas. These have ranged from domestic matters, such as health care, pensions, and education, to determining the constitutionality of national peace processes, the breadth of military power, and the validity of constitutional reforms that establish the broad structures of government.

These high courts are specially constructed to review the constitutionality of legislation and ultimately to regulate the boundaries of political institutions.[1] Besides ruling on important issues that face a nation, such as inequality, health care, and electoral processes, constitutional courts are thought to provide legitimacy to the lawmaking process (Stone Sweet 2000), to balance the interests of the elected branches (Landes and Posner 1975; Whittington 2005), and to protect underrepresented minority interests (Ely 1980). These functions are increasingly important in light of democratic backsliding in many countries (Ginsburg and Moustafa 2008; Scheppele 2018). At the same time, these courts may "judicialize politics" by inducing judges, rather than elected lawmakers, to make (or veto) laws (Shapiro 1980; Stone Sweet 2000; Garoupa and Ginsburg 2015).

Justification for the Book

Despite the rising importance of these courts, systematic and rigorous comparative studies are a relatively recent phenomenon (but see Ginsburg 2003; Alarie and Green 2017). Many of the extant studies employing various empirical methods focus only on one or a limited number of courts. The authors of the region-specific essays in this volume identify this as a recurring theme. From such singular studies of courts' and individual judges' behavior, however, we have learned that there is great diversity among national high courts. These courts differ in terms of their specific review powers, the manner in which judges are appointed, and the manner in which judicial review can be triggered (i.e., from referral from specific government actors to citizen complaints) (see Ríos-Figueroa 2011; Brinks and Blass 2017). Scholars propose that these and many additional factors may drive the behavior of high courts and their judges on specific courts. Whether these influences are generalizable to a larger cross-section of courts, however, remains an unanswered empirical question. Likewise, some of the extant studies analyze either individual judges' behavior or that of the court as a whole, but the linkages between these levels of analysis are underexplored. We argue that for some important research questions, it is necessary to develop theories that not only encompass comparative research, but also explain the relationship between individual judges' preferences and those of the collegial courts within which they work.

Through the course of creating this volume, we have found that there are very few studies that compare a large number of countries and courts. While there are multiple theories about judicial behavior, many of which have comparative implications or have been tested on a limited number of other jurisdictions, the scholarship on the behavior of high courts and judges is fragmented. To complicate matters, theories of judicial behavior not only fail to transcend a select sample of courts studied but often fail to cut across academic fields, adding to the disjointed nature of the analysis of high court judicial behavior. This is not to say that there is not rigorous work being done to explain behavior on individual courts or small samples, but rather, it is difficult to know whether the results from such studies travel outside their specific contexts. We, therefore, believe that the enterprise of comparative empirical work is sorely needed but requires testable hypotheses that cross borders, examine comparable data, and offer a deep understanding of the sociolegal contexts being analyzed.

With such challenges confronting comparative empirical research, scholars may ask, why bother. We believe that such comparative research, incorporating an understanding of both individual judges' and courts' behavior, is needed to assess a variety of pressing questions that cannot be answered with single- or limited-country studies. One persistent question is what constitutional and institutional design features allow constitutional judges and courts to fulfill their roles in checking other government actors, upholding nations' constitutions, protecting minority interests, and fortifying the legitimacy of institutions. Often, policymakers and foreign assistance providers have rushed to adopt constitutions and constitutional courts that have worked well in specific situations with little understanding or empirical evidence about whether these same institutions will travel well in other contexts.

An example of the need for such research can be found in post-Soviet Bulgaria. Following its democratic transition, a new constitutional court was created to check the powers of other elected actors, and the country adopted other Western-inspired reforms allowing the country to gain European Union member status. However, because reforms were transplanted from other systems with little acknowledgment of Bulgaria's prior and persistent Soviet-styled institutions, such as the powerful Procurator General, conflicts have arisen between the Procurator General and institutionally independent judges. This in turn has called into question whether incomplete reforms and a lack of acknowledgment of Soviet-styled institutions have inhibited the country's democratic development (see Bagashka and Tiede 2021). With rigorous comparative research, policymakers could be more informed about whether the situation in Bulgaria can be remedied and what paths may prove more successful for a host of countries that have also held onto some institutions existing prior to democratic transitions.

Comparative work can also help us better understand which features of constitutional courts garner the most public support for constitutional judges and courts and democratic institutions more generally, as well as in which specific sociopolitical contexts. This may be especially important when judges and courts are threatened with punishment from strong executives or legislatures, as seen in countries such as Venezuela, Hungary, Poland, and Pakistan, in which strong executives are threatening judges, removing them, or packing the courts. Comparative work also might suggest how constitutional courts and their judges can best cope with problems occurring in highly divided or polarized societies. While it has been suggested that certain inclusive appointment mechanisms may allow a court and its judges to represent more diverse interests, without comparative, empirical testing it is difficult to ascertain whether such inclusive rules do in fact alleviate the tensions of a divided society or under what conditions they may do so.

Furthermore, scholars studying one or just a few countries have developed theories about how and when judges and courts are more or less independent, assertive, or deferential to elected politicians. For example, McCubbins, Noll, and Weingast (1995, 2006) argue in reference to the US Supreme Court that courts are more assertive or independent under a fragmented government because the government is unable to coordinate actions to punish courts and judges. Similar arguments have been made by Iaryczower, Spiller, and Tommasi (2002) for Argentina's Supreme Court and by Scribner (2011) for the Chilean Supreme Court. While the fragmentation theory appears to explain a good deal of behavior in presidential regimes, Stone Sweet (2000) suggests that fragmented government may have the opposite effect in parliamentary systems where minority and coalition governments often must compromise on policy issues. Under such conditions, constitutional courts will be less likely to strike down the resulting laws because the laws themselves reflect the wide societal consensus on policy needed to create an enacting coalition. Scholarship by Herron and Randazzo (2003) on political fragmentation in Eastern European high courts seems to also suggest that fragmentation has no effect on Eastern European high courts declaring laws unconstitutional. Hilbink (2012) argues that fragmented government is neither a necessary nor sufficient condition for high court independence in a sample of presidential and parliamentary regimes that includes Costa Rica, France, Italy, India, Israel, Tanzania, Spain, and Chile.

The above patchwork of inconsistent results calls out for more cross-national work. As Vanberg (2015) points out, the assumptions that underlie fragmentation and other theories that explain how courts work in a single country might not hold in other governmental contexts. Questioning long-established theories for single-country studies is important for our knowledge of judicial behavior to move forward. However, without comparative research, it may be difficult to get any real purchase on the answers. As seen from just a few examples, comparative empirical work is needed to answer pressing issues related to governance and accountability. With comparative research, we can broaden our understanding of how judges and courts behave, asking more ambitious questions and developing generally applicable theories of how courts work in context.

FOCUS OF THE BOOK

We focus on the benefits of comparative judicial behavior work, but it would be naïve to think that the enterprise does not also involve some costly tradeoffs. First, comparative work, especially large-N studies, requires that researchers aggregate their data and lose much of the rich specificity found in their country- or court-level analyses. There is an inevitable degree of loss of institutional details. Second, as Driscoll suggests in the her essay, comparative work comes with significant barriers to entry, such as legal and country-level expertise, knowledge of formal and informal mechanisms inside and outside of courts, and in the case of judge-level behavioral analyses, detailed research to ascertain judges' individual attributes, characteristics, and preferences (see Driscoll, this volume). Third, comparative work cannot answer all questions that scholars and policymakers may have. As a result, the actual need or desire for comparative work depends acutely on whether the research questions themselves require such a framework.

Despite these challenges, understanding the behavior of judges and courts is paramount to understanding issues of institutional design and legitimacy and the ability of courts to weaken or fortify governance. Furthermore, comparative work may help determine what conditions are necessary for constitutional courts and judges to impact policy when deciding some of the most divisive issues facing society today. It is this urgent need to begin to be able to approach such important issues that we have taken on what seems to be a Sisyphean task. In this volume, our goals are modest. We attempt to introduce the study of comparative judicial behavior to scholars, students, and policymakers by providing a preliminary snapshot of the state of the field, with guidance in both theory-building and methods.

In short, through this volume, we propose to provide some preliminary answers to the following questions: How do we study courts comparatively? How does the extant literature on courts in specific regions inform comparative analyses? What are the costs and benefits of comparative analysis? And how might researchers overcome some of the barriers to entering a field of study that requires such immense levels of knowledge? While the volume looks to provide a discussion of the extant literature and its challenges, we hope this book is seen more broadly as a platform for diving into the challenging but fruitful study of comparative courts.

Understanding high court behavior is intrinsically a multidisciplinary endeavor. Political scientists have an important role both in the development of theories about judicial behavior as well as debating the consequences of behavior on politics. Economists, lawyers, sociologists, and other social scientists play a significant role in diversifying methods and implications. The fields of law and politics, law and economics, law and society, and empirical legal studies provide fundamental tools and perspectives to assist scholars in establishing a comprehensive view of high court behavior. Our book, both in the backgrounds of the authors and the approaches we take, reflects the multidisciplinary nature of the project.

The study of high court behavior relates to many areas of scholarship. The most immediate is scholarship on judicial behavior. For example, a recent edited volume by Howard and Randazzo (2018) looks at theory and methodology for studying judicial behavior in a very broad sense, focusing on courts at different levels of adjudication (mostly United States), not primarily at judicial behavior in constitutional or high courts as we do. An earlier edited book by Kapiezewski, Silverstein, and Kagan (2013) focuses on the roles of judges and courts in both politics and policy in new, restored, and established democracies. More specifically, this edited volume, uses rich descriptions to show the role that courts and judges play in "arenas of political contention," areas of conflict between new and old political regimes, different levels of government or power within a nation, between religious and secular values, as well as other areas of conflict. As such, this important edited volume emphasizes judicial behavior and courts (not just high courts as we do) with a more specific focus on qualitative methodologies (while we focus on quantitative or statistical approaches).

Another important area of scholarship that our book relates to is comparative constitutional law, an emerging field as described by Hirschl (2014). Empirical research is acknowledged by this author as an important methodology, although comparative institutional analysis and comparative case analysis are more typical approaches that scholars have taken in comparative constitutional law. Our book, instead, has a focus on the use of statistical methods to gain insight into the broader empirical realities of judicial behavior in the high court context. There is a clear growing use of statistical methods in comparative law (Spamann 2015) and in comparative constitutional law (Elkins, Ginsburg, and Melton 2009; Law and Versteeg 2012). Our book is related to this trend in the method but not necessarily in the particular objective. Unsurprisingly, high court behavior can be understood as an important area of research in both comparative law and comparative constitutional law. However, we are specifically interested in determinants of how judges and courts behave and decide and less in particular laws or procedures or in cross-country comparisons of constitutional rules.

There is also a large body of social science examining courts more generally. For example, scholars of authoritarianism look to courts as they seek to understand how autocracies function (for example, Ginsburg and Moustafa 2008; Scheppele 2018). Scholars of ethnic politics point to courts as places where bias and social control manifest (Posner 2005). Political economists are again trying to understand the role courts play in economic regulation and development (Djankov et al. 2003). All of these perspectives on courts are more focused on the general interaction of courts with salient social phenomena, including democratization and development, and less on specific determinants of judicial behavior.

PLAN OF THE BOOK

To provide a comprehensive perspective of comparative high court behavior, the book has three main themes: theory, region-specific studies, and methodology. These themes assist the reader in understanding the current state of the field and developing their own research agenda.

Theoretical Foundations of High Court Behavioralism

Scholars have developed different theories to explain the exercise of constitutional review. The early theories tended to focus on the study of the US Supreme Court, and later, on the American federal judiciary. These theories were not developed with a comparative intent. To bridge the gap, the opening essay by Kornhauser makes three fundamental contributions. First, Kornhauser places the most common theories of judicial behavior in context and critiques them. These early theories fall into three main camps: formalism, attitudinalism, and variations of agency theory, with the goal of explaining individual judges' behavior.

Kornhauser's second main contribution is to develop a strategy for linking individual judicial behavior to a court's overall decisions. A collegial court is not simply a sum of individual views but rather a particular institution with complex mechanisms that aggregate judicial preferences in a particular manner. It is possible to argue that the determinants of individual judicial behavior and collegial courts' decision-making are multiple. They include preferences but also rules and procedures (i.e., internal constraints), political context (i.e., external constraints), and legal tradition and models of decision-making. Kornhauser explains the comparative implications of these determinants by recognizing how they coexist in different ways across jurisdictions. Kornhauser develops a rich analytical framework to precisely derive comparative implications from these varying combinations of determinants. The ultimate goal of a theoretical analysis, though, is to generate testable hypotheses. No comparative empirical scholarship can be successfully developed without sound theoretical work that identifies determinants and a nexus of causality. The third contribution made in Kornhauser's essay is a basic framework for a comparative theory of courts. This should assist scholars with their search for sound, testable hypotheses used in quality empirical research.

The essay by Kornhauser easily convinces the reader that scholars need to converge on a general theory of judicial behavior and not a jurisdiction-based model (that is, a theoretical model based on individual jurisdictions). While comparative constitutional law and comparative judicial politics generate deep understandings of courts and their decision-making, as seen in our regional-specific essays, a good comparative theory must transcend localities to allow for some generality across jurisdictions. For example, a thesis of a court's exceptionalism is incompatible with a theory of general judicial behavior with comparative usefulness. Generality, of course, can lose touch with significant institutional details when abstraction is taken too far. Therefore, inevitably, a balance between generality and attention to country-specific realities should be achieved.

Judicial Behavior by Country and Region

National high courts are key political actors in their respective systems of government. The decisions by national high courts receive regular media attention because they play such a significant role in debates within society and politics, as mentioned earlier in this essay. All around the world, there is a general perception that high courts have emerged as significant political actors. This perception is further substantiated by leaders with authoritarian tendencies who have tried to reduce these courts' power specifically because they pose a threat to these leaders' agendas. Thus, understanding how courts make decisions and to what effect provides vital information about larger issues of governance.

In the regional-specific essays, leading scholars from across a number of disciplinary backgrounds share key insights about the institutional design, sociolegal context, and practical barriers to empirical research in their regions of expertise. All of these essays address the same set of key questions:

+ What is the breadth and scope of the literature in the region or country dealing with judicial behavior on high courts?
+ What are the general gaps or unresolved theoretical puzzles in the region or country?
+ What general empirical strategies have been used?
+ What are the general challenges regarding research in this region?
+ What are possible proposals for areas of future research to unite the field of judicial behavior?
+ What are the methodological challenges in these regions of study (i.e., issues of causation, measurement, and the availability of data to assess the theoretical claims)?

Each country or regional essay provides a systematic analysis of the state of the literature. The authors also suggest future areas for research, mindful of the local and institutional differences among courts in the region. Our experts share their country-specific knowledge to help lower the barriers for comparative scholars, allowing them to develop multi-country studies across regions. In other words, scholars who study courts in one region can learn about work being done in other countries and regions with similar (and dissimilar) institutional structures. This provides a platform for scholars to expand their research across regions while helping them to predict potential threats to the generalizability of their own theories and measures.

The region-specific essays are not intended to be primers on the nuts and bolts of particular court systems. Court structures and rules can change, and an exhaustive review of the structure and processes of the various high courts is beyond the scope of this work. This information is important for any research endeavor, of course, so we direct readers to national websites or organizations, such as the Constitute Project.[2] The regional essays instead provide individual in-depth overviews of the state of the art quantitative literature by region, capturing the complexity of the field and the innovations and challenges faced by regional- or country-specific scholars.

Our choice of regions to include in the region-specific essays was based on whether there was a substantial amount of literature on empirical judicial behavior to justify a separate country or regional essay. One of the purposes of the book is to provide readers with a view of the landscape of literature on high court behavior across the world. The differences in essay coverage and scope show that some regions have developed more advanced scholarship while other regions have not. For example, the volume has two essays on the American courts, the most studied region. One essay deals with the federal courts, including the US Supreme Court (Fischman), and one deals with state supreme courts (Hall). Readers may inquire why there is an essay on state supreme courts at all. Cross-national research to date has not included near the number of courts across which much of the state supreme court research compares. Indeed, the state supreme court research contains important lessons to help us understand how to identify and navigate around the barriers to large-N empirical research on judicial behavior. In her essay, Hall outlines the creative ways in which state supreme court research has overcome barriers similar to those that cross-national research must also overcome. For this reason, we think it is important to include this as a starting point to transition from a general discussion of the US-centric literature into the broader cross-national research context.

Single essays on the United Kingdom (Hanretty), Canada (Hausegger), Australia and New Zealand (Smyth), India (Parikh), and two European international courts (Carrubba and Fjelstul) were justified by the amount of scholarship on these regions or courts. Similarly, in certain instances, regions were merged together as there was not enough available research to justify a separate essay. For example, Bagashka and Garoupa's essay includes both Western and Eastern European high courts as well as those in Russia and in a few new independent states. The date of the creation of new independent states, to a large extent, drives this choice. Other regions, such as Latin America (Kapiszewski and Tiede), the Middle East (Aydin-Cakir), Asia (Lin and Ginsburg), and Africa (Lewis) include many studies on high court behavior, but no one country within these regions justifies a singular essay at this stage.

We should emphasize that the organization of region-specific essays largely reflects the current state of the art in empirical research. Due to data availability and other methodological constraints discussed in the final essay of the book, the vast majority of studies are focused on a very limited number of countries. For example, in their essay, Bagashka and Garoupa recognize that most European high courts have not been studied from a quantitative perspective. Smyth's essay focuses on Australia and New Zealand because there is extremely limited empirical literature on other common law jurisdictions such as Ireland, Cyprus, or Malta. Authors of essays on other regions make similar complaints. This does not mean that judicial behavior in such jurisdictions has not been the object of study with other approaches, qualitative, descriptive, or legalistic. It is the absence of statistical analysis for some countries and regions that concerns us in this book.

The bulk of the book, consisting of country- and region-specific essays, is unique in that it provides an analysis of the key academic literature by region. Readers may ask why we have surveyed the literature by world region rather than specific topics that concern a large range of countries. Thus far, concerted efforts to study the behavior of all these courts in a truly comparative manner with rigorous empirical methods has faced seemingly insurmountable challenges. The overall tendency is still for edited books to focus on collecting essays on single or a small number of courts or occasionally on a specific theme as discussed above. Unlike other important edited volumes, this book specifically deals with the empirical study of judicial behavior on high courts with a truly comparative agenda in mind. The book is distinct from the existing literature in that it grapples with the difficult questions of how to develop a theory of behavior that defies borders and takes advantage of rigorous methods and data availability to move this research agenda forward.

The choice to include regional analyses was based on our fundamental belief that true comparative work cannot be undertaken until the complexities of individual regions and courts is understood in a deep and meaningful way. Choices about research questions, data acquisition, and coding can be made only after researchers understand the courts and regions they are studying. Understanding court practices and what the academy believes is "important" to judicial decision-making in a particular region or in a particular court allows those seeking to conduct comparative work across regions to make decisions about what research questions are even possible to ask in such a diverse judicial world and to think about what kind of information or data is needed to answer such questions. For example, US scholars may be very familiar with how US Supreme Court judges reveal their opinions, generally joining the majority, concurring, or dissenting. These same scholars, wishing to undertake a study comparing the individual judges' decisions of the American high court to another high court may be surprised to find that in some countries, judges have considerably more options as to the form of their opinion and that in some countries, courts are not allowed to reveal dissenting opinions. Deciding whether a common coding scheme is possible would require in-depth knowledge, which we provide not by describing these unique institutional differences but by providing an analysis of whether judicial scholars classify these seemingly mundane differences as important. Thus, these essays provide a tool kit for regional scholars seeking to extend their research or for those just jumping into the field for the first time.

Methodological Advances and a Conundrum

A key reason for inertia in the comparative judicial arena is the fact that collecting data and amassing the necessary expertise in a number of countries is a daunting task for any individual researcher. Even if this could be accomplished, it is necessary to design theories and measurements that travel across varying institutional contexts. In short, there are important practical, theoretical, and methodological barriers that stand in the way of this kind of comparative research.

The book's final essays chart a path forward through the practical challenges of comparative empirical studies of judicial behavior. Driscoll's essay summarizes the key trends in the empirical study of judicial behavior and aggregates the lessons learned from the region-specific analyses. She closes by identifying the key underlying challenges of doing comparative work from an empirical perspective. Gill and Zorn's concluding essay provides an overview of the technological and methodological advancements that may lower these barriers. This essay discusses how new ways of gathering data may impact the way we conduct multi-country empirical research on judicial behavior, including the questions we ask and the levels of confidence we have in answering them.

Conclusion

The book develops over three themes—theory, detailed state of the art overviews by country or region (largely as a function of current scholarship), and methodology. Why this particular order? Why do we start with theory and conclude with methodological issues? As we have indicated, we need a good theory to generate hypotheses to be tested with emphasis on comparative aspects. Then we need excellent country studies to provide for appropriate background and to contextualize the collection of data for comparative empirical analysis. Only then are scholars ready to frame and discuss methodology. Specifically, empirical methodology requires theory and country-institutional understandings to complete the framework for true comparative empirical analysis. Altogether, these three elements—theory, country or regional knowledge, and methodology—are the bare bones of the successful study of high courts from a comparative and empirical perspective. By addressing all three together, we hope to reduce entry barriers and encourage innovative research strategies in this important field of study.

NOTES

1. Following the lead of several Western European countries, many countries have more recently created constitutional courts in Asia, Eastern Europe, Latin America and Africa (see Autheman 2004).
2. The Constitute Project is found at https://www.constituteproject.org/.

REFERENCES

Alarie, Benjamin, and Andrew J. Green. 2017. *Commitment and Cooperation on High Courts: A Cross-Country Examination of Institutional Constraints on Judges.* Oxford: Oxford University Press.

Autheman, Violet. 2004. *Global Lessons Learned: Constitutional Courts, Judicial Independence and the Rule of Law.* IFES Rule of Law White Paper Series. Washington, DC: IFES.

Bagashka, Tanya, and Lydia Tiede. 2021. "The Influence of Procurator Generals in Constitutional Review." *Journal of Law and Courts.*

Brinks, Daniel, and Abby Blass. 2017. "Rethinking Judicial Empowerment: The New Foundations of Constitutional Justice." *International Journal of Constitutional Law* 15: 296–331.

———. 2018. *The DNA of Constitutional Justice in Latin America: Politics, Governance, and Judicial Design.* Cambridge: Cambridge University Press.

Djankov, Simeon, Rafael La Porta, Florencio Lopez-de-Silanes, and Andrei Shleifer. 2003. "Courts." *Quarterly Journal of Economics* 118 (2): 453–517.

Elkins, Zachary, Tom Ginsburg, and James Melton. 2009. *The Endurance of National Constitutions.* Cambridge: Cambridge University Press.

Ely, John Hart. 1980. *Democracy and Distrust: A Theory of Judicial Review.* Cambridge: Harvard University Press.

Garoupa, Nuno, and Tom Ginsburg. 2015. *Judicial Reputation: A Comparative Theory.* Chicago: University of Chicago Press.

Ginsburg, Tom. 2003. *Judicial Review in New Democracies: Constitutional Courts in Asian Cases.* Cambridge: Cambridge University Press.

Ginsburg, Tom, and Tamir Moustafa, eds. 2008. *Rule by Law: The Politics of Courts in Authoritarian Regimes.* Cambridge: Cambridge University Press.

Herron, Erik, and Kirk Randazzo. 2003. "The Relationship between Independence and Judicial Review in Post-Communist Courts." *Journal of Politics* 65: 422–38.

Hilbink, Lisa. 2012. "The Origins of Positive Judicial Independence." *World Politics* 64: 587–621.

Hirschl, Ran. 2014. *Comparative Matters: The Renaissance of Comparative Constitutional Law.* Oxford: Oxford University Press.

Howard, Robert, and Kirk Randazzo, eds. 2018. *Routledge Handbook of Judicial Behavior.* New York: Routledge.

Iaryczower, Matias, Pablo Spiller, and Mariano Tommasi. 2002. "Judicial Independence in Unstable Environments, Argentina 1935–1998." *American Journal of Political Science* 46 (4): 699–716.

Kapieszewski, Diana, Gordon Silverstein, Robert Kagan, eds. 2013. *Consequential Courts: Judicial Roles in Global Perspective.* Cambridge: Cambridge University Press.

Landes, William, and Richard Posner. 1975. "The Independent Judiciary in an Interest-Group Perspective." *Journal of Law and Economics* 18: 875–91.

Law, David S., and Mila Versteeg. 2012. "The Declining Influence of the United States Constitution." *NYU Law Review* 87: 762–858.

McCubbins, Mathew D., Roger G. Noll, and Barry R. Weingast. 1995. "Politics and the Courts: A Positive Theory of Judicial Doctrine and the Rule of Law." *Southern California Law Review* 68: 1631–81.

———. 2006. "Conditions for Judicial Independence." *Journal of Contemporary Legal Issues* 15: 105–28.

Posner, Daniel N. 2005. *Institutions and Ethnic Politics in Africa.* New York: Cambridge University Press.

Ríos-Figueroa, Julio. 2011. "Institutions for Constitutional Justice in Latin America." In *Courts in Latin America,* edited by Gretchen Helmke and Julio Ríos-Figueroa, 27–54. New York: Cambridge University Press.

Scheppele, Kim Lane. 2018. "Autocratic Legalism." *University of Chicago Law Review* 85: 545–83.

Scribner, Druscilla. 2011. "Courts, Power and Rights in Argentina and Chile." In *Courts in Latin America,* edited by Gretchen Helmke and Julio Ríos-Figueroa, 248–77. New York: Cambridge University Press.

Shapiro, Martin. 1980. *Courts: A Comparative and Political Analysis*. Chicago: University of Chicago Press.

Spamann, Holger. 2015. "Empirical Comparative Law." *Annual Review of Law and Social Science* 11: 131–53.

Stone Sweet, Alec. 2000. *Governing with Judges: Constitutional Politics in Europe*. Oxford: Oxford University Press.

Vanberg, Georg. 2015. "Constitutional Courts in Comparative Perspective: A Theoretical Assessment." *Annual Review of Political Science* 18: 167–85.

Whittington, Keith. 2005. "'Interpose Your Friendly Hand': Political Supports for the Exercise of Judicial Review by the United States Supreme Court." *American Political Science Review* 99: 583–96.

Understanding Adjudication

LEWIS A. KORNHAUSER

A THEORY OF adjudication begins with two sets of three questions:
The first set asks about the behavior of *courts*. The second asks
about the behavior of *judges*. We thus have: What do courts and judges
do? What do courts and judges want? What constraints do courts and
judges face? Attitudinalism, the predominant social science account of
adjudication, has simple answers to these questions: Courts and judges
choose policies; they have preferences over policies, and, at least on
apex courts, they are unconstrained.[1]

These answers, even for apex courts, seem incomplete and misleading.
Constitutional drafters, legislators, and treaty signatories devote substantial resources to devising complex institutional structures, a meaningless
effort if the structure of institutions does not constrain the court. Judges
typically deny that courts are political bodies engaged in the naked ar-
ticulation of policy. They justify their decisions with long and complex
opinions. Thus, sustained attention to judicial activity suggests that these
six questions require more complex answers.

Attitudinalism, in recognition of this apparent gap in its explanations,
frequently posits a legal model with which to challenge its more real-
ist explanation. The legal model, however, is poorly specified and not
adequately tested against attitudinalism.[2]

Indeed, we require richer theories than attitudinalism both to approximate a legal model and to illuminate the processes of adjudication generally and of decision-making on apex courts in particular. Economists
and political scientists have begun to develop these richer models. This
essay introduces this theoretical literature. I focus on models of collegial
courts in which a panel of judges decides cases together. Apex courts
typically are collegial. The study of apex courts, however, also implicates

issues of hierarchy because apex courts generally sit atop a hierarchy or may hear cases in panels that are subject to plenary review.[3]

This essay has two aims. First, it sketches the diverse universe of apex courts in an effort to identify features that theory should incorporate and illuminate. Second, it outlines some richer theoretical structures that, with substantial work, might provide a more robust theory of courts and adjudication. I begin this exploration of theory by discussing first what judges do, then what constraints judges face, and finally what judges want. I then examine some models to illustrate these formal structures. I focus on formal models because they yield sharp predictions that can be brought to data.

The formal literature that I review largely studies federal or state courts in the United States. This focus, though explicable by the relative accessibility of data (and the national origins or residency of the authors), is unfortunate because apex courts elsewhere have significantly different internal structures and institutional settings. The extant literature reveals the importance of these institutional features on the behavior of courts and judges.[4]

Apex Courts

What is an apex court? Broadly, an apex court is a court of last resort that, typically, sits atop a judicial hierarchy. But this definition is too crude to capture the variety of courts that are of interest to scholars. A more restrictive definition would identify apex courts as courts of last resort over some, perhaps limited, domain.

Attempts at defining apex courts can await at least a brief examination of the set of courts that scholars have had in mind. Apex courts do not constitute a uniform set of courts. They come in a variety of forms and each requires special attention. The theoretical approach adopted here starts from the assumption that institutions—both "internal" and "external"—matter. Consequently, it is important to begin with some sense of the variety of apex courts.

Consider, for example, the United States. Each of the fifty states has an apex court that has the final say on disputes involving state law. The United States Supreme Court, by contrast, has final say on disputes that involve federal law. Each of these fifty-one courts is, in some sense, an apex court. The structure and decision procedures of these courts differ in important respects.

Or consider instead France. France has three national apex courts: the Cour de Cassation that sits atop the civil and criminal hierarchy, the Conseil d'Etat that sits atop the administrative law hierarchy, and the Conseil Constitutionel that has jurisdiction over questions of constitutional law.[5] The situation is more complex because France sits both in the EU and the set of countries that have signed the European Convention on Human Rights. It is thus subject to the jurisdiction of the European Court of Justice (ECJ) and the European Court of Human Rights (ECHR). Thus, the national apex courts are not at the top of the hierarchy relative to questions of European law. And with respect to questions of human rights law, the national apex courts, the ECJ, and the ECHR share jurisdiction.

The juridical situation for both France and the United States is, in fact, even more complex than the above description indicates. Both countries are subject to the jurisdiction of the appellate body of the World Trade Organization. And both may be subject to the jurisdiction of the International Court of Justice.[6]

We thus seem to have a plethora of apex courts with a set of conflicting jurisdictions and interrelations among the courts and other political institutions. Each of these courts has its own set of rules and regulations that govern its operations and decision-making. For the empiricist, this abundance of courts offers great opportunities to study the variation in behavior across these various institutions. For the theorist, however, it presents a challenge as any theory must be general enough to encompass institutional variation but specific enough to generate sharp predictions about behavior.

To begin, therefore, let us try to classify various institutional arrangements. Consider the following crude taxonomy: appointments and tenure, docket formation (including the court's jurisdiction), case-processing procedures, announcement procedures, enforcement mechanisms, and institutional settings. Each of these aspects of an apex court will affect both the behavior of the court and its judges and what parts of that behavior the analyst can observe.

What Do Courts and Judges Do?

Courts resolve disputes. The paradigmatic court resolves disputes between two parties. Carr, riding her bicycle, strikes and injures Baker. Baker complains; Carr denies responsibility. The parties bring their dispute to a third party—the court—to resolve. The court first determines what happened. It then determines whether, given the facts, the aggrieved party ("the plaintiff"), is entitled to recover from the other party. The court thus renders judgment or announces a disposition of the case. This disposition may be appealed to a higher court and, finally, in a system with more than two tiers, to an apex court.

Courts or judges often do more than render judgment. What gets done and by whom depends on the announcement procedures of the court. We may usefully distinguish three announcement protocols: seriatim courts, per curiam courts, and majoritarian courts. In both per curiam and majoritarian courts, in addition to a judgment, the court also offers reasons for its decision, and it sometimes announces a rule. In per curiam courts, the opinion of the court is often unsigned so no judge apparently gives reasons of her own. In majoritarian courts, the author of the opinion of the court is typically identified. Other judges on the court may also provide their own reasons for their decisions, either in dissent or in concurrence. The majority opinion, however, gives the court's reasons, not the author's.[7] In seriatim courts, each judge offers her own reasons for her dispositional vote but there are no reasons of the court.[8]

To understand in more depth what courts and judges do, we must specify the nature of the disputes that come before courts. Obviously, there are disputes between private individuals that rest either on judge-made or statutory law. In the modern state, however, many disputes arise from the administrative functions of the state. Administrative bodies often promulgate regulations and the validity of these regulations is challenged on procedural or substantive grounds. Finally, with the rise of judicial review and constitutional courts, many disputes concern the constitutionality of legislative or executive action. Table 1 summarizes the actions that courts or judges take in each instance.[9]

Each row in the table identifies a mode of judicial decision-making, that is, the grounds of decision in a dispute. The first row describes the structure of common law decision-making, and the second row describes the structure of statutory interpretation. The next two rows consider two distinct modes of judicial review of administrative action. The penultimate row depicts the structure of ex post judicial review. Finally, the bottom row describes a decision mode that distinguishes those constitutional courts that have the authority to rule on the constitutionality of legislative or executive action before that statute or action takes effect. The French Conseil Constitutionel, for example, has this authority.

TABLE 1. Modes of judicial decision-making

Mode	Actors	Judicial action	Status quo
Common law	J	Disposition	None
Statutory interpretation	Panel of judges or H, S, P, J	Disposition plus rule	None
Administrative law: Procedure	A, J	Disposition (judicial veto)	Judicial decision may restore a prior rule
Administrative law: Substantive	H, S, P, A, J	Disposition plus block veto	Judicial veto resets to the prior rule but blocks some rules
Ex post constitutional review	J, L or J, P	Disposition plus block veto	Judicial veto resets to the prior rule but blocks some rules
Ex ante constitutional review	J, L	Policy or block veto	Interpretation sets a new policy but a judicial veto resets to the prior rule while blocking some rules

A = Administrative Agency, H = House, J = Judiciary, L = Legislature, P = President, S = Senate

Subsequent columns briefly identify some salient features of the different modes of adjudication. Consider, for example, the first row that identifies a mode of common law adjudication. In this mode, the court acts alone, (relatively) unconstrained by the presence of other (political) actors. This fact is recorded in the second column, labeled "Actors," and in the case of common law is indicated by "J" alone. At least in a seriatim court, the court simply renders judgment by announcing a disposition. In a majoritarian court, it might also announce a rule. The third column, "Judicial action," reflects this feature of the model. Finally, "Status quo," the last column, indicates that every decision of a common law court changes the law because it alters the body of case law. As the other rows indicate, this feature is not shared by all the other modes.

More generally, the second column indicates the political actors involved in the adjudication. The behavior of the court and individual judges on the court is constrained by the presence of non-judicial actors such as the legislature (or house and senate) and the president.

As apex courts decide collegially, other judges on the panel constrain both the behavior of the court and of individual judges. This column identifies the set of actors that populate the typical formal model of the phenomenon.

The third column identifies the action taken by the judge or the court. The fourth column points to one immediate consequence of the decision taken in column three: what is the state of the law after the court acts? Initial models of collegial courts imported the models developed to study the US Congress and were developed in light of congressional voting procedures that follow Robert's Rules of Order. Under such procedures, the final legislative vote pairs a final, amended bill against the status quo; if the bill fails, the status quo remains unchanged. Courts, however, follow different procedures.

In all instances but one, after a judicial decision, the legal situation never reverts to the legal status quo ante. Even when the court strikes an administrative regulation or a statute on constitutional grounds, the legal terrain shifts at least minimally from its prior state because the decision constrains the future actions of the agency or the legislature. But the legal terrain may change more dramatically when the court announces an interpretation of a statute because that interpretation may implement a policy different from the one apparently enacted by the legislature.

Ex ante constitutional review, the last row in the table, places courts in a distinctive decisional setting. Typically, courts resolve disputes between parties. The resolution of the dispute requires the court first to apply or attempt to apply prevailing law to the events that gave rise to the dispute. In ex ante constitutional law, by contrast, the dispute before the court is simply an extension of the disagreement over the appropriate policy the legislature should have adopted. Whether the court rules that the adopted statute violates the constitution will depend on how the statute is interpreted, but the court engages in the process of interpretation in a factual vacuum.[10]

In all other instances, the facts of the case play an important role in adjudication. The case should also play an important role in models of judicial behavior. Both models and experience suggest that, even when judges care primarily about policy, the specific case heard in part determines which rule or policy a court announces.

What Constraints Do Courts and Judges Face?

Judges face two types of constraints: external and internal. External constraints arise from outside actors, whether individuals or institutions. Internal constraints derive from the people, practices and rules within the court itself. I discuss each in turn.

External Constraints

Apex courts face a number of external constraints. First, either the constitution or statutes specify the terms and conditions of judges' employment. Appointment and tenure provisions may affect judges' incentives and influence what cases they hear and how they resolve them. Some judges have life tenure. Some judges are appointed by political or nonpartisan actors for either fixed or renewable terms. Others, including judges on some apex courts, are subject to periodic or retention elections.[11]

The political branches have very limited control over judges appointed to life terms, though such judges may have a political affinity to or feel an obligation to the appointing officials. These judges, like most judges on apex courts, are still subject to removal by impeachment in some jurisdictions and by other means elsewhere.[12] Such extreme removal procedures may influence the decisions of judges on politically controversial cases.[13] Similarly, judges subject to retention elections may face pressures in cases that raise politically explosive issues.[14]

Judges that are appointed for a fixed term also may face incentives from other political actors or the public. A judge who wants reappointment may consider the interests of the party that reappoints. Even a judge who cannot be reappointed typically has a life after her tenure on the bench. She may consider how her rulings will affect her political future or her future practice or other future employment practices. These concerns, of course, may be difficult to tie to specific behaviors in identified cases.

Judges may face constraints from political actors in other ways, as well. The legislature, for instance, may control the jurisdiction of the court. In cases of statutory interpretation, the legislature has the power to replace the court's interpretation by amending the statute. In cases of administrative review, the agency may be able to conform its procedures to those required or to reframe a rejected rule; and, again, the legislature, can amend the statute to grant more clearly the relevant authority to the agency.[15] Even constitutional decisions may be overruled through the amendment procedures.[16]

Different political structures will thus yield different constraints. Contrast, for example, the presidential system of the United States to the parliamentary system of the United Kingdom. The parliamentary system imposes greater constraints on the UK Supreme Court because legislation is much easier to pass in a parliamentary system than in the presidential system of the United States.[17]

Outside actors determine, at least in part, the set of cases the court decides. A court cannot decide a case it cannot hear. Typically, the litigants determine the docket of the court. On some international courts, the parties must consent to jurisdiction. In other instances, the decision of a single litigant can bring a case to the court. The rules governing appeals thus have an important influence on the size and composition of the court's caseload. In some jurisdictions and on some international courts, other courts refer cases or issues to the apex court. National courts in the European Union, for example, refer cases involving European law to the European Court of Justice.[18] Constitutional courts with ex ante review may receive cases from legislators.

Finally, external agents enforce judicial orders. For example, if, after judgment, the defendant fails to pay plaintiff damages in a private suit, the sheriff (in the United States) enforces the judgment. More significantly, when a court rules against a government, it has no power to enforce compliance with its judgment.[19]

Internal Constraints

Judges generally do not decide alone. Even a single judge may be subject to review by a higher court or by a future court. Hierarchical control may even play a role on apex courts as some apex courts sit both in panels and en banc. Decisions of panels may be directly appealable to the full bench or indirectly reviewable should the issue arise again and be referred to the bench rather than a panel. Moreover, when a judge sits on a panel or en banc, the court decides together, at least on the disposition and possibly on the court's reasons for the disposition. Each judicial system has a distinctive set of rules and practices that construct the court's decisions from the decisions of the individual judges. Each set of rules constitutes the internal constraints faced by the judges on the court.

These internal constraints identify the court's decision procedure. This procedure has at least two important elements; the first determines the court's agenda while the second determines the court's rule of decision.

The agenda identifies the set of decisions that the court takes collectively. It may decide collectively on the disposition of the case only or on both the disposition of the case and the reasons underlying the disposition. The agenda determines to some extent the announcement procedure of the court. Further, the agenda may disaggregate the decision on the case into a series of decisions on component issues.[20]

Common law courts typically have adopted majority rule to resolve questions on the agenda. The rule of decision in many civilian courts, however, is not clear. Civilian courts such as the French Cour de Cassation issue a single, unsigned opinion. Ostensibly, the decision rule is unanimity or consensus, but the announcement procedure conceivably masks underlying disagreement of the judges hearing the case. On some courts, decisions that strike down a statute as unconstitutional require a supra-majority vote. In any case, these voting rules serve as a primary element in many formal models of collegiality.

What Do Courts and Judges Want?

Models of judicial behavior must address the central question: what do judges want, or, what objective do courts pursue? Different answers to this question suggest very different empirical strategies. Regardless of the answer, however, the model must link the judicial preferences to the actions that judges take.

The imputation of a preference to a judge requires decisions along multiple dimensions. First, one must identify the domain of preference, the set of objects over which the agent has preferences. Second, one must identify the judicial attitude toward her actions. Finally, one must decide how heterogeneous judicial preferences are.

Heterogeneity

Political scientists typically view judicial systems as a political venue. This perspective implicitly makes two important assumptions. First, it assumes that courts are an arena of interests rather than judgments. The analyst thus naturally assumes that judges have preferences over policies rather than render judgment over the correct disposition of a case—or the announcement of the correct rule. *Preference* here simply refers to the idea that each judge has a subjective ranking over the relevant domain. Judges on a collegial court with preferences over policies, for instance, then compromise on a policy of the court. Similarly, one would model the vertical relation between the apex court and lower courts as a principal-agent relation in which the two have conflicting interests or preferences.

Most models of collegial courts are political models. Carrubba et al. (2012), Cameron and Kornhauser (2012), and Parameswaran, Cameron, and Kornhauser (2021) offer models of bargaining on collegial courts.

Alternatively, an analyst might understand the judicial system as a *team* in the economic sense of Marschak and Radner (1972). All the agents on a team have a common set of preferences over a common domain. They may have different information or beliefs, or different action sets. The team faces a set of coordination problems that the team structure at least partially resolves. Kornhauser (1995) offers an informal account of a common law judicial system as a team.

Judges that share an understanding of their role have a common objective. We might understand that aim as getting it right or rendering the judgment required by law. Here *judgment* refers to some objective, or intersubjective, standard that all aim at. Participants in a legal practice often understand the law in this way, as having correct answers to legal questions. This tradition is particularly strong in civil law jurisdictions. Iaryczower and Shum (2012) provide a model of civil law adjudication on a collegial court that illustrates this approach. Attitudinalists often contrast their political approach to a legal model that is left largely unspecified. A more compelling theoretical account of a legal model would further develop the approach of a team seeking to get it right.

We shall use the term *preferences* to refer both to preferences understood as the ranking derived from the agent's interests and to judgments understood as her assessment of the correct outcome.

Judicial Attitude

A judge may vote either expressively or consequentially. When a judge votes expressively, she cares about her own action. When she votes consequentially, she cares about the action of the court, the judicial system, or the behavior induced by the court's action.

To understand these distinctions better, it is helpful to elaborate on the decision environments sketched in the prior subsection. One may usefully distinguish three types of collegial court: seriatim courts, per curiam courts, and majoritarian courts. These courts are distinguished by their methods of opinion announcement.

English appellate courts, which are collegial, are the paradigmatic seriatim court. In traditional English practice, after the court hears a case, each judge renders judgment; she offers an opinion that identifies *her* preferred disposition and her reasons for that disposition, often including the identification of her preferred rule. The judge might have preferences over three different domains. She might care about the disposition that *she* endorses. She might care about the disposition of the *court*. Or she may care about the rule that *she* announces. When she cares about *her* actions, we say her preferences are *expressive*. When she cares about the *action of the court*, we say her preferences are *consequential*. Notice that the judge cannot have consequential preferences over the court's rule because in English practice there is neither a rule of the court nor an opinion of the court, only the separate opinions of each judge on the panel. The rule of the instant case is constructed ex post by each judge sitting on a subsequent case for which the instant case might serve as a precedent.[21]

Per curiam courts provide a stark contrast to seriatim courts. The French Cour de Cassation is the paradigmatic per curiam court. It issues a single, anonymous opinion of the court that identifies the disposition of the case and offers a very sparse, single-sentence reason for the decision. Here we may observe little more than the action of the court so it seems natural to impute consequential preferences to each judge. A judge, of course, may nonetheless have expressive preferences over her dispositional vote and over different grounds on which the Cour might rest its judgment. The judge here would be expressing her preferences to other members of the court but her preferences would not be observable, except in limited circumstances, to the public or the analyst.[22]

Majoritarian courts have adopted a procedure intermediate to those of per curiam and seriatim courts. The Supreme Court of the United States is the paradigmatic majoritarian court. It (typically) announces a majority opinion—or an opinion of the Court—that is signed. Indeed, each justice that endorses that opinion is identified.[23] In addition, the dispositional vote of every judge is identified, and often one or more justices publish a dissenting or a concurring opinion. In this context, we might attribute expressive or consequential preferences (or both) over either dispositions or rules.

The Domain of Preference

I have suggested that, on a collegial court or within a judicial system as a whole, judges may have conflicting preferences or harmonious ones and that such preferences may be either expressive or consequential. And I have noted that the structure and conventions of different judicial systems push toward different attributions because of what behaviors each system makes readily available to the public and, hence, to analysts. I have not, however, systematically discussed the object of judicial preference: What do judges want? This question lies at the heart of models of judicial behavior.

Theorists typically identify one or more of four domains of preference: (1) dispositions, (2) policies, (3) social consequences, and (4) narrow self-interest understood as an interest in pecuniary gains and leisure.[24] These domains are interrelated in complex ways, and consequently some models impute preferences over complex domains that include more than one of the four domains identified above.[25]

Broadly, one might adopt one of three approaches to attribute preferences to judge. In the first approach, the kitchen-sink model, judicial preferences reflect everything that the judge might conceivably care about. In the second approach, the action space model, the domain of judicial preferences is defined directly over the set of actions available to the judge. In the third approach, the fundamental preferences approach, the domain of judicial preferences derives from a more holistic consideration of the problem to be analyzed.

The kitchen-sink approach may initially appear attractive because of its realism. But the approach is neither very well-specified nor tractable.[26] The action space model may seem to identify a natural domain of judicial preferences—the set of actions from which the judge chooses. This choice perhaps makes sense when judges have a simple action set, such as choosing dispositions and policies. Such a set of actions makes sense when the agent has expressive preferences over dispositions or policies. A judge with expressive preferences acts non-strategically and these simple action sets are straightforward.

But to understand strategic interactions, consequential preferences over dispositions or policies are typically not isomorphic to preferences over the judge's strategy space. In Cameron, Kornhauser, and Parameswaran (2019), for example, each judge has fundamental preferences over dispositions. Though her behavioral action space is the set of dispositions, her full strategy space is a much more complex object as, in principle, her choice at any point may be a function of the history of the prior decisions of the court.

It thus makes sense to identify a sensible domain over which the judge may have fundamental preferences. One identifies this domain by careful consideration of the environment in which the agent chooses and the choice set available to the agent. Institutional features of the judiciary will identify considerations that will be particularly relevant to the judge. In the federal judicial system of the United States, for example, judges have life tenure, essentially fixed salaries, and little prospect of promotion. A labor market theory of behavior here would be likely to yield little insight as there will be few, if any, connections between what judges and courts do and typical economic incentives. It thus makes sense to explore the way in which preferences over dispositions, policies, or social consequences influence judicial behavior. In a civilian jurisdiction, on the other hand, where judges are typically embedded in a bureaucracy, attention to the evaluative criteria used within the bureaucracy to assign judges to courts may be sensible.[27]

Figure 1, taken from Cameron and Kornhauser (2017b), provides a crude representation of some of the interactions. To understand the figure, start with the middle box that represents the case x and the case space X. Cases are distributed with density $f(x)$. These cases arise from disputes generated at time 0 by the social behaviors that the leftmost box represents. Some of these disputes are brought to court. The rightmost box represents the judicial processes that resolve the disputes. The court then resolves these disputes, announcing dispositions $d(x)$ and rules $r(x,y)$. These judicial acts then influence social behavior through a process represented in the leftmost box by $z(x)$ (which has distribution $Z(x)$). These social behaviors induce a new set of grievances and, in conjunction with the previous judicial decisions, a new set of litigated disputes, at least some of which are resolved by the judicial system.

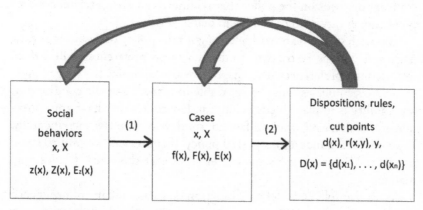

FIG. 1. Judicial actions and social consequences
Social behaviors generate cases, via law enforcement and private legal actions. In turn, cases generate judicial actions. Then, via feedback (the larger arrows in the figure), judicial actions affect social behaviors and cases.

A judge might have preferences over one or more elements in each of these boxes. For an economist, the social consequences in the leftmost box or dockets in the middle box comprise the obvious domain of preference. For political scientists, policies or rules in the rightmost box constitute the obvious domain of preference. For lawyers, either dispositions or rules comprises an appropriate domain of preference.

The domains of dispositions, policy, and social consequences are intertwined. A judicial policy, after all, is simply a function from the space of cases to the set of dispositions. Moreover, the enactment of a policy induces actions from public officials and private individuals that produce the social consequences of concern to the judge.

In many contexts, there are several reasons to take preferences over dispositions as fundamental. First, it is not clear how a court can commit to any rule that it announces. The problem emerges most clearly when different panels may hear an identical case or when the personnel of an en banc court changes over time. Second, judges rarely have the appropriate information from which to determine the social consequences of various rules that they might announce (even if they could commit to them). Third, if one assumes that the judge has fundamental preferences over dispositions, there is a natural way to derive preferences over policies: integrate the judge's evaluation of all dispositions dictated by a policy over the set of cases that the judge will hear.[28] These policy preferences, of course, are contingent on the distribution of cases that the court will (potentially) confront. If the set of cases that the judge will confront depends on the policy that is announced, then preferences over policies may vary with the policy in place.

The analyst, on the other hand, might take policy preferences as fundamental. Under restrictive conditions these preferences will induce well-defined preferences over dispositions, specifically, the judge's preferences over policies must be separable in cases.[29] But the condition of separability is implausible for common law courts that have any consequential concerns. Common law courts develop the law incrementally. Each decision announces a partial policy. If courts can commit to these partial policies then the sequence of cases that the court decides may matter.

As an example, consider a jurisdiction that has a regime of negligence with contributory negligence. Suppose Judge A's ideal doctrine sets the standards of care at the levels that minimize total social costs. Suppose the first case sets the standard of care for defendants too low. It is not obvious that Judge A should still prefer to set the standard of care for plaintiffs at the social cost–minimizing level; if plaintiff and defendant care are substitutes, she should prefer a policy that sets the plaintiff's standard of care above the first-best standard. This view of what the optimal continuation of a partial rule to which the court is committed implies that the judge will not have well-defined preferences over dispositions.

Suppose now the analyst attributes to each judge fundamental preferences over social consequences. There is again a natural way to derive preferences over policies: the judge should prefer policy A to policy B if and only if she prefers the social consequences induced by policy A over those induced by policy B. This procedure succeeds as long as neither policy A nor B interacts in a complex way with policies C, D, or E to which the court or the legislature is already committed. If these interactions exist, then the judge may not have well-defined preferences over policies.

Finally, recall that in the prior subsection, I noted that judges on seriatim courts could only have expressive preferences over rules while their preferences over dispositions might be either expressive or consequential. Judges on per curiam courts presumably must have only consequential preferences over dispositions and rules as they only act collectively.

Some Models

Attitudinalism

Attitudinalism derives from a simple stimulus response model of behavioral psychology. At its origins, the case facts constituted the stimulus that provoked the response of a judicial decision. But the formulation leaves unclear which judicial response is relevant. The most natural interpretation identifies the response as the judge's disposition of the case. Empirical work has in fact apparently adopted this approach. The rhetoric, however, often suggests interpreting the judicial response as the judge's choice of policy.[30] More recent practice that scales judicial votes to approximate and quantify the ideology of judges suggests that the domain of preference is a more abstract object—the set of policy evaluations—as the scaling applies across a range of cases that raise dramatically different issues.[31]

Scaling methods assume that judges vote sincerely. This assumption suggests that judges have expressive rather than consequential preferences. Moreover, apex courts are the most natural arena of application of attitudinalism because judges on these courts are less constrained than lower courts. Indeed, the implementations of the theory assume that these judges face no constraints. This is a big assumption because, as noted above, even apex courts are subject to legislative and public oversight. Moreover, apex courts are typically collegial; if judicial preferences are the least bit consequential—i.e., concerned with the decision of the *court*—then each judge is constrained by the other judges with whom she decides. The current literature has focused on defining and improving the measures of judicial ideological preferences.[32]

Labor Market Theories

Models of judicial behavior that rely exclusively on narrowly self-interested preferences are rare because it is difficult to tie these narrowly self-interested preferences, typically for leisure and income, to the decisions that judges render. A judge's income is not, except perhaps in corrupt legal systems, tied to her vote on the disposition or the rule that she announces.

There are two models, however, that have cleverly deduced some consequences of a pure labor market theory. Cooter (1983) was inspired by a practice in California that permitted parties to rent judges. This practice introduced private competition to the public system of adjudication. Cooter models this competition. He finds that private judges have a strong incentive to be impartial in order to attract future business. Moreover, he argues that this impartiality induces private judges to announce efficient rules. Competition then communicates this incentive to public judges.

Ash and Macleod (2015) offer a more concrete and fully specified model of the framework introduced in Epstein, Landes, and Posner (2013). They specify a utility function that depends on the allocation of time across judicial and non-judicial activities. They also assume that judges have preferences over how to allocate time across cases, with judges preferring to spend time on hard or important cases. They then use variation and change across the apex courts of the states of the United States in compensation, appointment rules, and caseloads to estimate the effects of compensation on judicial behavior.

These models share important features. First, each is comparative. It extracts information about the effects of external constraints by comparing across institutional regimes. Studying a single system from this perspective will be difficult unless that system has experienced a sufficient number of changes in the compensation structure of judges. The federal system in the United States poses particular challenges for this approach because federal judges are largely insulated from standard economic incentives (and their access to outside income is also severely limited by statute). Empirical investigations of the labor model in the federal system must thus rely on changes in the costs of decision or the amount of resources allocated to judges. One might, for instance, study how the change in the authorized number of clerks affected the productivity of judges.

Second, neither model has implications for the specific decisions, whether disposition or choice of rule, that judges make. This silence on the politically salient actions of judges arises because, again absent corruption, there is no link between case outcomes and pecuniary reward.

Social Consequences

Models that attribute to judges preference exclusively over social consequences are also extremely rare. The rarity here derives from the difficulty in tying judicial decisions to social consequences. In most cases, this social process is extremely complex and difficult to disentangle. Only very simple models provide a sufficiently short causal chain between the judicial decision and the social consequence.

Parameswaran (2018) illustrates this approach. He offers a model in which a single agent's choice imposes external costs on society. The judge seeks to maximize social welfare, which depends on the agent's choice of action. The judge acts under uncertainty; she does not know what the optimal choice of the agent is, but she has the opportunity to learn over time through setting the standard of care. This model is very elegant, but it would be difficult to apply to a broad data set of decisions of an apex court.

Gennaioli and Shleifer (2007) and Fernandez and Ponzetto (2010) adopt a somewhat different approach. In these models, a judge is drawn from a population of judges who differ in the way in which they weight type one and type two errors.

Disposition Only

A few models assume that judges have preferences solely over dispositions. In these models, the effective constraints derive from the collegial interaction of judges. As an example, consider Cameron, Kornhauser, and Parameswaran (2019), who model a court that decides cases in panels of varying composition (as some apex courts do). Judges have competing consequential preferences over dispositions. Moreover, judges only decide on dispositions. The model identifies conditions under which the court will adhere to a practice of stare decisis and hence implement a rule that no faction on the court would choose to implement if it were acting unilaterally. As noted earlier, one might understand this model as one of a seriatim court.

Lax (2007) also considers a model in which judges have preferences solely over dispositions and decide only on dispositions.[33] He identifies conditions under which a median judge exists in the sense that the implicit rule of the court corresponds to the ideal rule of that judge. The important result is that the implicit rule need not correspond to the ideal rule of *any* judge and will typically be more complex than the rule of any judge.

Policy Only

Some political models assume that judges have consequential preferences over policies. Hammond, Bonneau, and Sheehan (2005) and Jacobi (2009) offer median judge models of adjudication on the US Supreme Court. In these models, judges have preferences over a one-dimensional policy space and the court chooses a policy according to unspecified, but Condorcet-consistent, procedure. Unfortunately, procedures on the US Supreme Court and other apex courts are not obviously Condorcet-consistent.

Models of separation of powers provide a more influential example of political models that assume judges have consequential preferences only. The original models, Marks (2012) and Ferejohn and Shipan (1990), assume that the court consists of a single judge, and they investigate how the presence of a legislature and executive constrains the court and affects its decision-making. Spiller and Spitzer (1995) examine the voting behavior of judges on collegial courts in a similar separation-of-powers setting. They allow judges to have either expressive or consequential preferences over policies. They investigate how the behavior of the court changes as the attribution of preferences changes.

Hybrid Models

Most models of collegial courts assume a more complex domain of preference. Fischman (2008, 2011) provides a striking example of this behavior. Fischman assumes, again in a political model, that judges have consequential preferences over dispositions and over the costs of dissent (which judges are permitted to express publicly). This political model thus incorporates aspects of a labor theory into the argument. He then identifies conditions under which unanimity occurs even though one or more of the judges would decide differently were she deciding alone. He then estimates his model using immigration cases from the Ninth Circuit.

At the other extreme, Carrubba et al. (2012) consider preferences over a very complex domain. Each judge has both expressive and consequential preferences over policies, expressive preferences over dispositions, and labor theory preferences over the cost of writing a concurring or dissenting opinion. Results derive from the constraint that only judges in the dispositional majority may participate in the consequential choice of the court's policy. This constraint, which better captures the dynamics of opinion writing on the US Supreme Court, implies that judicial behavior does not conform to the behavior of the median judge on the court. More importantly, the policy announced by the court depends on the location of the case that it hears.

Parameswaran, Cameron, and Kornhauser (2019) consider preferences over a domain of preferences of intermediate complexity. Judges have consequential preferences over policies and expressive preferences over dispositions. As in Carrubba et al. (2012), only those judges in the dispositional majority participate in the consequential choice of policy. Parameswaran, Cameron, and Kornhauser (2019), however, explicitly model the process of policy formation. They conclude that the policy chosen corresponds to neither the ideal policy of the median judge on the court nor the ideal policy of the median judge in the dispositional majority. Moreover, the announced policy depends on the location of the case heard.

Vanberg (2001) models constitutional review in a parliamentary system. He studies the behavior of the court, not the individual judges as the court is modeled as a unitary actor—one might say as a per curiam court. Legislature and court have preferences over policies but both agents suffer external costs when their preferences are unsatisfied.[34] The model studies the degree of judicial deference as a function of public support for the court and the extent to which the public can observe whether the legislature has complied with the court's ruling.

Concluding Remarks

In the last twenty-five years, the theory of judicial behavior has blossomed with a plethora of new approaches to understanding the behavior of courts and the judges who compose them. As yet, there is neither a comprehensive theory nor a consensus model. This disarray has several reasons. First, the complexity and variety of judicial institutions make them both an interesting object of study and a difficult one. Second, models of judicial behavior typically isolate one or two causal mechanism from the complex processes that produce judicial behavior. One should expect multiple models of a single court, each of which identifies distinct influences on judicial behavior. Moreover, current models suggest the important role that institutions play in structuring judicial behavior. As apex courts exhibit a diverse set of institutional structures, each of which requires distinct modeling approaches, a comprehensive theory will require much time, thought, and effort to develop.

Current theory has primarily focused on the US Supreme Court. That Court, however, has a very peculiar, majoritarian structure with distinctive features of appointment, tenure, jurisdiction, and decisional rules. Many, if not most, apex courts have very different structures and face very different external constraints. Understanding judicial behavior on these courts (as well as understanding the behavior of the court as a whole) will require the development of new classes of models. Fortunately, as the prior discussion indicates, the current literature has identified the necessary elements from which one can build such models. Every model should specify the agents and their preferences, the set of actions available to them, and the environment in which they act. The prior discussion identifies a range of choices to be made at each step.

This bare description in fact provides leverage on several issues that students of apex courts often confront. Consider first the question of judicial activism. How should we define it? How do we measure it? Which courts exhibit it? Presumably, judicial activism reflects at least a disposition of a court to strike down legislation.

Political models of adjudication suggest one approach to understanding judicial activism. A court is more likely to strike down legislation on constitutional grounds when the views of the court differ dramatically from the views of the legislature and the court has the opportunity to strike down legislation. The mechanism of appointments and tenure clearly influence the likelihood that court and legislative views will diverge. If political institutions make appointments and tenure is short, one would expect the interests of court and legislature to be reasonably aligned. But if appointment is relatively insular or tenure is long, one might expect divergence to occur. In any case, this crude approach suggests that activist courts should emerge when this divergence of interests occurs, for whatever reasons. Internal features of the court may also impede or facilitate activism. Some courts require a supermajority vote to invalidate legislation on constitutional grounds, and this requirement will imply that the divergence between court and legislature will have to be greater before judicial activism is observed.

Embedding this idea in a model will reveal complexities. The legislature might act strategically by framing legislation in ways that avoid the court ruling the statute unconstitutional. Similarly, the court may act strategically to avoid repercussions from the legislature. These strategic interactions are complex and require care to analyze. A formal model would facilitate such analysis and would identify courts and periods when one would be more likely to observe activism.

This discussion also illustrates difficulties in doing comparative law. Institutions with dramatically different designs might yield similar judicial behavior depending on how design features interact and the external constraints that the judicial systems face.

Finally, I note two areas in which the theory requires substantial development. First, as mentioned earlier, in many models the policy and the disposition chosen may depend on the case before the court. This docket dependence creates a problem of time consistency of the court. In particular, how can a court commit to pursuing a consistent policy over time?[35] Second, doctrine and its development play an important role in all legal systems. It has, however, received little attention in the literature. Kornhauser (1992b) and Landa and Lax (2009) provide related frameworks in which to think about doctrine, but much work remains to be done.

Notes

Charles Cameron provided comments on an earlier draft.
1. I am overstating the clarity of attitudinalism's answers to these three questions. Attitudinalism's answers to the first and the second questions equivocate over dispositions and policies.
2. Cameron and Kornhauser (2017c) discuss this issue at length in section 4.
3. Apex courts that sit in panels and in plenary sessions may also present some hierarchical issues. Moreover, as apex courts sit over time, they present some problems that would arise even on a single-judge court that persisted over time.

4. Much of the literature reviewed is set in case space rather than policy space. For a review of the case space approach to modeling courts, see Cameron and Kornhauser (2017a, 2017b) and Lax (2011).

5. This description ignores the Tribunal des Conflits that resolves jurisdictional conflicts between the Cour de Cassation and the Conseil d'Etat.

6. France is also subject to the International Criminal Court.

7. The author of the majority opinion may also author a concurrence that provides the author's as distinct from the court's reasons. This practice is not uncommon on the US Court of Appeals for the DC Circuit but quite rare on the US Supreme Court.

8. In English practice, lawyers and judges talk as if there were an opinion of the court, but each judge in effect constructs retrospectively an opinion of the court from the opinions each judge issued in the precedent case.

9. This table is adapted from Cameron and Kornhauser (2017d).

10. Substantive administrative review shares some of these features as, in the United States, review often occurs in the context of an appeal from the rule-making process of the agency.

11. On elections, see for example Huber and Gordon (2004). On non-partisan elections, see Canes-Wrone and Clark (2009). On retention elections, see Canes-Wrone, Clark, and Park (2012). Maskin and Tirole (2004) provide theoretical grounding for the contrast between electoral accountability and unaccountable judges.

12. Members of international courts may not be subject to impeachment but they may be subject to removal by other means. The International Court of Justice, for example, allows for removal of a judge when the other judges on the bench unanimously conclude that she cannot fulfill her obligations.

13. After the Pennsylvania Supreme Court struck down the redistricting map of the state on grounds that it violated the state constitution, the Republican-controlled legislatures began impeachment proceedings against the four judges who voted to strike the statute.

14. For example, in California, justices of the state supreme court are subject to an uncontested retention election every twelve years. Failure to gain a majority vacates the seat. After she voted to strike down the death penalty, Chief Justice Rose Bird of the California Supreme Court failed to receive a majority of votes cast in a highly disputed retention election.

15. Eskridge and Ferejohn (1992) exemplify this in the US context. Carrubba, Gabel, and Hankla (2008) empirically study the European Court of Justice in this framework.

16. Some apex courts, such as the Constitutional Court of Colombia and the Indian Supreme Court, have held that certain core provisions of the constitution are non-amendable in which case the decisions of the reviewing court would be final.

17. Prior to the UK entry into the EU, UK courts could not exercise judicial review of parliamentary action. Upon entry to the EU, UK courts could, of course, rule that a statute failed to conform to EU law.

18. Ramos Romeu (2002) and Carrubba and Murrah (2005) study this referral process.

19. The constraints a court faces depend in part on what the judges and the court care about. The text assumes that judges and the court care about the court's actions, crudely understood. But, as the next section discusses, the court may care about the social consequences of its actions. In this instance, the court is constrained by the social processes that transform its decisions into social consequences. The court, therefore, does not through its decision unilaterally determine the social consequences; the social consequences result from the response of private citizens and public officials.

20. On some courts, the choice between case-by-case and issue-by-issue adjudication is not the result of a centralized rule that governs each case before the court but arises from the decentralized choices of individual judges on how to count the votes of their colleagues. For further discussion, see Kornhauser and Sager (1993).

21. More broadly, the significance of the instant case for the law is constructed by each lawyer and each citizen from the multiple opinions offered by the judges who decided the instant case. It is this procedure that motivates Dworkin's theory of adjudication as expressed in Dworkin (1975, 1986).

22. On this division between the public and private expressions and deliberations of the Cour de Cassation, see Lasser (2005).

23. A majority opinion is announced in roughly 95 percent of cases.

24. Epstein, Landes, and Posner (2013) introduce a catch-all utility function that represents, in their view, a comprehensive self-interested set of interests. For a critique, see Cameron and Kornhauser (2017c).

25. It is interesting to note that prior work on judicial preferences rarely, if ever, suggests preferences over dispositions. Baum (1994), for instance, surveys the literature and identifies four classes of concerns that might enter the judge's preferences: the content of the decision, life on the court, career, and personal standing. The discussion of the content of the decision identifies only preferences over policy and accuracy in the interpretation of the law. He attributes this latter preference only with lower court and non-federal judges. He also does not link accuracy to preferences over dispositions.

26. Virtually no author adopts this approach. Epstein, Landes, and Posner (2013) perhaps come closest as they define a very capacious labor market model of judicial behavior in which a judge cares about job satisfaction, internal reputation, and external reputation (among other things). But the authors derive no implications from this model.

27. See, for example, Ramseyer and Rasmusen (2003).
28. For further discussion, see Cameron, Kornhauser, and Parameswaran (2019) and Ainsley, Carrubba, and Vanberg (2015).
29. The separability of policy preferences over rules means that a judge prefers disposition one to disposition two, regardless of the disposition in other cases. The set of separable preferences is small in the set of all possible policy preferences. When we fix the distribution of cases, the derived preferences over policies discussed above are separable.
30. Thus, when studying a majoritarian court, rather than coding the judge's dispositional votes, the analyst should code the judge's decision to join one or more opinions.
31. For further discussion of policy evaluation, see Kornhauser (2007). The attention to scaling judicial attitudes has unfortunately deflected attention from the role of facts as the stimulus to judicial action.
32. See Fischman and Law (2009) for a critical review of the literature.
33. A part of the paper discusses rule choice.
34. The policy space is dichotomous as is the action space of the court. Thus, formally, the court could be choosing a disposition rather than a policy.
35. This problem is distinct from the possibility of path dependence. For a simple condition that implies path independence in the case-by-case development of the law, see Kornhauser (1992a).

References

Ainsley, Caitlin, Clifford Carrubba, and Georg Vanberg. 2015. "Preferences over Legal Rules and Non-Median Outcomes on Collegial Courts." Working paper. https://wp.nyu.edu/faspepl2015/wp-content/uploads/sites/1915/2015/05/ACV_Draft_2015.pdf.

Ash, Elliot, and W. Bentley Macleod. 2015. "Intrinsic Motivation in Public Service: Theory and Evidence from State Supreme Courts." *Journal of Law and Economics* 58: 863–913.

Baum, Lawrence. 1994. "What Judges Want: Judge's Goals and Judicial Behavior." *Political Research Quarterly* 47 (3): 749–68.

Cameron, Charles M., and Lewis A. Kornhauser. 2012. "Modeling Collegial Courts (3): Judicial Objectives, Opinion Content, Voting and Adjudication Equilibria." NYU School of Law, Public Law Research Paper No. 12-52; NYU Law and Economics Research Paper No. 12-34. http://dx.doi.org/10.2139/ssrn.2153785.

———. 2017a. "Chapter 2: What Courts Do . . . And How to Model It." NYU Law and Economics Research Paper. http://dx.doi.org/10.2139/ssrn.2979391.

———. 2017b. "Chapter 3: What do Judges Want?" NYU Law and Economics Research Paper. http://dx.doi.org/10.2139/ssrn.2979419.

———. 2017c. "Rational Choice Attitudinalism?" *European Journal of Law and Economics* 43 (3): 535–54.

———. 2017d. "Theorizing the Supreme Court." In *The Oxford Research Encyclopedia on Politics.* http://dx.doi.org/10.1093/acrefore/9780190228637.013 .264.

Cameron, Charles M., Lewis A. Kornhauser, and Giri Parameswaran. 2019. "Stare Decisis and Judicial Log-Rolls: A Gains-from-Trade Model." *Rand Journal of Economics* 50: 505–31.

Canes-Wrone, Brandice, and Tom S. Clark. 2009. "Judicial Independence and Non-Partisan Elections." *Wisconsin Law Review* 2009: 21–65.

Canes-Wrone, Brandice, Tom S. Clark, and Jee-Kwang Park. 2012. "Judicial Independence and Retention Elections." *Journal of Law Economics and Organization* 28 (2): 211–34.

Carrubba, Clifford, Barry Friedman, Andrew Martin, and Georg Vanberg. 2012. "Who Controls the Content of Supreme Court Opinions?" *American Journal of Political Science* 56 (2): 400–412.

Carrubba, Clifford, Matthew Gable, and Charles Hankla. 2008. "Judicial Behavior Under Political Constraints: Evidence from the European Court of Justice." *American Political Science Review* 102 (4): 435–52.

Carrubba, Clifford, and Lacey Murrah. 2005. "Legal Integration and Use of the Preliminary Ruling Process in the European Union." *International Organization* 59: 399–418.

Cooter, Robert D. 1983. "The Objectives of Private and Public Judges." *Public Choice* 41: 107–32.

Dworkin, Ronald M. 1975. "Hard Cases." *Harvard Law Review* 88 (6): 1057–109.

———. 1986. *Law's Empire.* Cambridge, MA: Harvard University Press.

Epstein, Lee, William Landes, and Richard Posner. 2013. *The Behavior of Federal Judges: A Theoretical and Empirical Study of Rational Choice.* Cambridge, MA: Harvard University Press.

Eskridge, William N., Jr., and John Ferejohn. 1992. "The Article I, Section 7 Game." *Georgetown Law Journal* 80: 523–64.

Ferejohn, John, and Charles Shipan. 1990. "Congressional Influence on Bureaucracy." *Journal of Law, Economics, and Organization* 6: 1–20.

Fernandez, Patricio, and Giacomo A. M. Ponzetto. 2010. "Stare Decisis: Rhetoric and Substance." *Journal of Law Economics and Organization* 28 (2): 313–36.

Fischman, Joshua. 2008. "Decision Making Under a Norm of Consensus: A Structural Analysis of Three-Judge Panels." Paper Presented at the First Annual Conference on Empirical Legal Studies. http://papers.ssrn.com/sol3 /papers.cfm?abstract_id=912299.

———. 2011. "Estimating Preferences of Circuit Judges: A Model of Consensus Voting." *Journal of Law and Economics* 54 (4): 781–809.

Fischman, Joshua, and David Law. 2009. "What is Judicial Ideology and How Should We Measure It?" *Washington University Journal of Law and Policy* 29: 133–214.

Gennaioli, Nicola, and Andri Shleifer. 2007. "The Evolution of the Common Law." *Journal of Political Economy* 115: 43–68.

Hammond, Thomas, Chris Bonneau, and Reginald Sheehan. 2005. *Strategic Behavior and Policy Choice on the U.S. Supreme Court.* Palo Alto CA: Stanford University Press.

Huber, Gregory A., and Sanford C. Gordon. 2004. "Accountability and Coercion: Is Justice Blind When It Runs for Office?" *American Journal of Political Science* 48 (2): 247–63.

Iaryczower, Matias, and Matthew Shum. 2012. "The Value of Information in the Court: Get it Right, Keep it Tight." *American Economic Review* 102 (1): 202–37.

Jacobi, Tonja. 2009. "Competing Models of Judicial Coalition Formation and Case Outcome Determination." *Journal of Legal Analysis* 1 (2): 411–58.

Kornhauser, Lewis A. 1992a. "Modeling Collegial Courts I: Path Dependence." *International Review of Law and Economics* 12: 169–85.

———. 1992b. "Modeling Collegial Courts II: Legal Doctrine." *Journal of Law Economics and Organization* 8 (3): 441–70.

———. 1995. "Adjudication by a Resource-Constrained Team." *Southern California Law Review* 68: 1605–29.

———. 2009. "Modeling Courts." In *Theoretical Foundations of Law and Economics,* edited by Mark D. White, 1–20. New York: Cambridge University Press.

Kornhauser, Lewis A., and Lawrence Gene Sager. 1993. "The One and the Many: Adjudication in Collegial Courts." *California Law Review* 81: 1–59.

Landa, Dimitri, and Jeffrey Lax. 2009. "Legal Doctrine on Collegial Courts." *Journal of Politics* 3: 946–63.

Lasser, Mitchel de S.-O.-I'E. 2005. *Judicial Deliberations: A Comparative Analysis of Judicial Transparency and Legitimacy.* Oxford: Oxford University Press.

Lax, Jeffrey. 2007. "Constructing Legal Rules in Appellate Courts." *American Political Science Review* 101 (3): 591–604.

———. 2011. "The New Judicial Politics of Legal Doctrine." *Annual Review of Political Science* 14: 131–57.

Marks, Brian A. 2012. "A Model of Judicial Influence on Congressional Policy Making: Grove City College v. Bell." *Journal of Law, Economics, and Organization* 31 (4): 843–75.

Marschak, Jacob, and Roy Radner. 1972. *Economic Theory of Teams.* New Haven: Yale University Press.

Maskin, Eric, and Jean Tirole. 2004. "The Politician and the Judge." *American Economic Review* 94 (4): 1034–54.

Parameswaran, Giri. 2018. "Endogenous Cases and the Evolution of Common Law." *RAND Journal of Economics* 49: 791–818.

Parameswaran, Giri, Charles M. Cameron, and Lewis A. Kornhauser. 2021. "Bargaining and Strategic Voting on Appellate Courts." *American Political Science Review*, 1–16. https://doi.org/10.1017/S0003055421000083.

Ramos Romeu, Francisco. 2002. "Judicial Cooperation in the European Courts: Testing Three Models of Judicial Behavior." *Global Jurist Frontiers* 2 (1): 1535–653.

Ramseyer, Mark, and Eric B. Rasmusen. 2003. *Measuring Judicial Independence: The Political Economy of Judging in Japan.* Chicago: University of Chicago Press.

Spiller, Pablo, and Matthew L. Spitzer. 1995. "Where is the Sin in Sincere? Sophisticated Manipulation of Sincere Judicial Voters (With Applications to Other Voting Environments)." *Journal of Law, Economics, and Organization* 11 (1): 32–63.

Vanberg, Georg. 2001. "Legislative-Judicial Relations: A Game-Theoretic Approach to Constitutional Review." *American Journal of Political Science* 45 (2) 346–61.

The US Supreme Court and Other Federal Courts

JOSHUA FISCHMAN

THE EMPIRICAL study of United States federal courts has thrived for decades in political science departments. As empirical research has developed in the legal academy, judicial behavior research has evolved into a more interdisciplinary enterprise. Legal scholars, many of whom have training in the social sciences, have joined political scientists in studying empirically how courts decide cases.

While greater interdisciplinarity offers more diverse perspectives, it can also give rise to tensions. Scholars from various disciplines pursue different research questions, apply different methodological approaches, and publish in different journals. While nearly every empirical project requires some simplifying assumptions, political scientists and legal scholars may disagree about what kinds of assumptions are acceptable.

The empirical literature on federal courts is far too voluminous to cover comprehensively here; Epstein (2005) and Whittington, Kelemen, and Caldeira (2010) provide more detailed discussions of the literature. This essay describes some active areas of research on federal courts, widely used methodological approaches, and pressing challenges in current judicial behavior research.

JUDICIAL BEHAVIOR RESEARCH IN FEDERAL COURTS: A BRIEF OVERVIEW

Much of the empirical research on federal judges investigates how they decide cases, particularly voting on the merits. This literature focuses primarily on three types of determinants of judicial decision-making.

The first are judges' innate preferences, often described as "attitudes" or "ideology." The second are strategic considerations, such as constraints posed by colleagues, other levels of the judicial hierarchy, other branches of government, or public opinion. The third category consists of legal considerations, such as doctrine, precedents, and legal texts.

Innate Preferences

Literature on judicial preferences has often characterized judges as policy makers, akin to legislators. Dating back to foundational work by Pritchett (1948) and Schubert (1965), Supreme Court scholars have analyzed the justices' votes to map them on a policy spectrum. Studies of the "attitudinal model" (Segal and Spaeth 2002) demonstrate that these innate preferences explain a large proportion of the divisions among the justices of the Supreme Court. The ideal point estimates of Martin and Quinn (2002) have become the dominant measure of ideology on the Supreme Court.

Much empirical research on the federal courts of appeals has demonstrated a strong correspondence between judicial voting behavior and ideology, typically as measured by the party of a judge's appointing president (Cross and Tiller 1998; Revesz 1997; Sunstein et al. 2006). Other studies have explored differences in judicial voting behavior by gender (Boyd, Epstein, and Martin 2010; Peresie 2005) and race (Cox and Miles 2008; Kastellec 2013; Scherer 2004). A few studies have explored other determinants of judicial behavior, such as religion (Sisk, Heise, and Morriss 2004), prosecutorial experience (Robinson 2011), or having daughters (Glynn and Sen 2015).

There have been fewer studies of political judging in district courts (e.g., Ashenfelter, Eisenberg, and Schwab 1995; Rowland and Carp 1996.) Much of the empirical literature on district courts has focused on sentencing tendencies and inter-judge disparity (e.g., Schanzenbach 2005; Waldfogel 1998), perhaps because of the ready availability of data and the importance of this research for sentencing reform.

Strategic Behavior

A rich literature in positive political theory uses game-theoretic models to explain judicial behavior. Such models view judges as "policy seekers" (Epstein and Knight 1998) who are potentially constrained by other actors. These judges behave strategically, anticipating the reactions of other actors, to pursue results that will be closest to their own policy preferences. Although much of this literature has relied on formal modeling, a growing strand tests these models empirically.

For example, a series of articles has examined whether the Supreme Court behaves strategically by considering the possibility of congressional override when the Court interprets statutes (Bailey and Maltzman 2011; Bergara, Richman, and Spiller 2003; Spiller and Gely 1992). Others have considered whether courts exercising judicial review consider the potential response of Congress (Harvey and Friedman 2006; Sala and Spriggs 2004) or public opinion (Giles, Blackstone, and Vining 2008; McGuire and Stimson 2004).

A second area of empirical research on strategic judging examines interactions between judges on different levels of the judicial hierarchy, such as whether judges' decisions are influenced by the prospect of reversal by a higher court (Boyd 2015; Fischman and Schanzenbach 2011; Klein and Hume 2003). Other studies examine strategic reactions among judicial colleagues on multi-member courts (Hettinger, Lindquist, and Martinek 2006; Maltzman, Spriggs, and Wahlbeck 2000). A large literature on "panel effects" in circuit courts examines how judges' votes are influenced by the presence of liberal or conservative panel colleagues (Revesz 1997; Sunstein et al. 2006). According to the "whistleblowing hypothesis," judges use dissents as signals to higher courts that the majority decision warrants review (Cross and Tiller 1998; Beim and Kastellec 2014; Beim, Hirsch, and Kastellec 2016). This theory combines collegial influences within multi-member courts and strategic behavior within the judicial hierarchy.

Further studies have demonstrated similar effects of having panel colleagues who are female (Boyd, Epstein, and Martin 2010) or African American (Kastellec 2016), although these effects may be due to deliberation rather than strategy. Fischman (2015) interprets these effects as channeled through colleagues' votes rather than characteristics, finding that these effects are largely uniform across characteristics and case types. He contends that panel effects may simply be the result of a strong norm of consensus in the circuit courts, similar to the norm that existed in the Supreme Court in earlier eras (Epstein, Segal, and Spaeth 2001; Post 2001).

Legal Sources

Judges often insist that they are applying law conscientiously in every case (e.g., Edwards 1998). Nevertheless, there is only a relatively small empirical literature examining legal influences on judicial behavior. Prominent examples include studies examining the influence of legally meaningful facts on Supreme Court decisions in Fourth Amendment cases (Segal 1984) and death penalty cases (George and Epstein 1992). Spaeth and Segal (1999) examine whether Supreme Court precedents override the ideological views of dissenting justices in subsequent cases. Richards and Kritzer (2002) develop the concept of "jurisprudential regimes," where legal precedents affect the relevance of case facts in subsequent cases and demonstrate their existence in the First Amendment context. Bartels (2009) examines how precedents influence the degree of ideological voting. Gilbert (2011) examines state court challenges to referenda under the "single subject rule," which requires that every ballot initiative be restricted to a single subject. He uses student surveys to construct measures of the legal merits of these challenges and found that these measures had a significant impact on the decisions in three state supreme courts.

Behavior Other than Merits Voting

Although judicial behavior studies often focus on merits voting, there are several smaller literatures that examine other forms of judicial behavior. Many of these literatures have focused on particular stages of the judicial decision-making process, such as decisions to review, oral argument, opinion assignment and drafting, deciding whether opinions should be published, and the use of precedent. Studies of judicial agenda-setting often focus on decisions by the Supreme Court to grant certiorari (Black and Boyd 2012; Black and Owens 2009; Caldeira and Wright 1988; Goelzhauser 2011) or decisions by the courts of appeals to grant en banc review (Clark 2009; Giles, Walker, and Zorn 2006).

A growing literature has examined oral argument at the Supreme Court. Some studies have found that the number of questions asked at argument predicts the final disposition (Epstein, Landes, and Posner 2013; Johnson et al. 2009) and the formation of coalitions (Black, Johnson, and Wedeking 2012). Feldman and Gill (2019) find that female justices are interrupted more often than male justices.

Judicial politics research has also examined the process of opinion assignment and authorship. Farhang, Kastellac, and Wawro (2015) find that female and liberal circuit judges are more likely to be assigned opinions in sexual harassment cases when plaintiffs prevail. Maltzman, Spriggs, and Wahlbeck (2000) explore strategic interactions in the formation of coalitions and the drafting of opinions in the Supreme Court. Bonneau et al. (2007) and Carrubba et al. (2012) have investigated whether the opinion author can move the holding closer to the author's own ideal point. In the circuit courts, where a majority of decisions are unpublished, scholars have examined how judges bargain over whether to publish a decision (Hazelton, Hinkle, and Jeon 2016; Law 2005).

Many studies have focused directly on judicial citations, typically to measure the quality of judges and the prominence of cases. For example, Choi and Gulati (2004) propose using circuit judges' citation counts as measures of judicial quality for selecting Supreme Court justices. With additional collaborators, they use citation counts to compare the quality of elected versus appointed judges (Choi, Gulati, and Posner 2008) and male versus female judges (Choi et al. 2011). Cross and Spriggs (2010) identify the most important decisions of the Supreme Court on the basis of citation counts. Fowler et al. (2007) construct more sophisticated measures of case importance using network analysis of citations.

General Gaps and Unresolved Questions

There is a widespread understanding that judicial decisions are influenced by judges' internal preferences, strategic considerations, and legal sources. Beyond this basic understanding, there is much disagreement. For example, attitudinalists emphasize the role of internal preferences (Segal and Spaeth 2002) while others see a larger role for strategical and legal considerations. Empirical research has not established *how much* each of these influences matter in general or how their influence varies by context.

There are many reasons why this question is difficult to answer. The effects of law, attitudes, and strategy are not directly measurable. The meaning of the law is often disputed in litigated cases, so there are no objective variables that represent the "law" in every case. Attitudes are similarly latent variables, estimated through models that require strong assumptions. Evidence of strategic behavior is often inferred from ideological interactions among multiple actors. Such evidence, however, is only as credible as the ideology variables on which it relies. Finally, these influences cannot be measured on a common scale that would facilitate direct comparison.

These concepts are not necessarily even distinct. If precedent constitutes a signal from a higher court to a lower court (Bueno de Mesquita and Stephenson 2002; McNollgast 1995), does following that precedent constitute strategic or legal behavior? Are beliefs about the proper exercise of judicial review attitudinal or legal? Similarly, if a legal change grants judges more policy discretion, is the exercise of this discretion attitudinal or legal?

Each of these influences on judicial behavior might be more properly characterized as bundles of influences. Judges might react differently to different kinds of legal sources, such as statutes, constitutional provisions, or judicial precedent. Judicial strategy may vary with context. Judicial attitudes may be more varied and subtle than the widely used liberal-conservative spectrum.

Although there is evidence that the Supreme Court is constrained by the political branches and public opinion, current research cannot convincingly say if this effect is large or small. Similar important questions relate to the judicial hierarchy: Do lower courts comply with Supreme Court decisions for strategic reasons or because of an internal duty to obey higher court precedent? If compliance is largely strategic, how does the Supreme Court enforce it? As a general matter, to what extent do game-theoretic models actually explain judicial behavior?

Such questions are relevant to many policy debates about the judicial role and the institutional design of the judiciary. For instance, debates about the proper scope of judicial review depend in part on how courts exercise judicial review and how the political branches modify their decisions accordingly. Debates about allocation of authority within the judicial hierarchy depend on empirical questions about how judges in each branch interact with the others. Similarly, the proper scope of deference to administrative agencies depends on how courts exercise review of agency decisions and how agencies modify their behavior in anticipation. Addressing such questions may require more refined approaches to modeling judicial behavior.

Although ideology measures and empirical strategies for studying judging have become increasingly sophisticated, further refinement may be necessary to make headway on some of these questions. As discussed below, commonly used ideology measures are adequate for testing theories but may not be precise enough to credibly estimate the magnitude of various influences on judicial behavior.

Empirical Strategies for Studying Judicial Behavior

Empirical research on judging in federal courts exploits a wide variety of methods. Regression has been a dominant statistical technique for several decades, but recent research has also exploited Markov Chain Monte Carlo methods, structural estimation, and text analysis. Recent research has also paid closer attention to issues relating to causal inference.

Many important influences on judicial behavior—most prominently, ideology—are not directly measurable. Researchers have addressed the measurement of ideology in two ways. First, they have identified variables that serve as proxies for ideology. Second, they have estimated ideology scores from judges' voting behavior. Each of these approaches has strengths and weaknesses.

Proxy Variables for Ideology

Proxy variables for judicial ideology are derived from sources other than a judge's voting behavior. A primary advantage of these measures is that because they are exogenous to judges' voting behavior they can be used in causal models to predict judges' votes or to control for their ideological tendencies in examining other behavioral phenomena. By contrast, measures that are derived from judges' votes cannot be used in subsequent analyses to explain the judges' voting behavior in a causal model (Fischman and Law 2009).

The most commonly used proxy variable is the party of a judge's appointing president. Although somewhat crude, this variable has shown to be a valid predictor of behavior in many courts and areas of law (Pinello 1999). The party variable is especially convenient for studies of three-judge panels, where the number of Democratic and Republican appointees provides an intuitive heuristic for panel ideology. Studies of Supreme Court justices often use Segal-Cover scores as proxies for ideology. These scores, which are derived from newspaper editorials about justices during the nomination process (Segal and Cover 1989), capture the views of newspaper editorial boards about the nominees' perceived liberalism or conservatism.

Giles-Hettinger-Peppers (GHP) scores for circuit judges incorporate information about a judge's home-state senator into the ideology measure (Giles, Hettinger, and Peppers 2001). The rationale for this measure is that presidents will defer to senators of the same party with regard to nominations within a particular state. Thus, when there is a single home-state senator of the same party as the appointing president, the GHP approach assigns the judge the same ideological "common space" score as the senator (Poole and Rosenthal 1997). When both senators come from the same party as the president, then the judge's GHP score is the average of the senators' common space scores. When there are no home-state senators of the same party, the judge is assigned the same common space score as the appointing president.

GHP scores, along with the related Judicial Common Space (JCS) measure (discussed below), have become commonly used proxy measures in recent years. Nevertheless, there has been very little testing about whether, or under what circumstances, the GHP measure outperforms the party variable. Indeed, several studies reported no improvement in goodness of fit over the party variable (Fischman and Law 2009).

Two recently developed measures have not yet been widely adopted but may play a more prominent role in future research. The Clerk-Based Ideology (CBI) score (Bonica et al. 2017) estimates judges' ideology from the political contributions of their law clerks. Cope and Crabtree (2020) use surveys of practicing lawyers published in the Almanac of the Federal Judiciary (AFJ) to construct ideology scores. Both the CBI and the AFJ scores have the potential to span all levels of the federal judicial hierarchy, including district courts.

Ideology Measures Derived from Behavior

Behaviorally derived ideology measures treat ideology as a latent variable that is estimated from the voting alignments in cases. For the Supreme Court, the Martin-Quinn scores (Martin and Quinn 2002) use a one-dimensional Bayesian model that estimates justices' ideal points from the Court's non-unanimous decisions. The model is based on item response models used to analyze legislative roll calls and it is estimated using a Markov Chain Monte Carlo method. The ideal points are dynamic in that they change over time as the ideology of justices evolves.

The justices' ideologies cannot be estimated precisely. Rather, the Bayesian model estimates a posterior distribution for each judge's ideal point. The commonly used Martin-Quinn scores are the means of these estimated distributions. Martin and Quinn report posterior standard deviations and quantiles, which can conceivably be used for hypothesis testing on the latent ideology parameters. However, many studies simply plug the posterior means into regression models to represent ideology.

Because the Martin-Quinn scores are derived from votes, they are reliable predictors of future voting behavior. They have superior predictive power relative to Segal-Cover scores (Fischman and Law 2009). However, because they are derived from votes, there is an inherent circularity in using them to "explain" votes. Furthermore, the Martin-Quinn model relies on assumptions of unidimensionality and sincere voting, so these scores should not be used to test these assumptions.

Estimating the ideology of circuit judges from their votes requires a different approach. Ideal point models such as Martin and Quinn (2002) make inferences about ideology from judicial disagreement. Voting in circuit courts does not conform with these models for two reasons. First, because of the strong norm of consensus in the circuit courts, circuit judges publicly disagree in only a tiny proportion of decisions; Epstein, Landes, and Posner (2013, 264–65) report that 2.7 percent of circuit court decisions during the period 1990–2007 had dissenting opinions. Nevertheless, the unanimous decisions are not always easy cases (Fischman 2015); many studies show significant differences between Democratic- and Republican-dominated panels, even in unanimous decisions. Second, the circuit courts decide almost all decisions in three-judge panels. Given the low rate of dissent, many pairs of judges participate together only rarely in non-unanimous decisions.

Studies of ideological voting in circuits courts exploit the random assignment of cases to panels (e.g., Revesz 1997; Sunstein et al. 2006). In contrast to ideal point models such as Martin and Quinn (2002), the inferences are largely drawn from differences in voting behavior *between* panels rather than *within* panels. The "consensus voting" model developed in Fischman (2011) estimates a voting model for three-judge panels in which dissent is costly. By incorporating random assignment and costly dissent, the model draws inferences from behavioral differences within and between panels. Unlike Martin-Quinn, however, the "consensus voting" model requires outcomes to be coded as liberal or conservative and is therefore also sensitive to the assumption of unidimensionality.

Bridging Measures

Much of the literature on strategic judging examines interactions between branches of government or between tiers of the judicial hierarchy. Such studies require ideology measures that span these different actors. The "Judicial Common Space" (JCS) scores map Supreme Court justices and circuit court judges in the same ideological space (Epstein et al. 2007). These scores merge the GHP scores for circuit judges and the Martin-Quinn scores for Supreme Court justices, using a transformation to map the two scores in the same space. Justices who were nominated when presidents were not constrained by the Senate serve as bridging observations; these justices have GHP scores derived from the president's ideology as well as Martin-Quinn scores derived from their subsequent voting behavior on the Court.

Using an ideal point model similar to the Martin-Quinn model, Bailey (2007) generates ideal points for Supreme Court justices, members of Congress, and presidents in a common one-dimensional ideological space. Bailey uses bridging observations, such as solicitor general filings, amicus briefs filed by members of Congress, and roll-call votes and public statements by expressly approving or disapproving of Supreme Court decisions. Bailey also uses Supreme Court decisions on related issues to bridge justices across different time periods.

Challenges and Areas for Future Progress

Although judicial politics scholars have made important strides in operationalizing and quantifying many of the important influences on judicial behavior, there remain many persistent measurement challenges. Progress will no doubt require further methodological innovation and also closer integration between theory and empirics. One cannot establish the validity of a measure until one has properly specified the construct that the measure is supposed to represent (Fischman 2013).

More refined measures of ideology and more nuanced coding of cases may be necessary to make further progress on some of the important questions about judicial behavior. Measurement error and incorrectly specified models lead to bias, so it is important to have a sense of the magnitude of this bias. This may require more careful examination of the assumptions that are used to generate such measures. The following sections discuss a few areas that may be fruitful to consider in future research.

Dimensionality of Judicial Ideology

A common assumption is that judicial ideology is one-dimensional. With respect to the Supreme Court, this claim finds some support in Grofman and Brazill (2002), who claim that a unidimensional model explains a large proportion of the variance in voting behavior in various natural courts from 1953 until 1991. Although widely cited, this claim is hardly conclusive. Grofman and Brazill find that a two-dimensional model provides some improvement in fit over a one-dimensional model, but there are no established criteria for determining how many dimensions are sufficient.

The assumption of unidimensionality is critical for a variety of applications. If ideology is unidimensional and preferences are single-peaked, then a decision by a multi-member court will be determined by its median member. The identity of the median would be critically important in understanding the decisions of the court (Grofman and Brazill 2002; Martin, Quinn, and Epstein 2005). On the other hand, if the court is multidimensional, then many pathologies of social choice can arise, such as Condorcet cycling and the doctrinal paradox (Kornhauser 1992). Agenda-setting rules will play a much larger role because decisions may depend on the order in which issues are addressed.

Several recent studies have challenged the commonly held view that ideology is one-dimensional in the Supreme Court. Lauderdale and Clark (2012) estimate separate one-dimensional models for different issue areas in the Supreme Court Database and find different ideological orderings and different medians for the various issue areas. Peress (2009) develops a random-effects model for estimating ideal points in small chambers. In applying this model to the Supreme Court, he finds that the Court had at least two dimensions from 2001 to 2005. Using multidimensional scaling, Fischman (2019) also finds a two-dimensional voting structure between 1994 and 2015.

Although there are lingering questions about the dimensionality of the Supreme Court, to my knowledge there has been no careful examination of the dimensions of the ideology space in district or circuit courts. In circuit courts, scaling methods such as those used by Grofman and Brazill (2002) or Peress (2009) could easily be applied to en banc decisions. The approach of Lauderdale and Clark (2012) could be modified to apply to district judges and three-judge panels. If these courts are unidimensional, then the ideological orderings should be similar across issue areas.

The dimensionality of judicial ideology also has important implications for measurement strategies. The Martin-Quinn scores depend on an assumption that the justices occupy a one-dimensional issue space, while the Judicial Common Space scores assume the justices and circuit judges occupy the *same* one-dimensional space. Similarly, many game-theoretic models of separation of powers (e.g., Eskridge and Ferejohn 1992; Ferejohn and Shipan 1990) assume that the Court and Congress occupy the same one-dimensional space. Deviations from strict unidimensionality may not be fatal for these literatures, however, it is difficult to assess without further examination. At a minimum, such studies could be restricted to particular issue areas where unidimensionality is more plausible.

Databases

Empirical research on federal courts has benefited enormously from widely used databases. The Supreme Court Database (Spaeth et al. 2017) provides detailed information on all Supreme Court decisions from the 1946 to the 2016 terms. The availability of this data has facilitated numerous empirical studies of the Court and also easy replication.

However, some commentators have questioned the ideological coding of decisions in the database, arguing that they suffer from "confirmation bias" or ignore multiple issues that are present in cases (Harvey and Woodruff 2013; Shapiro 2009). To some extent, such debates can never be conclusively settled. Whenever cases present multiple issues, the relative importance of these issues is inherently subjective. Perhaps future iterations of the Database can clarify when the ideological direction is clear and when it is contestable. Another approach would be to code issues separately so that decisions can include both liberal and conservative components. (The database allows for multiple issues per case but codes such issues very infrequently.) Issue coding would also facilitate more careful study of particular doctrinal issues. For example, in a study of the evolution of the standing doctrine, Ho and Ross (2010) generate a detailed issue-by-issue coding of each decision, distinguishing justices' votes on the merits from standing issues such as particularized injury or redressability.

The Court of Appeals Database includes a random sample of decisions from the federal courts of appeals from the period 1925 to 2002 (Kuersten and Haire 2007; Hurwitz and Kuersten 2012). This database includes fifteen cases per year 1925–60 and thirty cases per year 1961–2002, a tiny fraction of the total number of decisions decided by the courts of appeals. While this database has proven useful for testing models of voting behavior, the small sample size is less useful for studying adjudication in particular areas of doctrine.

In the circuit and district courts, there are still limitations on the availability of the decisions themselves. Ongoing advances in textual analysis should enable the collection and analysis of more comprehensive and detailed databases of decisions in the courts of appeals. Issue-by-issue coding will be especially important in the court of appeals, given the large number of issues that can be present in each case.

Bridging the Supreme Court and Circuit Courts

One important objective for future research is to develop richer data sets and modeling techniques to bridge the Supreme Court and circuit courts. Although the Judicial Common Space scores have served this purpose in recent years, it should be possible to construct more nuanced measures that exploit the rich data on judicial decisions in the courts of appeals. Bridge observations occur when the Supreme Court decides a case that was also decided in the courts of appeals, so it may be necessary to code cases by issues. A circuit panel may resolve multiple issues in an appeal, but the Supreme Court may only grant certiorari on one or two of these issues. The circuit panel may also be influenced by circuit precedent on a particular issue, whereas the Supreme Court would not be bound by the same precedent.

Analysis of Legal Texts

Although judicial decisions consist of text, they derive their social meaning in a variety of ways: as dispositions of disputes between particular litigants, as resolutions of particular legal issues, as precedents in a web of law, and sometimes as statements of the values central to our legal system. Until recently, empirical researchers relied exclusively on hand-coding to distill these meanings from judicial opinions. This process is inherently laborious, limiting the size of data sets that could be analyzed. It is also subjective and can be difficult to replicate.

Recent advances in methods of text analysis have the potential to revolutionize the study of judicial decisions. Such methods have already been employed to assess the clarity of judicial opinions (Goelzhauser and Cann 2014; Owens and Wedeking 2011) or whether judges allow clerks to author their opinions (Carlson, Livermore, and Rockmore 2016; Rosenthal and Yoon 2011). Hinkle and Nelson (2018) use text analysis to show that dissents using more distinctive words and emotional language generate more subsequent citations. These methods also have potential for estimating the ideological location of judicial opinions. For example, Hinkle et al. (2012) find that district judges strategically use more hedging language to avoid reversal when they are more ideologically distant from the circuit median. Future research in judicial politics will likely depend less on subjective assessment of cases and more on sophisticated algorithms for processing texts.

Conclusion

Recent events, both in the United States and around the globe, provide a stark reminder that the issues highlighted in this chapter are not merely academic. The increasing politicization of the judiciary (Devins and Baum 2017) and growing dysfunction in the confirmation process raise important questions about the influence of attitudes versus legal sources in judicial decision-making. Countering the aggressive expansion of executive power and threats to judicial independence will similarly require a nuanced understanding about how courts respond strategically to external forces. More credible methods will provide more credible answers to many of the most pressing questions facing the federal judiciary and courts around the world.

References

Ashenfelter, Orley, Theodore Eisenberg, and Stewart J. Schwab. 1995. "Politics and the Judiciary: The Influence of Judicial Background on Case Outcomes." *Journal of Legal Studies* 24: 257–81.

Bailey, Michael A. 2007. "Comparable Preference Estimates across Time and Institutions for the Court, Congress, and Presidency." *American Journal of Political Science* 51: 433–48.

Bailey, Michael A., and Forrest Maltzman. 2011. *The Constrained Court: Law, Politics, and the Decisions Justices Make*. Princeton: Princeton University Press.

Bartels, Brandon. 2009. "The Constraining Capacity of Legal Doctrine on the U.S. Supreme Court." *American Political Science Review* 103: 474–95.

Beim, Deborah, Alexander V. Hirsch, and Jonathan P. Kastellec. 2016. "Signaling and Counter-Signaling in the Judicial Hierarchy: An Empirical Analysis of *En Banc* Review." *American Journal of Political Science* 60: 490–508.

Beim, Deborah, and Jonathan P. Kastellec. 2014. "The Interplay of Ideological Diversity, Dissents, and Discretionary Review in the Judicial Hierarchy: Evidence from Death Penalty Cases." *Journal of Politics* 76: 1074–88.

Bergara, Mario, Barak Richman, and Pablo T. Spiller. 2003. "Modeling Supreme Court Strategic Decision Making: The Congressional Constraint." *Legislative Studies Quarterly* 28: 247–80.

Black, Ryan C., and Christina L. Boyd. 2102. "US Supreme Court Agenda Setting and the Role of Litigant Status." *Journal of Law, Economics, & Organization* 28: 286–312.

Black, Ryan C., Timothy R. Johnson, and Justin Wedeking. 2012. *Oral Arguments and Coalition Formation on the U.S. Supreme Court: A Deliberate Dialogue*. Ann Arbor: University of Michigan Press.

Black, Ryan C., and Ryan J. Owens. 2009. "Agenda-Setting in the Supreme Court: The Collision of Policy and Jurisprudence." *Journal of Politics* 71: 1062–75.

Bonica, Adam, Adam S. Chilton, Jacob Goldin, Kyle Rozema, and Maya Sen. 2017. "Measuring Judicial Ideology Using Law Clerk Hiring." *American Law and Economics Review* 19: 129–61.

Bonneau, Chris W., Thomas H. Hammond, Forrest Maltzman, Paul J. Wahlbeck. 2007. "Agenda Control, the Median Justice, and the Majority Opinion on the U.S. Supreme Court." *American Journal of Political Science* 51: 890–905.

Boyd, Christina L. 2015. "The Hierarchical Influence of Courts of Appeals on District Courts." *Journal of Legal Studies* 44: 113–41.

Boyd, Christina L., Lee Epstein, and Andrew D. Martin. 2010. "Untangling the Causal Effects of Sex on Judging." *American Journal of Political Science* 54: 389–411.

Bueno de Mesquita, Ethan and Matthew Stephenson. 2002. "Informative Precedent and Intrajudicial Communication." *American Political Science Review* 96: 755–66.

Caldeira, Gregory A., and John R. Wright. 1988. "Organized Interests and Agenda Setting in the U.S. Supreme Court." *American Political Science Review* 82: 1109–27.

Carlson, Keith, Michael A. Livermore, and Daniel Rockmore. 2016. "A Quantitative Analysis of Writing Style on the U.S. Supreme Court." *Washington University Law Review* 93: 1461–510.

Carrubba, Cliff, Barry Friedman, Andrew Martin, and Georg Vanberg. 2012. "Who Controls the Content of Supreme Court Opinions?" *American Journal of Political Science* 56: 400–412.

Choi, Stephen J., and Mitu Gulati. 2004. "Choosing the Next Supreme Court Justice: An Empirical Ranking of Judge Performance." *Southern California Law Review* 78: 23–118.

Choi, Stephen J., Mitu Gulati, Mirya Holman, and Eric A. Posner. 2011. "Judging Women." *Journal of Empirical Legal Studies* 8: 504–32.

Choi, Stephen J., G. Mitu Gulati, and Eric A. Posner. 2008. "Professionals or Politicians: The Uncertain Empirical Case for an Elected Rather than Appointed Judiciary." *Journal of Law, Economics, & Organization* 26: 290–336.

Clark, Tom S. 2009. "A Principal-Agent Theory of En Banc Review." *Journal of Law, Economics, & Organization* 25: 55–79.

Cope Kevin L., and Charles Crabtree. 2020. "An Expert-Sourced Measure of Judicial Ideology." *University of Virginia Law & Economics Research Paper No. 2020-19.* https://papers.ssrn.com/abstract=3739518.

Cox, Adam B., and Thomas J. Miles. 2008. "Judging the Voting Rights Act." *Columbia Law Review* 108: 1–54.

Cross, Frank B., and James F. Spriggs II. 2010. "The Most Important (and Best) Supreme Court Opinions and Justices." *Emory Law Journal* 60: 407–502.

Cross, Frank B., and Emerson H. Tiller. 1998. "Judicial Partisanship and Obedience to Legal Doctrine: Whistleblowing on the Federal Courts of Appeals."
Yale Law Journal 107: 2155–76.

Devins, Neal, and Lawrence Baum. 2017. "Split Definitive: How Party Polarization Turned the Supreme Court into a Partisan Court." *Supreme Court
Review* 2017: 301–65.

Edwards, Harry T. 1998. "Collegiality and Decision Making on the D.C. Circuit." *Virginia Law Review* 84: 1335.

Epstein, Lee, ed. 2005. *Courts and Judges.* Hampshire: Ashgate.

Epstein, Lee, and Jack Knight. 1998. *The Choices Justices Make.* Washington,
DC: CQ Press.

Epstein, Lee, William M. Landes, and Richard A. Posner. 2013. *The Behavior of
Federal Judges: A Theoretical and Empirical Study of Rational Choice.* Cambridge: Harvard University Press.

Epstein, Lee, Andrew D. Martin, Jeffrey A. Segal, and Chad Westerland. 2007.
"The Judicial Common Space." *Journal of Law, Economics, and Organization*
23: 303–25.

Epstein, Lee, Jeffrey A. Segal, and Harold J. Spaeth. 2001. "The Norm of Consensus on the U.S. Supreme Court." *American Journal of Political Science* 45
(2): 362–77.

Eskridge, William N., Jr., and John Ferejohn. 1992. "The Article I, Section 7
Game." *Georgetown Law Journal* 80: 523–64.

Farhang, Sean, Jonathan P. Kastellec, and Gregory J. Wawro. 2015. "The Politics
of Opinion Assignment and Authorship on the US Court of Appeals: Evidence from Sexual Harassment Cases." *Journal of Legal Studies* 44: S59–S85.

Feldman, Adam, and Rebecca D. Gill. 2019. "Power Dynamics in Supreme
Court Oral Arguments: The Relationship between Gender and Justice-to-
Justice Interruptions." *Justice System Journal* 40: 173–95.

Ferejohn, John, and Charles Shipan. 1990. "Congressional Influence on Bureaucracy." *Journal of Law, Economics, and Organization* 6: 1–20.

Fischman, Joshua B. 2011. "Estimating Preferences of Circuit Judges: A Model
of Consensus Voting." *Journal of Law and Economics* 54: 781–809.

———. 2013. "Reuniting 'Is' and 'Ought' in Empirical Legal Scholarship." *University of Pennsylvania Law Review* 162: 117–68.

———. 2015. "Interpreting Circuit Court Voting Patterns: A Social Interactions
Framework." *Journal of Law, Economics, and Organization* 31 (4): 808–42.

———. 2019. "Politics and Authority in the U.S. Supreme Court." *Cornell Law
Review* 104: 1513–92.

Fischman, Joshua B., and David S. Law. 2009. "What Is Judicial Ideology,
and How Should We Measure It?" *Washington University Journal of Law and
Policy* 29: 133–214.

Fischman, Joshua B., and Max M. Schanzenbach. 2011. "Do Standards of Review Matter? The Case of Federal Criminal Sentencing." *Journal of Legal Studies* 40: 405.

Fowler, James, Timothy Johnson, James Spriggs II, Sangick Jeon, and Paul Wahlbeck. 2007. "Network Analysis and the Law: Measuring the Legal Importance of Precedents at the U.S. Supreme Court." *Political Analysis* 15: 324–46.

George, Tracey E., and Lee Epstein. 1992. "On the Nature of Supreme Court Decision Making." *American Political Science Review* 86: 323–37.

Gilbert, Michael D. 2011. "Does Law Matter? Theory and Evidence from Single Subject Adjudication." *Journal of Legal Studies* 40 (2): 333–65.

Giles, Micheal W., Bethany Blackstone, and Richard L. Vining. 2008. "The Supreme Court in American Democracy: Unraveling the Linkages Between Public Opinion and Judicial Decision Making." *Journal of Politics* 70: 293–306.

Giles, Micheal W., Virginia Hettinger, and Todd Peppers. 2001. "Picking Federal Judges: A Note on Policy and Partisan Selection Agendas." *Political Research Quarterly* 54: 623–41.

Giles, Micheal W., Thomas G. Walker, and Christopher Zorn. 2006. "Setting a Judicial Agenda: The Decision to Grant En Banc Review in the U.S. Courts of Appeals." *Journal of Politics* 68: 852–66.

Glynn, Adam N., and Maya Sen. 2015. "Identifying Judicial Empathy: Does Having Daughters Cause Judges to Rule for Women's Issues?" *American Journal of Political Science* 59 (1): 37–54.

Goelzhauser, Greg. 2011. "Avoiding Constitutional Cases." *American Politics Research* 39: 483–511.

Goelzhauser, G., and D. M. Cann 2014. "Judicial Independence and Opinion Clarity on State Supreme Courts." *State Politics & Policy Quarterly* 14: 123–41.

Grofman, Bernard, and Timothy J. Brazill. 2002. "Identifying the Median Justice on the Supreme Court through Multidimensional Scaling: Analysis of 'Natural Courts,' 1953–1991." *Public Choice* 112: 55–79.

Harvey, Anna, and Barry Friedman. 2006. "Pulling Punches: Congressional Constraints on the Supreme Court's Constitutional Rulings, 1987–2000." *Legislative Studies Quarterly* 31: 533–62.

Harvey, Anna, and Michael J. Woodruff. 2013. "Confirmation Bias in the United States Supreme Court Judicial Database." *Journal of Law, Economics, and Organization* 29: 414–60.

Hazelton, Morgan, Rachael K. Hinkle, and Jee Seon Jeon. 2016. "Sound the Alarm? Judicial Decisions Regarding Publication and Dissent." *American Political Research* 44: 649–81.

Hettinger, Virginia A., Stefanie A. Lindquist, and Wendy L. Martinek. 2006. *Judging on a Collegial Court: Influences on Appellate Decision Making.* Charlottesville: University of Virginia Press.

Hinkle, Rachael K., Andrew D. Martin, Jonathan David Shaub, Emerson H. Tiller. 2012. "A Positive Theory and Empirical Analysis of Strategic Word Choice in District Court Opinions." *Journal of Legal Analysis* 4: 407–44.

Hinkle, Rachael K., and Michael J. Nelson. 2018. "How to Lose Cases and Influence People." *Statistics, Politics and Policy* 8: 195–221.

Ho, Daniel E., and Erica Ross. 2010. "Did Liberal Justices Invent the Standing Doctrine? An Empirical Study of the Evolution of Standing, 1921–2006." *Stanford Law Review* 62: 591–667.

Hurwitz, Mark S., and Ashlyn Kuersten. 2012. "Changes in the Circuits: Exploring the Courts of Appeals Databases and the Federal Appellate Courts." *Judicature* 96: 23–34.

Johnson, Timothy R., Ryan C. Black, Jerry Goldman, and Sarah A. Treul. 2009. "Inquiring Minds Want to Know: Do Justices Tip Their Hands with Questions at Oral Argument in the U.S. Supreme Court Empirical Research on Decision-Making in the Federal Courts." *Washington University Journal of Law & Policy* 29: 241–62.

Kastellec, Jonathan P. 2013. "Racial Diversity and Judicial Influence on Appellate Courts." *American Journal of Political Science* 57: 167–83.

———. 2016. "Race, Context, and Judging on the Courts of Appeals: Race-Based Panel Effects in Death Penalty Cases." https://papers.ssrn.com/sol3/papers.cfm?abstract_id=2594946.

Klein, David E., and Robert J. Hume. 2003. "Fear of Reversal as an Explanation of Lower Court Compliance." *Law & Society Review* 37: 579–606.

Kornhauser, Lewis A. 1992. "Modelling Collegial Courts. II. Legal Doctrine." *Journal of Law, Economics, & Organization* 8: 441–70.

Kuersten, Ashlyn K., and Susan B. Haire. 2007. "Update to the United States Courts of Appeals Database, 1997–2002." *Judicial Research Initiative.* http://artsandsciences.sc.edu/poli/juri/appct.htm.

Lauderdale, Benjamin E., and Tom S. Clark. 2012. "The Supreme Court's Many Median Justices." *American Political Science Review* 106: 847–66.

Law, David S. 2005. "Strategic Judicial Lawmaking: Ideology, Publication, and Asylum Law in the Ninth Circuit." *Immigration and Nationality Law Review* 26: 275.

Maltzman, Forrest, James F. Spriggs II, and Paul J. Wahlbeck. 2000. *Crafting Law on the Supreme Court.* Cambridge: Cambridge University Press.

Martin, Andrew D., and Kevin M. Quinn. 2002. "Dynamic Ideal Point Estimation via Markov Chain Monte Carlo for the U.S. Supreme Court, 1953–1999." *Political Analysis* 10 (2): 134–53.

Martin, Andrew D., Kevin M. Quinn, and Lee Epstein. 2005. "The Median Justice on the United States Supreme Court." *North Carolina Law Review* 83: 1275–321.

McGuire, Kevin T., and James A. Stimson. 2004. "The Least Dangerous Branch Revisited: New Evidence on Supreme Court Responsiveness to Public Preferences." *Journal of Politics* 66: 1018–35.

McNollgast. 1995. "Politics and the Courts: A Positive Theory of Judicial Doctrine and the Rule of Law." *Southern California Law Review* 68: 1631–83.

Owens, Ryan J., and Justin P. Wedeking. 2011. "Justices and Legal Clarity: Analyzing the Complexity of U.S. Supreme Court Opinions." *Law & Society Review* 45 (4): 1027–61.

Peresie, Jennifer L. 2005. "Female Judges Matter: Gender and Collegial Decision Making in the Federal Appellate Courts." *Yale Law Journal* 114: 1759–90.

Peress, Michael. 2009. "Small Chamber Ideal Point Estimation." *Political Analysis* 17 (3): 276–90.

Pinello, Daniel R. 1999. "Linking Party to Judicial Ideology in American Courts: A Meta-Analysis." *Justice System Journal* 20: 219–54.

Poole, Keith T., and Howard Rosenthal. 1997. *Congress: A Political-Economic History of Roll Call Voting*. New York: Oxford University Press.

Post, Robert C. 2001. "The Supreme Court Opinion as Institutional Practice: Dissent, Legal Scholarship, and Decisionmaking in the Taft Court." *Minnesota Law Review* 85: 1267–1390.

Pritchett, C. Herman. 1948. *The Roosevelt Court*. New York: MacMillan.

Revesz, Richard L. 1997. "Environmental Regulation, Ideology, and the D.C. Circuit." *Virginia Law Review* 83: 1717–72.

Richards, Mark J., and Herbert M. Kritzer. 2002. "Jurisprudential Regimes in Supreme Court Decision Making." *The American Political Science Review* 96 (2): 305–20.

Robinson, Rob. 2011. "Does Prosecutorial Experience 'Balance Out' a Judge's Liberal Tendencies?" *The Justice System Journal* 32 (2): 143–68.

Rosenthal, Jeffrey S., and Albert H. Yoon. 2011. "Detecting Multiple Authorship of United States Supreme Court Legal Decisions Using Function Words." *Annals of Applied Statistics* 5: 283–308.

Rowland, C. K., and Robert A. Carp. 1996. *Politics and Judgment in Federal District Courts*. Lawrence, KS: University Press of Kansas.

Sala, Brian R., and James F. Spriggs. 2004. "Designing Tests of the Supreme Court and the Separation of Powers." *Political Research Quarterly* 57 (2): 197–208.

Schanzenbach, Max. 2005. "Racial and Sex Disparities in Prison Sentences: The Effect of District-Level Judicial Demographics." *The Journal of Legal Studies* 34 (1): 57–92.

Scherer, Nancy. 2004. "Blacks on the Bench." *Political Science Quarterly* 119: 655.

Schubert, Glendon A. 1965. *The Judicial Mind: The Attitudes and Ideologies of Supreme Court Justices, 1946–1963*. Evanston: Northwestern University Press.

Segal, Jeffrey A. 1984. "Predicting Supreme Court Cases Probabilistically: The Search and Seizure Cases, 1962–1984." *American Political Science Review* 78: 891–900.

Segal, Jeffrey A., and Albert D. Cover. 1989. "Ideological Values and the Votes of U.S. Supreme Court Justices." *American Political Science Review* 83: 557–65.

Segal, Jeffrey, and Harold Spaeth. 2002. *The Supreme Court and the Attitudinal Model Revisited*. New York: Cambridge University Press.

Shapiro, Carolyn. 2009. "Coding Complexity: Bringing Law to the Empirical Analysis of the Supreme Court." *Hastings Law Review* 60: 477–540.

Sisk, Gregory C., Michael Heise, and Andrew P. Morriss. 2004. "Searching for the Soul of Judicial Decisionmaking: An Empirical Study of Religious Freedom Decisions." *Ohio State Law Journal* 65: 491–614.

Spaeth, Harold, Lee Epstein, Ted Ruger, Jeffrey Segal, Andrew D. Martin, and Sara Benesh. 2017. Supreme Court Database v.2017 r.01. http://scdb.wustl.edu/data.php.

Spaeth, Harold J., and Jeffrey A. Segal. 1999. *Majority Rule or Minority Will: Adherence to Precedent on the U.S. Supreme Court*. Cambridge: Cambridge University Press.

Spiller, Pablo T., and Rafael Gely. 1992. "Congressional Control or Judicial Independence: The Determinants of U.S. Supreme Court Labor-Relations Decisions, 1949–1988." *RAND Journal of Economics* 23: 463–92.

Sunstein, Cass R., David Schkade, Lisa M. Ellman, and Andres Sawicki. 2006. *Are Judges Political? An Empirical Analysis of the Federal Judiciary*. Washington, DC: Brookings Institution Press.

Waldfogel, Joel. 1998. "Does Inter-Judge Disparity Justify Empirically Based Sentencing Guidelines?" *International Review of Law and Economics* 18: 293–304.

Whittington, Keith E., R. Daniel Kelemen, and Gregory A. Caldeira, eds. 2010. *The Oxford Handbook of Law and Politics*. New York: Oxford University Press.

State Supreme Courts in the United States

The Comparative Advantage

MELINDA GANN HALL

IN STRUCTURE and focus, the scientific literature on state supreme courts in the United States is comparative.[1] From research designs utilizing single states, strategically chosen subsets of courts or states, or large-N studies of all fifty-two courts of last resort, state supreme courts serve as an outstanding analytical device for developing and testing theories of judicial decision-making focused on context. Because of the wide array of variations across the states in the factors associated with appellate court justices' choices, alternative accounts of judging can be placed in head-to-head competition, and both micro-level and macro-level influences can be assessed, all within single models. In this regard, studies of state supreme courts generate a wide range of interesting propositions relevant for exploring judicial choice in judiciaries across the globe, and vice versa.

Of course, studies of US state high courts have limitations compared with some types of cross-national comparisons. The political, economic, and social features unique to the United States generally and each state specifically restrict the range of subjects available for scientific scrutiny, just as the generalizability of empirical findings are bound by the particular configurations of the nation and the states themselves. Except with changes over time or with abrupt disruptions or upheavals, every nation is limited in this way.

Even so, there are considerable comparative advantages of using subnational courts in the United States as a theoretical and methodological device for constructing general theories of politics, as the impressive body of work on these fascinating institutions reveals. Within this rapidly developing body of research are sophisticated theories linking judicial behavior not only with the laws governing disputes and the justices' individual preferences but also with the broader context within which courts and judges operate, including basic organizational structures, procedural rules utilized by courts to build dockets and decide cases, recruitment and retention processes for staffing the bench, and the external political, economic, and social climates in which courts are situated.

The theoretical propositions and empirical findings from studies of state supreme courts provide valuable insights into the role of judicial and non-judicial factors in shaping the fundamental functions of appellate courts and the behavior of those who staff the bench. Furthermore, because the US states provide fifty distinct contexts at once, studies of state supreme courts can serve as models for how to conduct theoretically driven systematic comparative research while informing some of the most significant debates about law, courts, and politics.

This essay surveys a select set of challenges and principal topics in the state supreme court literature, much of which can help illuminate the politics of courts and judicial behavior in similar non-US contexts. As an interesting contrast to most nations, the discussion also includes a review of the impact of electoral politics on judicial choice. Although most judges around the world are not elected, these studies highlight goals beyond legal policy and personal preferences that can influence the choices of judges, as well as the significance of the political contexts within which judging occurs, including relative degrees of judicial independence.

Capitalizing on the Context of the US States

Especially since the emergence of the modern scientific literature in the 1980s, scholars of state supreme courts have embraced complex models of judicial choice and the quantitative methodologies required to test them. In fact, the perennial debate about judiciaries across the globe simply is absent—the debate between proponents of legal doctrine as the primary explanation for the decisions of judges (usually described as the legal model) and those who place an emphasis on judges' personal preferences (typically labeled the attitudinal model).

Instead, even the earliest empirical studies of state supreme courts situated these institutions squarely within their internal and external environments, noting the incentives and constraints these factors place on judges wishing to pursue their own preferences while maintaining fidelity to law. For instance, early seminal works considered the varying power of these institutions to thwart the rulings of the United States Supreme Court and shape state and national legal policies generally (e.g., Canon 1973), while others evaluated factors specific to the external environments of states affecting the propensity to dissent (e.g., Canon and Jaros 1970). Although numerous theoretical perspectives were, and continue to be, explicated in this body of work, viewing judicial choice in isolation from the political context has not been typical.

There are many explanations for this interesting deviation from US Supreme Court studies, which still constitute the most sizable proportion of the work done in the law and courts field. Most obvious is the place of state supreme courts in the appellate hierarchy. Although unlikely, state supreme courts can be reviewed and reversed by the US Supreme Court on matters of federal law, which creates an incentive for state supreme court justices to consider the likelihood of reversal when deciding some cases, including many state criminal appeals. Moreover, unlike judges appointed to the federal courts with lifetime tenure, the majority of state supreme court justices are elected through various mechanisms, thereby introducing democratic accountability and the desire to retain office into the judicial calculus.

From a different perspective, although research on state supreme courts naturally has borrowed from the US Supreme Court literature and from legal scholars generally, this work has also drawn from Americanists specializing in state politics and its various subfields, including legislative politics, public policy, campaigns and elections, interest groups, public opinion, and political parties. These various subfields all were attentive to the different political, economic, and social conditions characterizing the states, as well as the possible impact of these features on elite behavior and the functions and interactions of institutions.

Specifically with regard to state supreme courts, the extraordinary variations across the states were obvious in, among other things, the backgrounds and experiences of justices staffing the bench, the methods for selecting and retaining justices, the laws governing the disputes, the ways in which courts are organized and operate, and the various political, economic, and social conditions in each particular state. Hypothesizing that these various factors might matter was intrinsic to the research attempting to explain judicial behavior and often required accessing research, including theory and methods, from outside the law and courts subfield. Likewise, these variations were widely acknowledged as an outstanding laboratory for investigations into questions about the impact of context on judicial politics and for developing theories that effectively integrate micro-level and macro-level forces influencing judicial choice.

In these endeavors, serious momentum in the forward march of scientific discovery came with rational choice approaches to the study of state supreme courts (e.g., Brace and Hall 1993; Hall and Brace 1999). Generally speaking, rational choice theory, or the strategic model in its various manifestations, posits that political actors are instrumentally rational and that individual behavior and collective outcomes are contingent on the rules of the game created by institutions and other contextual circumstances. Among other things, institutions shape goals and create incentives and disincentives for particular choices.[2]

Assuming that not all decisions are strategic, researchers attempted to assess when and why state supreme court justices might engage in strategic behavior, typically by choosing alternatives that do not fit well with personal preferences. These models included the requisite legal factors and individual preferences, as well as a variety of institutional and other contextual variables both internal and external to courts. Thus, strategic models started with the most fundamental components of the legal model and attitudinal model but went beyond these simple accounts by connecting the pursuit of preferences and fidelity to law to the broader environments within which judges were working.

Rational choice approaches are especially well suited to state supreme courts not only because of the variations across judiciaries and states but also because these models allow for multiple goals, including reelection, progressive ambition, and administrative efficiency. Most state supreme court justices are elected, and the scientific literature has placed a considerable emphasis on how the various alternative forms of judicial selection and reselection shape the choices of courts and judges and influence their primary goals.

Table 1 illustrates some of these notable differences across courts and states. First, consider the various methods used for reselection to state supreme courts and the justices' terms of office. Remarkably, only three states provide lifetime tenure. Otherwise, state supreme court justices must be reelected in partisan, nonpartisan, or retention elections, or reselected by state political elites, which include the legislature, governor, or some sort of commission. Thus, career ambitions seem likely in these institutions.

Table 1 also shows how state supreme courts differ on the professionalization dimension, or the extent to which these institutions have the

Table 1. Selected features of US state supreme courts and the US states

State	Court reselection	Court term	Court professionalization	GDP in millions of dollars	Budget power	Legislative partisanship
Alabama	Partisan election	6	0.513	205,625	Yes	Republican
Alaska	Retention election	10	0.690	50,404	Yes	Republican
Arizona	Retention election	6	0.598	305,849	Yes	Republican
Arkansas	Nonpartisan election	8	0.506	121,383	No	Republican
California	Retention election	12	1.004	2,622,731	Yes	Democratic
Colorado	Retention election	10	0.485	322,644	No	Divided
Connecticut	Reappointment	8	0.571	259,918	No	Divided
Delaware	Reappointment	12	0.618	71,453	Yes	Democratic
Florida	Retention election	6	0.707	926,049	No	Republican
Georgia	Nonpartisan election	6	0.644	531,302	Yes	Republican
Hawaii	Reappointment	10	0.532	84,671	No	Democratic
Idaho	Nonpartisan election	6	0.512	68,377	No	Republican
Illinois	Retention election	10	0.690	796,012	No	Democratic
Indiana	Retention election	10	0.578	347,249	Yes	Republican
Iowa	Retention election	8	0.460	185,183	No	Republican
Kansas	Retention election	6	0.477	150,576	Yes	Republican
Kentucky	Nonpartisan election	8	0.621	196,681	Yes	Republican
Louisiana	Partisan election	10	0.677	236,999	No	Republican
Maine	Reappointment	7	0.406	59,295	No	Divided
Maryland	Retention election	10	0.513	382,437	Yes	Democratic
Massachusetts	Life	Life	0.575	505,776	Yes	Democratic
Michigan	Nonpartisan election	8	0.878	490,238	Yes	Republican
Minnesota	Nonpartisan election	6	0.586	339,096	No	Republican

State	Court reselection	Court term	Court professionalization	GDP in millions of dollars	Budget power	Legislative partisanship
Mississippi	Nonpartisan election	8	0.360	108,495	No	Republican
Missouri	Retention election	12	0.640	299,113	Yes	Republican
Montana	Nonpartisan/Retention if unopposed	8	0.473	46,227	Yes	Republican
Nebraska	Retention election	6	0.562	117,446	No	Unicameral Nonpartisan
Nevada	Nonpartisan election	6	0.407	146,278	Yes	Democratic
New Hampshire	Life	Life	0.694	77,208	Yes	Republican
New Jersey	Reappointment	7	0.712	575,331	Yes	Democratic
New Mexico	Partisan/Retention if unopposed	8	0.466	93,594	Yes	Democratic
New York	Reappointment	14	0.724	1,500,055	No	Divided
North Carolina	Nonpartisan election	8	0.548	521,621	No	Republican
North Dakota	Nonpartisan election	10	0.253	53,453	Yes	Republican
Ohio	Nonpartisan election	6	0.601	626,622	Yes	Republican
Oklahoma	Retention election	6	0.445	181,278	No	Republican
Oregon	Nonpartisan election	6	0.526	228,886	No	Democratic
Pennsylvania	Retention election	10	0.876	719,834	Yes	Republican
Rhode Island	Life	Life	0.530	57,529	No	Democratic
South Carolina	Reappointment	10	0.728	209,859	No	Republican
South Dakota	Retention election	8	0.336	48,354	Yes	Republican
Tennessee	Retention election	8	0.717	331,868	No	Republican
Texas	Partisan election	6	0.670	1,599,283	No	Republican
Utah	Retention election	10	0.329	157,671	No	Republican
Vermont	Reappointment	6	0.352	31,091	Yes	Democratic

(continued)

TABLE 1. Selected features of US state supreme courts and the US states (*continued*)

State	Court reselection	Court term	Court professionalization	GDP in millions of dollars	Budget power	Legislative partisanship
Virginia	Reappointment	12	0.661	492,932	Yes	Republican
Washington	Nonpartisan election	6	0.640	476,770	Yes	Democratic
West Virginia	Nonpartisan election	12	0.813	72,861	Yes	Republican
Wisconsin	Nonpartisan election	10	0.629	313,088	Yes	Republican
Wyoming	Retention election	8	0.394	38,328	No	Republican

Sources: Court reselection and term: Hall (2018b), based on data reported by the American Judicature Society. Court professionalization: Squire (2008, 228–29), showing scores based on salary, docket control, and staff. State GDPs: generated using the interactive data tool from the Bureau of Economic Analysis at https://apps.bea.gov/itable/index.cfm. Budget power: Gubernatorial budget reduction power independent of legislative approval (Perkins 2018). Legislative partisanship: 2018 data reported by the National Conference of State Legislatures at http://www.ncsl.org/Portals/1/Documents/Elections/Legis_Control_04118_26973.pdf.

capacity to do their jobs effectively. Professionalization includes salary, staff, and docket control (Brace and Hall 2001; Squire 2008). Table 1's column labeled "Court professionalization" displays the Squire Index (Squire 2008), which ranges from 0.253 (least professionalized) to 1.004 (most professionalized) as standardized against the US Supreme Court. Professionalized state supreme courts have a greater capacity to attract quality members, decide cases more efficiently and effectively, and use dockets strategically to sidestep political controversy (Brace and Hall 2001; Hall 2015). Professionalization also promotes the incumbency advantage in judicial elections (Hall 2014b, 2015).

Variations in the wealth of states are also displayed in table 1, shown as state gross domestic product (GDP) in millions of US dollars. Overall, the states range from a low of $31 billion in Vermont to $2.6 trillion in California (now the fifth largest economy in the world [Bureau of Economic Analysis]). These variations should, among other things, shape the types of issues and parties involved in the disputes, the capacity of states to fund their judiciaries, and a host of other factors relevant to judicial decision-making.

For a different look at the states, table 1 contains information about gubernatorial power and partisan control of state legislatures, both of which influence, among other things, the potential for retaliation for unpopular judicial decisions. Governors in twenty-seven states have the power to reduce the state's budget, including funding for the judiciary, without legislative approval. At the same time, almost all state legislatures are currently controlled by a single party, although states vary on which party. Unified legislatures increase the likelihood of a legislative response to undermine court decisions or otherwise attack the judiciary, which may have political repercussions for compliance with court decisions and the electoral fates of individual justices.

In short, by evaluating multiple goals in models that allow for the interplay of a host of factors internal and external to judiciaries, studies of state supreme courts have produced a fascinating body of work illustrating the remarkable complexities of the judicial calculus. Although judges outside the United States are rarely elected, other features common to state supreme courts can be found in nations across the globe, including career concerns brought about by a variety of circumstances, including relative degrees of judicial independence.

CHALLENGES IN STUDYING STATE SUPREME COURTS: LOGISTICS AND MEASUREMENT

Two particularly daunting obstacles have impeded the advancement of empirical scholarship on state supreme courts, problems endemic to studies of courts everywhere. The first is logistical: the absence of scientific infrastructure in the form of easily assembled or readily available data on all of these institutions or at least a sizable proportion of them (see, e.g., Brace and Hall 2000). The second is empirical: measuring key concepts effectively, especially the various types of preferences relevant to judicial choice, including those of the justices, other political elites, and the public. Similarly, various components of the legal model have proven challenging to operationalize, although advances have been made.

Regarding readily accessible data, the multiple types of variations that make state supreme courts intrinsically interesting and excellent avenues for comparative inquiry also render studying these institutions profoundly difficult. In the absence of central repositories, studying state supreme courts initially required gathering data from multiple and varied sources on a project-by-project basis, entirely at the cost of the investigators. For scholars interested in the behavior of the individual justices rather than court behavior at high levels of aggregation, this meant having to rely, for the most part, on intensive case studies of single states or projects focused on small numbers of states selected to maximize variations on key dimensions. With regard to sheer volume alone, state supreme courts collectively decide thousands of cases annually, in contrast to the US Supreme Court, which now decides fewer than one hundred per term.

Selecting cases carefully by substantive issue also was necessary given the range of topics decided by state supreme courts. In this regard, the death penalty and abortion have been especially popular as a research focus because of the political salience of these issues. On the death penalty and abortion, state political elites and state voters have preferences and are attentive, and various types of electoral effects and other political maneuverings, if any, are likely to be present.

Furthermore, not much was known about state supreme courts, including basic things such as docket composition, rules for granting discretionary review, caseload management techniques, opinion assignment practices and other internal operating procedures, selection and reselection practices, terms of office, judicial salaries and other resources provided to the state judiciary, rules governing the participation of amicus curiae, and biographical information about the justices. In other words, a great deal of description was necessary before researchers knew what to code and before any kind of testing could occur. For fifty states, this translated into extraordinary hours of work piecing together sources across the states, which were not standardized or complete.

But even with these substantial obstacles, scholars of state supreme courts managed to devise effective strategies for constructing data sets that would facilitate rigorous tests of hypotheses about institutions and other contextual features. With thoughtful designs, state supreme court studies evaluated the impact of all of the major forces affecting judicial politics and behavior systematically in single models, allowing direct competition among leading hypotheses. From a scientific perspective, this is the most fundamental advantage of studying state courts: the analytical and theoretical leverage obtained in these designs.

After individual scholars made progress in constructing unique data sets limited in temporal scope and subject matter that still could be used to produce theoretically compelling results, the scientific community was convinced of the utility of such work and its theoretical payoffs. This breakthrough came in the form of the State Supreme Court Data Project, launched in 1996.[3] Seven years in production and sponsored primarily by the National Science Foundation, the Data Project produced a database consisting of the cases decided by all fifty-two state supreme courts from 1995 through 1998. Though modest on the temporal dimension, 423 items of information were coded about each case (the unit of analysis), including appellate history, various facts about the dispute itself, traits of the litigants, the primary issues decided on appeal, the decisions and opinions of the courts, and the votes of the individual justices. The Data Project also included detailed information about the personal and professional backgrounds of the justices and various features of the courts and states. Thus, since the mid-2000s and for the first time, new generations of scholars (and established scholars as well) have had ready access to comprehensive data on state supreme courts and the opportunity to expand their horizons beyond the US Supreme Court and the legal and attitudinal models. The sizable body of work advancing knowledge utilizing the Data Project speaks for itself.

The next significant innovation in infrastructure came in 2013, when Matthew E. K. Hall and Jason Windett (2013) capitalized on automated textual analysis to collect and code the cases decided by all state supreme courts from 1995 through 2010. These data and the tools developed to assemble them represent a sea change in the profession and are likely to revolutionize the study of state supreme courts and other political institutions. Thus, the tedious and time-consuming process of investigators reading and coding cases may quickly be relegated to the past, although coding case outcomes still remains somewhat illusive with this technology.

The second significant challenge in studying state supreme courts relates to the measurement of key concepts, particularly the preferences of judges and various components of the legal model. Fortunately, as with data availability, considerable progress on measurement has occurred over the past several decades.

One of the most pivotal concerns in judicial politics research is accurately measuring the individual justices' preferences. Various efforts to capture judicial preferences utilize previous votes (e.g., Brace and Hall 1997; Hall 1992), journalists' perceptions of the justices at the time of their accession to office (e.g., Traut and Emmert 1998), and various social background traits. Regarding backgrounds, these variables were used as surrogates for preferences but also were considered by some to influence judicial behavior independent of preferences. On issues such as the death penalty, criminal cases generally, gender discrimination, and obscenity, studies of case outcomes and dissent have documented that social background variables influence judicial choice. These include religion (Songer and Tabrizi 1999), gender (Songer and Crews-Meyer 2000; Szmer, Christensen, and Kaheny 2015), and race (Bonneau and Rice 2009; Songer and Crews-Meyer 2000; Szmer, Christensen, and Kaheny 2015).

In this work, the trait used most frequently as a surrogate for each justice's ideological preferences has been political party affiliation or, when not known, the partisanship of the appointing governor (e.g., Brace and Hall 1995; Hall and Brace 1992, 1994). Unfortunately for many reasons, partisan affiliations are far from perfect. For one thing, partisan affiliations are difficult to identify in states in which the justices are elected in nonpartisan elections, and in other states partisanship has not consistently comported with national trends (e.g., the historic outliers of conservative southern Democrats and liberal northeastern Republicans).

Brace, Langer, and Hall (2000) attempted to address this problem by estimating contextually based party-adjusted judge ideology scores (PAJID), which blend measures of the justices' partisan affiliations with measures of state citizen or elite ideology (Berry et al. 1998), depending on the method of initial accession to the bench. More recently, Bonica and Woodruff (2014) have developed common space measures of the justices' ideal points based on campaign contributions. At about the same time, Windett, Harden, and Hall (2015) used justices' votes to generate dynamic ideal points mapped to a common space.

At present, no single measure perfectly captures the elusive concept of judicial preferences, and each is based on a series of simplifying assumptions necessary to generate the scores. However, each year brings innovations and new data upon which to build.

Another principal concept presenting measurement challenges concerns the legal model and the problem of adequately reflecting the impact of law on judicial choice. On this issue, specific case facts have been used successfully to predict both the exercise of judicial review in state supreme courts (Emmert 1992) as well as the disposition of cases (e.g., Brace and Hall 1993, 1997; Emmert 1992; Emmert and Traut 1994; Hall and Brace 1996). Other studies on a variety of topics measure legal influences by coding state constitutional provisions (Flemming, Holian, and Mezey 1998; Kassow, Songer, and Fix 2012), statutory language (Randazzo, Waterman, and Fix 2011), and support from amici (Kane 2017; Songer and Kuersten 1995).

Beyond preferences and legal factors essential to the attitudinal and legal models, there have been impressive advances on other key concepts presenting measurement challenges in studies of state supreme courts. These include, for example, robust measures of various internal operating rules (Hall 1990; Hughes, Wilhelm, and Vining 2015; McConkie 1976), case salience (Vining and Wilhelm 2011), supreme court electoral competitiveness (Hall 2015), supreme court prestige (Caldeira 1983; Comparato 2002), lower court and supreme court professionalization (Brace and Hall 2001; Squire 2008), and selection and retention systems (Goelzhauser 2018; Hall 2015). Additionally, progress has been made by scholars of state politics in measuring key variables beyond the judiciary, such as public opinion (Brace et al. 2002) and legislative professionalization (Squire 2017).

Although some of the logistical difficulties and measurement challenges in studying state supreme courts have been addressed in numerous creative ways, ongoing efforts are needed to generate new data archives and improved measures of the variables of greatest theoretical significance. To be sure, these same challenges are present whenever scholars take on any relatively unexplored court or sets of courts, but the notable advances already achieved in studies of state supreme courts and the fascinating questions posed therein should serve as encouragement to undertake these pursuits, not only in the US but around the world.

INSTITUTIONAL ARRANGEMENTS IN THE STATE SUPREME COURT LITERATURE

The range of subjects in studies of state supreme courts is considerable and well beyond the scope of this essay.[4] Overall, scholars have devoted the lion's share of attention to the causes and consequences of dissent (including opinion writing) at the individual and aggregate level (e.g., Boyea 2007; Brace and Hall 1990; Hall 1987a; Hall and Brace 1989; Matthew Hall and Windett 2016; Leonard and Ross 2014; Romano and Curry 2020), as well as explaining individual and collective decisions on the merits of the cases (e.g., Bonneau and Rice 2009; Brace and Boyea 2008; Brace and Hall 1993, 1995, 1997; Canes-Wrone, Clark, and Kelly 2014; Hall 2014a; Hall and Brace 1992, 1994).

Other topics include separation-of-powers games in state government, including the willingness of courts to docket controversial cases (Brace, Hall, and Langer 1999; Langer 2002), overturn legislative majorities (Brace, Hall, and Langer 1999; Langer 2002), and uphold challenges to executive power (Johnson 2015). Some work explores internal dynamics, including who sits as chief justice (Langer et al. 2003). Still other research looks at how courts affect other institutions, including the likelihood of drawing fire from the legislature in the form of court-curbing legislation (Leonard 2016), as well as the process of legislative bill introduction and enactment (Wilhelm 2009). From a policy perspective, topics include the consequences of judicial elections on state tort law (Baum, Klein, and Streb 2018), ideological congruence on state supreme courts (Boyea 2010), treatment of US Supreme Court precedent (Fix and Kassow 2020), and the conditions under which judges and courts support or abrogate fundamental civil rights and liberties (e.g., Beavers and Walz 1998; Gryski, Main, and Dixon 1986; Hume 2013; Lewis, Wood, and Jacobsmeier 2014; Zschirnt 2016). As a final example, the impact of nonelective judicial retention procedures has been addressed (e.g., Brace, Hall, and Langer 1999; Langer 2002; Romano and Curry 2020), revealing strategic behavior by justices to avoid reappointment denials (Gray 2017; Johnson 2015; Shepherd 2009), much in the same vein as elected justices seeking to avoid defeat at the polls.

In this sizable body of work, institutional arrangements and other contextual features have figured prominently in producing multiple goals for the justices and in shaping the effects of case facts and the justices' preferences. Excellent representations of this point are studies focused on strategic voting by state supreme court justices to minimize electoral opposition on issues salient to the public. This work specifically assesses the relationship between electoral responsiveness and a variety of conditions in the electoral environment, including single-member districts, approaching the end of a term (i.e., last two years), narrow vote margins in the previous election (i.e., unsafe seats), inexperience in seeking reelection, and short terms (Hall 1985, 1987a, 1987b, 1992, 1995).

Generally, earlier research (e.g., Brace and Hall 1990, 1993, 1995, 1997; Hall and Brace 1989, 1992, 1994) established that judicial choice is a complex interaction of the preferences and characteristics of the justices (e.g., seniority, age, prosecutorial experience, partisan affiliations, previous votes), various case facts and other legal variables (e.g., crime and victim characteristics related to aggravating and mitigating circumstances in death penalty cases), institutional arrangements (e.g., selection and retention systems, terms of office, opinion assignment practices, and voting rules), and external environments surrounding courts (e.g., state partisan competition, state electoral competition, public opinion, citizen and elite ideology, and divided government). Although not every study of state supreme court decision-making includes the four fundamental pillars of the justices' preferences, institutional arrangements, state environmental features, and legal pressures, many do integrate these features and concomitantly assume multiple goals, thus providing compelling and sophisticated representations of the judicial calculus.

As an indicator of the diversity of such considerations, table 2 lists a selection of key contextual variables employed in studies of state supreme court decision-making. Generally, courts and states differ noticeably from each other, and some of these differences can be, and have been, examined in empirical models. Of course, there are still many features remaining to be explored.

ELECTORAL POLITICS AND STATE SUPREME COURT DECISION-MAKING

Although studies of state supreme court decision-making vary widely with regard to the specific propositions tested and methods applied, perhaps the central theme in the empirical scholarship on these institutions is this: the methods by which justices are initially chosen and then retained have a profound impact on the choices justices make. Certainly the initial work done in the 1980s and 1990s (e.g., Brace and Hall 1993,

Table 2. Select contextual variables in state supreme court decision-making studies

Individual-level electoral variables	Institutional features of courts	Characteristics of states
Approaching the end of a term (last two years)	Amicus participation rules	Budget size and features
	Caseload size	Citizen ideology
	Chief Justice power	Crime/murder rate
Experience in seeking reelection	Chief Justice selection methods	Direct democracy provisions
		Electoral competition
Initially appointed to an elected seat	Court ideology/partisan distribution	Elite ideology
		Gubernatorial budget power
Lame duck (retiring or otherwise leaving office)	Court reputation	Lawyers per capita
	Intermediate appellate court	Legislative professionalism
	Mandatory retirement	Partisan competition
Prior election to a non-judicial office	Number of justices	Population characteristics
	Opinion assignment rules	Education
Unsafe seat (previous vote percentage)	Professionalization	Percent Democratic
	Lower court	Racial diversity
	State Supreme Court	Religion
	Remuneration (including retirement benefits)	Urbanism
		Wealth
	Rules governing vote order	Public opinion
	Selection and retention methods	State constitutional provisions
	Single member vs. multi-member constituency	State statutory provisions
	Term of office	Timing of state supreme court elections
	Torts as a percentage of the docket	Unified vs. divided government

1995; Hall 1987a, 1987b, 1992, 1995; Hall and Brace 1992, 1994, 1996; Traut and Emmert 1998) placed a sharp focus on selection politics. Contemporary work has also retained and expanded this focus, including examining the elections themselves and the conventional wisdom surrounding these races (e.g., Bonneau and Hall 2009; Bonneau, Hall, and Streb 2011; Hall 2014b, 2015). Although not necessarily specifically designed as tests of electoral politics hypotheses, these studies of state supreme court decision-making nonetheless have produced a complex and nuanced body of empirical results about the impact of elections on various aspects of judicial politics.

Specifically, as described by Hall (2018a), recent work has established that various electoral practices, conditions, and concerns influence the justices' votes on issues highly salient to the public and political elites, including the death penalty (e.g., Canes-Wrone, Clark, and Kelly 2014; Hall 2014a), criminal cases (e.g., Bonneau and Rice 2009; Savchak and Barghothi 2007), civil litigation between asymmetric power litigants (e.g., Brace and Hall 2001), and abortion (e.g., Caldarone, Canes-Wrone, and Clark 2009). Electoral politics also shape dockets (e.g., Brace and Hall 2001; Brace, Hall, and Langer 2001; Langer 2002), consensus and dissent (e.g., Boyea 2007), judicial review (Brace, Hall, and Langer 2001; Langer 2002), justices' tenure (Boyea 2011; Hurwitz and Curry 2016), diversity among justices (Goelzhauser 2011), adherence to precedent (Comparato and McClurg 2007; Hoekstra 2005), the likelihood of amici curiae participation and their impact (Kane 2017, 2018), and ideological congruence among justices (Boyea 2010). Electoral politics even influence opinions and the opinion writing process in state supreme courts, including the willingness of justices to write separate concurring and dissenting opinions (Leonard and Ross 2014; Romano and Curry 2020), opinion length (Leonard and Ross 2016), opinion clarity (Goelzhauser and Cann 2014), the extent to which justices adopt text from lower court opinions (Savchak and Bowie 2016), and the linguistic strategies used in framing opinions (Romano and Curry 2020).

To wit, state supreme court justices are strategic actors situated within complex environments characterized by a mass of countervailing pressures. As one particular case in point of the consequences of selection and retention mechanisms, judicial elections bring public preferences into sharp focus for the justices, resulting in judicial decisions more consistent with citizen ideology (e.g., Brace and Hall 2001; Savchak and Barghothi 2007) and public opinion (Brace and Boyea 2008; Caldarone, Canes-Wrone, and Clark 2009; Hall 1992, 1995, 2014a). Additionally, justices in unsafe seats strategically retire rather than risk being ousted from office (Hall 2001), but mandatory retirement provisions free the justices from their electoral shackles and thus fundamentally negate the representative function (Hall 2002, 2014a).

Although most judges worldwide are not elected, career concerns of all sorts, including career advancement, may be highly relevant to other institutions. Certainly courts operate in a wide range of environments, many of which can be hypothesized to influence judicial politics, including the degree to which courts are insulated from external pressures. Studies of state supreme courts can help to inform these inquiries.

CONCLUSION

Studies of state supreme courts in the United States have provided some sophisticated and insightful propositions about judicial politics, including the impact of a wide array of institutional arrangements and other environmental factors working to shape the decisions of judges and the operations of state judiciaries. Still, there is so much more to be learned about state supreme courts. Perhaps the biggest payoffs will come from combining theories that continue to unite micro-level and macro-level approaches with research designs that capitalize on variations across the states. Extant work provides numerous excellent examples of the utility of this approach and the potential for future comparative explorations. But even with studies of single courts, whether in a US state or in any nation where institutional factors cannot be assessed directly because of the lack of variation, attention to the institutional features of the judiciary and the broader contexts within which those courts are situated can improve theory and help place results properly in the literature.

One avenue for future research with big potential payoffs is examining judicial behavior in areas of law not salient to the public and other state office holders. Although controversial hot-button issues such as capital punishment, abortion, and judicial review cases have been evaluated for scientifically compelling reasons (e.g., understanding the electoral incentive and separation-of-powers games), little is known about the decisions of judges and courts and the determinants of those decisions on more routine matters of law. Some exceptions to the lack of attention to non-salient issues include research by Cann and Wilhelm (2011) and Langer (2002), but most issues on the dockets of state supreme courts have received scant or no attention from scholars interested in judicial choice. Much more work is needed to understand the conditions under which justices respond to external pressures, if at all, when few are watching, including voters and the other branches of government.

Overall, exciting possibilities are on the horizon given recent advances in big data technologies that are revolutionizing the way judicial decisions are being collected and coded, thereby freeing researchers from more pedestrian tasks and providing information of astonishing range and detail. These new tools will facilitate comparisons across courts in unprecedented ways and will inspire new theoretical approaches and more sophisticated understandings of judicial politics. These technologies are available to study all courts in which the decisions of judges are publicly available, at least for some of the docket. Thus, state supreme court scholars are not the only beneficiaries of these recent innovations in the study of law and courts, as numerous studies of other institutions clearly demonstrate.

Most fundamentally, research on US state supreme courts is comparative. As such, scholars interested in nations beyond the United States may find these studies relevant. Through enhanced dialog and scholarly exchange among judicial politics scholars across the globe, the possibilities for scientific advancement are extraordinary.

Notes

1. This essay builds upon, and draws from, Hall (2018a), which provides a detailed extensive review of the research on state supreme courts.
2. Empirical studies of the US Supreme Court, including the attitudinal model, were initially grounded in social-psychological theory. Exceptions include Murphy (1964) and Rohde (1972a, 1972b).
3. The State Supreme Court Data Project was conducted from 1996 through 2003 at Michigan State University with Melinda Gann Hall as co-principal investigator and Rice University with Paul Brace as co-principal investigator. Originally coded with each case as the unit of analysis, the Data Project has been converted to the individual level by flipping the original data set and adding an array of individual justice variables. The Data Project is available online at https://www.ruf.rice.edu/~pbrace/statecourt/.
4. Hall (2018a) provides a comprehensive list of publications on state supreme courts and a discussion of these works.

References

Baum, Lawrence, David Klein, and Matthew J. Streb. 2018. *The Battle for the Court: Interest Groups, Judicial Elections, and Public Policy*. Charlottesville: University of Virginia Press.

Beavers, Staci L., and Jeffrey S. Walz. 1998. "Modeling Judicial Federalism: Predictors of State Court Protections of Defendants' Rights under State Constitutions, 1969–1989." *Publius* 28 (Spring): 43–59.

Berry, William D., Evan J. Ringquist, Richard C. Fording, and Russell L. Hanson. 1998. "Measuring Citizen and Government Ideology in the American States, 1960–93." *American Journal of Political Science* 42 (January): 327–48.

Bonica, Adam, and Michael J. Woodruff. 2014. "A Common-Space Measure of State Supreme Court Ideology." *Journal of Law, Economics, and Organization* 31 (3): 472–98.

Bonneau, Chris W., and Melinda Gann Hall. 2009. *In Defense of Judicial Elections*. New York: Routledge.

Bonneau, Chris W., Melinda Gann Hall, and Matthew J. Streb. 2011. "White Noise: The Unrealized Effects of *Republican Party of Minnesota* v. *White* on Judicial Elections." *Justice System Journal* 32 (3): 247–68.

Bonneau, Chris W., and Heather Marie Rice. 2009. "Impartial Judges? Race, Institutional Context, and U.S. State Supreme Courts." *State Politics & Policy Quarterly* 9 (Winter): 381–403.

Boyea, Brent D. 2007. "Linking Judicial Selection to Consensus: An Analysis of Ideological Diversity." *American Politics Research* 35 (September): 643–70.

Boyea, Brent D. 2010. "Does Seniority Matter? The Conditional Influence of State Methods of Judicial Retention." *Social Science Quarterly* 91 (March): 209–27.

Boyea, Brent D. 2011. "Time Served in State Supreme Courts: Mapping the Determinants of Judicial Seniority." *Justice System Journal* 32 (1): 44–61.

Brace, Paul, and Brent D. Boyea. 2008. "State Public Opinion, the Death Penalty, and the Practice of Electing Judges." *American Journal of Political Science* 52 (April): 360–72.

Brace, Paul, and Melinda Gann Hall. 1990. "Neo-Institutionalism and Dissent in State Supreme Courts." *Journal of Politics* 52 (February): 54–70.

Brace, Paul, and Melinda Gann Hall. 1993. "Integrated Models of Judicial Dissent." *Journal of Politics* 55 (November): 914–35.

Brace, Paul, and Melinda Gann Hall. 1995. "Studying Courts Comparatively: The View from the American States." *Political Research Quarterly* 48 (March): 5–29.

Brace, Paul, and Melinda Gann Hall. 1997. "The Interplay of Preferences, Case Facts, Context, and Structure in the Politics of Judicial Choice." *Journal of Politics* 59 (November): 1206–31.

Brace, Paul, and Melinda Gann Hall. 2000. "Comparing Courts Using the American States." *Judicature* 83 (March-April): 250–66.

Brace, Paul, and Melinda Gann Hall. 2001. "'Haves' Versus 'Have Nots' in State Supreme Courts: Allocating Docket Space and Wins in Power Asymmetric Cases." *Law & Society Review* 35 (2): 393–413.

Brace, Paul, Melinda Gann Hall, and Laura Langer. 1999. "Judicial Choice and the Politics of Abortion: Institutions, Context, and the Autonomy of Courts." *Albany Law Review* 62 (April): 1265–303.

Brace, Paul, Melinda Gann Hall, and Laura Langer. 2001. "Placing Courts in State Politics." *State Politics & Policy Quarterly* 1 (Spring): 81–108.

Brace, Paul, Laura Langer, and Melinda Gann Hall. 2000. "Measuring the Preferences of State Supreme Court Judges." *Journal of Politics* 62 (May): 387–413.

Brace, Paul, Kellie Sims-Butler, Kevin T. Arceneaux, and Martin Johnson. 2002. "Public Opinion in the American States: New Perspectives Using National Survey Data." *American Journal of Political Science* 46 (January): 173–89.

Caldarone, Richard P., Brandice Canes-Wrone, and Tom S. Clark. 2009. "Partisan Labels and Democratic Accountability: An Analysis of State Supreme Court Abortion Decisions." *Journal of Politics* 71 (April): 560–73.

Caldeira, Gregory A. 1983. "On the Reputation of State Supreme Courts." *Political Behavior* 5 (1): 83–108.

Canes-Wrone, Brandice, Tom S. Clark, and Jason P. Kelly. 2014. "Judicial Selection and Death Penalty Decisions." *American Political Science Review* 108 (February): 23–39.

Cann, Damon M., and Teena Wilhelm. 2011. "Case Visibility and the Electoral Connection in State Supreme Courts." *American Politics Research* 39 (May): 557–81.

Canon, Bradley C. 1973. "Reactions of State Supreme Courts to a U.S. Supreme Court Civil Liberties Decision." *Law & Society Review* 8 (Fall): 109–34.

Canon, Bradley C., and Dean Jaros. 1970. "External Variables, Institutional Structure, and Dissent on State Supreme Courts." *Polity* 3 (Winter): 175–200.

Comparato, Scott A. 2002. "On the Reputation of State Supreme Courts Revised." Paper delivered at the Annual Meeting of the Midwest Political Science Association, Chicago, IL, April 25–28.

Comparato, Scott A., and Scott D. McClurg. 2007. "A Neo-Institutional Explanation of State Supreme Court Responses in Search and Seizure Cases." *American Politics Research* 35 (September): 726–54.

Emmert, Craig F. 1992. "An Integrated Case-Related Model of Judicial Decision Making: Explaining Supreme Court Decisions in Judicial Review Cases." *Journal of Politics* 54 (May): 543–52.

Emmert, Craig F., and Carol Ann Traut. 1994. "The California Supreme Court and the Death Penalty." *American Politics Quarterly* 22 (January): 41–61.

Fix, Michael, and Benjamin Kassow. 2020. *U. S. Supreme Court Doctrine in State High Courts.* New York: Cambridge University Press.

Flemming, Gregory N., David Holian, and Susan Gluck Mezey. 1998. "An Integrated Model of Privacy Decision Making in State Supreme Courts." *American Politics Quarterly* 26 (January): 35–58.

Goelzhauser, Greg. 2011. "Diversifying State Supreme Courts." *Law & Society Review* 45 (September): 761–81.

Goelzhauser, Greg. 2018. "Classifying Judicial Selection Institutions." *State Politics & Policy Quarterly* 18 (2): 174–92.

Goelzhauser, Greg, and Damon M. Cann. 2014. "Judicial Independence and Opinion Clarity on State Supreme Courts." *State Politics & Policy Quarterly* 14 (2): 123–41.

Gray, Thomas. 2017. "The Influence of Legislative Reappointment on State Supreme Court Decision-Making." *State Politics & Policy Quarterly* 17 (3): 275–98.

Gryski, Gerard S., Eleanor C. Main, and William J. Dixon. 1986. "Models of State High Court Decision Making in Sex Discrimination Cases." *Journal of Politics* 48 (February): 143–55.

Hall, Matthew E. K., and Jason Harold Windett. 2013. "New Data on State Supreme Court Cases." *State Politics & Policy Quarterly* 13 (4): 427–45.

Hall, Matthew E. K., and Jason Harold Windett. 2016. "Discouraging Dissent: The Chief Judge's Influence in State Supreme Courts." *American Politics Research* 44 (4): 682–709.

Hall, Melinda Gann. 1985. "Docket Control as an Influence on Judicial Voting." *Justice System Journal* 10 (Summer): 243–55.

Hall, Melinda Gann. 1987a. "Constituent Influence in State Supreme Courts: Conceptual Notes and a Case Study." *Journal of Politics* 49 (November): 1117–24.

Hall, Melinda Gann. 1987b. "An Examination of Voting Behavior in the Louisiana Supreme Court." *Judicature* 71 (June): 40–46.

Hall, Melinda Gann. 1990. "Opinion Assignment Procedures and Conference Practices in State Supreme Courts." *Judicature* 73 (January): 209–14.

Hall, Melinda Gann. 1992. "Electoral Politics and Strategic Voting in State Supreme Courts." *Journal of Politics* 54 (May): 427–46.

Hall, Melinda Gann. 1995. "Justices as Representatives: Elections and Judicial Politics in the American States." *American Politics Quarterly* 23 (October): 485–503.

Hall, Melinda Gann. 2001. "Voluntary Retirements from State Supreme Courts: Assessing Democratic Pressures to Relinquish the Bench." *Journal of Politics* 63 (November): 1112–40.

Hall, Melinda Gann. 2002. "Assessing the Consequences of Mandatory Retirement on State High Courts: Judicial Behavior under the Condition of the Terminal Term." Paper presented at the Annual Meeting of the Midwest Political Science Association, Chicago, IL, April 25–28.

Hall, Melinda Gann. 2014a. "Representation in State Supreme Courts: Evidence from the Terminal Term." *Political Research Quarterly* 67 (June): 335–46.

Hall, Melinda Gann. 2014b. "Televised Attacks and the Incumbency Advantage in State Supreme Courts." *Journal of Law, Economics, & Organization* 30 (March): 138–64.

Hall, Melinda Gann. 2015. *Attacking Judges: How Campaign Advertising Influences State Supreme Court Elections*. Stanford, CA: Stanford University Press.

Hall, Melinda Gann. 2018a. "Decision Making in State Supreme Courts." In *Routledge Handbook of Judicial Behavior*, edited by Robert M. Howard and Kirk A. Randazzo, 301–20. New York: Routledge Press.

Hall, Melinda Gann. 2018b. "State Courts: Politics and the Judicial Process." In *Politics in the American States: A Comparative Analysis* (11th ed.), edited by Virginia Gray, Russell L. Hanson, and Thad Kousser, 275–302. Washington, D.C: CQ Press.

Hall, Melinda Gann, and Paul Brace. 1989. "Order in the Courts: A Neo-Institutional Approach to Judicial Consensus." *Western Political Quarterly* 42 (September): 391–407.

Hall, Melinda Gann, and Paul Brace. 1992. "Toward an Integrated Model of Judicial Voting Behavior." *American Politics Quarterly* 20 (April): 147–68.

Hall, Melinda Gann, and Paul Brace. 1994. "The Vicissitudes of Death by Decree: Forces Influencing Capital Punishment Decision Making in State Supreme Courts." *Social Science Quarterly* 75 (March): 136–51.

Hall, Melinda Gann, and Paul Brace. 1996. "Justices' Responses to Case Facts: An Interactive Model." *American Politics Quarterly* 24 (April): 237–61.

Hall, Melinda Gann, and Paul Brace. 1999. "State Supreme Courts and Their Environments: Avenues to General Theories of Judicial Choice." In *Supreme Court Decision Making: New Institutionalist Approaches*, edited by Cornell W. Clayton and Howard Gillman, 281–300. Chicago: University of Chicago Press.

Hoekstra, Valerie. 2005. "Competing Constraints: State Supreme Court Responses to Supreme Court Decisions and Legislation on Wages and Hours." *Political Research Quarterly* 58 (June): 317–28.

Hughes, David A., Teena Wilhelm, and Richard L. Vining, Jr. 2015. "Deliberation Rules and Opinion Assignment Procedures in State Supreme Courts: A Replication." *Justice System Journal* 36 (4): 395–410.

Hume, Robert. 2013. *Courthouse Democracy and Minority Rights: Same-Sex Marriage in the States*. New York: Oxford University Press.

Hurwitz, Mark S., and Todd A. Curry. 2016. "Strategic Retirements of Elected and Appointed Justices: A Hazard Model Approach." *Journal of Politics* 78 (October): 1061–75.

Johnson, Gbemende. 2015. "Executive Power and Judicial Deference: Judicial Decision Making on Executive Power Challenges in the American States." *Political Research Quarterly* 68 (March): 128–41.

Kane, Jenna Becker. 2017. "Lobbying Justice(s)? Exploring the Nature of Amici Influence in State Supreme Court Decision Making." *State Politics & Policy Quarterly* 17 (3): 251–74.

Kane, Jenna Becker. 2018. "Informational Need, Institutional Capacity, and Court Receptivity: Interest Groups and Amicus Curiae in State High Courts." *Political Research Quarterly* 71 (4): 881–94.

Kassow, Benjamin, Donald R. Songer, and Michael P. Fix. 2012. "The Influence of Precedent on State Supreme Courts." *Political Research Quarterly* 65 (2): 372–84.

Langer, Laura. (2002). *Judicial Review in State Supreme Courts: A Comparative Study*. Albany: SUNY Press.

Langer, Laura, Jody McMullen, Nicholas P. Ray, and Daniel D. Stratton. 2003. "Recruitment of Chief Justices on State Supreme Courts: A Choice Between Institutional and Personal Goals." *Journal of Politics* 65 (August): 656–75.

Leonard, Meghan E. 2016. "State Legislatures, State High Courts, and Judicial Independence: An Examination of Court-Curbing Legislation in the States." *Justice System Journal* 37 (1): 53–62.

Leonard, Meghan E., and Joseph V. Ross. 2014. "Consensus and Cooperation on State Supreme Courts." *State Politics & Policy Quarterly* 14 (1): 3–28.

Leonard, Meghan E., and Joseph V. Ross. 2016. "Understanding the Length of State Supreme Court Opinions." *American Politics Research* 44 (July): 710–33.

Lewis, Daniel C., Frederick S. Wood, and Matthew L. Jacobsmeier. 2014. "Public Opinion and Judicial Behavior in Direct Democracy Systems: Gay Rights in the American States." *State Politics & Policy Quarterly* 14 (4): 367–88.

McConkie, Stanford S. 1976. "Decision Making in State Supreme Courts." *Judicature* 59 (February): 337–43.

Murphy, Walter F. 1964. *Elements of Judicial Strategy.* Chicago: University of Chicago Press.

Perkins, Heather. 2018. "State Executive Branch." In *Book of the States 2017.* Lexington, KY: Council of State Governments.

Randazzo, Kirk A., Richard W. Waterman, and Michael P. Fix. 2011. "State Supreme Courts and the Effects of Statutory Constraint: A Test of the Model of Contingent Discretion." *Political Research Quarterly* 64 (December): 779–89.

Rohde, David W. 1972a. "Policy Goals and Opinion Coalitions in the Supreme Court." *Midwest Journal of Political Science* 16 (May): 208–24.

Rohde, David W. 1972b. "Policy Goals, Strategic Choice and Majority Opinion Assignments in the U.S. Supreme Court." *Midwest Journal of Political Science* 16 (November): 652–82.

Romano, Michael K., and Todd A. Curry. 2020. *Creating the Law: State Supreme Court Opinions and the Effects of Audiences.* New York: Routledge.

Savchak, Elisha Carol, and A. J. Barghothi. 2007. "The Influence of Appointment and Retention Constituencies: Testing Strategies of Judicial Decision-making." *State Politics & Policy Quarterly* 7 (Winter): 394–415.

Savchak, Elisha Carol, and Jennifer Barnes Bowie. 2016. "A Bottom-Up Account of State Supreme Court Opinion Writing." *Justice System Journal* 37 (2): 94–114.

Shepherd, Joanna M. 2009. "Are Appointed Judges Strategic Too?" *Duke Law Journal* 58: 1589–626.

Songer, Donald R., and Kelley A. Crews-Meyer. 2000. "Does Judge Gender Matter? Decision Making in State Supreme Courts." *Social Science Quarterly* 81 (September): 750–62.

Songer, Donald R., and Ashlyn Kuersten. 1995. "The Success of *Amici* in State Supreme Courts." *Political Research Quarterly* 48 (March): 31–42.

Songer, Donald R., and Susan J. Tabrizi. 1999. "The Religious Right in Court: The Decision Making of Christian Evangelicals in State Supreme Courts." *Journal of Politics* 61 (May): 507–26.

Squire, Peverill. 2008. "Measuring the Professionalization of U.S. State Courts of Last Resort." *State Politics & Policy Quarterly* 8 (Spring): 223–38.

Squire, Peverill. 2017. "A Squire Index Update." *State Politics & Policy Quarterly* 17 (4): 361–71.

Szmer, John, Robert K. Christensen, and Erin B. Kaheny. 2015. "Gender, Race, and Dissensus on State Supreme Courts." *Social Science Quarterly* 96 (June): 553–75.

Traut, Carol Ann, and Craig Emmert. 1998. "Expanding the Integrated Model of Judicial Decision Making: The California Justices and Capital Punishment." *Journal of Politics* 60 (November): 1166–80.

Vining, Richard L., and Teena Wilhelm. 2011. "Measuring Case Salience in State Courts of Last Resort." *Political Research Quarterly* 64 (September): 559–72.

Wilhelm, Teena. 2009. "Strange Bedfellows: The Policy Consequences of Legislative Judicial Relations in the American States." *American Politics Research* 37 (January): 3–29.

Windett, Jason H., Jeffrey J. Harden, and Matthew E. K. Hall. 2015. "Estimating Dynamic Ideal Points for State Supreme Courts." *Political Analysis* 23 (Summer): 461–69.

Zschirnt, Simon. 2016. "Gay Rights, the New Judicial Federalism, and State Supreme Courts: Disentangling the Effects of Ideology and Independence." *Justice System Journal* 37 (4): 348–66.

Examining the Empirical Study of the Supreme Court of Canada

LORI HAUSEGGER

CREATED IN 1875, and not officially supreme until 1949,[1] the Supreme Court of Canada (SCC) is a relatively young institution, but one that provides some great theory-testing opportunities. The role of the Supreme Court changed dramatically with the adoption of the 1982 Charter of Rights and Freedoms,[2] allowing for a before and after picture in terms of court prominence and power. The SCC is also arguably one of the most similar systems to the United States Supreme Court, providing a natural testing ground to the plethora of judicial behavior theories developed in that country. It is surprising, therefore, that there are not more comparative studies of the two courts and two systems. Indeed, I would argue that the study of the Canadian Supreme Court itself is still in a relatively early stage with room for more work in a variety of areas.

This essay traces the research areas where judicial behavior studies have been done on the Canadian Court, then discusses some of the gaps that still need to be filled and the challenges that face scholars as they attempt to fill them. Interestingly, Canadian and American scholars have tended to approach the study of courts differently, with Canadians much less likely to use quantitative methods in large-N studies. As Americans have started to turn their attention to the Canadian courts, more questions are receiving quantitative attention.

Judicial Behavior on the Supreme Court of Canada

Dubbed the "quiet court in an unquiet country" the Supreme Court of Canada until the 1970s was really a minor player in Canadian politics, "a small and undistinguished body that limited itself to giving short, technical (and, to laypeople, virtually unreadable) decisions" (McCormick 2000, 3). Political scientists left the study of legal issues to the law schools for much of the time period between World War II and the passage of the Charter (Russell 1986). While there was the occasional piece in the behavioralist tradition (see, for example, Peck's 1967 piece applying scalogram analysis to the SCC), there was little empirical work done on the Supreme Court and judicial behavior by either political scientists or law professors. Indeed, as late as 1986, Peter Russell wrote that the "empirical investigation of courts and judicial behaviour . . . has been slowly emerging as a distinct field of interest . . . [but one that] remains very much at the margin of political science" (5).

In the three decades since Professor Russell's comment, the Supreme Court's role in the Charter era has expanded, and it has become a powerful policy-making institution in Canada. Its decisions receive considerable attention from the media and have a significant impact on Canadian life (for a recent look at the court's policy impact in a variety of issue areas see the edited volume of Macfarlane 2018). With this change, empirical work on the Supreme Court has increased significantly. Canadian scholars have tended to focus more on qualitative studies, often using interviews and surveys to dig into judicial decision-making. While a few have undertaken questions using quantitative methods (for example, Alarie and Green from the University of Toronto's law school), most quantitative work by Canadians has focused more on descriptive statistics (see, for example, the extensive work by Peter McCormick).

More recently, American scholars have moved into the study of the Canadian Supreme Court, particularly those interested in testing the traveling power of theories of judicial behavior developed in the United States. The approach of most of these scholars has been heavily quantitative (see, for example, work by Roy Flemming and by Donald Songer, Matthew Wetstein, and Cynthia Ostberg). The distinction between the Canadian and American scholars is interesting and will be addressed more in the Empirical Strategies section below.

Regardless of approach, the studies of the past three decades have helped us gain a better understanding of the Supreme Court of Canada— from the decision to grant leave to appeal, to the decisions once leave is granted. However, while studies have covered a wide variety of areas in the judicial behavior realm, many of these have not been explored very deeply. With the exceptions perhaps of the influence of policy preferences on decisions and the dialog between the court and Parliament, most areas have very few studies dedicated to them.

After a brief (and likely incomplete)[3] survey of what has been done in judicial behavior (from the appeal decision to the outcome of the case), I will discuss some of the areas that may be in need of further study.

COURT PROCESSES

By Leave Decisions

Canadian scholars have examined the decision-making of Supreme Court justices at the leave to appeal stage primarily through the use of interviews (Greene et al. 1998; Macfarlane 2012a). Roy Flemming, one of the first Americans to turn his attention to Canada in the post-Charter years, studied this stage of decision-making extensively (2000, 2004; Flemming and Krutz 2002a, 2002b). His book-length treatment does make use of interviews but also uses logit regression models in his attempts to determine the influences on decisions.

Flemming's study is particularly interesting as it attempts to apply American theories of judicial behavior in the Canadian context. Flemming (2004) took factors found to be important in the certiorari decisions of the United States Supreme Court and tested them on the Supreme Court of Canada. He found some factors—for example, jurisprudential factors—had more influence in Canada than in the United States. He also discovered the importance of country-specific factors. He highlighted Canada's use of panels of three justices to rule on leave to appeal (rather than all nine justices) because he found different panels used different criteria in making their decisions.

Perhaps more noteworthy, Flemming also discovered that some theories of decision-making might work in other contexts but in different ways. For example, Flemming (2004) found that a strategic explanation argued to have some explanatory power in the United States—prediction of the court's vote on the merits (the "will I win" consideration)—did not make sense in Canada where panels were so much the norm that the three justices could not predict who would sit with them on the merits. However, that did not mean strategic considerations did not exist; they were just different. Flemming suggested that a justice who did not want to grant leave, but was outnumbered by the preferences of the rest of the panel, might vote strategically and join their colleagues making it a unanimous outcome. He argued that since the chief justice might not assign a justice to hear a case they had voted to deny leave, a potentially dissenting justice had an incentive to go along with the others and increase his or her chance of sitting on the panel and having input at the merits stage. Given the SCC's convention of asking for volunteers to write decisions, this strategic vote at the appeal stage would open the possibility of significant input on the outcome of the case.

In the years since Flemming's book *Tournament of Appeals*, there has been only limited attention to this aspect of judicial decision-making. Macfarlane (2012a) and Songer et al. (2012) addressed the topic through interviews, asking justices what influenced their vote to grant an appeal. Using data primarily from 1990 to 2011, Alarie and Green (2017) examined how the rules and processes of different courts (of which Canada was one) might affect their approach to accepting cases.

Once Leave Is Granted

For cases granted leave,[4] the chief justice of the Supreme Court decides the size of the panel and who will sit on it. In 1991, Andrew Heard drew attention to the potential impact of the use of panels in the Charter era. Since then the decision-making behind panel size and panel makeup has been studied both qualitatively (Greene et al. 1998; Macfarlane 2012a) and quantitatively (see Hausegger and Haynie 2003; Songer et al. 2012; Alarie, Green, and Iacobucci 2015). These studies have suggested that the Court is more likely to sit en banc when a Charter issue is in play and when an intervener is present,[5] and is more likely to sit as a panel for "appeal as of right" cases (Songer et al. 2012; Alarie, Green and Iacobucci 2015).

Referencing the American literature on panel assignments in the US Federal Court of Appeals (primarily the Fifth Circuit) during the civil rights era, studies of the Supreme Court of Canada's panel assignments have tested for the influence of policy preferences. There is a suggestion from the research that SCC chief justices (at least in the time period studied) were more likely to assign justices with similar policy preferences to panels in civil rights and liberties cases (Hausegger and Haynie 2003). Studies have also suggested that a justice's home province, expertise, and gender may influence their appointment to a panel (Hausegger 2000). More recent chief justices have preferred larger panels, but Chief

Justice McLachlin (2000–2017) was the first chief justice able to achieve en banc hearings more often than seven-member panels, and then only in some of her terms. This achievement is in need of further study.

In terms of judicial opinions and the Supreme Court's output, Peter McCormick probably has more data, and has written more empirical studies, than any other scholar. He has examined voting coalitions (see, for example, McCormick 1998), levels of disagreement between the justices (see, for example, McCormick 2004, 2003), the influences behind separate concurrences (McCormick 2005, McCormick 2008), and the use of anonymous decisions by the court (McCormick and Zanoni 2020). McCormick has also spent considerable time studying the use of citations by justices (1995, 2009).

McCormick's studies, while data rich, tend not to utilize quantitative models. In many of these areas, American scholars have stepped in. For example, Donald Songer and his coauthors, Szmer and Johnson (2011), examined the causes behind dissent in the Canadian Supreme Court. Using logit models, they discovered that political conflict, panel size, legal ambiguity, and the leadership style of a chief justice are all related to the likelihood of dissent. More recently, Johnson and Reid (2020) used similar methods to add gender to this list of factors, and found gender diversification to significantly impact the dissenting behavior of the court.

Determinants of Judicial Decision-Making: Inside Influences

Policy Preferences

Until relatively recently, Canadian scholars had not spent significant time studying the ideology of Supreme Court justices. Indeed, Canadian scholars long suggested that even the Supreme Court's ideological predilections were not readily apparent or consistent. Much of the work on policy preferences and their impact on judicial behavior at the Canadian Supreme Court has been done by American scholars. For example, Ostberg and Wetstein (2007) tested the American attitudinal model on the Canadian court for decisions made by that court between 1984 and 2003. These scholars found ideology played a significant role in some issues, areas (criminal and economic) but not others (civil liberties). The authors concluded that in Canada, the attitudinal model "is more complex and less pronounced than found in the United States" (Ostberg and Wetstein 2007, 216).

Songer (2008) used both interviews and quantitative models to examine the Supreme Court broadly. As part of his study, he also tested the attitudinal model. His findings were similar to those of Ostberg and Wetstein. However, Songer argued that judicial attitudes did not appear to explain unanimous decisions on the court. When the two sets of authors combined with Susan Johnson for a 2012 book, they concluded that Canadian Supreme court justices do not "simply adhere to rote liberal or conservative stances across multiple issue dimensions. Rather, their voting behavior reflect[s] a more nuanced, multi-dimensional ideological approach to the contested cases" (Songer et al. 2012, 172; see also Alarie and Green 2009). These findings suggest the need for care when constructing measures of ideology across countries.

Strategic Decision-Making

Strategic considerations have received a lot of attention in the American literature on judicial decision-making, both in terms of individual justices considering their colleagues' positions, and the US Supreme Court as an institution considering the political environment. Both of these strategic dimensions have received less attention in Canada. The studies by Flemming (2004), Songer (2008), and Ostberg and Wetstein (2007) all address the possibility that individual justices act strategically. Susan Johnson (2012) examines two periods of institutional change for the Supreme Court (1949 and 1982) and uses quantitative models to suggest the SCC justices do vote strategically. Knopff, Baker, and LeRoy (2009) explore the judicial rhetoric used in the *Sauve v. Canada* (Chief Electoral Officer) cases (*Sauve I and II*) to suggest that Supreme Court justices engage in strategic coalition building. However, when Massie, Randazzo, and Songer (2014) examined Supreme Court retirements, they found no evidence of strategic retirements for either partisan or policy purposes.

From an institutional perspective, Radmilovic's deep dive into the *Quebec Secession Reference* case leads him to argue that Canadian justices undertake strategic behavior in order to further the Court's institutional legitimacy (2010). Similarly, Knopff, Baker, and LeRoy (2009) suggest the Supreme Court justices have been strategic with their use of judicial rhetoric in some of their high-profile cases (for example, the *Patriation Reference*; see also the discussion in Russell's 1983 article, "Bold Statecraft, Questionable Jurisprudence"). Emmett Macfarlane (2012b) found that the Supreme Court's Charter-related security decisions, post 9/11, have been marked by deference and judicial minimalism, with the court being very conscious about institutional roles in the security area. While these studies have contributed to our understanding of strategic decision-making in Canada, this is definitely an area where there is room for further work.

Background Characteristics

Tate and Sittiwong (1989) were some of the first American scholars to test American theories of the influences of background characteristics—the personal attributes model—on Canadian justices. Their quantitative analysis of non-unanimous cases between 1949 and 1985 suggested that religion, region, and previous political and judicial experience had an impact on the justices' decision-making in economic and civil liberties cases.

While Songer and Johnson (2007) suggested that religion might be a time-bound influence, their more recent work with Ostberg and Wetstein (2012) found that Catholics and non-Catholics did vote significantly differently in criminal and civil liberties cases. Songer et al. (2012) also found that Ontario justices "stood out" from justices originating in other regions in terms of their support for criminal defendants and rights claimants. Schertzer (2016) examined Quebec justices as representatives of Quebec through a review of the justices' own statements and their jurisprudence in decisions important to Quebec. He discovered that these justices appeared to conceive of representation differently and regard Quebec's place in Canada differently as well.

Since Tate and Sittiwong's study, more attention has been directed at the influence of gender on decision-making. Rosalie Abella (who now sits on the SCC) has stated that every "decisionmaker who walks into a courtroom to hear a case is armed not only with the relevant legal texts, but with a set of values, experiences and assumptions that are thoroughly embedded" (1987, 8). The first female Supreme Court justice in Canada, Bertha Wilson, agreed, noting that while there are whole areas of law, such as contracts, that do not seem to have a "uniquely feminine perspective," there are other areas that have a "distinctly male perspective" (1990).

Wilson's suggestion seems to have been borne out in the literature. Songer and Johnson (2007), for example, found that the women on the SCC have tended to vote more liberally than their male colleagues in civil liberties cases but exhibited little difference in economic or criminal cases. Ostberg and Wetstein (2007) reported similar findings from their quantitative models.

Scholars have also turned their attention to other behavior by women judges, examining their dissent behavior (Belleau and Johnson 2008;

Johnson and Reid 2020) and their opinion writing (McCormick 2013). And there has been work on the effect of women lawyers on judicial decision-making before the SCC (Kaheny, Szmer, and Sarver 2011). Indeed, the impact of gender has inspired cross-national studies as well. For example, Johnson and Songer's 2009 study found gender differences across more policy areas in the SCC than in the US Supreme Court, where party played a more important role.

Overall, there has been a reasonable amount of work on some background characteristics in Canada and little to none on others (for example, the impact of the professional background of judges as crown or defense attorneys). Thus, there is room for more work to be done.

DETERMINANTS OF JUDICIAL DECISION-MAKING: OUTSIDE INFLUENCES

Interveners

The rules for interveners (the equivalent of an American amicus curiae) have shifted over the years, and non-government interveners appearing before the Supreme Court are a much more recent phenomenon. Early work took a more descriptive analysis of intervener participation, often making arguments about the normative dimensions of allowing groups access (see, for example, Brodie 2002; Hein 2001). Most of the empirical study of interveners before the Supreme Court is relatively recent. These studies suggest interveners do affect judicial decision-making. For example, Alarie and Green (2010) used quantitative analysis to find that justices with more liberal voting records voted more conservatively when a conservative intervener was present in the case.

Other Canadian studies of the influence of interveners on the court tend to focus on one group, or a particular issue area, to determine intervener impact (see for example, Radmilovic 2013, on governments; Manfredi 2004, on feminist groups; Watchel and Hennigar 2014, on Christian conservative groups). These studies suggest groups have had success as interveners before the court but leave open the question of how they are influencing the justices.

Governments

Much of the Canadian scholarship on governments and their relations to the SCC has been focused on the "dialog" between the two institutions (see for example, Hogg and Bushell 1997; Hogg, Bushell, and Wright et al. 2007; Manfredi and Kelly 1999; Hennigar 2004; Kelly 2005; Clarke

2006). The dialog literature grew out of a Hogg-Bushell argument that concerns about the undemocratic nature of judicial review under the Charter were overblown because elected officials had the capacity to respond to Supreme Court decisions. This argument sparked over a decade of back and forth between scholars, making the "dialog" literature some of the most refined on the SCC. While much of this literature has a more normative focus, there were discussions that had implications for strategic decision-making and the impact of court outcomes. For instance, would justices be more prone to "activism" because of the potential for governments to respond (particularly using section 33, the "notwithstanding clause"[6]). Or would justices be more deferential, especially in "second look" cases where a modified law has come back to the court? As noted in the Strategic Decision-Making section above, there is also a limited literature that more broadly examines the influence that the court's external political environment may have on its decisions.

Outside of the dialog and external environment literature, consideration of government-court relations is more limited. Peter McCormick (1993) examined the party capability theory and government success before the SCC, and there has been some quantitative work on the influence of governments as interveners before the court (see for example Radmilovic 2013). Matthew Hennigar and James Kelly have also written extensively on the federal government's decisions to appeal to the SCC and their treatment once there.

Gaps in the Literature

It is difficult to talk about gaps in the literature in Canada since the field is still relatively young. The passage of the Charter of Rights and Freedoms in 1982 spiked interest in the courts in Canada. So while we have seen a lot of work since the 1980s, there are areas of judicial behavior that have not received attention and many others that have room for more. As scholars continue to focus on the different questions, there will be necessary refinements of measurement and theory.

An example of an area needing more study is the leave to appeal stage of Supreme Court decision-making. As discussed above, in 2004 Flemming found that the American version of strategic explanations did not work at the leave stage in Canada—primarily because justices were unable to predict who would sit on a panel with them at the merits stage. However, we now know that in the later terms of Chief Justice McLachlin's tenure

(McLachlin retired in December 2017), the court sat en banc more than at any previous time since the enactment of the Charter. Has that change in an institutional feature affected judicial behavior at the leave to appeal stage? Or are Canadian justices still less likely to be strategic in their granting behavior?

The leave to appeal stage is also an area where professional court staff play a significant role. This staff—and their influence on judicial behavior—have been under-studied. Indeed, the inner workings of the court's processes from granting leave to opinion assignment are not illuminated very well yet. While we now know more about how chief justices decide on panels, we know little about the impact of oral arguments on the justices and even less about the influences on the opinion assignment process. We know from judicial interviews that SCC justices often volunteer to write an opinion (Greene et al. 1998; Songer 2008), but it would be interesting to have access to the actual numbers so we could determine when and how often the chief justice assigns. Have SCC chief justices been strategic in using their power to influence case decisions through opinion assignments?

Of course, there always needs to be more work refining the measurement of judicial preferences and the influences of other background characteristics. For example, there is little work in Canada on whether judicial behavior changes over a justice's time on the bench (but see Ostberg, Wetstein, and Ducat [2003] who apply American theories of "freshman effects" to Canada). Given the complexity found by Ostberg, Wetstein, and others for the impact of ideology on the Canadian bench—and the long term justices typically sit for—this adds another wrinkle into predictive models.

In terms of background characteristics, the Supreme Court has had four women justices for a number of years now and it is likely they bring different experiences to their decision-making—particularly in issue areas where gender is most relevant. We now have a few studies on this influence. However, other aspects of a justice's background should also affect their world view. One background factor that might have major implications in decision-making is professional background. Criminal cases make up about 35 percent of the SCC's docket most years. Do justices with crown or defense backgrounds approach these cases differently? Do justices with experience in criminal law get more deference from their colleagues, thus skewing decision-making models? As more years pass since the adoption of the Charter, we should have more variation between justices in order to test these kinds of influences.

Looking outward, the relationship between judicial decision-making and outside influences also seems underdeveloped. While Canadian scholars have spent a significant amount of time writing about the dialog that may exist between the Supreme Court and Parliament, much less has been done on the connection between public opinion and judicial decision-making. And if one conceives of judicial audiences similarly to Larry Baum's suggestions (social and professional groups, policy groups, the media; 2006), very little work has been done at all (although see Riddell and Morton's 1998 article coding law review articles for comparison with doctrinal development).

Finally, as in most countries, the law and courts literature in Canada has focused primarily on the Supreme Court with much less work being done on lower courts. Even the interaction between these lower courts and the Supreme Court (and any hierarchical effect) is under-studied in Canada. The focus on the high court makes sense given its position as the final court of appeal. However, with the SCC making fewer than one hundred decisions a year, the provincial courts of appeal are effectively the last resort of most cases. Given the increased importance of these courts—and the policy implications of their decisions—more scholarly work on their decision-making is needed.

EMPIRICAL STRATEGIES USED ON THE CANADIAN COURTS

As mentioned above, empirical strategies differ between Canadian and American scholars studying the Supreme Court of Canada. American scholars have primarily examined the court through quantitative analysis of large-N studies. Canadian scholars, by contrast, have primarily focused more on qualitative approaches. There are exceptions on both sides, of course. But for the most part, Canadian scholars have not enthusiastically embraced quantitative techniques in the study of judicial behavior. I find this very interesting given the proximity of the countries and the many similarities between the doctoral training in each.

Perhaps this has something to do with the growth of the study of the courts in Canada. Peter Russell—considered by many to be the grandfather of the law and courts field in political science—arrived at the University of Toronto to teach his first course in 1958. That class was Canadian Government and Politics, and like many academics teaching their first class, Russell was one week ahead of the students in the book. When he reached the point in the semester where he was supposed to discuss the Constitution, Russell discovered that the Supreme Court of Canada had become the final court of appeal in 1949. He asked his colleagues what had happened at the Court since 1949 and was told that was for the lawyers. If he wanted to know, they suggested, "go talk to Bora Laskin," a law professor at the University of Toronto Law School (and a future chief justice of the Supreme Court of Canada). Laskin gave Russell material to read and allowed him to sit in on his "Constitutional Law" class (the above discussion relies on Peter Russell's direct communication with the author, 2018). Presumably the material given to Russell by this learned law professor was not influenced by the "behavioural revolution" taking place in the United States at that time but instead included books on legal philosophy and constitutionalism.

Russell notes that in the 1960s a few political scientists like Sidney Peck and Donald Fouts attempted to apply some of the quantitative techniques gaining ground in the United States (1986, 12). However, these attempts at "quantitative analysis of judicial behaviour did not stimulate a great deal of interest" (Russell 1986, 12). Russell argues that "[b]ecause quantitative techniques usually dealt with judges' vote rather than with their reasons, it was recognized that they could not provide an adequate account of the significance of the decisions. Nor could they provide explanations of judicial decision making" (1986, 13). Indeed, by the mid-1970s, this kind of research was no longer being done on judicial decision-making in Canada. Since most of the law and courts political scientists that emerged after Russell were either trained by him or heavily influenced by his work, this meant a whole generation of scholars doing empirical work on the Supreme Court did not undertake quantitative techniques in their analyses. This has left most of the large-N quantitative work to American scholars.

CHALLENGES FACED BY RESEARCHERS
Data Access

Accessing data on the Supreme Court of Canada is easier than ever before. Until the mid-1990s, one had to physically go to the court and sit in the library while court staff brought you boxes of factums (case briefs) for you to look at and code. The Supreme Court "modernized" in the mid-1990s to . . . microfilm! Scholars had to go to the basement of the Supreme Court and look through microfilm—photocopying the needed pages. Today, however, the Supreme Court has all the party and intervener factums for cases on their website for all to access. Thus, access to case material is no longer the same obstacle it was to research on the court. It is still time-consuming and potentially expensive to collect though (if you pay for assistance), and grants in this area are not plentiful.

While the actual case material is now easier to access, data from "behind the scenes" is still difficult. We know little about opinion assignment and preliminary votes because only the justices attend conferences and, unlike their American counterparts, Canadian justices do not have the convention of providing their notes and papers to an archival site. The court itself apparently has an archivist who, among other things, interviews outgoing chief justices and keeps a record of the court (Ian Greene, direct communication with author, 2018). But this type of archival material was, until recently, unknown to scholars and is not available to the general public. Indeed, in May 2018, the *Globe and Mail* reported on an agreement between the Supreme Court of Canada and Library and Archives Canada that included a "50-year embargo on public access to files related to the deliberations of the judges, from the time they rule on a case" (Fine 2018).

Thus, much of what we know about any behind-the-scenes processes or decision-making comes from surveys of court personnel and interviews with the justices themselves. While surveys and interviews often provide rich material about the justices and the courts they sit on, these sources do have drawbacks in that they rely on someone's memory and their willingness to share honestly (or even to be aware of what is influencing their behavior). More problematically, these methods of data collection may present a difficulty to future researchers as judges and justices throughout Canada (like other Canadians!), are becoming more and more reluctant to complete surveys and allow interviews. The justices are also often highly skeptical of empirical (particularly quantitative) work on the courts—especially when it suggests non-legal factors, such as gender, may play a role in their decisions.

Broader Issues

An interesting issue for the study of Canadian courts more generally is the lack of Canadian universities training political scientists in the law and courts field today. Many of the pioneers in the field are now retired (Russell, Greene, McCormick, Baar). The second generation is also retiring or in administrative positions (for example, Knopff, Morton, Manfredi), and for those following, many are not in PhD-granting institutions, so that leaves a limited number still taking students. While scholars studying public policy, federalism, and other fields tangentially related to the courts continue to train students, those directly in the fields of law and courts are small in number and may be shrinking. This trend will be important to watch as political scientists (like any field) bring a unique perspective to studies of the court.

CHALLENGES FOR COMPARATIVE RESEARCH

Studying courts comparatively with their differing selection systems, institutional rules, and country characteristics presents a great opportunity to identify the effects of different arrangements. Comparative study should help make connections between processes, rules, and behavior. For example, different countries make different choices about the amount of political input to allow in the judicial selection process and the group representation to emphasize. What do these choices mean for judicial behavior once those selected are on the bench?

The challenge is in doing these comparative studies well. How do we capture comparable measures while still being sensitive to country-specific issues? Examining studies of the chief justice's decision-making in setting panels helps illustrate some of the difficulty of doing comparative research—particularly large-N quantitative research. Panel size and composition can be affected by random factors such as illness and off-court commitments, and if a justice is missing for long enough, models ignoring this fact can be misleading. For example, in Canada, for a period of time in the late 1980s, at least two justices were unable to sit: Justice Gerald Le Dain suffered a "major depressive illness," and Justice Jean Beetz was diagnosed with cancer (Sharpe and Roach 2003). Chief Justice Brian Dickson, therefore, was really starting with a bench of seven when setting panels. Can comparative models accurately illuminate decision-making while not taking these types of issues into account?

An added difficulty in comparative research is finding measures that work in different countries—and using measures that make sense in the country's context. For example, measures of policy preferences have been refined greatly in the United States, but many studies have used party of the appointing president as a proxy. When American scholars have studied the courts in Canada, they have tended to bring that measure with them. However, party affiliates are appointed to the Canadian courts at a lower rate than in the United States, and it is not uncommon to have a judge appointed to a lower court by one party and elevated to a higher court by another (Hausegger et al. 2010). How do we ensure that measures are capturing what we intend?

Comparative research is obviously a valuable enterprise but one that we need to approach carefully. We need to move away from a "have methods, will travel" approach to one that allows measures that are sensitive to country-specific factors but still generalizable enough to get an understanding of the impact of different institutional structures, processes, and behaviors.

NOTES

I would like to thank Nuno Garoupa, Rebecca Gill, Lydia Tiede, and the other authors in this collection for helpful comments on an earlier version of this essay. I also thank Peter Russell and Ian Greene for agreeing to speak to me about the state of the field. Finally, I thank Troy Riddell and Matthew Hennigar for providing insights on this essay.

1. Before 1949, Canadian cases could be appealed beyond the Supreme Court of Canada to Britain, where the Judicial Committee of the Privy Council (JCPC) acted as the final court of appeal.

2. In 1982, Canada repatriated its Constitution, bringing it home from Britain. The Constitution Act, 1982, included a Charter of Rights and Freedoms, which guaranteed, among other things, freedom of expression and religion, democratic rights, legal rights, equality rights, and language rights. Although Canadian courts were active in the federalism area before 1982, the Charter gave courts the authority to declare laws in violation of rights and strike down laws. Canadian courts have played a much more active policy-making role since its passage.

3. In particular, there may be some literature from francophone Quebec scholars that I am missing.

4. The SCC also hears roughly 20 percent of its docket "by right." These cases have not received extensive study but tend instead to be treated as an independent variable in studies of judicial decision-making (e.g., an influence on the size of the panel hearing a case). In addition, the court has the power to decide reference cases, a form of abstract judicial review. Although they involve some of the most controversial issues in Canadian politics, these cases have been largely neglected by law and court scholars. For two recent analysis, see Puddister 2019 and Mathen 2019.

5. An intervener is an interested third party participating in a case. This is similar to an amicus curiae in the United States, although interveners are not as prevalent as amici even at the Supreme Court level. Interveners are extremely rare at the leave to appeal stage.

6. Section 33, the notwithstanding clause, allows the federal or provincial governments to declare that a piece of legislation will operate "notwith-standing" a court ruling that it violates s. 2, or ss. 7–15 of the Charter of Rights and Freedoms. This declaration must be renewed every five years.

References

Abella, Rosalie. 1987. "The Dynamic Nature of Equality." In *Equality and Judicial Neutrality*, edited by Sheilah Marin and Kathleen Mahoney, 3–9. Toronto: Carswell.

Alarie, Benjamin, and Andrew Green. 2009. "Policy Preference Change and Appointments to the Supreme Court of Canada." *Osgoode Hall Law Journal* 47: 1–46.

Alarie, Benjamin, and Andrew Green. 2010. "Interventions at the Supreme Court of Canada: Accuracy, Affiliation, and Acceptance." *Osgoode Hall Law Journal* 48: 381–410.

Alarie, Benjamin, and Andrew Green. 2017. *Commitment and Cooperation on High Courts*. New York: Oxford University Press.

Alarie, Benjamin, Andrew Green, and Edward Iacobucci. 2015. "Panel Selection on High Courts." *University of Toronto Law Journal* 65: 335–81.

Baum, Lawrence. 2006. *Judges and Their Audiences: A Perspective on Judicial Behaviour*. Princeton: Princeton University Press.

Belleau, Marie-Claire, and Rebecca Johnson. 2008. "Judging Gender: Difference and Dissent at the Supreme Court of Canada." *International Journal of the Legal Profession* 15: 55–71.

Brodie, Ian. 2002. *Friends of the Court: The Privileging of Interest Group Litigants in Canada*. Albany: SUNY Press.

Clarke, Jeremy. 2006. "Beyond the Democratic Dialogue, and towards a Federalist One: Provincial Arguments and Supreme Court Responses in Charter Litigation." *Canadian Journal of Political Science* 39: 293–314.

Fine, Sean. 2018. "Supreme Court of Canada to Keep Records of Deliberations Secret for at Least 50 Years." *Globe and Mail*, 14 May 2018.

Flemming, Roy B. 2000. "Processing Appeals for Judicial Review: The Institutions of Agenda Setting in the Supreme Courts of Canada and the United States." In *Political Dispute and Judicial Review: Assessing the Work of the Supreme Court of Canada*, edited by Hugh Mellon and Martin Westmacott. Scarborough, Ont.: Nelson Thomson Learning.

Flemming, Roy. 2004. *Tournament of Appeals: Granting Judicial Review in Canada*. Vancouver: UBC Press.

Flemming, Roy, and Glen S. Krutz. 2002a. "Repeat Litigators and Agenda Setting on the Supreme Court of Canada." *Canadian Journal of Political Science* 35: 811–33.

Flemming, Roy, and Glen S. Krutz. 2002b. "Selecting Appeals for Judicial Review in Canada: A Replication and Multivariate Test of American Hypotheses." *Journal of Politics* 64: 232–48.

Greene, Ian, Carl Baar, Peter McCormick, George Szablowski, and Martin Thomas. 1998. *Final Appeal: Decision-Making in Canadian Courts of Appeal.* Toronto: Lorimer.

Hausegger, Lori. 2000. "Panel Selection and the Canadian Supreme Court: Neutral Assignment or the Exercise of Power." Paper presented at the Annual Meeting of the Southern Political Science Association, Atlanta.

Hausegger, Lori, and Stacia Haynie. 2003. "Judicial Decisionmaking and the Use of Panels in the Canadian Supreme Court and the South African Appellate Division." *Law and Society Review* 37: 635–57.

Hausegger, Lori, Troy Riddell, Matthew Hennigar, and Emmanuelle Richez. 2010. "Exploring the Links Between Party and Appointment: Canadian Federal Judicial Appointments from 1989 to 2003." *Canadian Journal of Political Science* 43: 633–59.

Heard, Andrew. 1991. "The Charter in the Supreme Court of Canada: The Importance of Which Judges Hear an Appeal." *Canadian Journal of Political Science* 24: 289–307.

Hein, Gregory. 2001. "Interest Group Litigation and Canadian Democracy." In *Judicial Power and Canadian Democracy*, edited by Paul Howe and Peter Russell, 214–54. Montreal: McGill-Queen's University Press.

Hennigar, Matthew. 2004. "Expanding the 'Dialogue' Debate: Canadian Federal Government Responses to Lower Court Charter Decisions." *Canadian Journal of Political Science* 37: 3–21.

Hogg, Peter, and Allison A. Bushell. 1997. "The Charter Dialogue between Courts and Legislatures (or Perhaps the Charter Isn't Such a Bad Thing after All)." *Osgoode Hall Law Journal* 35: 75–124.

Hogg, Peter, and Allison A. Bushell, and Wade K. Wright. 2007. "Charter Dialogue Revisited—or 'Much Ado About Metaphors.'" *Osgoode Hall Law Journal* 45: 1–65.

Johnson, Susan W. 2012. "The Supreme Court of Canada and Strategic Decision Making: Examining Justices' Voting Patterns during Periods of Institutional Change." *American Review of Canadian Studies* 42: 236–56.

Johnson, Susan W., and Rebecca A. Reid. 2020. "Speaking Up: Women and Dissenting Behavior in the Supreme Court of Canada." *Justice System Journal.* https://doi.org/10.1080/0098261X.2020.1768185.

Johnson, Susan W., and Donald Songer. 2009. "Judge Gender and the Voting Behavior of Justices on Two North American Supreme Courts." *Justice System Journal* 30: 265–79.

Kaheny, Erin, John Szmer, and Tammy Sarver. 2011. "Women Lawyers Before the Supreme Court of Canada." *Canadian Journal of Political Science* 44: 83–109.

Kelly, James B. 2005. *Governing with the Charter: Legislative and Judicial Activism and Framers' Intent.* Vancouver: UBC Press.

Knopff, Rainer, Denis Baker, and Sylvia LeRoy. 2009. "Courting Controversy: Strategic Judicial Decision Making." In *Contested Constitutionalism: Reflections on the Canadian Charter of Rights and Freedoms,* edited by James Kelly and Christopher Manfredi, 66–85. Vancouver: UBC Press.

Macfarlane, Emmett. 2012a. *Governing from the Bench: The Supreme Court of Canada and the Judicial Role.* Vancouver: UBC Press.

Macfarlane, Emmett. 2012b. "Failing to Walk the Rights Talk Post 9/11 Security Policy and the Supreme Court of Canada." *Review of Constitutional Studies* 16: 159–79.

Macfarlane, Emmett. 2018. *Policy Change, Courts and the Canadian Constitution.* Toronto: University of Toronto Press.

Manfredi, Christopher. 2004. *Feminist Activism in the Supreme Court: Legal Mobilization and the Women's Legal Education and Action Fund.* Vancouver: UBC Press.

Manfredi, Christopher, and James B. Kelly. 1999. "Six Degrees of Dialogue: A Response to Hogg and Bushell." *Osgoode Hall Law Journal* 37: 513–27.

Massie, Tajuana, Kirk Randazzo, and Donald Songer. 2014. "The Politics of Judicial Retirement in Canada and the United Kingdom." *Journal of Law and Courts* 2: 273–99.

Mathen, Carissima. 2019. *Courts without Cases: The Law and Politics of Advisory Opinions.* Oxford: Hart Publishing Ltd.

McCormick, Peter. 1993. "Party Capability Theory and Appellate Success in the Supreme Court of Canada, 1949–1992." *Canadian Journal of Political Science* 26: 523–40.

McCormick, Peter. 1995. "The Supreme Court Cites the Supreme Court: Follow-Up Citation on the Supreme Court of Canada, 1989–1993." *Osgoode Hall Law Journal* 33: 453–86.

McCormick, Peter. 1998. "Birds of a Feather: Alliances and Influences on the Lamer Court, 1990–1997." *Osgoode Hall Law Journal* 36: 339–68.

McCormick, Peter. 2000. *Supreme at Last: The Evolution of the Supreme Court of Canada.* Toronto: Lorimer.

McCormick, Peter. 2003. "With Respect . . . Level of Disagreement on the Lamer Court 1990–2000." *McGill Law Journal* 48: 89–116.

McCormick, Peter. 2004. "Blocs, Swarms and Outliers: Conceptualizing Disagreement on the Modern Supreme Court of Canada." *Osgoode Hall Law Journal* 42: 99–138.

McCormick, Peter. 2005. "The Choral Court: Separate Concurrence and the McLachlin Court, 2000–2004." *Ottawa Law Review* 37: 1–33.

McCormick, Peter. 2008. "Standing Apart: Separate Concurrences and the Modern Supreme Court of Canada, 1984–2006." *McGill Law Journal* 53: 137–66.

McCormick, Peter. 2009. "American Citations and the McLachlin Court: An Empirical Study." *Osgoode Hall Law Journal* 47: 83–129.

McCormick, Peter. 2013. "Who Writes: Gender and Judgment Assignment on the Supreme Court of Canada." *Osgoode Hall Law Journal* 51: 595–626.

McCormick, Peter, and Marc D. Zanoni. 2020. *By the Court: Anonymous Judgments at the Supreme Court of Canada.* Vancouver: UBC Press.

Ostberg, Cynthia L., and Matthew E. Wetstein. 2007. *Attitudinal Decision Making in the Supreme Court of Canada.* Vancouver: UBC Press.

Ostberg, Cynthia L., Matthew E. Wetstein, and Craig Ducat. 2003. "Acclimation Effects on the Supreme Court of Canada: A Cross Cultural Examination of Judicial Folklore." *Social Science Quarterly* 84: 704–22.

Peck, Sidney. 1969. "A Scalogram Analysis of the Supreme Court of Canada." In *Comparative Judicial Behavior: Cross-Cultural Studies of Political Decision Making in the East and West,* edited by Glendon Schubert and David J. Danelski, 293–324. New York: Oxford University Press.

Puddister, Kate. 2019. *Seeking the Court's Advice: The Politics of the Canadian Reference Power.* Vancouver: UBC Press.

Radmilovic, Vuk. 2010. "Strategic Legitimacy Cultivation at the Supreme Court of Canada: Quebec Secession Reference and Beyond." *Canadian Journal of Political Science* 43: 843–69.

Radmilovic, Vuk. 2013. "Governmental Interventions and Judicial Decision Making: Supreme Court of Canada in the Age of the Charter." *Canadian Journal of Political Science* 46: 323–44.

Riddell, Troy Q., and F. L. Morton. 1998. "Reasonable Limitations, Distinct Society and the Canada Clause: Interpretive Clauses and the Competition for Constitutional Advantage." *Canadian Journal of Political Science* 31: 467–93.

Russell, Peter. 1983. "Bold Statecraft, Questionable Jurisprudence." In *And No One Cheered: Federalism, Democracy and the Constitution Act,* edited by Keith Banting and Richard Simeon, 210–38. Toronto: Methuen.

Russell, Peter. 1986. "Overcoming Legal Formalism: The Treatment of the Constitution, the Courts and Judicial Behaviour in Canadian Political Science." *Canadian Journal of Law and Society* 1: 5–33.

Schertzer, Robert. 2016. "Quebec Justices as Quebec Representatives: National Minority Representation and the Supreme Court of Canada's Federalism Jurisprudence." *Publius* 46: 539–67.

Sharpe, Robert J., and Kent Roach. 2003. *Brian Dickson: A Judge's Journey.* Toronto: University of Toronto Press.

Songer, Donald. 2008. *The Transformation of the Supreme Court of Canada: An Empirical Examination.* Toronto: University of Toronto Press.

Songer, Donald, and Susan W. Johnson. 2007. "Judicial Decision Making in the Supreme Court of Canada: Updating the Personal Attribute Model." *Canadian Journal of Political Science* 40: 911–34.

Songer, Donald, and Susan W. Johnson, C. L. Ostberg, and Matthew Wetstein. 2012. *Law, Ideology and Collegiality: Judicial Behaviour in the Supreme Court of Canada.* Montreal: McGill-Queens University Press.

Songer, Donald, John Szmer, and Susan W. Johnson. 2011. "Explaining Dissent on the Supreme Court of Canada." *Canadian Journal of Political Science* 44: 389–409.

Tate, Neal C., and P. Sittiwong. 1989. "Decision-Making in the Canadian Supreme Court: Extending the Personal Attributes Model across Nation." *Journal of Politics* 51 (4): 900–16.

Watchel, Chance Minnett, and Matthew Hennigar. 2014. "Righteous Litigation: An Examination of Christian Conservative Interest Group Litigation before the Appellate Courts of Canada, 1982–2009." In *Modern Canada: 1945 to the Present,* edited by Catherine Briggs. Toronto: Oxford University Press.

Wilson, Bertha. 1990. "Will Women Judges Really Make a Difference?" *Osgoode Hall Law Journal* 28: 507–22.

Empirical Studies of Judicial Behavior and Decision-Making in Australian and New Zealand Courts

RUSSELL SMYTH

THE PURPOSE of this essay is to provide an overview of the empirical literature on judicial behavior and decision-making for courts in Australia and New Zealand.[1] Both are common law countries with stable legal systems derived from the English system. In neither country are judges elected at any level. Australia has a federal court structure, in which the High Court of Australia is the final court of appeal.[2] New Zealand has a single judicial hierarchy, in which the Supreme Court of New Zealand is the final court of appeal.[3] The picture that emerges from the review is that in Australia, and even more so in New Zealand, the empirical literature on judicial behavior is fairly thin.[4] For several theories in law, economics, and political science that could be tested with data, there are no studies at all for Australian and New Zealand courts, and for others there are just a few studies. I discuss various reasons why this is the case and the challenges to overcoming it. One of the most important reasons for this situation is that the number of people doing empirical work on Australasian courts lack critical mass. This lack of depth in the literature on Australasian courts means that it lacks the richness evident in studies for jurisdictions, such as the United States, for which there is a much larger group of scholars doing empirical work. Most of the main measures that have been refined in the US empirical literature, such as attitudinal and ideology measures, are not well developed in the Australian and New Zealand literature, and for most topics, the small number of studies makes it difficult to draw robust general conclusions.

The Empirical Literature on Judicial Behavior in Australian Courts

The empirical literature on judicial behavior in Australia dates from the late 1960s. Most of the early empirical literature on judicial behavior in Australia, which was published from the late 1960s and through the 1970s, adopted scalogram (or jurimetric) analysis, which had been pioneered by Glendon Schubert in a series of studies for the United States Supreme Court. Schubert (1968a, 1968b, 1969a, 1969b), examined the relationship between background characteristics of the High Court judges and voting behavior along a continuum from authoritarianism to collectivism. Schubert's approach, or some variant thereof, was adopted and applied in studies by Douglas (1969) and, most notably, Blackshield (1972, 1977, 1978). Between these studies, there are scalogram analyses for the Latham Court (1935–52), Dixon Court (1952–64) and Barwick Court (1964–81) (see Blackshield 2001; Gill 2002, 2009; Turner 2015 for summaries of these studies). Related research used another strand of jurimetrics, pioneered by Fred Kort, to develop mathematical models of judicial voting in an effort to predict future voting outcomes on the High Court (Tyree 1977, 1981; for more details, see Blackshield 2001; Gill 2002, 2009).

In the 1980s and 1990s there were few studies examining judicial behavior in Australia (Blackshield 2001; Gill 2002, 2009; Turner 2015). This situation has been attributed to a lack of statistical training among legal scholars in Australia and concerns about the ability of scalogram analysis to provide new insights into judicial behavior (Blackshield 2001; Gill 2009). To these points, I would add that few social scientists in Australia seemed interested in judicial behavior in this period and there was a general mistrust of attempts to apply models developed in the US literature on judicial politics to Australia. Similarly, US political scientists did not start turning their attention to the High Court until the 2000s.

In the late 1990s, a new series of studies emerged examining voting behavior on the High Court. These studies focused on the evolution of voting blocks in an attempt to find who was the most influential Justice on the court (Lynch 2003; Smyth 1999a, 2001c, 2002c). These studies cover the Latham Court (Smyth 2001c, 2002c), the Mason Court (1987–95) (Smyth 1999a), and the first five years of constitutional cases in the Gleeson Court (1998–2003) (Lynch 2003). A related set of studies has examined dissenting (Narayan and Smyth 2004; Smyth 2003a, 2004, 2005b) and joining (Pierce 2008) behavior on the High Court and its determinants. Lynch (2005) examined whether the justices disagreed—dissent or write separate judgments—more often in constitutional cases than in other areas of the law. Smyth and Narayan (2004) used time series techniques to date structural breaks in the dissent rate and examined the effect of leadership on variations in the dissent rate on the court over the twentieth century. Other related studies include Gill (2002), who analyzed patterns of decision-making using multidimensional scaling; Gill (2009), who considered determinants of "liberal votes" between 1964 and 2003; and Weiden (2011), who examined the role of attitudinal and ideological factors in influencing whether judges invalidate legislation.

Another set of studies have examined trends in caseload and decision-making on the High Court over time. Groves and Smyth (2004) considered changing patterns in judgment writing from the beginning of the court in 1903 until 2001. Lynch (2003) and then the annual Lynch and Williams studies have produced annual statistics on the court's constitutional decisions since 1998.[5] Pierce (2006, chap. 4) considered trends in constitutional cases over time as well as consideration of specific provisions (e.g. S. 51, 92) and amicus participation. Gill, Pierce, and Weiden (2011) examined trends in the caseload of the court over the period 1976–98. Gill, Pierce, and Weiden also considered other aspects of decision-making and presented trends on a number of issues (e.g., reported versus unreported decisions, appellant winning percentage, cases heard in the court's original jurisdiction, and "left leaning" decisions), drawing on the High Courts' Judicial Database.

A large number of studies have used judicial citations to examine various aspects of judicial behavior. One set of such studies have analyzed what the High Court cites and changing patterns in citation practice over time (Lefler 2011; Nielsen and Smyth 2008; Schultz 2016; Smyth 1998, 1999d, 2000d, 2001d; Smyth and Nielsen 2019; von Nessen 1992). Such studies have extended to examining citation patterns in the Federal Court of Australia (Smyth 2000a, 2000d), the state Supreme Courts (Fausten, Nielsen, and Smyth 2007; Smyth 1999b, 1999c, 2001a, 2007, 2008, 2009a, 2009b, 2009c, 2009d; Smyth and Fausten 2008), and the District Court of New South Wales (Smyth 2018). Other studies used judicial citations to rank judges according to their judicial influence or prestige (Smyth 2000b, 2001b), examined the determinants of judicial influence and prestige (Bhattacharya and Smyth 2001b; Smyth and Bhattacharya 2003a), and examined the relationship between aging and judicial productivity (Bhattacharya and Smyth 2001a; Smyth and

Bhattacharya 2003b). Kendall (2011) and Smyth (2000d) used citation analysis to examine the use of economics in decision-making. Smyth and Mishra (2010) used coordinate judicial citations to examine the prestige of state supreme courts, while Smyth and Mishra (2011) analyzed the determinants of the transmission of precedent across state supreme courts. Flanagan and Ahern (2011) administered a survey to High Court judges to get their views on citing foreign law as a source of persuasive authority as part of a multi-country study.

In other areas, there are just a few studies. Examples include the determinants of judicial retirement (Kerby and Banfield 2014; Maitra and Smyth 2005a); whether there is a consensual norm on the High Court (Gill 2011; Narayan and Smyth 2005; Smyth 2002b), and party capability theory (Haynie et al. 2013; Sheehan and Randazzo 2012; Smyth 2000c). Some studies have used methods from computational linguistics to examine the prevalence of ghost writing on the High Court (Seroussi, Smyth, and Zukerman 2011) and the author of joint judgments (Partovi et al. 2017). Sheldon (1967) examined the responsiveness of the High Court to public opinion, focusing on the decision in the *Communist Party* case.[6] Nielsen and Smyth (2019) administer a survey to examine public awareness of the High Court. In follow-up studies, Krebs, Nielsen, and Smyth (2019) and Nielsen, Robinson, and Smyth (2020) administered surveys to examine judicial legitimacy on the High Court.

In yet other areas, there is only one study. These areas include acclimation (or freshman) effects on the High Court (Smyth 2002a), determinants of appeal success from the High Court to the Judicial Committee of the Privy Council (Pierce 2006, chap. 4), barrister gender and litigant success in the High Court (Mishra and Smyth 2014), and examination of whether the High Court is countermajoritarian (Smyth and Mishra 2015). Tutton, Mack, and Roach Anleu (2018) examined judicial demeanor during oral argument using audiovisual recordings of the High Court's hearings. Smyth and Mishra (2009) examine the determinants of how judges allocate their time between publishing their decisions and leisure, using a sample of county court judges from Victoria. Booth and Freyens (2014a, 2014b) examined the effect of appointing party and employment history on the outcome of labor disputes for a sample of arbitration decisions of the Fair Work Commission.

The Empirical Literature on Judicial Behavior in New Zealand Courts

There is a relatively small empirical literature on the courts and judicial behavior in New Zealand. There are a few studies examining different aspects of citation practice, focused primarily on the Court of Appeal (Allan Huscroft, and Lynch 2005; Richardson 2001; Smyth 2000e, 2001e). Smyth (2003b) analyzed the relationship between judicial citations and case complexity in the Court of Appeal. Kendall (2011) compared the use of economics in judicial reasoning in New Zealand with Australia and the United States. New Zealand judges were also included in Flanagan and Ahern's (2011) multi-country survey of judicial attitudes to citing foreign precedent. Richardson (2001) presented data on trends in judgment writing on the Court of Appeal, while Richardson (2009) empirically analyzed appeals from the Court of Appeal to the Judicial Committee. Kerby and Banfield (2014), as part of their comparative study with the High Court of Australia and Supreme Court of Canada, examined the determinants of voluntary resignation on the Court of Appeal. Maitra and Smyth (2005b) examined the determinants of promotion from the High Court to Court of Appeal. A related study is Cooter and Ginsburg (1996), who used a game theory network and included New Zealand (and Australia) in their multi-country study of why judicial activism varies across countries.

There are a few empirical-based studies of the Supreme Court. Russell and Barber (2015) gave an empirical overview of the decisions of the Supreme Court. Hammond (2013) examined citations to academic authorities in the Supreme Court. Evans and Fern (2015) and Norling (2015) analyzed special leave applications considered by the Supreme Court.

What Are the Remaining Gaps in the Literature?

With the exception of one or two areas, such as citation practice, there are a dearth of studies for most topics for the High Court of Australia. This observation applies even more so for the New Zealand Court of Appeal and New Zealand Supreme Court. For several topics, there are only one or two studies for courts in Australia and New Zealand. This means that pretty much on all topics, the nuances have not been explored and we do not have a critical mass of evidence from which to draw firm conclusions. Where we do have studies for Australia, theory-building is curtailed because those studies are restricted to the High Court in Australia. For example, there is just the one study examining the effect of barrister gender on outcomes and it is for the High Court (Mishra and Smyth 2014). The obvious, and interesting, extension would be to test the effect of barrister gender on outcomes in the Family Court of Australia, in which there are a much higher proportion of female barristers and judges. Even in areas like party capability theory, for which there are a few studies for the High Court of Australia, the literature only uses the "basic" variables. Hence, the richness in the literature that has developed in the party capability literature in the United States is largely missing the Australian and New Zealand contexts.

A related issue is that because there are few studies in general, the methodological advances in how we measure specific variables that have been incorporated into the US literature are missing in the literature on the Australian and New Zealand courts. For instance, among the few studies for the High Court of Australia that test the attitudinal model, most measure ideology by party of appointment (eg, Booth and Freyens 2014a, 2014b; Smyth 2005b). There are few studies that measure judicial ideology using more sophisticated approaches, such as original content analysis of newspapers (e.g., Weiden 2011; Mishra and Smyth 2014).

In Australia, with few exceptions mainly focused around citation practices, the state supreme courts are largely unexplored. While in the United States a large literature has evolved for the state courts, testing a range of theories, on the basis that in many instances state judges have different incentives, this is missing in Australia. This observation applies a fortiori to the district courts (County Court in Victoria) and the magistrates courts (Local Court in New South Wales), as well as the federal court, federal circuit court, and family court. For the latter two, I am not aware of any empirical studies of decision-making or judicial behavior at all. For the state supreme courts and district courts, in which the serious crime is tried, there are no studies of what defendant and judge characteristics determine sentence length. There has been a significant increase in the number of female trial judges in the state supreme courts and district courts across Australia, but there are no studies of whether this affects case outcomes. These observations are also true for the courts of general jurisdiction in New Zealand. In New Zealand, there are very few studies of decision-making in the Supreme Court, despite there now being fourteen years of data for the court. The High Court in New Zealand has a provision to draw on lay judges from a panel of experts in certain types of cases, such as antitrust cases.[7] The role of such judges is to assist with interpreting expert evidence. It would be interesting to examine how lay judges affect the outcome of such cases.

With a few exceptions (see e.g., Sheldon 1967; Cooter and Ginsburg 1996; Flanagan and Ahern 2011; Gill, Pierce, and Weiden 2011; Kendall 2011; Haynie et al. 2013; Kerby and Banfield 2014; Weiden 2011), the High Court of Australia, New Zealand Court of Appeal, nor New Zealand Supreme Court have been included in comparative studies. This has also limited theory-building. The theoretical basis to most studies of judicial behavior in Australia and New Zealand has been borrowed from the US context (see e.g., Pierce 2008). More generally, judicial behavior and decision-making in Australia and New Zealand is undertheorized.

WHAT EMPIRICAL STRATEGIES HAVE BEEN USED?

Most of the literature is quantitative in nature. Some of the literature, and in particular most of that published in the law reviews, present statistics in tabular form without using statistical methods to analyze the data. Early studies for the High Court of Australia used jurimetrics. Most of the more recent studies for Australian and New Zealand courts that use statistical methods use standard multiple regression. Some studies use time series econometrics (e.g., Smyth and Narayan 2004), survival analysis (Maira and Smyth 2005a, 2005b), multidimensional scaling (Gill 2002) or machine-learning methods developed in computational linguistics (Seroussi, Smyth, and Zukerman 2011; Partovi et al. 2017). Nielsen, Robinson, and Smyth (2020) employed an experiment in a survey.

There is a lack of panel data models. Smyth and Mishra (2011) used panel data modeling to examine the transfer of interstate precedent across Australian state supreme courts, but I am not aware of other panel data studies. As a federation with a small number of states and territories (six states and two territories), constructing panel data sets should be much easier than in the United States with its fifty states. The further application of panel data for the Australian states and territories represents an opportunity to use Australian data to make methodological advances in the manner in which we model judicial behavior.

There are a small number of studies that have used qualitative techniques to examine different aspects of judicial behavior. The most prominent example of an Australian study is Pierce (2006), who interviewed eighty-two current or retired High Court judges, federal court judges, and state and territory supreme court judges as part of his study of the Mason Court (see also Pierce 2002). Flanagan and Ahern (2011) administered a survey to Australian and New Zealand judges to ascertain their view on citing foreign precedent. Tutton, Mack, and Roach Anleu (2018) used observational methods to study judicial demeanor on the High Court of Australia. Another example for the Australian lower courts is the Magistrates Research Project, conducted at Flinders University by Sharyn Roach Anleu and Kathy Mack. These authors have published a series of studies based on interviews with magistrates and ethnographic data; they examined how magistrates explain their decisions in court, magistrates' job satisfaction, and the role of magistrates in orchestrating social change (e.g., Roach Anleu and Mack 2005, 2007, 2015).

CHALLENGES WITH DATA

One source of public data on the High Court of Australia is the National Science Foundation High Courts database. Several of the US researchers on the High Court have used this database (e.g., Gill 2002, 2009; Gill, Pierce, and Weiden 2011; Haynie et al. 2013; Sheehan, Gill, and Randazzo 2012). However, Lynch (2014) is critical of the manner in which High Court decisions in the database have been coded. He points out various problems with the subject categories.

Most researchers, though, have collected and maintained their own data sets (e.g., Kerby and Banfield 2014; Pierce 2008). Almost all studies use data collected from the law reports. The Australasian Legal Institute website represents a rich source of raw data.[8] Most of the courts also have their own websites with electronic versions of their judgments.

It takes time, or considerable dollars spent on research assistants, though, to convert the raw data into usable data sets. Collaborative research on the High Court would benefit from having a central repository into which the privately maintained data sets used in published studies could be placed.[9] The Edward A. Clark Center for Australian and New Zealand Studies at the University of Texas at Austin is developing data sets for New Zealand and Australian courts. As of March 2018, the Clark Center High Court data set contains data on a number of variables for all High Court decisions reported in the *Commonwealth Law Reports* over the period 2008 to 2017. Among others, these variables include (1) a media-based measure of a decision's political salience, (2) the number and identities of interveners, (3) a code for each decision's policy content, (4) the laws at issue, coded by policy content,

(5) the number and identities of the participating judges, and (6) the vote margins. Policy codes are assigned according to the codebook used by the Australian Policy Agendas Project. When completed, the data set will be made freely available to the public on the Comparative Agendas Project's website.[10]

A second Australian data set being compiled by the Clark Center includes data on every article published in *The Australian* over the period 1996 to 2017. The data set includes (1) article title, (2) article authors, (3) newspaper edition, (4) section, (5) page number, (6) word length, and (7) names of decisions discussed. Comparable data is being collected for the *Sydney Morning Herald* over a longer period, 1970 to 2017.[11]

The Clark Center is also compiling similar databases for cases decided in the New Zealand Supreme Court from its inception in 2004 through to 2017 and for New Zealand Supreme Court cases reported in the *New Zealand Herald* over the same period. This data is already starting to be used in new research produced at the Clark Center.[12]

Testing of some models (e.g., attitudinal versus legal model) requires background data on judges. There are some useful sources of bibliographic data on judges. Judicial biography is a relatively new endeavor in Australia (see Burnside 2009; Josev 2017), although there are now book-length treatments, including in some cases multiple books, for several High Court judges (e.g., Barton, Gaudron, Griffith, Higgins, Isaacs, Latham, Dixon, Evatt, Barwick, Murphy, Gibbs, Deane, Stephen, Wilson, Gaudron, and Gleeson). Blackshield, Coper, and Williams (2001) have detailed entries on each of the High Court of Australia judges up to when their book was published. Another potentially useful source of bibliographic data is the New Zealand Women Judges Oral Histories Project, which provides extensive information on New Zealand's women lawyers admitted between 1897 and 1958 and female judges appointed since 1975 (see Chan 2014; Geenty 2017). Zoe Robinson, at the School of Political Science at the Australian National University, is developing a database on the High Court of Australia, modeled on the Supreme Court database. When complete, it will obviously contain very detailed biographical details on the judges as well as very detailed sets of variables on a host of other issues.

Other Challenges

Traditionally, in Australia and New Zealand, relatively few economists or political scientists have been interested in judicial behavior (see Turner

2015; Varuhas 2005).[13] As a consequence, there is no real tradition of multidisciplinary research agendas. More generally, the leading Australian law reviews and the academic legal community in Australia are not particularly open to the study of the courts and judicial behavior using regression analysis or more advanced statistical modeling. When US political scientists have adopted quantitative empirical methods to study the High Court of Australia (Pierce 2006, chap. 4; Sheehan, Gill, and Randazzo 2012), book reviews of these volumes by prominent Australian legal scholars published in Australian law reviews have been highly critical of the use of multiple regression (Twomey 2007; Lynch 2014). This reflects a lack of statistical training among Australian and New Zealand legal academics. It also reflects the dominance of black-letter law reasoning in Australia and New Zealand.[14] This sort of thinking is reflected in a speech given by Virginia Bell, a current puisne justice of the High Court of Australia. Her Honor states, "the community is uninterested in the judges. . . . . because of an unstated acceptance that [their] *decisions are made on legal merit and not on the political or ideological sympathies of the judge*" (Bell 2017, 6, emphasis mine). This seems a remarkable statement given the amount of empirical evidence to the contrary for Australian courts and tribunals alone (see e.g., Weiden 2011; Booth and Freyens 2014a, 2014b). Yet, in perpetrating the myth that judges are apolitical, such sentiment generates hostility to examining judicial behavior. The line becomes, there is no point examining judicial behavior because judges are apolitical in applying the law. Attempts to apply theories developed in the US literature are often dismissed on the basis that they do not reflect the apolitical nature of Australian judges. Hence, while one can still publish empirical work on judicial behavior in Australia and New Zealand in economics and political science journals, this does not help to break down barriers between disciplines.

Conclusion

In this essay, I have reviewed the empirical literature on judicial behavior and decision-making in Australian and New Zealand courts. While there are more studies for Australian courts, and the High Court of Australia in particular, than the Supreme Court of New Zealand or New Zealand Court of Appeal, there are relatively few studies for both jurisdictions, compared with other countries, such as the United States. This situation can be seen as an opportunity for scholars interested in comparative judicial politics. We need more comparative studies for

Westminster systems. The Supreme Court of New Zealand and High Court of Australia represent interesting comparison points with the Supreme Court of Canada and the Supreme Court for the United Kingdom, but with rare exceptions (Hanretty 2013, 706, fig. 1; Kerby and Banfield 2014), such comparisons have not been made. But, more than this, we need more studies in which testable theories developed in the social sciences are examined for Australasian courts. Such studies should attempt to incorporate methodological advances in measurement in the empirical legal studies literature for other countries. More studies of this sort would not only increase our understanding of judicial behavior in Australia and New Zealand, but add to the stock of evidence for countries other than the United States.

NOTES

I thank Nuno Garoupa, Vinod Mishra, Ingrid Nielsen, and participants in the National Science Foundation workshop, Facilitating Empirical Studies of Judicial Behavior on Constitutional Courts from a Comparative Perspective, Texas A&M School of Law in Fort Worth, May 11–12, 2018, for helpful comments on earlier versions of this essay. I also thank Rhonda Evans for furnishing information on data sets being compiled at the Edward A. Clark Center for Australian and New Zealand Studies at the University of Texas, Austin.

1. For a more general discussion of judicial behavior with particular reference to Australia and New Zealand see Smyth (2005a).
2. Before 1975, litigants could appeal from the High Court to the Judicial Committee of the Privy Council. Between 1975 and 1986, litigants could appeal from the state supreme courts to either the High Court or Judicial Committee creating a "bizarre situation of dualism—and potential conflict—at the apex of the Australian hierarchy of courts" (Blackshield et al. 2001a, 560). The right of appeal from state supreme courts to the Judicial Committee was abolished in 1986. Below the High Court sits the states and territories' court hierarchies consisting of, in each of the state and territories, the Court of Appeal, Supreme Court, District Court (County Court in Victoria), and Magistrates Court (Local Court in New South Wales). Sitting alongside the states and territories' court hierarchies, below the High Court, is the Federal Court of Australia, established in 1976; the Family Court of Australia, established in 1975, the jurisdiction of which is limited to family law matters; and the Federal Circuit Court of Australia, established in 1999 to ease the workload of the Federal Court.
3. The Supreme Court of New Zealand was established in 2004, replacing the Judicial Committee of the Privy Council as the final court of

appeal. Below the Supreme Court, in descending order, are the courts of general jurisdiction are the New Zealand Court of Appeal, New Zealand High Court, and New Zealand District Court. While, prior to 2004, the Judicial Committee was the final court of appeal, the Court of Appeal was often viewed as the de facto final court in New Zealand (Harris 2007) with few appeals from the Court of Appeal to the Judicial Committee, particularly in criminal cases (Richardson 2009).

4. Albeit, not as thin as in some other wealthy Commonwealth and former Commonwealth countries, such as Cyprus, Ireland and Malta. There is very little empirical work for these jurisdictions at all. One exception is Elgie et al. (2018) who examine partisan decision-making on the Irish Supreme Court.

5. Lynch and Williams produce annual statistics for the High Court's constitutional decisions in the tradition of the annual *Harvard Law Review* statistics for the US Supreme Court. The most recent statistics for 2016 are published in Lynch and Williams (2017). That study has a complete record of previous studies in the appendix.

6. *Australian Communist Party v. Commonwealth*, 82 C.L.R. 1

7. https://www.courtsofnz.govt.nz/the-courts/high-court/cases-to-court #lay-members-of-the-high-court.

8. http://www.austlii.edu.au.

9. An impediment to this idea is that some of the data sets will be lost or in paper form. Unfortunately, most of the raw data I have is in paper form. Other data have been lost when laptops have died.

10. http://www.comparativeagendas.net/.

11. The Clark Center databases on the High Court and Australian newspapers have been used in a series of conference papers by Rhonda Evans and coauthors (see e.g., Evans 2017, 2017a; Evans and Dwidar 2016, 2016a; Evans and Joyce 2013).

12. See e.g., Evans and Eissler (2015), Evans and Fern (2014), and Rowe (2018).

13. Judicial views on law and economics in Australasia have also been very mixed. Sir Ivor Richardson, president of the New Zealand Court of Appeal from 1996 to 2002, was a champion of law and economics (Richardson 1999, 2002) and the greater use of empirical methods to analyze the courts' output (Richardson 2001, 2009). In Australia, Sir Anthony Mason (Mason 1991), chief justice of Australia 1987–1995, and James Spigelman (Spigelman 1991), chief justice of New South Wales from 1998–2011, have been critical of the claims of law and economics, while Michael Kirby (Kirby 1999), puisne justice of the High Court 1996–2009, has been more supportive of using law and economics in decision-making, while still rejecting some of its more extreme claims.

14. There are some indications this might be starting to change in some of the law reviews. The *University of New South Wales Law Review* is one leading

Australian law review that seems more open to publishing quantitative
work. A recent example, albeit not on judicial behavior, is Poynton et al.
(2018).

References

Allan, J., G, Huscroft, and W. Lynch. 2005. "The Citation of Overseas Authority
in Rights Litigation in New Zealand: How Much Bark—How Much Bite?"
Otago Law Review 11 (1): 433–68.

Bell, V. 2017. "Examining the Judge: Launch of Issue 40(2) of the UNSW Law
Journal." Sydney, 29 May. Transcript available on the High Court website
at https://cdn.hcourt.gov.au/assets/publications/speeches/current-justices
/bellj/bellj29May2017.pdf.pdf.

Bhattacharya, M., and R. Smyth. 2001a. "Aging and Productivity Among Judges:
Some Empirical Evidence from the High Court of Australia." *Australian
Economic Papers* 40 (2): 199–212.

Bhattacharya, M., and R. Smyth. 2001b. "The Determinants of Judicial Influence and Prestige: Some Empirical Evidence from the High Court of Australia." *Journal of Legal Studies* 30 (1): 223–52.

Blackshield, A. R. 1972. "Quantitative Analysis: The High Court of Australia
1964–69." *Lawasia* 3: 1–66.

Blackshield, A. R. 1977. "Judges and the Court System." In *Labor and the Constitution 1972–1975: The Whitlam Years in Australian Government*, edited by
G. Evans, 105–30. Melbourne: Heinemann.

Blackshield, A. R. 1978. "X/Y/Z/N Scales: The High Court of Australia,
1972–1976." In *Understanding Lawyers: Perspectives on the Legal Profession in
Australia*, edited by R. Tomasic, 133–57. Sydney: Allen & Unwin.

Blackshield A. R. 2001. "Jurimetrics." In *Oxford Companion to the High Court
of Australia*, edited by Anthony Blackshield, Michael Coper, and George
Williams. Melbourne: Oxford University Press.

Blackshield A. R, M. Coper, and J. Goldring. 2001a. "Privy Council, Judicial Committee of the." In *Oxford Companion to the High Court of Australia*, edited by Anthony Blackshield, Michael Coper, and George Williams,
560–664. Melbourne: Oxford University Press.

Blackshield, A. R., M. Coper, and G. Williams, eds. 2001b. *Oxford Companion to
the High Court of Australia*. Melbourne: Oxford University Press.

Booth, J. and B. Freyens. 2014a. "A Study of Political Activism on Labour
Courts." *Economics Letters* 123: 370–73.

Booth, J. and B. Freyens. 2014b. "Ideology and Judicial Decision Making in Australian Labour Courts." Mimeo, Centre of Law & Economics, Australian
National University.

Burnside, S. 2009. "Griffith, Isaacs and Australian Judicial Biography: An Evo-
lutionary Development?" *Griffith Law Review* 8: 151–84.

Chan, E. 2014. "Women Trailblazers in the Law: The New Zealand Women Judges Oral Histories Project." *Victoria University of Wellington Law Review* 45: 407–36.

Cooter, R. D., and T. Ginsburg. 1996. "Comparative Judicial Discretion: An Empirical Test of Economic Models." *International Review of Law and Economics* 16: 295–313.

Douglas, R. N. 1969. "Judges and Policy on the Latham Court." *Politics* 4 (1): 20–41.

Elgie, R., A. McAuley, and E. O'Malley. 2018. "The (Not-so-surprising) Nonpartisanship of the Irish Supreme Court." *Irish Political Studies* 33 (1): 88–111.

Evans, R. 2017. "Measuring the Political Salience of Decisions of the High Court of Australia: Does the American Measure Travel?" Paper presented at Australian Society for Quantitative Political Science, Wellington, New Zealand, 11–12 December 2017.

Evans, R. 2017a. "A New Measure of Judicial Power: The High Court of Australia 2016." Paper presented at Australian and New Zealand Studies Association of North America, Washington, DC, 21–23 February 2017.

Evans, R., and M. Dwidar. 2016. "Converging Agendas? A Study of Issue Attention Across the High Court of Australia and the New Zealand Court of Appeal." Paper presented at the 9th Annual Comparative Agendas Conference, Geneva, Switzerland, 27–29 June 2016.

Evans, R., and M. Dwidar. 2016a. "The High Court of Australia's Policy Agenda, 1970–2015." Paper presented at Australian and New Zealand Studies Association of North America, Winter Park, FL, 4–6 February 2016.

Evans, R., and R. Eissler. 2015. "Policy Agendas of National Courts: Australia and New Zealand Compared." Paper presented at the 8th Annual Comparative Policy Agendas Conference, Lisbon, Portugal, 22–24 June 2015.

Evans, R., and S. Fern. 2014. "Does Size Matter? Agenda-Setting on the New Zealand Supreme Court." Paper presented (with Sean Fern) at Midwest Political Science Association, Chicago, IL, 3–6 April 2014.

Evans, R., and S. Fern. 2015. "From Applications to Appeals: A Political Science Perspective on the New Zealand Supreme Court's Docket." In *The Supreme Court of New Zealand 2004–2013*, edited by M. R. Russell and M. Barber, 33–60. Wellington: Thomson Reuters.

Evans, R., and S. Joyce. 2013. "The High Court of Australia's Agenda-Setting Role." Paper presented at Law & Society Association Annual Meeting, Boston, MA, 30 May–2 June 2013.

Farrell, J., and R. Smyth. 2014. "Trends in Co-authorship in the Australian Group of Eight Law Reviews." *Monash University Law Review* 39 (3): 815–37.

Fausten, D., I. Nielsen, and R. Smyth. 2007. "A Century of Citation Practice on the Supreme Court of Victoria." *Melbourne University Law Review* 31 (2): 733–804.

Flanagan, B., and S. Ahern. 2011. "Judicial Decision-Making and Transnational Law: A Survey of Common Law Supreme Court Judges." *International Comparative Law Quarterly* 60: 1–28.

Galligan, B. 1987. *Politics of the High Court: A Study of the Judicial Branch of Government in Australia*. St. Lucia: University of Queensland Press.

Geenty, K. 2017. "Oral Histories of Pioneering Women Judges Recorded." New Zealand Law Society. https://www.lawsociety.org.nz/news/legal-news/oral-histories-of-pioneering-women-judges-recorded.

Gill (Wood), R. 2002. "Dimensions of Decision Making: Determining the Complexity of Politics on the High Court of Australia." http://ssrn.com/abstract=1539886.

Gill (Wood), R. 2009. "The Fading Utility of the Australian Legalist Story: Using Social Background Theory to Explain Outcomes on the High Court." http://ssrn.com/abstract=1539885.

Gill, R. 2011. "Consensus or Ambivalence? Why Court Traditions Matter." http://ssrn.com/abstract=1881961.

Gill (Wood), R., J. L. Pierce, and D. L. Weiden. 2011. "Empirical and Legal Trends At the High Court of Australia." http://ssrn.com/abstract=1985814.

Groves, M., and R. Smyth. 2004. "A Century of Judicial Style: Changing Patterns in Judgment Writing on the High Court 1903–2001." *Federal Law Review* 32 (2): 255–80.

Hammond, G. 2013. "Judges and Academics in New Zealand." *New Zealand Universities Law Review* 25: 681.

Hanretty, C. 2013. "The Decisions and Ideal Points of British Law Lords." *British Journal of Political Science* 43 (3): 703–16.

Harris, B. 2007. "Judicial Activism and New Zealand's Appellate Courts." In *Judicial Activism in Common Law Supreme Courts*, edited by Bruce Dickson, 273. Oxford University Press, Oxford.

Haynie, S. L., K. Randazzo, R. S. Sheehan, and D. R. Songer. 2013. "Winners and Losers in Appellate Case Outcomes: A Comparative Perspective." Paper presented at the Annual Meeting of the APSA, Chicago.

Josev, T. 2017. "Judicial Biography in Australia: Current Obstacles and Opportunities." *University of New South Wales Law Journal* 40 (2): 842.

Kendall, K. 2011. "The Use of Economic Analysis in Court Judgments: A Comparison Between the United States, Australia and New Zealand." *Pacific Basin Law Journal* 28: 107–47.

Kerby, M., and A. C. Banfield. 2014. "The Determinants of Voluntary Judicial Resignation in Australia, Canada and New Zealand." *Commonwealth & Comparative Politics* 52 (3): 335–57.

Kirby, M. 1999. "Law and Economics in the Courts: Is There Hope?" In *The Second Wave of Law and Economics*, edited by Megan Richardson and Gillian Hadfield. Sydney: Federation Press.

Krebs, S., I. Nielsen, and R. Smyth. 2019. "What Determines Institutional Legitimacy of the High Court of Australia?" *Melbourne University Law Review* 43 (2): 605–53.

Lefler, R. 2011. "A Comparison of Comparison: Use of Foreign Case Law as Persuasive Authority by the United States Supreme Court, the Supreme Court of Canada, and the High Court of Australia." *Southern California Interdisciplinary Law Journal* 11: 165.

Lynch, A. 2003. "The Gleeson Court on Constitutional Law: An Empirical Analysis of its First Five Years." *University of New South Wales Law Journal* 26: 32–65.

Lynch, A. 2005. "Does the High Court Disagree More Often in Constitutional Cases? A Statistical Study of Judgment Delivery 1981–2003." *Federal Law Review* 33: 485–523.

Lynch, A. 2014. Review of *Judicialization of Politics: The Interplay of Institutional Structure, Legal Doctrine and Politics on the High Court of Australia*, by Reginald S. Sheehan, Rebecca D. Gill, and Kirk A. Randazzo. *Adelaide Law Review* 34: 465–71.

Lynch, A. and G. Williams. 2017. "The High Court on Constitutional Law: The 2016 and French Court Statistics." *University of New South Wales Law Journal* 40 (4): 1468–91.

Maitra, P., and R. Smyth. 2005a. "Determinants of Retirement on the High Court of Australia." *Economic Record* 81 (254): 193–203.

Maitra, P., and R. Smyth. 2005b. "Judicial Independence, Judicial Promotion and the Enforcement of Legislative Wealth Transfers—An Empirical Study of the New Zealand High Court." *European Journal of Law and Economics* (2004) 17 (2): 209–35.

Mishra, V., and R. Smyth. 2014. "Barrister Gender and Litigant Success on the High Court of Australia." *Australian Journal of Political Science* 49 (1): 1–21.

Mason, A. F. 1991. "Law and Economics." *Monash University Law Review* 17 (2): 167–81.

Narayan, P. K., and R. Smyth. 2004. "What Explains Dissent on the High Court of Australia? An Empirical Assessment Using a Cointegration and Error Correction Approach." *Journal of Empirical Legal Studies* 4 (2): 401–25.

Narayan, P. K., and R. Smyth. 2005. "The Consensual Norm on the High Court of Australia: 1904–2001." *International Political Science Review* 26 (2): 147–68.

Nielsen, I., Z. Robinson, and R. Smyth. 2020. "'Keep Your (Horse) Hair On?' Experimental Evidence on the Effect of Exposure to Legitimizing Symbols on Diffuse Support for the High Court." *Federal Law Review* (in press).

Nielsen, I., and R. Smyth. 2008. "One Hundred Years of Citation of Authority on the Supreme Court of New South Wales." *University of New South Wales Law Journal* 31 (1): 189–214.

Nielsen, I., and R. Smyth. 2019. "What Does the Australian Public Know about the High Court?" *Federal Law Review* 47 (1): 31–63.

Norling, O. 2015. "The First 1000 Decisions of the Supreme Court of New Zealand: A Study in How the Court Grants Leave." PhD diss., University of Otago.

Patapan, H. 2000. *Judging Democracy: The New Politics of the High Court of Australia*. Cambridge: Cambridge University Press.

Partovi, P., R. Smyth, I. Zukerman, and J. Valente. 2017. "Addressing 'Loss of Identity' in the Joint Judgment: Searching for 'the Individual Judge' in the Joint Judgments of the Mason Court." *University of New South Wales Law Journal* 40 (2): 670–711.

Pierce, J. 2002. "Interviewing Australia's Senior Judiciary." *Australian Journal of Political Science* 37 (1): 131–42.

Pierce, J. 2006. *Inside the Mason Court Revolution: The High Court of Australia Transformed*. Carolina Academic Press.

Pierce, J. 2008. "Institutional Cohesion in the High Court of Australia: Do American Theories Travel Well Down Under?" *Commonwealth and Comparative Politics* 46 (3): 318–40.

Posner, R. 1997. "The Future of the Law and Economics Movement in Europe." *International Review of Law and Economics* 17: 3.

Poynton, S., J. Chan, M. Vogt, A. Grunseit, and J. Bruce. 2018. "Assessing the Effectiveness of Wellbeing Initiatives for Lawyers and Support Staff." *University of New South Wales Law Journal* 41 (2): 584–619.

Richardson, I. 1999. "Law, Economics and Judicial Decision-Making." In *The Second Wave of Law and Economics*, edited by Megan Richardson and Gillian Hadfield, 129–52. Sydney: Federation Press.

Richardson, I. 2001. "Trends in Judgment Writing in the New Zealand Court of Appeal." In *Legal Method in New Zealand*, edited by Rick Bigwood, 261–82. Auckland: Butterworths.

Richardson, I. 2002. "Law and Economics—And Why New Zealand Needs It." *New Zealand Business Law Quarterly* 8 (2): 151.

Richardson, I. 2009. "The Permanent Court of Appeal: Surveying the 50 Years." In *The Permanent New Zealand Court of Appeal: Essays on the First 50 Years*, edited by Rick Bigwood, 297. Hart Publishing, Oxford.

Roach Anleu, S., and K. Mack. 2005. "Magistrates Everyday Work and Emotional Labour." *Journal of Law and Society* 32: 590–614.

Roach Anleu, S., and K. Mack. 2007. "Magistrates, Magistrates Courts and Social Change." *Law & Policy* 29: 183–209.

Roach Anleu, S., and K. Mack. 2015. "Performing Authority: Communicating Judicial Decisions in Lower Criminal Courts." *Journal of Sociology* 51: 1052–69.

Rowe, R. 2018. "Courting the Media: Does the New Zealand Supreme Court Shape News Coverage of its Decisions?" Unpublished manuscript. Clark Center, University of Texas, Austin.

Russell, M. R., and M. Barber. 2015. Empirical Analysis of Supreme Court Decisions. In *The Supreme Court of New Zealand 2004–2013*, edited by M. R. Russell and M. Barber, 1–32. Wellington: Thomson Reuters.

Schubert, G. 1968a. "Political Ideology on the High Court." *Politics* 3 (1): 21–40.

Schubert, G. 1968b. "Opinion Agreement Among the High Court Justices." *Australian and New Zealand Journal of Sociology* 4: 2–17.

Schubert, G. 1969a. "Judicial Attitudes and Policy-making in the Dixon Court." *Osgoode Hall Law Journal* 7: 1–30.

Schubert, G. 1969b. "Two Causal Models of Decision-making by the High Court of Australia." In *Comparative Judicial Behavior: Cross-Cultural Studies of Judicial Decision-making in the East and the West*, edited by G. Schubert, and D. J. Danelski, 335–66. New York: Oxford University Press.

Schultz, K. 2016. "Backdoor Use of Philosophers in Judicial Decision-Making? Antipodean Reflections." *Griffith Law Review* 25: 441.

Seroussi, Y., R. Smyth, and I. Zukerman. 2011. "Ghosts from the High Court's Past: Evidence from Computational Linguistics for Dixon Ghosting for McTiernan and Rich." *University of New South Wales Law Journal* 34 (3): 984–1005.

Sheehan, R., R. Gill, and K. A. Randazzo. 2012. *Judicialization of Politics: The Interplay of Institutional Structure, Legal Doctrine and Politics on the High Court of Australia*. Carolina Academic Press, 2012.

Sheehan, R., and K. A. Randazzo. 2012. "Explaining Litigant Success in the High Court of Australia." *Australian Journal of Political Science* 47 (2): 239–55.

Sheldon, C. H. 1967. "Public Opinion and High Courts: Communist Party Cases in Four Constitutional Systems." *Western Political Quarterly* 20: 341.

Smyth, R. 1998. "Academic Writing and the Courts: A Quantitative Study of the Influence of Legal and Non-Legal Periodicals in the High Court." *University of Tasmania Law Review* 17 (2): 164–85.

Smyth, R. 1999a. "Some are More Equal than Others—An Empirical Investigation into the Voting Behaviour of the Mason Court." *Canberra Law Review* 6 (1 and 2): 193–218.

Smyth, R. 1999b. "What do Intermediate Appellate Courts Cite? A Quantitative Study of the Citation Practice of Australian State Supreme Courts." *Adelaide Law Review* 21 (1): 51–80.

Smyth, R. 1999c. "What do Judges Cite? An Empirical Study of the 'Authority of Authority' in the Supreme Court of Victoria." *Monash University Law Review* 25 (1): 29–53.

Smyth, R. 1999d. "Other than 'Accepted Sources of Law'? A Quantitative Study of Secondary Source Citations in the High Court." *University of New South Wales Law Journal* 22 (1): 19–59.

Smyth, R. 2000a. "The Authority of Secondary Authority: A Quantitative Study of Secondary Source Citations in the Federal Court." *Griffith Law Review* 9 (1): 25–52.

Smyth, R. 2000b. "Who Gets Cited? An Empirical Study of Judicial Prestige in the High Court." *University of Queensland Law Journal* 21 (1): 7–22.

Smyth, R. 2000c. "The 'Haves' and the 'Have Nots'—An Empirical Study of the Rational Actor and Party Capability Hypotheses in the High Court 1948–1999." *Australian Journal of Political Science* 35 (2): 255–74.

Smyth, R. 2000d. "Law or Economics? An Empirical Investigation of the Impact of Economics on Australian Courts." *Australian Business Law Review* 28 (1): 5–21.

Smyth, R. 2000e. "Judicial Citations—An Empirical Study of Citation Practice in the New Zealand Court of Appeal." *Victoria University of Wellington Law Review* 31 (4): 847–95.

Smyth, R. 2001a. "Citation of Judicial and Academic Authority in the Supreme Court of Western Australia." *University of Western Australia Law Review* 30 (1): 1–27.

Smyth, R. 2001b. "Judicial Prestige: A Citation Analysis of Federal Court Judges." *Deakin Law Review* 6 (1): 120–48.

Smyth, R. 2001c. "Judicial Interaction on the Latham Court: A Quantitative Study of Voting Patterns on the High Court 1935–1950." *Australian Journal of Politics and History* 47 (3): 330–48.

Smyth, R. 2001d. "Citations by Court." In *Oxford Companion to the High Court of Australia*, edited by Tony Blackshield, Michael Coper, and George Williams, 98–99. Melbourne: Oxford University Press.

Smyth, R. 2001e. "Judicial Robes or Academic Gowns?—Citations to Secondary Authority and Legal Method in the New Zealand Court of Appeal." In *Legal Method in New Zealand*, edited by Rick Bigwood, 101–29. Auckland: Butterworths.

Smyth, R. 2002a. "Acclimation Effects for High Court Justices 1903–1975." *University of Western Sydney Law Review* 6: 167–90.

Smyth, R. 2002b. "Historical Consensual Norms in the High Court." *Australian Journal of Political Science* 37 (2): 255–66.

Smyth, R. 2002c. "Explaining Voting Patterns on the Latham High Court 1935–50." *Melbourne University Law Review* 26 (1): 88–109.

Smyth, R. 2003a. "Explaining Historical Dissent Rates in the High Court of Australia." *Journal of Commonwealth and Comparative Politics* 41 (2): 83–114.

Smyth, R. 2003b. "Case Complexity and Citation of Judicial Authority—Some Empirical Evidence from the New Zealand Court of Appeal." *Murdoch E-Law Journal* 10 (1): http://www.murdoch.edu.au/elaw/indices/issue/v10n1.html.

Smyth, R. 2004. "What Explains Variations in Dissent Rates? Time Series Evidence from the High Court." *Sydney Law Review* 26 (2): 221–40.

Smyth, R. 2005a. "Do Judges Behave as *Homo economicus* and, If So, Can We Measure Their Performance? An Antipodean Perspective on a Tournament of Judges." *Florida State University Law Review* 32 (4): 1299–330.

Smyth, R. 2005b. "The Role of Attitudinal, Institutional and Environmental Factors in Explaining Variations in Dissent Rates on the High Court of Australia." *Australian Journal of Political Science* 40 (4): 519–40.

Smyth, R. 2007. "The Citation Practices of the Supreme Court of Tasmania, 1905–2005." *University of Tasmania Law Review* 26 (1): 34–62.

Smyth, R. 2008. "A Century of Citation of Case-Law and Secondary Authority in the Supreme Court of Western Australia." *University of Western Australia Law Review* 34 (1): 145–67.

Smyth, R. 2009a. "Trends in Citation Practice of the Supreme Court of Queensland over the Course of the Twentieth Century." *University of Queensland Law Journal* 28 (1): 39–79.

Smyth, R. 2009b. "Citation to Authority on the Supreme Court of South Australia: Evidence from a Hundred Years of Data." *Adelaide Law Review* 29 (1): 113–66.

Smyth, R. 2009c. "Citations of Foreign Decisions in Australian State Supreme Courts over the Course of the Twentieth Century: An Empirical Analysis." *Temple International & Comparative Law Journal* 22 (2): 409–436.

Smyth, R. 2009d. "Citing Outside the Law Reports: Citations of Secondary Authorities on the Australian State Supreme Courts Over the Twentieth Century." *Griffith Law Review* 18 (3): 692–724.

Smyth, R. 2018. "What Do Trial Judges Cite? Evidence from the New South Wales District Court." *University of New South Wales Law Journal* 41: 211.

Smyth, R., and M. Bhattacharya. 2003a. "What Determines Judicial Prestige? An Empirical Analysis for Judges of the Federal Court of Australia." *American Law and Economics Review* 5 (1): 233–62.

Smyth, R., and M. Bhattacharya. 2003b. "How Fast Do Old Judges Slow Down? A Life Cycle Study of Aging and Productivity in the Federal Court of Australia." *International Review of Law and Economics* 23 (2): 141–64.

Smyth, R., and D. Fausten. 2008. "Coordinate Citations between Australian State Supreme Courts over the Twentieth Century." *Monash University Law Review* 34 (1): 53–74.

Smyth, R., and V. Mishra. 2009. "The Publication Decisions of Judges on the County Court of Victoria." *Economic Record* 85 (271): 462–71.

Smyth, R., and V. Mishra. 2010. "The Prestige of Australian State Supreme Courts over the Twentieth Century." *Australian Journal of Political Science* 45 (3): 323–36.

Smyth, R., and V. Mishra. 2011. "The Transmission of Legal Precedent across the Australian State Supreme Courts over the Twentieth Century." *Law & Society Review* 45 (1): 139–70.

Smyth, R., and V. Mishra. 2015. "Judicial Review, Invalidation and Electoral Politics: A Quantitative Survey." In *The High Court, the Constitution and Australian Politics*, edited by Rosiland Dixon and George Williams, 18–37. Melbourne: Cambridge University Press.

Smyth, R., and P. K. Narayan. 2004. "Hail to the Chief! Leadership and Structural Change in the Level of Consensus on the High Court of Australia." *Journal of Empirical Legal Studies* 1 (2): 399–427.

Smyth, R., and I. Nielsen. 2019. "The Citation Practices of the High Court of Australia: 1905–2015." *Federal Law Review* (in press).

Spiegelman, J. 2001. "Economic Rationalism and the Law." *University of New South Wales Law Journal* 24: 200.

Turner, R. 2015. "The High Court of Australia and Political Science: A Revised Historiography and New Research Agenda." *Australian Journal of Political Science* 50 (2): 347–64.

Tutton, J., K. Mack, and S. Roach Anleu. 2018. "Judicial Demeanour: Oral Argument in the High Court of Australia." *Justice System Journal* 39 (3): 273–99.

Twomey, A. 2007. Review of *Inside the Mason Court Revolution: The High Court of Australia Transformed*, by Jason Pierce. *Melbourne University Law Review* 31 (3): 1175–86.

Tyree, A. 1977. "The Geometry of Case Law." *Victoria University of Wellington Law Review* 4: 403.

Tyree, A. 1981. "Fact Content Analysis of Case Law: Methods and Limitations." *Jurimetrics Journal* 22: 1.

Varuhas, Jason N. (2005). "One Person Can Make a Difference: An Individual Petition System for International Environmental Law." *New Zealand Journal of Public and International Law* 3 (2): 329–72.

von Nessen, P. E. 1992. "The Use of American Precedents by the High Court of Australia, 1901–1987." *Adelaide Law Review* 181.

Weiden, D. L. 2011. "Judicial Politicization, Ideology and Activism in the High Courts of the United States, Canada and Australia." *Political Research Quarterly* 64 (2): 335–47.

Empirical Studies of Judicial Behavior in the United Kingdom

CHRIS HANRETTY

ALL JURISDICTIONS have judges who doubt the value of social scientific research, either generally or as applied to the judiciary. In the United Kingdom, judicial dubiety has historically been high, negatively impacting studies of the judiciary (Darbyshire 2011, 3). This picture is slowly changing, and judges have become more open to academics. This is particularly true of judges on the UK's Supreme Court (established 2009). Judges' greater openness has led to greater interest in judicial behavior amongst social scientists and to greater use of social scientific methods by lawyers.

This essay reviews the empirical study of UK judicial behavior. I begin by describing the UK legal system and the empirical study of law in the United Kingdom. I go on to describe some of the topics in judicial behavior that have been analyzed. Having mentioned some of the key findings, I describe the empirical strategies that have most commonly been used and some challenges to such research. I note methodological problems having to do with causation and measurement, and I suggest a key theme (specialization) that can offer a (partial) account of judicial behavior in (some) judicial systems.

THE UK LEGAL SYSTEM

The UK legal system is composed of three systems (the English and Welsh legal system, the Scottish legal system, and the Northern Irish legal systems), with common elements that operate atop (the UK Supreme

Court) or parallel to (employment and immigration tribunals) these distinct systems.

In England and Wales, important cases are heard at first instance in the High Court. They may be appealed to the Court of Appeal and/or the Supreme Court of the United Kingdom (UKSC). The High Court is divided into several divisions that reflect patterns of legal specialization. The Court of Appeal is divided into civil and criminal divisions. The Northern Irish system follows the structure of the English and Welsh system, except that there is no equivalent specialization at first instance.

Scottish courts are more firmly divided into civil and criminal courts. The High Court of the Justiciary hears appeals in criminal cases. The Court of Session is both a first-instance (Outer House) and appellate court (Inner House). Court of Session decisions may be appealed to the UKSC. Decisions of the High Court of the Justiciary may not be appealed to the UKSC unless they involve a human rights or devolution issue.

The UKSC hears appeals from these courts and from other UK-wide tribunals. It also hears reference questions concerning devolution issues (analogous to, but narrower than, advisory opinions in the Canadian context). The UKSC was created in 2009 to replace the Appellate Committee of the House of Lords (the "Law Lords"). The UKSC is a general appellate court rather than a constitutional court. Compared to other common law courts of final appeal, it hears more cases that deal with ordinary questions of family, criminal, civil or administrative law, and fewer "constitutional" cases. This comparison is made more complicated by the fact that the United Kingdom lacks a codified constitution, which makes it difficult to say which legal claims are constitutional in nature.

Since the United Kingdom has no codified constitution, and given a long-standing belief in parliamentary sovereignty, in theory no court is able to set aside primary legislation. Where primary legislation conflicts with EU law, courts may disapply the legislation because Parliament would never implicitly do anything that would conflict with the United Kingdom's obligations as an EU member state. This, in practice, allows courts to set aside such legislation. Where primary legislation conflicts with the European Convention on Human Rights, the court may declare that the legislation is incompatible with the Convention. These declarations do not mean that legislation ceases to apply, but it does create strong political incentives for the government to change the law. Courts generally prefer to interpret laws in ways that are Convention-compatible rather than issue declarations of incompatibility.

Judges are generally appointed following an open call for applications and review by a non-political panel of assessors with a strong judicial component. In England and Wales, appointments to the High Court and Court of Appeal are made by the Judicial Appointments Commission. This commission is composed of fifteen members, of whom five must be current judges and five must be lay members. Similar bodies exist for Scotland and Northern Ireland. In theory, these bodies merely nominate candidates; in practice, their nominations are almost always accepted.

Appointments to the UKSC are more ad hoc. Applications from individuals who meet the qualifying requirements are reviewed by a selection committee ordinarily composed of the president of the court, one member each from the judicial appointments commissions of England and Wales, Scotland, and Northern Ireland, and one further senior judge. Judges are almost always appointed from the Court of Appeal or the highest appellate court in their jurisdiction. The committee recommends a name to the Lord Chancellor (a member of the government), but the Lord Chancellor has always approved this name. When the Lord Chancellor approves the committee's choice, this name is forwarded on to the Prime Minister. Between them, judges must "have knowledge of, and experience of practice in, the law of each part of the United Kingdom" (section 25 of the Constitutional Reform Act of 2005, as amended by the Crime and Courts Act 2013).

THE EMPIRICAL STUDY OF THE LAW IN THE UNITED KINGDOM

Generally, research into the law carried out in UK universities and departments of law is more oriented toward the social sciences than it has been in the past and is more oriented toward the social sciences than, say, research in German law schools (Siems and Mac Síthigh 2012, 672). However, this orientation does not always bring with it a thoroughgoing empiricism in the way many would understand it.

Adler and Simon (2014), citing MacCormick (1994), distinguish between "law in social science" and other approaches to the study of law (fundamental values and principles, doctrinal law, or "law in action"). They then go on to distinguish "empirical" and "non-empirical" modes of sociolegal inquiry. They define the "empirical" mode to include "large-scale quantitative hypothesis-testing research" and "small scale qualitative hypothesis-generating research" (Adler and Simon 2014, 176). Yet many of the articles in journals of sociolegal studies fit neither mold. Articles on "Love as a Disadvantage in Law" (Grossi 2018) or "Alternative

Business Forms and the Contestation of Markets" (Boeger 2018), to take
two recent articles from the *Journal of Law and Society* (*JLS*), are not empirical in the sense implicitly used by Adler and Simon (2014). Indeed,
Adler and Simon (2014) go on to argue that fewer than one in seven
articles in *JLS* are empirical in their sense (the majority of which are
quantitative in nature).

Within the field of sociolegal studies (both in its empirical and non-
empirical modes), judicial behavior has *not* been a primary concern.
Sociolegal scholars have had an admirable concern for law as it is experienced by everyday litigants, in family, housing, or social security cases.
Insofar as sociolegal study is concerned with elites, it often focuses on the
professional closure project pursued by solicitors and barristers (Abel
2003; Zimdars 2010; Zimdars 2011; Blackwell 2017).

Empirical study of judicial behavior is therefore a minority interest
amongst law faculties in the United Kingdom and amongst sociolegal
scholars more generally. Research into the law by *other disciplines* is fitful.
Criminologists have it best: there is abundant literature on sentencing
decisions. However, most sentencing data does not record information
on the sentencing judge. This means that although there are some fascinating aggregate trends (judges responded to well-publicized riots in
London by increasing the probability of awarding a custodial sentence;
see Pina-Sánchez, Lightowlers, and Roberts 2017), criminology says little
about the role of judges in observed outcomes. Political scientists have
evinced little interest: "The UK courts have, at least until quite recently,
largely been treated as very marginal if not completely irrelevant to the
academic study of UK politics" (Drewry 2009, 439). Finally, although
there are notable exceptions, law and economics as a field has yet to
tackle firmly the subject of judicial behavior.

BREADTH AND SCOPE OF THE LITERATURE ON JUDICIAL BEHAVIOR

The UK literature on judicial behavior is broad, in that it has analyzed
several distinct judicial behaviors. However, the literature is not deep:
there has been little sustained engagement with any particular behavior.
The papers that I cite below do not engage with one another, or even cite
one another. Thus, although there have been papers on judicial appointment, judicial language, judicial dissent, and judges' votes, this research
has not been cumulative.

Appointments

There has been considerable research into judicial appointments (Malleson 2009). The earliest such research analyzed the appointment of judges by ministers, acting upon judges' recommendations (Tate 1975, 1992). This research finds that appointment to the Court of Appeal or the House of Lords is heavily influenced by social standing. These findings (which concern the method of appointments used before 2005) are borne out by more recent research (Hanretty 2015b; Blanes i Vidal and Leaver 2011). There have been no studies yet of judicial appointment under the post-2005 system, but Blanes i Vidal and Leaver (2011) find that the advantage had by "elite" candidates diminished when the 2005 system was first proposed.

Politics plays a very limited role. Hanretty (2015b) finds that parties had "favorites," in the sense that they were more likely to pick Court of Appeal judges previously appointed by co-partisans compared to judges appointed by the opposing side. In this he disagrees with Salzberger and Fenn (1999, 844), who argue that judges were more likely to be promoted the more they ruled in favor of the government, whatever its partisan complexion. Politics does not explain judicial retirements: Massie, Randazzo, and Songer (2014), using the same strategic retirement models used successfully in the United States, find "no evidence of strategy to achieve political objectives ... [judges instead] stay as long as possible or retire for personal reasons" (274).

Language and Citation

Setting apart from its literary merit (Coleman 2000), language in judicial and non-judicial settings has been analyzed by social scientists interested in judges' values and by those interested in theories concerning judicial citation. In her article on the values held by UKSC justices, Cahill-O'Callaghan (2013) combines a content analysis of one notable "close-call" (the 5–4 split in *JFS* [2009] UKSC 15) with a survey of academics in Cardiff Law School. Sentence fragments were coded according to whether they indicated one of ten different value orientations identified by Schwartz (1992). The analysis shows differences between the judges in the majority (who emphasized *universalism*) from those in the minority (who emphasized *tradition*). This matches the survey findings: academics who reported greater attachment to tradition were significantly more likely to agree with the minority (Kendall's $\tau=0.657$, n$=18$, $p=0.002$). The great value of the paper lies in the close and attentive analysis of a single case: a recent book extends the analysis (Cahill-O'Callaghan 2020). The key challenge is assessing whether legal language has independent force. Judges may simply have preferences over legal outcomes and then reach for the values language that best exemplifies that outcome.

The historical overlap between the legislature and the judiciary means that we can also analyze judges' words in a political setting. O'Brien (2016) analyzes the parliamentary contributions of the Law Lords—that is, those members of the upper chamber of Parliament who had been given life peerages in order that they might serve on the UK court of final appeal, the Appellate Committee of the House of Lords. O'Brien (2016) provides descriptive statistics on the rate at which judges intervened in legislative debates. He argues that "the most active judicial peers were conservative in their politics," but judgments regarding judges' political orientations are based on biographies and expert commentary, and are used to predict how often judges speak in Parliament. Judges' speeches are not used to make inferences about judges' politics.

Citations are a distinctive but not unique component of judicial language. Patterns of citations can reveal distinctive political or value orientations. The decision to cite one authority rather than another can help us position judges in a complex issue space (Clark and Lauderdale 2010). Analysis of the citation patterns of English and British judges has concentrated on two things: the degree of participation of British judges in a cross-national citation network (Gelter and Siems 2013; Siems 2010), and the degree to which citations reflect another network formed by patterns of on-the-job interaction (Blanes i Vidal and Leaver 2012). In particular, Blanes i Vidal and Leaver (2012) find that judges are more likely to cite and follow opinions by judges with whom they have recently worked or with whom they are scheduled to work. They find no support for the claim that judges are more likely to cite when one of the litigants is a "political" litigant, which is at odds with some claims regarding the presence of defensive citation practices where the risk of political overrule is higher.

VOTES

The most important and most studied aspect of judicial behavior concerns the votes of judges, and in particular decisions to allow or dismiss appeals. These votes can also be characterized as votes in the majority or in the minority, votes for or against the liberal outcome (where that applies), or votes for or against governmental action (in cases with government litigants). Each of these characterizations has a court-level analog. In this section, I describe only those articles which analyze the votes of individual judges.

Dissenting Votes

Hanretty (2013) analyzes the votes of judges in non-unanimous cases before the House of Lords between 1968 and 2003 (the period covered by the High Courts Judicial Database). He analyzes these votes using a standard item response model, which links whether or not a judge dissented as a function of the judge's ideal point, the location of the case, and the degree to which that case discriminates with respect to some underlying dimension. He finds that a one-dimensional item response model, which recovers judges' political positions in other jurisdictions, fails to recover any such differences in the United Kingdom. The fit of the model is poor, and the judge "locations" cannot be interpreted as positions in any political space, but rather reflect judges' propensity to dissent.

A more recent analysis of dissenting votes on the UKSC by the same author comes to a different conclusion. Hanretty (2020, chap. 8) analyzes dissents in decisions taken by the UKSC, and finds that judges *can* be positioned from left to right. He argues that judges' positions are political and cannot be interpreted as doctrinal differences regarding the proper degree of discretion to be given to government.

Votes for or against the Government

Arvind and Stirton (2016) analyze all non-unanimous cases of the House of Lords and UKSC in which a state body features as litigant. The model uses the same parameters as an item response model, but the outcome variable is recorded differently: the outcome is given a score of 2 if the state body won, a 1 if the state body recorded a partial win, or a 0 if the state body lost. In modeling these outcomes, they are able to position judges on a "red-light/green-light scale" (Harlow and Rawlings 2006), with some judges prepared to grant state actors considerably more latitude ("green-light" judges like Lords Brown, Rodger, Carswell and Walker), and others more restricted in their approach ("red-light" judges). They show that the recovered judge positions are not correlated with dissent but are correlated with the proportion of pro-state decisions each judge reaches.

In certain respects, the outcome of this analysis resembles the outcomes Robertson (1998) analyzes in his study of the decisions of the

House of Lords between 1986 and 1995. Robertson uses multiple discriminant analysis to assess whether the (assumed random) presence of Judge X on the panel made a difference to the probability of a pro-state ruling in tax and public law cases, for the plaintiff in constitutional and civil liberties cases, and for defendants in criminal trials. The coefficients for these different analyses are then combined using factor analysis to show that judges' preferences can be represented in two underlying dimensions: egalitarianism and constitutionalism.

Votes for or against the Liberal Outcome

Iaryczower and Katz (2015) extend the standard ideal point model by incorporating an element of learning. Judges receive a "private" signal which indicates whether case-specific information favors one alternative (allowing or dismissing) or another. Judges' private information may be close to the unobserved "true" value (precise judges) or far from it (imprecise judges). Iaryczower and Katz (2015) are thus able to recover both judge positions on a left-right scale and in terms of precision (more or less precise judges).

In order to fit this model, Iaryczower and Katz (2015), like Arvind and Stirton (2016), are required to code cases in a particular direction. They use the same liberal/conservative coding used in the High Courts Judicial Database (HCJD), though they note that "for about a third of the individual decisions, the liberal-conservative classification taken from the HCJD does not coincide with the labeling obtained from the IRT [item response theory] model, the largest proportion of them involving public law appeals" (77).

They argue that a combined learning plus ideology model substantially outperforms a spatial model, and they reach several ancillary conclusions based both on the judge ideology parameters ("no statistically significant differences . . . between judges with and without political experience, or between Conservative and Liberal/Labour nominees"), and on the judge sensitivity parameters (experience increases sensitivity, sensitivity is higher in commercial cases and lowest in other cases).

Outcomes

Just as researchers have studied the votes of individual judges under different classifications, so too have researchers studied court-level outcomes. Blanes i Vidal and Leaver (2015) studied whether or not the Court of Appeal's Civil Division decided to allow or dismiss appeals from first instance courts as a function of whether or not the judges on the panel have worked, or are scheduled to work, with the author of the first instance opinion. (This is possible because High Court judges are occasionally asked to sit on the Court of Appeal.) Although the paper is about appeals, the authors motivate the issue as a specific example of a broader phenomenon of (potentially biased) peer review. They find substantial effects: "the proportion of reviewer affirmances is 30% points higher in the group where reviewers know they will soon work with their reviewee, relative to groups where such interaction is absent" (431).

Hanretty (2014) examines outcomes in the House of Lords between 1968 and 2003, using data from the HCJD. He tests whether "haves" came out ahead—that is, whether governmental and corporate litigants won out over individuals. The principal finding—that governmental litigants, but not corporate litigants, enjoy such an advantage—has not been borne out by more recent research in the UKSC (Hanretty 2020), which finds no such advantage.

GAPS AND UNRESOLVED PUZZLES—WHAT PREFERENCES? AND IS IT PREFERENCES OR ROLE?

It should be clear from the section on the analysis of dissent that there is disagreement over whether judges have political preferences. Hanretty (2013) suggests they do not; Arvind and Stirton (2016) suggest judges have doctrinal preferences only; and Hanretty (2020) and Iaryczower and Katz (2015) claim that judges do have left/right (or liberal/conservative) preferences. In my view, this debate exists in part because of a problem of measurement: we are not very good at operationalizing liberal or left-leaning decisions. I say more about this later.

There is a related debate about whether it is proper to conceive of judges as having preferences, as opposed to roles. Most quantitative empirical legal studies use the language of preferences, but an alternative approach (both in the social science and in the study of judges) views judges principally as actors playing different roles. Judges are therefore part of a dialog (Paterson 2013) or "multilogue."

Role-based explanations are often clearer. The great advantage of a preference-based account of judicial behavior is that everything and nothing may enter into a judge's utility function, from questions of high policy to what the judge had for breakfast that morning (Epstein and Knight 2013). Those who instead adopt a logic of "appropriateness" (March and Olsen 2004) have a seemingly simpler task of finding the role adopted by each actor at any given moment, and deducing from that role the appropriate actions.

Gaps and Unresolved Puzzles—The Study of Lower Courts

One gap concerns our knowledge of appellate courts below the level of the UKSC. Although it is natural that researchers should be interested in the UKSC as the apex court of the United Kingdom, the appellate courts may be more useful for the testing of general or partial theories concerning judicial behavior. As I discuss below, there is some evidence from the Court of Appeal for England and Wales that the assignment of judges to cases is near-random for at least part of the legal year, and randomness has been a key aid in testing claims about the impacts of judges. The larger volume of cases heard by the Court of Appeal (around one thousand cases per year) means that it is possible for researchers either to examine homogeneous groups of cases (immigration appeals) or to identify smaller effects. Those who have looked at tribunals have often been able to identify judge effects fairly cleanly (Blackwell 2013).

Empirical Strategies Used

The primary empirical strategy for researching judicial behavior has arguably been extensive elite interviewing (Paterson 2013) coupled with close observation (Darbyshire 2011). Paterson (2013) also uses archival research, but there is no tradition that says that judges should archive their personal papers. Only a few judges have deposited notebooks, which are analogous to the notebooks of Justices Burton or Blackmun on the Supreme Court of the United States.

Concerning quantitative work, general regression analyses of judicial decisions exist (Hanretty 2014, 2020), but usually these models are not identified so as to recover causal parameters. Work by Blanes i Vidal and Leaver is exceptional in this regard.

Item response models have been used by several authors. This is one of the benefits of the United Kingdom being a laggard with respect to the empirical study of judicial behavior—it has been able to steal advanced techniques without first working through more basic efforts.

Some methods that have not been used as much as might be expected include the content analysis of large corpora and network analysis of citations. Network analysis has been used for specific questions (Gelter and Siems 2013; Siems 2010), but there has been no general attempt at scaling citations. Content analysis similarly has been applied, but typically only at the level of the individual case (Cahill-O'Callaghan 2013).

GENERAL CHALLENGES REGARDING RESEARCH ON JUDICIAL BEHAVIOR

Social scientific research has both internal and external challenges. The main external challenge is the limited variation in judges' characteristics. The main internal challenges concern training, funding, and suitable publication outlets.

Variation in Judges' Characteristics

There is a considerable amount of research on the impact of judges' characteristics on their decisions. The main characteristics researched have included gender, race, age, and education. The UK judiciary has limited diversity with respect to all of these characteristics. This makes it difficult or impossible to study the impact of such characteristics.

GENDER

The first female Law Lord was Baroness Hale. She was appointed in 2004. This was twenty-three years after the first female appointee to the Supreme Court of the United States (Sandra Day O'Connor); twenty-two years after the first female appointee to the Supreme Court of Canada (Bertha Wilson); seventeen years after the first female appointee to the High Court of Australia (Mary Gaudron); and fifteen years after the first female appointee to the Supreme Court of India. Brenda Hale remained the only female member of the Appellate Committee, and the only member of the UKSC, until Lady Black was appointed to the court in 2017. Until this point, it was impossible to make claims about the impact of gender on judicial behavior at the apex of the UK court system because any claims about gender would have been a combination of claims about gender and claims about Baroness Hale.

ETHNICITY

There are no Black or minority ethnic members of the UKSC. There is one Black or minority ethnic member of the Court of Appeal (Rabinder Singh).

EDUCATION

The educational background of judges on the UKSC is narrow. A majority of the judges attended either Oxford or Cambridge. Only three out of the twelve judges have not, and two of them went to universities that are socially elite (Hughes and Black studied at Durham). Second, an overwhelming majority of the judges attended socially exclusive private schools.

AGE

Because appointment to the UKSC is generally promotion from the Court of Appeal, appointees tend to be older than had they been appointed directly from the High Court or from other areas of legal practice. The youngest judge appointed to the UKSC, Lord Reed, was fifty-five when he was appointed; the ages of the most recent appointees (Kitchin, Sales, Hamblen) were sixty-three, fifty-six and sixty-two. The judicial retirement age of seventy means that average tenure on the court will now be between eight and twelve years.

Training, Funding, and Getting Published

The empirical study of judicial behavior involves different disciplines: the techniques of analysis of at least one social science, combined with a knowledge of the law. The literature that I have summarized above is either interdisciplinary or cross-disciplinary. By an interdisciplinary approach, I mean one that blends insights from multiple disciplines. By a cross-disciplinary approach, I mean an approach that views the subject matter of one discipline from the perspective of another discipline.

Interdisciplinary work is generally demanding and less likely to receive funding (Bromham, Dinnage, and Hua 2016). Where researchers' home discipline is in law, researchers may require training in the particular methodologies of the social sciences. Paterson and Darbyshire picked up the techniques of qualitative sociology and anthropology "on the job"; Blackwell and Stirton trained as lawyers but passed through the orbit of the London School of Economics and picked up some taste for quantitative methods there; and Cahill-O'Callaghan previously trained as a biologist. The need for additional training for interdisciplinary researchers housed in law is not unique to the United Kingdom, but it is aggravated by the structure of university education. Here, undergraduates pick a major and do not take courses in other subjects unless they explicitly pick a joint degree. Additionally, law is an undergraduate degree rather than a postgraduate qualification.

It is also not clear (at least for quantitative research) what suitable outlets are. *Public Law* and *Modern Law Review* have made game attempts at publishing quantitative work, and *Public Law* went so far as to publish an article employing item response models estimated using Markov Chain Monte Carlo (Arvind and Stirton 2016), but such articles are rare.

Methodological Challenges—Causation

When considering causation, it is helpful to consider two ways of studying causation: forward causal inference (sometimes described as "the effects of causes") and reverse causal inference ("the causes of effects," or "what explains this outcome?") (Gelman and Imbens 2013). Forward causal inference is carried out using both experimental and observational data. Reverse causal inference is generally only carried out using observational data. Although I believe that modeling observed outcomes (who wins in appeal cases?) offers useful evidence concerning reverse causal inference, in this section I am primarily interested in forward causal inference, or attempts to know the effects of particular causes or interventions.

Forward causal inference on "the effects of judges" has proved remarkably convincing in other jurisdictions, where circumstances permit. In particular, the random assignment of judges to cases has allowed very strong conclusions to be drawn regarding the impact of judges. These conclusions subsequently condition the work of theory- and model-building that characterizes reverse causal inference.

The gold standard for forward causal inference is the randomized controlled trial. Data from a randomized controlled trial allows us to be confident than any systematic differences in outcomes between randomized control and treatment groups must be the result of the treatment rather than any other factors. If those other factors had systematic effects, this would indicate that randomization had failed.

Natural experiments arise in the law where judges are randomly allocated to cases. In the United States, several (but not all) circuits of the United States Court of Appeals randomly assign judges to panels (Hall 2010). This allows for the effects of specific judges to be estimated and for the average causal effects of judge characteristics (such as being nominated by a Republican president or being male) to be estimated (Sunstein et al. 2007). This design has been successfully exported to other jurisdictions where judges are randomly assigned.

The problem in the United Kingdom is that we either know that judges are assigned non-randomly, or we know that assignment is partly random, or we do not know whether assignment is random or not. In the UKSC, we know that judges are assigned to hear cases at least partly on the basis of their specialization in the relevant area of law and partly on the basis of having participated in the earlier permission to appeal stage. This has been shown qualitatively by Paterson (2013) and quantitatively by Hanretty (2020, chap. 5).

In the Court of Appeal of England and Wales, we know that assignment is *partly* random. This question has been dealt with extensively by Blanes i Vidal and Leaver (2015). They focus on the Civil Division of the Court of Appeal, which they argue is "self-contained." Blanes i Vidal and Leaver (2012) describe the panel formation procedure as follows:

> the task of forming the panel falls to the . . . Listing Officer who is an employee of the court . . . Our conversations with a listing officer . . . suggest that the principles underlying panel formation run as follows. First, only "ticketed" judges can be chosen. Second, whenever possible, allocation follows the "cab-rank principle". As judges dispose of their cases, they join the back of the rank and wait to receive a new case; as a case requiring a panel of size n arrives, the . . . Listing Officer matches it to the first n judges in the rank. Third, in the event of a tie (when more than n judges join the rank at the same time), the panel is formed at random (82).

They note that whilst strictly speaking, "it is the duration of the previous case that determines whether or not a judge will be assigned to a particular case," the allocations at the beginning of the year (more specifically, the Michaelmas term, which runs from October to December) seem to be random. They are able to test the randomness assumption by looking at the distributions of pairings of judges and the proportion of contentious cases heard by judges. In both cases, they show no significant (i.e., non-random) differences. This work implies that the effect of judges, or the average effects of judge characteristics (e.g., nominating party, gender, elite status) on particular types of outcome could be estimated for the Court of Appeal's Civil Division. For other high courts (i.e., the Court of Session, the Northern Irish Court of Appeal) we simply do not know by what procedure judges are assigned to cases. If random assignment is used, we may be missing a trick.

Methodological Challenges—Measurement

The benefit of randomization of judges to cases is that it allows us to draw inferences about the effect of judges on particular types of outcomes. However, there is no consensus in the literature about what kinds of outcomes we ought to be interested in or how these relate to theoretical constructs. The data that has been gathered to test associations with different outcomes has not been collected in a way which allows researchers to reuse their data with different types of outcomes.

For example, the theoretical construct at play in Iaryczower and Katz (2015) is judicial liberalism. The relationship between judicial liberalism and outcomes in particular cases is set by the codebook of the High Courts Judicial Database. Judicial liberalism involves the following:

+ decisions in favor of defendants in criminal cases
+ decisions in favor of individuals alleging that their civil rights were violated
+ decisions in favor of economic underdogs
+ decisions for injured parties in torts
+ decisions for copyright holders
+ decisions for the government, in public law cases
+ decisions for national government rather than subnational government

The problem with this list is that many instances of judicial liberalism have involved decisions against the government in public law cases, specifically cases involving immigration and asylum. Although the construct in principle applies equally well to the United Kingdom as to its home jurisdiction, the particular coding decisions made by the compilers of the HCJD don't travel.

Compare this with the constructs and measures used in Arvind and Stirton (2016). Here, the theoretical construct is red-light/green-light judicial permissiveness toward the state (though sometimes the language points more to deference to the executive). This construct is entirely coherent, but other authors might argue that this concept is internally heterogeneous—that, for example, decisions in favor of the Inland Revenue in tax cases are very different to decisions in favor of police constabularies (Robertson 1998).

These two schema are based on the *case categorization* and the *identity of the winning litigants*. There are other outcomes which cannot be based on the two factors. Poole and Shah (2011) collect information on two distinct outcomes in human rights cases: whether the litigant advancing a human rights related claim was successful (had its appeal allowed), and whether the human rights claim itself was successful. The two are different. Litigants who advance a human rights related claim can win for reasons other than their human rights claim.

Outcomes which relate to the *ratio* rather than just the case outcome are liable always to be application specific. For the rest, measuring the kinds of outcomes we are interested in requires, and ought always to be constructed from, some kind of moderately detailed taxonomy of cases, and detailed information on the identity of litigants. In table 1, I list the way in which, in my book, I attempt to assess left-leaning outcomes on this basis. As others have noted, the construction of general purpose legal taxonomies—and even more, legal taxonomies that work well across jurisdictions and legal families—is a very hard task, and it is unlikely that any taxonomy will command universal assent.

METHODOLOGICAL CHALLENGES—AVAILABILITY OF DATA

The United Kingdom is characterized by good public availability of the raw data of the analysis of judicial behavior coupled with limited availability of structured data. By the raw stuff of judicial behavior, I mean primarily the full text of the decisions reached by judges but also ancillary material (e.g., permission to appeal decisions, transcripts, etc.).

At the level of the UKSC, all court decisions are available in PDF format through the UKSC website. There are no unreported decisions. Video-recorded oral argument before the court is available for one year, but there are almost no transcripts. Information on the total population of cases where permission to appeal was sought is also available.

Regarding other courts, the British and Irish Legal Information Institute (www.bailii.org) has near-complete coverage of decisions of the Court of Appeal and the Court of Session. Although it is a voluntarily provided service, it has acquired semi-official status, such that the UKSC regularly links to HTML versions of its own judgments, and the appellate judgments it reviews, on its website. The only instances where decisions are missing are where the cases involved sensitive details of the litigants. Decisions made available on BAILII are not indexed by Google, and may not be scraped, precisely because information about named individuals may either be sensitive or become sensitive. This restriction would make it more difficult to run natural language processing on the full text of historical decisions.

TABLE I. Categorization of left-wing outcomes according to area of law and identity of litigants (A) and (B)

Area of law	(A)	(B)	Left-wing outcome
Public	Individual or association	Public authority	Win for individual or association
	Public authority	Company	Win for public authority
Family	Individual	Individual	Win for the mother (in care proceedings); win for the economic underdog in divorce and estates cases
	Public authority (care proceedings)	Individual	Win for public authority
Criminal	Individual	Prosecuting authorities	Win for the individual
Chancery	Company	Company	Win for the economic underdog
	Individual	Individual	Win for the economic underdog
	Individual or association	Company	Win for individual or association
Civil	Company	Company	Win for the economic underdog
	Individual	Individual	Win for the economic underdog
	Individual or association	Company	Win for individual or association
Tax law	Tax authorities	Individuals, associations, or companies	Win for tax authorities
Exceptions			Win for the party alleging human rights infringement in human rights cases
			Win for the defendant in defamation cases

As far as structured data is concerned, the picture is poorer. The High Courts Judicial Database (HCJD) covered decisions of the House of Lords between 1969 and 2003, though it did not always offer complete coverage. The format of the HCJD worked reasonably well, though there were questions about some of the free-text fields recording the names of the different barristers. The database did not, however, record characteristics of the case that were specific to the United Kingdom, such as findings of declarations of incompatibility, governmental actions which were ultra vires, and so on.

Hanretty (2020), which is a full analysis of all stages of decision-making at the UKSC, is accompanied by replication materials that cover the period 2009 to 2017. The format of the data follows, so far as is possible, the structure of the data contained in the HCJD.

AREAS OF FUTURE RESEARCH TO UNITE THE FIELD OF JUDICIAL BEHAVIOR

It's often said that where you stand depends on where you sit. My view based on the literature reviewed so far is that the field of judicial behavior should think more seriously about how where you stand depends on where you came from. Pre-appointment judicial careers are a growth area of research and have tremendous potential to explain judicial behavior.

I take as illustrations recent work that uses sequence analysis to reduce pre-appointment judicial careers to a limited number of types (Jäckle 2016; Kerby and Banfield 2013). Examples of such types might include the commercial lawyer who enters the judicial hierarchy at a senior level, the academic lawyer who alternates between the courtroom and the university, and the careerist judge who enters early and is steadily promoted. These types are general but can become more specific where courts are structured according to legal specialization.

I think that this research has potential because I have found in my own work that judges' paths prior to the bench matter greatly for their behavior. When I studied the Estonian Supreme Court (Hanretty 2015a), I found that the most notable difference was between judges in the different chambers of the court or between judges who had specialized in criminal, administrative, or civil law. Specialism is a key theme of Hanretty (2020): because of the structure of the (English) court system, judges are often appointed to the UKSC as family law, criminal law, or chancery law specialists.

Pre-appointment judicial careers thus seem to structure behavior in an important way in several courts. The pre-appointment judicial careers need not be orthogonal to political concerns—one's position in the labor market shapes one's politics, and so judges who have chosen to operate first as barristers in independent practice specializing in commercial litigation will have a different outlook to judges who have come from the public sector or academia. But focusing on careers offers a general approach not tied to any particular country.

REFERENCES

Abel, Richard L. 2003. *English Lawyers Between Market and State: The Politics of Professionalism.* Oxford University Press.

Adler, Michael, and Jonathan Simon. 2014. "Stepwise Progression: The Past, Present, and Possible Future of Empirical Research on Law in the United States and the United Kingdom." *Journal of Law and Society* 41 (2): 173–202.

Arvind, T. T., and Lindsay Stirton. 2016. "Legal Ideology, Legal Doctrine and the UK's Top Judges." *Public Law* July 2016: 418–436.

Blackwell, Michael. 2013. "Variation in the Outcomes of Tax Appeals Between Special Commissioners: An Empirical Study." *British Tax Review* 154 (2): 154–75.

Blackwell, Michael. 2017. "Starting Out on a Judicial Career: Gender Diversity and the Appointment of Recorders, Circuit Judges, and Deputy High Court Judges, 1996–2016." *Journal of Law and Society* 44 (4): 586–619.

Blanes i Vidal, Jordi, and Clare Leaver. 2011. "Are Tenured Judges Insulated from Political Pressure?" *Journal of Public Economics* 95 (7–8): 570–86.

Blanes i Vidal, Jordi, and Clare Leaver. 2012. "Social Interactions and the Content of Legal Opinions." *The Journal of Law, Economics, & Organization* 29 (1): 78–114.

Blanes i Vidal, Jordi, and Clare Leaver. 2015. "Bias in Open Peer-Review: Evidence from the English Superior Courts." *The Journal of Law, Economics, and Organization* 31 (3): 431–71.

Boeger, Nina. 2018. "Beyond the Shareholder Corporation: Alternative Business Forms and the Contestation of Markets." *Journal of Law and Society* 45 (1): 10–28.

Bromham, Lindell, Russell Dinnage, and Xia Hua. 2016. "Interdisciplinary Research Has Consistently Lower Funding Success." *Nature* 534 (7609): 684.

Cahill-O'Callaghan, Rachel J. 2013. "The Influence of Personal Values on Legal Judgments." *Journal of Law and Society* 40 (4): 596–623.

Cahill-O'Callaghan, Rachel J. 2020. *Values in the Supreme Court: Decisions, Division and Diversity.* Oxford: Hart.

Clark, Tom S., and Benjamin Lauderdale. 2010. "Locating Supreme Court Opinions in Doctrine Space." *American Journal of Political Science* 54 (4): 871–90.

Coleman, Brady. 2000. "Lord Denning & (and) Justice Cardozo: The Judge as Poet-Philosopher." *Rutgers LJ* 32: 485.

Darbyshire, Penny. 2011. *Sitting in Judgment: The Working Lives of Judges*. London: Bloomsbury Publishing.

Drewry, Gavin. 2009. "A Political Scientist's Perspective." In *The Judicial House of Lords 1876–2009*, edited by Louis Blom-Cooper, Brice Dickson, and Gavin Drewry, 439–53. Oxford: Oxford University Press.

Epstein, Lee, and Jack Knight. 2013. "Reconsidering Judicial Preferences." *Annual Review of Political Science* 16.

Gelman, Andrew, and Guido Imbens. 2013. *Why Ask Why? Forward Causal Inference and Reverse Causal Questions*. National Bureau of Economic Research.

Gelter, Martin, and Mathias M. Siems. 2013. "Language, Legal Origins, and Culture Before the Courts: Cross-Citations Between Supreme Courts in Europe." *Supreme Court Economic Review* 21 (1): 215–69.

Grossi, Renata. 2018. "Love as a Disadvantage in Law." *Journal of Law and Society* 45 (2): 205–25.

Hall, Matthew. 2010. "Randomness Reconsidered: Modeling Random Judicial Assignment in the US Courts of Appeals." *Journal of Empirical Legal Studies* 7 (3): 574–89.

Hanretty, Chris. 2014. "Haves and Have-Nots Before the Law Lords." *Political Studies* 62 (3): 686–97.

Hanretty, Chris. 2015a. "Judicial Disagreement Need Not Be Political: Dissent on the Estonian Supreme Court." *Europe-Asia Studies* 67 (6): 970–88.

Hanretty, Chris. 2015b. "The Appointment of Judges by Ministers: Political Preferment in England, 1880–2005." *Journal of Law and Courts* 3 (2): 305–29.

Hanretty, Chris. 2013. "The Decisions and Ideal Points of British Law Lords." *British Journal of Political Science* 43 (3): 703–16.

Hanretty, Chris. 2020. *A Court of Specialists: Judicial Behavior on the UK Supreme Court*. Oxford: Oxford University Press.

Harlow, Carol, and Richard Rawlings. 2006. *Law and Administration*. Cambridge University Press.

Iaryczower, Matias, and Gabriel Katz. 2015. "More than Politics: Ability and Ideology in the British Appellate Committee." *The Journal of Law, Economics, and Organization* 32 (1): 61–93.

Jäckle, Sebastian. 2016. "Pathways to Karlsruhe: A Sequence Analysis of the Careers of German Federal Constitutional Court Judges." *German Politics* 25 (1): 25–53.

Kerby, M., and A. Banfield. 2013. "A Sequence Analysis of Canadian Supreme Court Judicial Careers." Paper presented at ECPR General Conference, Bordeaux, September 4–7, 2013.

MacCormick, Neil. 1994. "Four Quadrants of Jurisprudence." In *Prescriptive Formality and Normative Rationality in Modern Legal Systems*, edited by W. Krawietz, N. MacCormick, and G. H. von Wright, 53–70. Berlin: Duncker and Humblot.

Malleson, Kate. 2009. "Who Goes Upstairs? Appointments to the House of Lords." In *The Judicial House of Lords*, edited by Louis Blom-Cooper, Gavin Drewry, and Brice Dickson, 112–21. Oxford: Oxford University Press.

March, James G., and Johan P. Olsen. 2004. "The Logic of Appropriateness." In *The Oxford Handbook of Political Science*, edited by Robert E. Goodin. Oxford: Oxford University Press.

Massie, Tajuana, Kirk A. Randazzo, and Donald R. Songer. 2014. "The Politics of Judicial Retirement in Canada and the United Kingdom." *Journal of Law and Courts* 2 (2): 273–99.

O'Brien, Patrick. 2016. "Judges and Politics: The Parliamentary Contributions of the Law Lords 1876–2009." *The Modern Law Review* 79 (5): 786–812.

Paterson, Alan. 2013. *Final Judgment: The Last Law Lords and The Supreme Court*. London: Bloomsbury Publishing.

Pina-Sánchez, Jose, Carly Lightowlers, and Julian Roberts. 2017. "Exploring the Punitive Surge: Crown Court Sentencing Practices Before and After the 2011 English Riots." *Criminology & Criminal Justice* 17 (3): 319–39.

Poole, Thomas, and Sangeeta Shah. 2011. "The Law Lords and Human Rights." *The Modern Law Review* 74 (1): 79–105.

Robertson, David. 1998. *Judicial Discretion in the House Of Lords*. Oxford: Clarendon Press.

Salzberger, Eli, and Paul Fenn. 1999. "Judicial Independence: Some Evidence from the English Court Of Appeal." *The Journal of Law and Economics* 42 (2): 831–47.

Schwartz, Shalom H. 1992. "Universals in the Content and Structure of Values: Theoretical Advances and Empirical Tests in 20 Countries." *Advances in Experimental Social Psychology* 25 (1): 1–65.

Siems, Mathias M. 2010. "Citation Patterns of the German Federal Supreme Court and of the Court of Appeal of England and Wales." *King's Law Journal* 21 (1): 152–71.

Siems, Mathias M., and Daithí Mac Síthigh. 2012. "Mapping Legal Research." *The Cambridge Law Journal* 71 (3): 651–76.

Sunstein, Cass R., David Schkade, Lisa M. Ellman, and Andres Sawicki. 2007. *Are Judges Political? An Empirical Analysis of the Federal Judiciary*. Brookings Institution Press.

Tate, C. Neal. 1975. "Paths to the Bench in Britain: A Quasi-Experimental Study of the Recruitment of a Judicial Elite." *Western Political Quarterly* 28 (1): 108–29.

Tate, C. Neal. 1992. "Recruitment to the British Appellate Judiciary, 1876–1972: Causal Models." *International Political Science Review* 13 (3): 249–67.

Zimdars, Anna. 2010. "The Profile of Pupil Barristers at the Bar of England and Wales 2004–2008." *International Journal of the Legal Profession* 17 (2): 117–34.

Zimdars, Anna K. 2011. "The Competition for Pupillages at the Bar of England and Wales (2000–2004)." *Journal of Law and Society* 38 (4): 575–603.

Empirical Studies of Judicial Behavior and Decision-Making on Indian Courts

SUNITA PARIKH

T HE MAIN focus of this essay will be on the Indian Supreme Court, since that is the object of the vast majority of scholarly research, but I will include discussions of lower-level courts as appropriate. Unlike the experiences of scholars of and in some developing countries, empirical research on Indian courts has a relatively long history and data are available, if not always easily analyzable. Indian High (State) Court and Supreme Court decisions are published annually in English, and the Supreme Court issues regular reports on the disposition of many types of cases. The background of justices on the high courts and Supreme Court are also publicly available.

Theoretically, it should be possible to collect and analyze a wide variety of variables on written opinions as well as on judges' characteristics and the overall caseloads of the courts. However, there are inconsistencies and gaps in aspects of these data, both over time and across categories, which limit the types of analysis that can be conducted. Keeping these limitations in mind, we can nevertheless suggest avenues for empirical research that is comparable to that done in the United States and other judicial regimes.

Contextual and Historical Background

The Indian Supreme Court was established in 1950 when the Constitution of India was enacted. It succeeded the Federal Court of India, an indigenous apex court created under the Government of India Act of 1935. The transition was almost seamless, as the sitting justices of the Federal Court transitioned to become justices of the new Supreme Court and began issuing decisions in its first year.

India's political system is federal, but unlike the United States, the judiciary comprises an integrated system with the Supreme Court at the apex, state high courts below it, and district and sub-districts courts below that (see Robinson 2016 for an overview). The Supreme Court has both appellate and original jurisdiction, and appeals can be made with or without the consent of the high courts. Justices must be selected from qualified jurists who have served for stipulated periods in lower courts, which results in a homogeneous pool of candidates and relatively short tenure on the Supreme Court given the required retirement age of sixty-five. The justices are officially selected by the president of India, but s/he is advised by the chief justice of India (CJI).

The Supreme Court comprises thirty-one justices, including the CJI, and sits in benches of two, three, or more members. The Constitution requires that cases with "constitutional import" be heard by a bench of at least five justices, and decisions that overrule precedent must be decided by a larger bench than the original ruling. The largest bench to hear a case was the thirteen-member bench constituted for the *Keshavananda Bharati* case, which considered an appeal to *Golak Nath*, itself an appeal of a chain of earlier cases. While constitution benches were relatively common during the first decades of the Court's existence, they have become much less frequent. Robertson found that less than 2 percent of cases were heard by constitution benches. At the same time, two-judge benches have become the modal bench size, in part due to the Court's ever-increasing caseload and regular attempts to reduce the large backlog of cases.

The Supreme Court's early decisions included controversial decisions that set the pattern for Court-Executive interactions and established a consensus view of the Court as a political (if not partisan) institution. Foundational research on the Court by scholars such as Rajeev Dhavan, Marc Galanter, Upendra Baxi, and George Gadbois departed from the "black-letter law" view of judicial decision-making to explore how the Court worked around and sometimes directly challenged the executive's expectation that it would defer in a wide range of policy areas.

Despite confronting a unitary executive and being constrained by norms of parliamentary deference (Dhavan 1977), the Court developed a range of approaches designed to increase its reach, authority, and legitimacy. Although the Court was granted explicit judicial review, the norms and constraints of its common law tradition mean that the Court must honor Parliament's powers of delegation except under a small set of circumstances; in response, decisions have stretched these circumstances as far as possible (Darnell and Parikh 2011). In the 1950s and 1960s, the Court continually ruled against legislation for violating the fundamental rights provisions of the Constitution, leading to a long list of "non-justiciable" subjects and numerous constitutional amendments. Executive-legislative conflict reached its apex in the *Golak Nath* and *Keshavananda Bharati* cases, when the Court asserted a "basic structure" doctrine and argued that certain parts of the Constitution were unamendable. In retaliation, the Indira Gandhi government bypassed the usual norms for appointing a CJI to select one considered more friendly to the government in the "supersession of judges" controversy (Austin 1999), and Parliament stripped the Court of its power of judicial review.

These unilateral executive actions proved to be short-lived, as the post-Emergency Janata government restored both judicial review and the norm of seniority in CJI selection. Bruised by these experiences and suffering a loss of legitimacy from the Court's compliance with Gandhi's Emergency provisions, the Court responded by greatly broadening the requirements for standing to bring a case and encouraged an increase in Public Interest Litigation (Epp 1998; Holladay 2012; Mate 2015; Moog 1998; Sathe 2002). Over the 1980s and 1990s the Court regained its depleted legitimacy and increased its authority. Whereas critics in the early years had accused justices of being elite and out of touch with the types of policies necessary for social change and economic development, now the charges were of judicial activism and "legislating from the bench" (Rao 2014). Chandra, Hubbard, and Kalantry argue, however, that the Court continues to be an important source of political access for less powerful Indians (2017). In the last few years, the Court has issued a range of decisions that have substantive and symbolic impact:

+ In 2017 a nine-judge bench overturned two earlier constitution-bench decisions and ruled that privacy was a fundamental right guaranteed under the Constitution.
+ In 2014 the Court recognized the existence of a "third gender" and ordered the government to treat its members as minorities, with all appropriate protections.
+ In 2013 the Court upheld the colonial-era prohibitions on sodomy specified in Section 377 of the Indian Penal Code.

✦ In 2013 the Court banned the use of "lal batti" (red light) beacons atop the cars of political VIPs, arguing that they display a "Raj mentality" and are the "antithesis of the concept of a Republic."

In recent years there have been two heated debates taking place within the Court: the first, which became highly public in January 2018, was about the CJI's impartiality in allocating cases to benches, while the second involved the propriety of different benches ruling more or less simultaneously on the same issue rather than referring cases to a larger bench. It is clear, therefore, that the question is not whether the Court is a political institution, but in what ways and under what conditions justices behave like political actors.

Breadth and Scope of Literature on Judicial Behavior

There has been a wide range of research on judicial behavior, some of which is theoretically informed and some of which is quantitative. Most theoretically informed analysis has drawn on law and society approaches rather than law and economics or empirical legal studies. The foundational scholars of the modern literature continue to hold a dominant position, with more recent research updating their findings or building on their analytical insights. There has not been much research that explicitly applies theories developed in other contexts to the Indian case (Darnell and Parikh 2011 is an exception). Nevertheless, empirically oriented studies provide a partial road map for future research and point to gaps in the currently available data.

Characteristics of Judges

Gadbois's research on the characteristics of Supreme Court judges remains the benchmark for individual-level studies (Gadbois 1968, 1969). Gadbois updated his earlier study in a later book, taking the biographical data of justices through 1989. Chandrachud has updated Gadbois's data through 2010, focusing on individual-level characteristics and regional representation (Chandrachud 2011a, 2011b). Mate has incorporated judges' "education, professional training, and socialization" into a theory of elite institutionalism to explain judicial decision-making (Mate 2015).

Gadbois and Chandrachud present aggregated and descriptive statistics on justices' characteristics, but neither conduct more sophisticated analysis on the data. To my knowledge, there are no statistical studies that employ justices' background characteristics as a variable, although scholars have become increasingly interested in the extent to which different caste, ethnic, regional, and gender categories are represented on the bench (Chandra, Hubbard, and Kalantry 2018). Moreover, there are no comparable studies of the individual background characteristics of judges below the Supreme Court level.

Appointments

The appointment of judges to the high courts and Supreme Court is governed by the Constitution and is quite specific. Candidates for the Supreme Court must have served (a) at least five years on a high court or (b) as a high court or Supreme Court advocate for at least ten years, and (c) should be a "distinguished jurist." For high courts, candidates must have served on a subordinate court for ten years or been a high court advocate for ten years. Appointments to both the Supreme Court and high courts are officially made by the president of India upon recommendations from a panel (known as the collegium) comprising the CJI and other senior justices. The Court has reaffirmed this process in the three cases (known as the *Judges* cases), and in 2016 it held unconstitutional both legislation (the NJAC Act) and a constitutional amendment establishing a commission that would include members of the political branches and civil society.

While there is a small but robust literature on the *Judges* cases and executive-judicial conflict over appointment control, it is primarily qualitative and descriptive. The lists provided to the president of India by the collegium are generally not made public except in the rare cases where disputes arise, as was the case in 1998 (Singh 1999). An overview of the appointments system and interbranch conflict over appointments can be found in Mittal (2019).

Workload and Backlog

Indian courts, from the Supreme Court down, are notorious for their heavy load of cases and the backlogs that arise as a result. The first Supreme Court comprised eight justices, but it has steadily increased to its current size of thirty-one. In its first term it accepted over one thousand admissions, and by 2014 the number had risen to over sixty thousand (Robinson 2016). It is difficult to estimate the exact number of cases the Court accepts, as Robinson details in his thorough examination of the Supreme Court's workload (2013a). However, it is clear that the Court has a consistent problem of admitting a huge number of cases that it cannot clear on a regular basis. The backlog has fluctuated over the years and diminished substantially in some periods, only to rise again.

The high courts face an even greater problem, as the Supreme Court's Annual Reports indicate; in the 2016–17 report the total backlog for India's twenty-four high courts was over 4.2 million pending cases (Supreme Court of India 2017). The causes are a combination of a large number of admitted cases and a shortage of justices in many of the high courts; each court has a set number of serving judges, ranging from a high of one hundred sixty on the Allahabad High Court to a low of two each on the Tripura, Meghalaya, and Manipur High Courts. The four oldest courts are Calcutta (thirty-three), Bombay (seventy-three), Madras (sixty), and Allahabad. As of 2016–17, there were vacancies in several courts, with heavy workloads and backlogs.

This area has received a fair amount of scholarly attention at every court level. Dhavan cautioned against the rising backlog four decades ago (Dhavan 1978, originally published under the name "Dhawan"), and Moog has written several articles on litigiousness, congestion, and backlog issues (Moog 1992, 1993, 1998) as well as on alternative judicial institutions (1991). More recently, in addition to Robinson's work, researchers have examined the effect of delays and vacancies at the district court level (Hazra and Micevska 2004; Micevska and Hazra 2004; Mathur and Prasath 2017; Ghosh 2015). Chemin (2010) examined the impact of reforms across court levels on economic activity, and Eisenberg, Kalantry, and Robinson analyzed the correlation between levels of litigation and measures of well-being (2012). Most recently, Chandra, Hubbard, and Kalantry have begun to publish the results of a sweeping study of the Supreme Court's caseload, characteristics of litigants, and subjects of litigation (2019).

Internal Organization

Robinson has examined the assignment of justices to benches and cases to benches in the Supreme Court (2013a, 2013b), and many scholars discuss how bench decisions matter (e.g., Mate 2015). In addition, Robinson et al. examined the decline in constitution benches over time (2011). However, despite the importance of this topic, there is little work beyond Robinson's that directly addresses these issues, and no research that I could find at the high and district court levels.

Outcomes: Voting, Concurrences, and Dissents

Studies of voting outcomes, especially with respect to concurring and dissenting opinions, go back at least to the work of Dhavan (1977) and especially Gadbois (1984). The latter's work on the decline of dissent has been supplemented in recent years by new studies by Gupta (1995), Robinson et al. (2011), Singh, Alam, and Juahari (2016), and Ashok (2017). Recent studies emphasize the extent to which the dominance of two-judge benches have limited incentives and opportunities for dissent. Ashok points out that if both justices issue separate, divergent opinions, the case must be referred to a larger bench for resolution. In addition, the decline of constitution benches, from nearly 37 percent of the docket in the 1950s and 1960s to less than 2 percent in recent years, has removed the most likely venue for dissents and concurrences to be produced (Ashok 2017).

While there are several quantitative studies on voting, some of which directly engage with theories developed outside the Indian context, most of this research provides descriptive statistics or at most some simple correlations. Ashok's study is noteworthy for engaging with the contemporary empirical legal studies literature.

Precedent

Numerous studies, especially those which look at voting outcomes and the effects of different sizes of benches, consider the issue of stare decisis (Robinson et al. 2011; Robinson 2013b; Ashok 2017; Mate 2015; *inter alia*). Green and Yoon (2016) directly address the topic in their examination of the effect of institutional structure on the workings of common law. Building on the theories of Landes and Posner and those of other US empirical legal scholars, and following Fowler and his colleagues' network analysis of the US Supreme Court (Fowler et al. 2007; Fowler and Jeon 2008), Green and Yoon predict that the system of precedents will work less well in India than in the United States or Canada. They find weak citation practices when looking at a large set of cases, but when they examine the one hundred most important cases, they find that citations to precedent more closely resemble other common law courts. Green and Yoon's study is noteworthy in that it employs multiple regression techniques.

Interbranch Conflict

Interbranch conflict has been the implicit focus of many studies of the Supreme Court since it was established, but it is usually explored historically, qualitatively, and/or narratively. Parikh (2009) and Darnell and Parikh (2011) have directly applied theories developed in the context of the US courts.

GAPS AND UNRESOLVED PUZZLES IN THE LITERATURE

Research on judicial ideology in terms of the positions of individual justices is almost nonexistent at any level of the judiciary. This is somewhat surprising because the wealth of written opinions and large number of justices over time should provide plenty of data from which ideology scores might be constructed for the Supreme Court, and there is little disagreement that justices and benches take positions that can be located on an ideological spectrum. In studies of issue areas, specific cases, and specific justices, there is frequently attribution of ideological positions by scholars and other observers, but these have not been systematically compiled or analyzed.

There is also no systematic research on judicial appointments at any level, although there is a small legal literature on the *Judges* cases. The collegium system of appointments, which has been in effect since 1993, has been scrutinized, especially since the legislative attempt to create a National Judicial Appointments Commission, but the opaque nature of the appointments process and the lack of availability of public data make appointments difficult to study.

The role of the chief justices (CJ) in both the Supreme Court and the high courts is both critical and paradoxical: critical because the CJ assigns cases and appoints justices to benches, paradoxical because the CJ is chosen by seniority and serves relatively short terms due to mandatory retirement, which inhibits their ability to build and maintain power. Nevertheless, while scholars have consistently explored the extent to which case and bench assignment have effects on judicial behavior and outcomes, there is no systematic study of CJs at any level. Similarly, as noted above, several scholars have examined the effect of benches on decisions and behavior, but not in any systematic, theoretically rigorous way (although the most recent work by Ashok, Green and Yoon, and Robinson goes some way toward doing so).

Finally, there is a shortage of systematic research on high courts, district courts, and alternative dispute resolution institutions such as administrative tribunals, Lok Adalats, Sharia courts, and the like, although the work that has been done is very good and can provide a foundation for more theoretically rigorous and empirically systematic extensions

(Whitson 1991; Galanter and Krishnan 2003; Xavier 2005; Redding 2012).

GENERAL EMPIRICAL STRATEGIES

Until quite recently, most published research on judicial behavior was based on textual analysis, elite interviewing, or participant observation. There were some exceptions, such as Gadbois's research on dissents and Dhavan's work on case backlog, but even these were primarily descriptions of aggregated data. The literatures were extensive and theoretically informed; they covered a wide variety of topics relevant to our understanding of judicial behavior, but they were not easily replicated and the data on which they were based were not made widely available.

In the past decade or so, the number of quantitative studies have increased, but the technical level has remained fairly basic. They are very worthwhile because we now have an understanding of patterns in decisions, appointments, caseload, and backlog, especially for the Supreme Court. The Court itself has been publishing annual reports with statistical information on a relatively regular basis, which will allow us to understand more data trends than ever. There are at least a few projects in progress on the Supreme Court and its predecessors which will provide aggregated data that can be analyzed in sophisticated ways, assuming the data are made publicly available.

GENERAL RESEARCH CHALLENGES

The biggest challenge in studying the Indian judiciary is the sheer size of the courts and the caseloads. The vast majority of work is done on the Supreme Court, which has issued tens of thousands of written or signed decisions and has admitted and disposed of many times that number. While we talk about "the Supreme Court" as an entity, we are really talking about justices who sit primarily in two-judge benches, many of whom have little interaction with each other, some of whom serve very short terms (the shortest have been less than a year). Scholars are well aware of this and take note of it in their research, but we have not developed a systematic way of incorporating that knowledge into our understanding of the behavior that interests us.

These challenges are even larger at the high court and district court levels. With twenty-four high courts and dozens of district courts, it is even more difficult to say anything about them as coherent institutions. The vast divergences in size, authority, and influence of the different high courts is obvious, and scholars have examined the relationships between them and the Supreme Court, but these analyses are usually focused on the Supreme Court.

The other major challenges lie in the availability and reliability of data on the different levels of the judiciary. Even the two major online repositories for the Supreme Court provide different numbers of reported and signed cases. Robinson (2013a) does an excellent job of showing the difficulties of reconciling different reporting systems across the different categories of admissions, and these become even greater if we want to analyze the Court over a longer period of time. Similar data for the high courts and district courts are correspondingly more uneven and more difficult to obtain.

Finally, given the historical reliance on qualitative, labor-intensive fieldwork, and interviewing techniques, it is difficult to estimate how much data can be gathered from public or semi-public sources. There are no publicly available databases of decisions comparable to US sources, for example. Proprietary databases of court decisions exist, but these present problems for scholars working in communities where providing data sets for replication purposes are expected or required.

METHODOLOGICAL CHALLENGES

The technical methodological challenges facing scholars of the Indian judiciary are probably less severe today than they have been in the past. Supreme Court and high court reports and publications are all available in English, which means translation issues do not arise. While there are inconsistencies in reporting, all written and signed decisions are available publicly and online and many other types of reports are being made available online as well. Text analysis and scraping techniques developed for large data repositories should make it easier to get at least a first cut at analyzable data. That said, the problems and errors that arise in existing algorithmically produced data sets will be magnified for Indian data because of its size (e.g., mistakes in issue area categorization will occur in greater numbers and require more labor to fix).

Once we move past publicly available data, the methodological challenges increase. To my knowledge, there is no norm governing deposit of retired judges' personal papers. The decision to allow scholars to look at the papers held by the Supreme Court and high courts rest with the justices and civil servants of those courts. The opacity of the decision-making process around practices such as bench assignment means that it is difficult to know how to model them or whether the same assumptions can be maintained across time.

Conclusion

There is a robust empirical literature on the Indian Supreme Court, and it provides a strong foundation on which to develop rigorous theoretical and empirical extensions. While there will be challenges in reconciling data across time and space, transparency in collection and analysis should mitigate the worst of these potential problems.

References

Ashok, K. 2017. "Disinclined to Dissent? A Study of the Supreme Court of India." *Indian Law Review* 1 (1): 7–35.

Austin, G. 1999. *Working A Democratic Constitution: The Indian Experience.* New Delhi and New York: Oxford University Press.

Chandra, A., W. H. Hubbard, and S. Kalantry. 2017. "The Supreme Court of India: A People's Court?" *Indian Law Review* 1 (2): 145–81.

Chandra, A., W. Hubbard, and S. Kalantry. 2019. "From Executive Appointment to the Collegium System: The Impact on Diversity in the Indian Supreme Court." *VRÜ Verfassung und Recht in Übersee* 51 (3): 273–89.

Chandra, A., W. H. J. Hubbard, and S. Kalantry, S. 2019. "The Supreme Court of India: An Empirical Overview of the Institution." In *A Qualified Hope: The Indian Supreme Court and Progressive Social Change*, edited by Gerald N. Rosenberg, Sudhir Krishnaswamy, and Shishir Bail, 43–76. Cambridge University Press.

Chandrachud, A. 2011a. "Regional Representation on the Supreme Court." *Economic and Political Weekly* 46 (20): 13–17.

Chandrachud, A. 2011b. "An Empirical Study of the Supreme Court's Composition." *Economic and Political Weekly* 46 (1): 71–77.

Chandrachud, A. 2014. *The Informal Constitution: Unwritten Criteria in Selecting Judges for the Supreme Court of India.* Oxford University Press.

Chemin, M. 2010. "Does Court Speed Shape Economic Activity? Evidence from a Court Reform in India." *The Journal of Law, Economics, & Organization* 28 (3): 460–85.

Darnell, A. W. and S. Parikh. 2011. "Judicial Stability During Regime Change: Apex Courts in India 1937–1960." In *Political Economy of Institutions, Democracy and Voting*, edited by Norman J. Schofield and Gonzalo Caballero, 119–36. Berlin: Springer Verlag.

Dhavan, R. 1977. *The Supreme Court of India: A Socio-Legal Analysis of its Juristic Techniques.* Bombay: NM Tripathi Pvt. Ltd.

Dhavan, R. 1978. *The Supreme Court under Strain: The Challenges of Arrears.* NM Tripathi Pvt. Ltd. Bombay.

Eisenberg, T., S. Kalantry, and N. Robinson. 2012. "Litigation as a Measure of Well-Being." *DePaul L. Rev.* 62: 247.

Epp, C. R. 1998. *The Rights Revolution: Lawyers, Activists, and Supreme Courts in Comparative Perspective.* Chicago: University of Chicago Press.

Fowler, J. H., T. R. Johnson, J. F. Spriggs, S. Jeon and P. J. Wahlbeck. 2007. "Network Analysis and the Law: Measuring the Legal Importance of Precedents at the US Supreme Court." *Political Analysis* 15 (3): 324–46.

Fowler, J. H., and S. Jeon. 2008. "The Authority of Supreme Court Precedent." *Social Networks* 30 (1): 16–30.

Gadbois, G. H. 1968. "Indian Supreme Court Judges: A Portrait." *Law and Society Review* 3 (2, 3): 317–36.

Gadbois Jr., G. H. 1969. "Selection, Background Characteristics, and Voting Behavior of Indian Supreme Court Judges, 1950–1959." In *Comparative Judicial Behavior,* edited by Glendon Schubert and David Danelski, 221–56. New York: Oxford University Press.

Gadbois Jr., G. H. 1984. "The Decline of Dissent on the Supreme Court, 1950–1981." In *Justice and Social Order in India,* edited by R. A. Sharma, 235–59. New Delhi: Intellectual Publishing House.

Gadbois Jr., G. H. 2011. *Judges of the Supreme Court of India: 1950–1989.* New Delhi: Oxford University Press.

Galanter, M., and J. K. Krishnan. 2003. "Debased Informalism: Lok Adalats and Legal Rights in Modern India." In *Beyond Common Knowledge: Empirical Approaches to the Rule of Law,* edited by Erik Gilbert Jensen and Thomas C. Heller, 96–141. Stanford: Stanford University Press.

Ghosh, H. 2015. "Gujarat's Courts Need 287 Years to Clear Pending Cases." *India Spend,* December 2, 2015. http://www.indiaspend.com/special-reports/gujarats-courts-need-287-years-to-clear-pending-cases-72726.

Green, A. J., and A. Yoon. 2017. "Triaging the Law: Developing the Common Law on the Indian Supreme Court." *Journal of Empirical Legal Studies* 14 (4): 683–715.

Gupta, V. K. 1995. *Decision Making in the Supreme Court of India: A Jurimetric Study.* Kaveri Books.

Hazra, A. K., and M. B. Micevska. 2004. *The Problem of Court Congestion: Evidence from Indian Lower Courts.* ZEF discussion papers on development policy 88. http://hdl.handle.net/10419/21844.

Holladay, Z. 2012. "Public Interest Litigation in India as A Paradigm for Developing Nations." *Indiana Journal of Global Legal Studies* 19 (2): 555–73.

Mathur, S., and R. Prasath. 2017. "Why Judicial Reform Should Start With Lower Courts." *India Spend,* March 31, 2017. http://www.indiaspend.com/cover-story/why-judicial-reform-should-start-with-lower-courts-79679.

Mate, M. 2015. "The Rise of Judicial Governance in the Supreme Court of India." *Boston University International Law Journal* 33: 169.

Mittal, Y. 2019. "Independence of Judiciary: An Epitome of 'Rule of Law' in India." *Journal of Constitutional Law and Jurisprudence* 1 (2): 1–5.

Moog, R. S. 1991. "Conflict and Compromise: The Politics of Lok Adalats in Varanasi District." *Law and Society Review* 25 (3): 545–69.

Moog, R. 1992. "Delays in the Indian Courts: Why the Judges Don't Take Control." *The Justice System Journal* 16 (1): 19–36.

Moog, R. 1993. "Indian Litigiousness and the Litigation Explosion: Challenging the Legend." *Asian Survey* 33 (12): 1136–50.

Moog, R. 1998. "Activism on the Indian Supreme Court." *Judicature* 82: 124.

Moog, R. 2001. "Judicial Activism in the Cause of Judicial Independence: The Indian Supreme Court in the 1990s." *Judicature* 85: 268.

Parikh, S. 2009. "Comparative Politics and the Study of Courts." Paper presented at the Political Science and Law Conference, Searle Center on Law, Regulation, and Economic Growth. Northwestern University School of Law, Chicago, IL, September 25–26.

Rao, K. C. 2014. "Role of Judicial Activism with Special Reference to India." *Editorial Board* 3 (10): 182.

Redding, J. A. 2012. "Secularism, the Rule of Law, and Shari'a Courts: An Ethnographic Examination of a Constitutional Controversy." *St. Louis ULJ* 57: 339.

Robinson, N. 2013a. "A Quantitative Analysis of the Indian Supreme Court's Workload." *Journal of Empirical Legal Studies* 10 (3): 570–601.

Robinson, N. 2013b. "Structure Matters: The Impact of Court Structure on the Indian and US Supreme Courts." *The American Journal of Comparative Law* 61 (1): 173–208.

Robinson, N. 2016. "Judicial Architecture and Capacity." In *The Oxford Handbook of the Indian Constitution*, edited by Sujit Choudhry, Madhav Khosla, and Pratap Bhanu Mehta, 330–48. New York: Oxford University Press.

Robinson, N., A. Agarwal, V. Bhandari, A. Goel, K. Kakkar, R. Muthalaly, V. Shivakumar, M. Sreekumar, S. Sreenivasan, and S. Viswanathan. 2011. "Interpreting the Constitution: Supreme Court Constitution Benches Since Independence." *Economic and Political Weekly* 46 (9): 27–31.

Sathe, S. P. 2002. *Judicial Activism in India*. Oxford University Press.

Singh, M. P. 1999. "Securing the Independence of the Judiciary: The Indian Experience." *Ind. Int'l & Comp. L. Rev.* 10: 245.

Singh, Y. P., A. Alam, and A. C. Jauhari. 2016. "Dissenting Opinions of Judges in the Supreme Court." *Economic and Political Weekly* 51 (5): 13–16.

Supreme Court of India. 2017. *Annual Report 2016–17*. SCI Publications.

Xavier, A. 2005. "Mediation: Its Origin and Growth in India." *Hamline J. Pub. L. & Pol'y* 27: 275.

Whitson, S. L. 1991. "Neither Fish, Nor Flesh, Nor Good Red Herring Lok Adalats: An Experiment in Informal Dispute Resolution in India." *Hastings Int'l & Comp. L. Rev.* 15: 391.

European International Courts

THE CJEU AND THE ECtHR

CLIFFORD CARRUBBA AND JOSHUA FJELSTUL

OVER THE last several decades, national governments have increasingly been choosing to create adjudicatory bodies, or courts, to help ensure fidelity to the international agreements they sign (Smith 2000; Carrubba and Gabel 2015). Two of the earliest—and most influential today—are the Court of Justice of the European Union (CJEU) and the European Court of Human Rights (ECtHR).[1] In this essay, we discuss three central features of the literature. First, we review the core questions scholars of these two courts have asked. Second, we review the main empirical strategies employed to answer these questions. In doing so, we also review the primary challenges in doing empirical work on these courts. And finally, we discuss future directions for the literature in terms of data innovations, theory innovations, and connecting to the domestic courts literature.

CORE QUESTIONS

The first, and foundational theoretical, question for any international court revolves around influence. Under what conditions and for what reasons can international courts influence state behavior? This question is both the obvious and the sensible starting point. Governments voluntarily sign international agreements. In doing so, they choose to create these courts. Once the system is in place, they voluntarily participate in the adjudicatory process. For the ECtHR and the CJEU, this means complying with an adverse ruling if one is made. Why would states do that?

Four types of arguments have been put forward to explain this process. These arguments have been extensively reviewed in Carrubba and Gabel (2017). Here we summarize that discussion.

The first type of argument is the legal and consent-based arguments. These arguments are predicated on the notion that international agreements by construction eliminate, or do not even provoke, issues of noncompliance. For example, the managerial model of international agreements argues that treaties are consent-based and designed to serve the interests of the states that signed the agreement. For this reason, we should only expect errors of application from things like honest mistakes in interpretation, sub-state actors who resist implementation, and so on. To the degree the national government can induce compliance, it will do so upon having the error pointed out in the adjudicatory process (e.g., Chayes and Chayes 1993). Others argue that the simple act of signing the agreement and the resultant legalization of the commitment are sufficient to induce a norm of compliance even if the national government does wish to deviate from prescribed behavior.

The second type of argument is about circumventing the state. In this argument, the threat of noncompliance is real but can be managed if international courts strategically partner with sub-state actors. An example of this strategy in action is the preliminary ruling system. The preliminary ruling system allows a national court to refer a case to the CJEU and ask for proper interpretation of EU law. The common understanding is that this system was originally conceived as a way to challenge the validity of international law. A national court could ask for an interpretation, and if it deemed that interpretation as inconsistent with national law, the national court could strike it down. The CJEU used case law to transform the preliminary ruling system into one in which private litigants instead could challenge national law as inconsistent with EU law. The court was successful because this interpretation gave any national court the power of judicial review over its own country's laws. This is a heady proposition for a lower court (see Burley and Mattli 1993; Alter 2001). Stone Sweet and Brunell (1998) provide another important argument following this logic. These scholars argue that international agreements are incomplete contracts. As a result, contractual disputes naturally arise, which an international court can resolve. The court's resolution provides legal rules and standards that fill in the incomplete contract. With greater clarity come expanded rights and new opportunities for vested interests to pursue. The consequence is that the actors that benefit from the agreement grow in power, and that power allows them to place increasing pressure on governments to further expand the vested interest's opportunities through expanded international agreements and laws. Stone Sweet and Brunell's application is the expansion of trade rights in the EU. The governments created an agreement that increased the ability of export-oriented firms to succeed. Those firms pushed on the boundaries and ambiguities of the agreement in court. The court expanded their rights. The firms grew in power and pushed for the governments to further expand their rights through treaty revision and secondary EU law. Thus, the court was able to get compliance with its vision for the EU by empowering sub-state allies to put domestic pressure on governments.

The third type of argument focuses on how courts help solve collective-action problems. International cooperation is often characterized by the prisoners' dilemma. Coordination on a set of policies can leave governments mutually better off, but each has an incentive to defect from that coordination. International agreements can help by codifying and coordinating expectations over what is not permissible under the agreement. Critically, these codified expectations allow states to coordinate punishment if someone violates the rules, and that threat of punishment can be enough to ensure the violation does not occur.

Signing the agreement, while helpful, is not enough. Treaties are incomplete contracts and monitoring and enforcement is costly. Further, over time the costs of compliance will vary, sometimes enough that the threat of punishment will not be enough to curtail defection, at least in the short run. Courts can help facilitate monitoring and enforcement, and they can act as a sort of release valve on the system. Litigants can bring challenges over potential violations to court (facilitating monitoring), states can participate in the litigation process (facilitating information transmission), and the court can then fill in the incomplete contract in a way that allows exceptions to potential application of the regime's rules when it appears the costs of compliance would be sufficiently high. As such, the court is a critical component to sustaining international cooperation. It helps facilitate enforcement but also tailors interpretation of the rules such that exceptions are allowed when necessary for the overall health of the system.

The final type of argument focuses on how agreements create credible commitments. Like the previous argument, this one starts from the first principle that international agreements help resolve collective-action problems. However, here the focus is on how signing the agreement can generate ex post costs for defection from the agreement. The generic example of this is a person tying her own hands by yielding a bond that is forfeit upon violation of the agreement to a third party. Scholars have applied this argument to human rights regimes in particular (e.g., Simmons 2009).

More recently, scholars have moved beyond the question of why these courts have influence. Instead they are looking at questions that one would expect to see in the domestic courts literature. They are examining the role and development of legal doctrine in judicial decision-making, the sources and impact of judicial preferences on judicial decision-making, and the institutional constraints on judicial decision-making. Importantly, these literatures implicitly take for granted court influence. This relationship between these two literatures is explored in more detail in Carrubba and Gabel (2017).

First, scholars are examining the role of precedent in international court decision-making. Scholars provide evidence that the ECtHR cites external case law (especially in separate opinions) to try to convince others to follow aggressive interpretations of international law (Voeten 2010). They also argue that internal citations are used to persuade domestic courts of the merits of their decision (Lupu and Voeten 2012). Related work can be found on the WTO (Pelc 2014).

Second, scholars are interested in the preferences and biases of individual judges. Historically, scholars have tended to argue that international court judges have a bias toward activism and expansive application of the laws they oversee. Work by Voeten (2007) demonstrates that the primary dimension of contestation in the ECtHR is over activism and whether a ruling expands the reach of the court. However, he also demonstrates that judges do not all have activist tendencies and that the interests of the appointing government predicts well a judge's preferences on this dimension. Work by Malecki (2012) that focuses on the CJEU comes to the same conclusions. Work by Voeten (2008) also shows a national bias in ECtHR judicial preferences. Fjelstul (2018) looks at the professional training of CJEU judges and finds that judges from common law member states cite precedent more frequently than judges from civil law member states and that common law judges have historically had a large influence on the court's jurisprudence.

Finally, scholars are drawing on the US separation of powers literature to examine if threats of legislative override impact CJEU decision-making. The European Parliament and the European Council of Ministers are the two main legislative bodies in the EU. They pass the secondary laws that the CJEU interprets and implements, and they can pass secondary laws to override CJEU interpretations of existing laws. Recent work by Martinsen (2015) and Larsson and Naurin (2016) find evidence that CJEU decisions are, in fact, sensitive to threats of override.

The gist of this section is that the questions scholars are asking about these international courts are fundamentally changing. Initially, the questions were all about whether and why these courts actually matter. Can they affect government behavior and why? Now scholars are focused on how judicial preferences, the structure of legal decision-making, and the institutional context within which courts operate affect judicial decision-making taking the authority of their decisions for granted.

From a theoretical perspective, this is a non-trivial leap. If decisions are enforced for exogenous reasons, such as norms of compliance, then the work follows sensibly. However, if compliance is a function of political factors, as in the collective-action literature, then there may be a fundamental interaction between the causes of compliance and the ways these other questions should be answered.

EMPIRICAL STRATEGIES

Empirical work on international courts is predominantly observational. Older work has often focused on case studies and taken a more historical approach. Since then, quantitative approaches have become more predominant. Across many of these observational studies, particularly in the study of the CJEU, strategic selection is a consistent and core empirical challenge.

Litigates in the EU, as in any legal system, always have an incentive to condition their decision to bring cases based on their beliefs about the likelihood of winning. The Commission has an incentive to be strategic in initiating infringement investigations, if and when to drop these investigations when governments are uncooperative, and whether to refer cases to the CJEU based on how they think the case will resolve in court (König and Mäder 2014; Fjelstul and Carrubba 2018). National courts have an incentive to refer cases to the CJEU based upon how they anticipate the CJEU is likely to rule. The General Court has an incentive to anticipate the reaction of the Court of Justice when ruling in cases that can be appealed. The CJEU has an incentive to act strategically based upon whether they anticipate the possibility that their rulings may not be followed.[2] This could be the because of the threat of noncompliance (Carrubba and Gabel 2015), or the threat of override (Martinsen 2015; Larsson et al. 2017). And, governments must make a strategic decision over whether to comply with an adverse ruling (Carrubba and Gabel 2015).

Generally speaking, scholars in this area have not taken advantage of causal inference techniques to deal with these sources of endogeneity. For example, to the extent that studies on compliance in the EU recognize that Commission selection in the infringement procedure is a problem (e.g., Hartlapp and Falkner 2009), they either dismiss it as unavoidable or attempt to treat it as a nuisance empirical problem (e.g., Hartlapp and Falkner 2009; Mbaye 2001; Börzel and Risse 2003; Sverdrup 2004; Hartlapp 2008) rather than as something to be theorized.

There are some exceptions. Carrubba (2005), König and Mäder (2014), and Fjelstul and Carrubba (2018) use an EITM approach.[3] By modeling the selection processes that cause endogeneity, these studies derive testable predictions that already incorporate potential bias. Carrubba and Gabel (2015) derive and test the hypothesis that the court is sensitive to the balance member state preferences and moderates its rulings accordingly. König and Mäder (2014) test the predictions of a reduced-form model of the infringement procedure and identify a compliance deficit caused by the Commission dropping cases. By incorporating the insights of Carrubba and Gabel (2015) and explicitly modeling each step in the infringement procedure, Fjelstul and Carrubba (2018) identify what we can and cannot learn from observable noncompliance data, finding that observable levels of noncompliance are uninformative but that the likelihood of progression through the infringement procedure can be informative, but only at certain stages.

Fjelstul (2018) uses matching techniques to estimate the effect of common law judges on the CJEU's use of precedent via several causal mechanisms. This paper uses matching as a pre-processing technique to create balanced treatment and control groups, simulating an experiment. Further afield from the CJEU, but related to the infringement procedure, Cheruvu and Fjelstul (2019) use a difference-in-differences analysis to identify the causal effect of a Commission initiative to improve response times in the infringement procedure. The volume of observational data available on the CJEU provides an opportunity to use various causal inference techniques to improve inference. We believe these approaches can and should increase in use as textual data proliferates.

Measuring Judicial Outcomes

Whether studying why international courts have influence or more traditional questions about judicial decision-making, scholars who study the CJEU tend to design empirical tests around three basic types of judicial outcomes: how the CJEU disposes of cases, the voting patterns of individual judges, and the use of citations in CJEU judgments. In this section, we highlight some of the research design and data-collection challenges that scholars face with respect to each of these outcomes. There are some exceptions that are worth noting, however. Carrubba and Gabel (2015)—in the only study on the judicial effectiveness of the CJEU—look at the effect of CJEU rulings on intra-EU trade.

Judgments

Some studies are interested in explaining how international courts dispose of cases, pairing data on the disposition with a variety of explanatory variables (e.g., Voeten 2008; Carrubba, Gabel, and Hankla 2008; Carrubba and Gabel 2015; Larsson and Naurin 2016). How rulings are coded can vary in these studies.

Studies take different approaches in terms of how to code outcomes of cases. Some studies try to stay close to the objectively observable characteristics, like whether the plaintiff or defendant won the case or legal issue (e.g., Carrubba, Gabel, and Hankla 2008; Carrubba and Gabel 2015). Frankenreiter (2018) follows Carrubba and Gabel (2015) and codes agreement between the CJEU judgment and the advocate-general opinion by the legal issue. Other studies code outcomes by some substantive characteristic like whether the outcome furthered European integration or limited it (Larsson and Naurin 2016). This second approach has the advantage of offering a more substantive interpretation of the results. However, it also comes with two potential costs. The first is that it can add noise, as coding cases on a pro- or anti-integration scale is far more subjective than coding whether the court agrees with the plaintiff or the defendant. The second is that it assumes that pro- or anti-integration is the relevant substantive dimension in the case. It may be that a left or right dimension would be more relevant.

Another potential source of disagreement relates to the unit of observation. One option is to code one outcome per case. Another is to code how the court disposes of each legal issue within a case. This second approach is predominant to date (e.g., Carrubba and Gabel 2015; Larsson and Naurin 2016; Frankenreiter 2018). This distinction can be important depending upon two factors. First, if cases consist of multiple legal issues, then how these issues are disposed of can vary within a case. Thus, the overall coding can miss potentially valuable nuance in the judicial decision. Second, if the covariates of interest also vary by legal issue, then the researcher can be adding noise to the coding scheme. For example, at the CJEU, government observations in a case can vary by legal issue. Sometimes they come out in favor of one side and sometimes the other, even within the same case. Of course, the appropriate unit of observation depends on the question.

Voting

As we discuss above, one recent strand of research on the CJEU imports questions from the literature on domestic courts to understand the extent to which the CJEU works like a domestic court. This includes questions about where judicial preferences come from and what the relevant dimensions of contestation are. Some studies try to tease out judicial preference orderings and dimensions of contestation (e.g., Voeten 2007; Malecki 2012). Others look for judge-specific sources of bias in judicial decision-making (Voeten 2008).

Looking at the literature on the US Supreme Court, scholars have developed sophisticated models to estimate time-varying and issue-specific judge positions using voting and citation data (e.g., Martin and Quinn 2002; Clark and Lauderdale 2010; Lauderdale and Clark 2012, 2014). Lauderdale and Clark (2016) even estimate case-specific judge positions using conditional autoregressive priors. These approaches have proven very productive in the US literature, but they do not translate to the CJEU context.

The problem with studying the preferences of individual CJEU judges is that votes are not made public and there are no dissenting or concurring opinions. (At the ECtHR, in contrast, votes are made public.) Malecki (2012) makes the only real progress on this issue to date. Using a hierarchical Bayesian item response theory (IRT) model, he takes advantage of variation in the composition of the chambers to estimate ideal points of Court of Justice judges even though we cannot observe individual votes. Malecki (2012) estimates judge preferences on a pro- or anti-Commission dimension. The key input to the model is whether or not the court sides with the Commission. This can vary by legal issue within a case, so Malecki uses data from Carrubba and Gabel (2015), who code agreement between the court and the Commission by legal issue.

Malecki (2012) made a huge stride forward in estimating the positions of CJEU judges despite the fact that voting data is not publicly available. However, there are several downsides to this approach that future research can address. One downside is that the ideological positions of appointing governments are inputs in the model, so we cannot use these positions to analyze whether there is a principal-agent problem between member state governments and the judges that they appoint.

A second downside is that Malecki's approach requires a considerable amount of hand-coded data. The IRT model requires data on whether the court agreed with the Commission's brief and the number of government briefs for and against the Commission for identification. Gabel, Hix, and Malecki (2007) use a similar identification strategy in a study of MEP roll-call behavior. Carrubba and Gabel (2015) hand code this information for all Court of Justice cases prior to 2000, but as we discuss below, there are challenges to extending this data.

A final downside is that this approach cannot be used to estimate a left or right dimension, as there is not a binary indicator of left or right preferences that we can use to estimate the IRT model. Scholars have shown that EU politics has both a pro- or anti-integration dimension and a right or left dimension (Hix, Noury and Roland 2006; Hix and Noury 2009). We expect there to be a right or left dimension reflected in CJEU judges' decisions. The extent to which the preferences of CJEU judges—and by extension, the CJEU—fall on a pro- or anti-integration dimension or a left or right dimension is an open empirical question that has big implications for how the CJEU resolves legal disputes between the Commission and member states.

A closely related question in the literature is whether advocates-general (AGs) are political (i.e., what dimension underlies their preferences). Carrubba and Gabel (2015) argue that AGs are largely apolitical and that AG opinion is a good control for the legal merits of the case, which is an important control in empirical work on the disposition of CJEU judgments. Frankenreiter (2018), on the other hand, develops an empirical test to see if advocates-general are political and finds a correlation between the ideological positions of AGs and their appointing member states. This test relies on party manifesto data (Volkens et al. 2017). Future work on the CJEU should further explore the political role of AGs by developing and testing theories of when CJEU judges are more or less likely to rely on AG opinions.

Citations

Scholars are interested in explaining variation in the degree to which international courts rely on precedent. Despite the fact that precedent is not binding in international law, international courts frequently cite case law to justify decisions. This is true of the CJEU, the International Court of Justice (ICJ), the European Court of Human Rights (ECtHR), and World Trade Organization (WTO) tribunals (Shahabuddeen 2007; Busch 2007; Lupu and Voeten 2012; Pelc 2014; Derlén and Lindholm 2014, 2015; Larsson et al. 2017; Fjelstul 2018). In fact, both the CJEU and ECtHR citation networks look very similar to the US Supreme Court citation network (Lupu and Voeten 2012; Larsson and Naurin 2016).

The literature provides several plausible theories of why civil law international courts cite precedent like common law domestic constitutional courts. First, international courts might cite precedent to ensure that the relevant body of law remains consistent and predictable over time (Lupu and Voeten 2012). Domestic constitutional courts share this concern (Fon and Parisi 2006; Helfer 2008). Second, international courts could cite precedent to justify their rulings to domestic courts, which they often rely on to enforce their rulings (Lupu and Voeten 2012). In this view, citations to existing case law can help domestic courts interpret the ruling of an international court, increasing the likelihood that a domestic court applies the law the way the international court wants it to be applied. Third, they might cite precedent to legitimize their rulings in the eyes of the public (Lupu and Voeten 2012).

These theories focus on the external politics of courts (i.e., how courts use precedent to affect outside political actors), but the internal politics of courts also play a role. International courts are unique in that judges come from different countries—and therefore different legal traditions. At the CJEU, judges from common law member states are more likely to cite precedent due to the principal of stare decisis (Fjelstul 2018). Internal politics also affect which cases are cited. CJEU judges are more likely to cite cases written by judges from member states with similar preferences as their own member state (Frankenreiter 2017).

The empirical approach to the study of citations at international courts is the same as the approach in the literature on domestic constitutional courts. Using network analysis, scholars identify how central a decision is to the citation network (e.g., Lupu and Voeten 2012). *Hubs* are decisions that cite many other judgments, and *authorities* are decisions that are cited by many other judgments. Good hubs cite good authorities and good authorities are cited by many good hubs. Cases that are well embedded in precedent are hubs and will have high hub scores.

Hub scores are calculated by looking at the entire citation network as a whole and therefore change over time as new cases are added. As such, hub scores can be calculated for all cases based on the network at the time that the most recent case in the sample was published or hub scores can be recalculated for all cases at the time each case in the sample was published, where the score used for each case is the score for that case at the time it was published. To avoid this issue, studies often use out degree (i.e., the number of other cases a case cites) as a simpler alternative measure (e.g., Larsson and Naurin 2016; Fjelstul 2019).

For example, in a study on the ECtHR, Lupu and Voeten (2012) use these statistics to evaluate a set of hypothesized predictors of citations, including the legal issues at hand, the article basis of the cases, whether the ECtHR is ruling against a government or overturning a preliminary objection, and whether the case comes from a common law country (which has a history of using precedent). In a similar study on the CJEU, Larsson and Naurin (2016) find that the Court of Justice is more likely to cite precedent when disagreeing with the Commission, the AG opinion, or the balance of member states (as indicated by third-party briefs).

Data Availability

A significant obstacle to conducting good empirical work in this area is data availability. Scholars generally rely on small, hand-coded samples that cover a limited time frame. Currently available data on the CJEU gives us only partial snapshots of the institutional processes we care about. This naturally limits the confidence we can have in the generalizability of empirical findings beyond the sample used.

The most comprehensive data sets on CJEU judgments are Carrubba and Gabel (2015), which is based on Carrubba, Gabel, and Hankla (2008), and Larsson and Naurin (2016). Both rely on hearing reports to identify the positions of the court, the AG, and member state governments. Both also use a legal issue as the unit of observation, instead of a case or judgment. Carrubba and Gabel (2015) cover all Court of Justice rulings from 1960 to 1999. They code whether the court agrees with the plaintiff, the Commission's brief (if applicable), and any third-party briefs.

Larsson and Naurin (2016) code references for preliminary rulings for which there was an oral hearing (since the source is the report for the hearing) from 1997 to 2008. The data covers 1,599 cases and 3,845 legal issues. It does not cover direct actions. Using the hearing reports, they identify the legal questions and code the position of each actor. Hearing reports are only publicly available until 1994, but the authors obtain them from the Swedish foreign ministry on the condition they are used only for research purposes. These are not available to other researchers. They also code the extent to which the court's ruling furthers European integration on a three-point scale. Since these data sets use hand-coded positions, extending either to cover additional cases would be difficult and time-consuming.

Other recent quantitative studies use smaller subsets based on Carrubba, Gabel, and Hankla (2008) or Carrubba and Gabel (2015). In estimating judge positions, Malecki (2012) uses a sample of 1,549 legal issues in Article 267 cases (references for preliminary rulings) between 1970 and 1997. Frankenreiter (2018) uses a sample of 1,085 legal issues across 501 cases, but this includes only references for preliminary rulings dealing with the four freedoms between 1997 and 2006. He hand codes agreement between the court's judgment and the AG's opinion for each legal issue.

Studies of noncompliance have also tended to rely on small, handcoded samples. For example, König and Mäder (2012) and König and Mäder (2014) use the decision-making in the European Union (DEU) data set, which includes estimated preferences for all member states and the Commission on all of the contested issues in a set of secondary laws (Thomson et al. 2012). Thus, the unit of observation is closer to Carrubba and Gabel (2015) in that documents are broken down by issue. The positions of each actor is exactly the type of information we would ideally want to have, but the DEU data set covers only a small sample of high-profile directives. There are nearly 4,000 directives and over 130,000 regulations.

The potential problem with limited samples is that the institutional environment of the CJEU has changed dramatically over time in ways that we expect will change the behavior of the actors we are interested in. For example, Carrubba et al. (2018) document how the court's chambers system has changed over time. There are significant changes over time in the rules that constrain how the court assigns cases to chambers; it has far more flexibility in more recent years. How we should expect the court to behave will, of course, depend on the institutional constraints that are operating at the time. Changes in institutional rules over time may or may not matter, depending on the specific questions a study is exploring, but we caution the use of a limited sample without carefully considering how the results may depend on the temporal context.

Existing data also neglect important areas of institutional activity entirely. For example, scholars have completely neglected the General Court, which has decided over five thousand cases since its creation in 1989. The General Court has jurisdiction over annulments at first instance, which play an important role in the evolution of EU law by providing the CJEU a mechanism to strike down secondary laws and other decisions by EU institutions, such as trademark decisions by the Office for Harmonization in the Internal Market (OHIM), that it believes are not compatible with the treaty. There are no publicly available data sets on the General Court.

While a necessary first step, it is not enough to have comprehensive data on CJEU judgments. Courts never operate in a vacuum. Even if we have comprehensive data on judicial outcomes in the EU, we know that courts make decisions based on outside political factors, and so we need data on those factors to test our theories. For example, the CJEU may be sensitive to threats of judicial override (Larsson and Naurin 2016).[4] To see if member states actually ever amend secondary laws or treaties after an adverse CJEU ruling, we would need data on successful and attempted amendments to secondary laws that have been the subject of litigation.

Data-collection efforts have increased dramatically over the last years. Larsson and Naurin (2016) extend Carrubba and Gabel (2015) with some important coding differences. Fjelstul and Carrubba (2018) collect data on every Commission infringement case from 2003 through 2015. Cheruvu and Fjelstul (2019) extend this data with additional observations and variables. Fjelstul (2018) provides data on which judges hear every Court of Justice cases from 1952 through 2016, including who the AG is and who the judge-rapporteur is. This is the most comprehensive data set of CJEU cases to date. Derlén and Lindholm (2014) collect data on the Court of Justice citation network. This covers citations to other Court of Justice cases, but not citations to General Court cases, secondary laws, or EU treaties. Larsson et al. (2017) combine citation data from Derlén and Lindholm (2014) with additional case-level data from Larsson and Naurin (2016). All of these studies are facilitating better empirical work on the CJEU.

NEXT STEPS

To conclude, we consider next steps the literature can take to address the theoretical and empirical challenges we have identified. We highlight three areas to focus on. First, scholars should invest in more comprehensive data collection using web-scraping and text mining techniques. Second, scholars should consider new theoretical approaches. Third, scholars should look for productive ways to connect the literature on domestic courts and international courts.

Data Collection

We anticipate that the future of data collection in this literature will revolve around text analysis (e.g., the processing of text using regular expressions and other methods). These techniques will allow scholars to improve the quantity and quality of data on the CJEU. The Commission provides free access to the full text of all EU documents and associated metadata through an online database called EUR-Lex. It takes a considerable amount work to collect EU legal documents, identify and extract the relevant text from those documents, clean that text, and compile it into a usable quantitative data set. Nevertheless, we think this approach will pay huge dividends.

Using text analysis to process the text of EU documents (and any associated metadata) provides several advantages over hand-coding. First, this approach can be comprehensive. Using these methods, we can collect, clean, and process more data faster. Second, it is more accurate. Conditional on the code being well-written, automating the process avoids human coding errors. Third, automated text processing greatly improves replicability. We can perfectly replicate the process of data collection and data cleaning by rerunning the code. Fourth, we do not need to conduct expensive and time-consuming inter-coder reliability tests, as we would with hand-coding.

With so much data potentially available from official sources like EUR-Lex, the question of what to collect and how to organize the information in a useful way to promote and facilitate theory-testing is a very important one. Of course, it depends on the theoretical questions that we want to be able to address. We think the biggest return will come from mapping the linkages between treaties, secondary law, and case law.

Courts never operate in a vacuum. We think courts make rulings based on founding treaties, precedent, existing laws, expectations about future laws (i.e., the threat of judicial override), and expectations of future treaty changes. One way forward, then, is to build toward a theory of the evolution of political systems. When do secondary laws generate court cases, and how do cases affect the future interpretation of secondary law? Can the CJEU cause member states to revise the treaty or secondary law by issuing adverse rulings? To what extent does the CJEU anticipate noncompliance, the possible creation of new secondary law, or new treaty revisions when issuing adverse rulings?

To answer these questions, CJEU researchers will need data on the linkages among treaties, secondary law, and case law. These sources of EU law all affect each other. Treaties and secondary laws can amend secondary laws, and case law can interpret or enforce treaties and secondary laws; court cases can annul secondary laws. New secondary law or treaty revisions can generate new case law, and new case law can prompt new secondary law or future treaty revisions. Legal principles and policies also link all of these documents together in complex ways. We can trace these linkages using citations. Secondary law frequently references treaties and other secondary law. Case law references other case law but also treaties and secondary law.

Fjelstul (2019) maps these kinds of linkages. He collects the text and metadata of all of these documents from EUR-Lex and uses text-analysis tools to build a comprehensive data set of the linkages between them. This is an incredibly data-intensive process. The data set covers over 4,000 EU treaty articles, nearly 4,000 directives, over 130,000 regulations, over 20,000 decisions, over 10,000 Court of Justice judgments, nearly 5,000 General Court judgments, over 8,000 AG opinions, over 140,000 implementing measures (national laws passed by member states to transpose directives), and over 30,000 national court decisions that apply EU law—nearly the entire body of EU law from 1952 through 2015 (a total of over 365,000 documents). Of note, we believe this is the first data set to cover the General Court. This data set provides a comprehensive picture of how the EU legal system has evolved over time.

There are many potential uses for this data. We can establish new stylized facts that can serve as the basis for new theory development. We can also develop and test theories about the evolution of the EU legal system. In particular, we can use this information to develop and test theories of how inter-state bargaining between EU member states over treaty articles (i.e., over the nature of the institutional constraints) or secondary laws (i.e., within current institutional constraints) generate political disputes, how the CJEU settles these disputes, and how the resolution of these disputes prompts member states to revise treaty articles and amend secondary laws.

Theoretical Challenges

There are significant challenges to developing the theories that we can test using this data. The literature sometimes uses formal models to derive testable predictions that incorporate selection problems. But formal models that accurately capture institutional processes, and therefore that accurately model strategic selection, can be very complex (e.g., Fjelstul and Carrubba 2018 versus König and Mäder 2014). Computational techniques are a currently under-utilized way to embrace this complexity. We can use computational simulations of game-theoretic equilibria to study policy-making, compliance, and dispute resolution. We can also use agent-based models that allow for a wider range of behavioral postulates than the utility maximization of game-theoretic models.

For example, Fjelstul and Carrubba (2018) accurately model all of the steps in the Commission's formal infringement procedure. König and Mäder (2014), in contrast, do not take into account the actual structure of the procedure, such as the fact that there are multiple stages (e.g., the letter of formal notice stage, the reasoned opinion stage, and the referral stage). Fjelstul and Carrubba (2018) incorporate an insight from Carrubba and Gabel (2015) that the court is sensitive to member states' costs of compliance. Accurately modeling the structure of the procedure greatly increases the complexity of our model, but the payoff is high. We are able to derive new testable predictions that are specific to our theory and, conditional on taking the model as true, we can make substantively important inferences about why member states are committing violations and how frequently the Commission fails to correct noncompliance. We use a computational simulation to derive a non-obvious, testable comparative static. The analytical solution, while it exists, is too complex to sign. Testing this computationally derived comparative static gives us more confidence in our model and allows us to make substantively important inferences conditional on the model being true.

Connecting across Literatures

Finally, consider how this literature can connect to the literature of domestic courts. We see two paths forward. Perhaps the most obvious way is to see how questions we have studied in the domestic courts' literatures are or are not playing out differently in the international courts' literature.

This path appears fruitful. For example, we are finding consistent evidence of a separation of powers constraint in the EU. If we are finding such a constraint with regards to implementation of EU law, why should we expect it to be different in other legislative systems? One can raise questions about the generalization, but it is indeed evidence in a certain direction. As another example, we are finding systematic bias in how international judges rule. To the degree these judges are comparable, this reinforces the perception that judges are influenced by factors outside of the legal merits of a case. We can imagine doing more work to see if patterns found at the domestic level follow through at the international one as well.

While useful, this first type of linkage is probably not the most fruitful. Rather, we believe there is much to learn from the international courts' literature that can and should be brought back to the domestic courts' literature. Specifically, the question of why we see compliance with international court rulings is potentially quite important for the domestic courts' literature. Scholars of domestic courts have long recognized this quandary. A whole literature on judicial impact studies when court rulings actually change behavior (e.g., Canon 1991; Wood and Waterman 1991; Epp 1998; Ellig 2001; Ohlhausen and Luib 2008; Ellig and Wiseman 2011). More recent work has focused on the question of government compliance specifically. Seminal work by Vanberg (2001, 2005) studies when the German federal government evaded its Supreme Court rulings. This was extended by Staton (2006, 2010) in studying the Mexican high court and then brought to the US context by Carrubba and Rogers (2003), Carrubba (2010), and Carrubba and Zorn (2010). Further, scholars are even looking at how "weak" international court with severe concerns about compliance can evolve into ones that look like "strong" domestic courts that do not have to worry about it as much (Carrubba 2009).

This work has brought the question of compliance with rule of law into focus in the domestic literature. However, it does not explore how the first principles of when compliance is a concern can and should inform how we study other questions. For example, how might it cause us to reexamine the question of when do judicial preferences matter. Or, alternatively, how may we revisit the question of what sorts of rules high courts establish in implementing secondary laws. It seems to us that these are potentially highly fruitful ways of taking seriously the underpinnings of judicial influence. After all, if our theories over these questions are inconsistent with foundational theories of compliance, something has to give.

Notes

1. The CJEU currently consists of two courts: the Court of Justice and the General Court. It previously consisted of the Civil Service Tribunal, which existed from 2005 to 2016. Prior to the Treaty of Lisbon (2009), the Court of Justice was known as the European Court of Justice (ECJ) and the General Court, established in 1989, was known as the Court of First Instance.
2. This translates to the ECtHR as well.
3. Empirical implications of theoretical models (EITM) is a research strategy in which scholars solve formal models, derive empirical implications, and then test those implications empirically.
4. Larsson and Naurin (2016) look at the court's behavior to find evidence that the court anticipates the threat of legislative override, but the authors do not provide any empirical evidence that overrides ever occur or are attempted.

References

Alter, Karen. 2001. *Establishing the Supremacy of European Law: The Making of an International Rule of Law in Europe.* Oxford, England: Oxford University Press.

Börzel, Tanja A., and Thomas Risse. 2003. "Conceptualizing the Domestic Impact of Europe." In *The Politics of Europeanization,* edited by Kevin Featherstone and Claudio M. Radaelli, 57–80. Oxford Scholarship Online. https://oxford.universitypressscholarship.com/view/10.1093/0199252092.001.0001/acprof-9780199252091-chapter-3.

Burley, Anne-Marie, and Walter Mattli. 1993. "Europe Before the Court: A Political Theory of Legal Integration." *International Organization* 47 (Winter): 41–76.

Busch, Marc L. 2007. "Overlapping Institutions, Forum Shopping, and Dispute Settlement in International Trade." *International Organization* 61 (4): 735–61.

Canon, Bradley. 1991. "Courts and Policy: Compliance, Implementation, and Impact." In *The American Courts: A Critical Assessment,* edited by John Gates and Charles Johnson. Washington, DC: Congressional Quarterly Press. 435–66.

Carrubba, Cliff. 2009. "A Model of Endogenous Development of Judicial Institutions in Federal and International Systems." *Journal of Politics* 71: 55–69.

Carrubba, Clifford J. 2005. "Courts and Compliance in International Regulatory Regimes." *Journal of Politics* 67 (3): 669–89.

Carrubba, Clifford J. 2010. "Federalism, Public Opinion, and Judicial Authority
in Comparative Perspective." *Mich. St. L. Rev.* 697.

Carrubba, Clifford J., and Matthew J. Gabel. 2015. *International Courts and the
Performance of International Agreements.* New York: Cambridge University
Press.

Carrubba, Clifford J., and Matthew Gabel. 2017. "International Courts: A Theoretical Assessment." *Annual Review of Political Science* 20: 55–73.

Carrubba, Clifford J., Matthew Gabel, Joshua C. Fjelstul, and Dani Villa. 2018.
"The Internal Organization of the European Court of Justice: Discretion,
Compliance, and the Strategic Use of Chambers." Working paper.

Carrubba, Clifford J., Matthew Gabel, and Charles Hankla. 2008. "Judicial Behavior under Political Constraints: Evidence from the European Court of
Justice." *American Political Science Review* 102 (4): 435–52.

Carrubba, Clifford, and James R Rogers. 2003. "National Judicial Power and the
Dormant Commerce Clause." *Journal of Law, Economics, and Organization* 19
(2): 543–70.

Carrubba, Clifford J., and Christopher Zorn. 2010. "Executive Discretion, Judicial Decision Making, and Separation of Powers in the United States." *Journal of Politics* 72 (3): 812–24.

Chayes, Abram, and Antonia Chayes. 1993. "On Compliance." *International
Organization* 47 (2): 175–205.

Cheruvu, Sivaram, and Joshua Fjelstul. 2019. "Can International Institutions
Help States to Comply with International Law? Encouraging Evidence from
the European Union's Pilot Program." Working paper.

Clark, Tom, and Benjamin Lauderdale. 2010. "Locating Supreme Court Opinions in Doctrine Space." *American Journal of Political Science* 54: 871–90.

Derlén, Mattias and Johan Lindholm. 2014. "Goodbye van Gend en Loos, Hello
Bosman? Using Network Analysis to Measure the Importance of Individual
CJEU Judgments." *European Law Journal* 20 (5): 667–87.

Derlén, Mattias, and Johan Lindholm. 2015. "Characteristics of Precedent: The
Case Law of The European Court of Justice in Three Dimensions." *German
Law Journal* 16: 1073.

Ellig, Jerome. 2001. *Dynamic Competition and Public Policy: Technology, Innovation, and Antitrust Issues.* Cambridge: Cambridge University Press.

Ellig, Jerry, and Alan E. Wiseman. 2011. *Competitive Exclusion with Heteroge-
nous Sellers: The Case of State Wine Shipping Laws.* Technical report AAWE
working paper.

Epp, Charles R. 1998. *The Rights Revolution: Lawyers, Activists, and Supreme
Courts in Comparative Perspective.* Chicago: University of Chicago Press.

Fjelstul, Joshua C. 2018. "Life After Brexit: The Impact of Common Law Judges
at the Court of Justice of the European Union." Working paper.

Fjelstul, Joshua C. 2019. "The Evolution of European Union Law: A New Dataset on the Acquis Communautaire." *European Union Politics* 20 (4): 670–91.

Fjelstul, Joshua C., and Clifford J Carrubba. 2018. "The Politics of International Oversight: Strategic Monitoring and Legal Compliance in the European Union." *American Political Science Review* 112 (3): 429–45.

Fon, Vincy, and Francesco Parisi. 2006. "Judicial Precedents in Civil Law Systems: A Dynamic Analysis." *International Review of Law and Economics* 26: 519–35.

Frankenreiter, Jens. 2017. "The Politics of Citations at the ECJ: Policy Preferences of EU Member State Governments and the Citation Behavior of Judges at the European Court of Justice." *Journal of Empirical Legal Studies* 14 (4): 813–57.

Frankenreiter, Jens. 2018. "Are Advocates General Political? Policy Preferences of EU Member State Governments and the Voting Behavior of Members of the European Court of Justice." *Review of Law & Economics* 14 (1).

Gabel, Matthew, Simon Hix, and Michael Malecki. 2007. "From Preferences to Behaviour: Comparing MEPs' Survey Responses and Roll-Call Voting Behavior." Tenth Biennial Conference of the European Union Studies Association.

Hartlapp, Miriam. 2008. "Extended Governance: Implementation of EU Social Policy in the Member States." In *Innovative Governance in the European Union*, edited by Ingeborg Tömmel and Amy Verdun, 221–36. Boulder: Lynne Rienner.

Hartlapp, Miriam, and Gerda Falkner. 2009. "Problems of Operationalization and Data in EU Compliance Research." *European Union Politics* 10 (2): 281–304.

Helfer, Laurence R. 2008. "Redesigning the European Court of Human Rights: Embeddedness as a Deep Structural Principle of the European Human Rights Regime." *European Journal of International Law* 19 (1): 125–59.

Hix, Simon, and Abdul Noury. 2009. "After Enlargement: Voting Patterns in the Sixth European Parliament." *Legislative Studies Quarterly* 34 (2): 159–74.

Hix, Simon, Abdul Noury, and Gerard Roland. 2006. "Dimensions of Politics in the European Union." *American Journal of Political Science* 50 (2): 494–511.

König, Thomas, and Lars Mäder. 2012. "Non-Conformable, Partial and Conformable Transposition: A Competing Risk Analysis of the Transposition Process of Directives in the EU15." *European Union Politics* 14(1):46–69.

König, Thomas, and Lars Mäder. 2014. "The Strategic Nature of Compliance: An Empirical Evaluation of Law Implementation in the Central Monitoring System of the European Union." *American Journal of Political Science* 58 (1): 246–63.

Larsson, Olof, and Daniel Naurin. 2016. "Judicial Independence and Political Uncertainty: How the Risk of Override Affects the Court of Justice of the EU." *International Organization* 70 (2): 377–408.

Larsson, Olof, Daniel Naurin, Mattias Derlén, and Johan Lindholm. 2017. "Speaking Law to Power: The Strategic use of Precedent of the Court of Justice of the European Union." *Comparative Political Studies* 50 (7): 879–907.

Lauderdale, Benjamin E., and Tom S. Clark. 2012. "The Supreme Court's Many Median Justices." *American Political Science Review* 106 (4): 847–66.

Lauderdale, Benjamin E., and Tom S. Clark. 2014. "Scaling Politically Meaningful Dimensions Using Texts and Votes." *American Journal of Political Science* 58 (3): 754–71.

Lauderdale, Benjamin E., and Tom S. Clark. 2016. "Estimating Vote-Specific Preferences from Roll-Call Data Using Conditional Autoregressive Priors." *Journal of Politics* 78 (4): 1153–69.

Lupu, Yonatan, and Erik Voeten. 2012. "Precedent in International Courts: A Network Analysis of Case Citations by the European Court of Human Rights." *British Journal of Political Science* 42 (2): 413–39.

Malecki, Michael. 2012. "Do ECJ Judges All Speak with the Same Voice? Evidence of Divergent Preferences from the Judgments of Chambers." *Journal of European Public Policy* 19 (1): 59–75.

Martin, Andrew D., and Kevin M. Quinn. 2002. "Dynamic Ideal Point Estimation via Markov Chain Monte Carlo for the US Supreme Court, 1953–1999." *Political Analysis* 10 (2): 134–53.

Martinsen, Dorte Sindbjerg. 2015. "Judicial Influence on Policy Outputs? The Political Constraints of Legal Integration in the European Union." *Comparative Political Studies* 48 (12): 1622–60.

Mbaye, Heather A. D. 2001. "Why National States Comply with Supranational Law." *European Union Politics* 2 (3): 259–81.

Ohlhausen, Maureen K., and Gregory P. Luib. 2008. "Moving Sideways: Post-Granholm Developments in Wine Direct Shipping and their Implications for Competition." *Antitrust Law Journal* 75 (2): 505–47.

Pelc, Krzysztof J. 2014. "The Politics of Precedent in International Law: A Social Network Application." *American Political Science Review* 10 8(3): 547–64.

Shahabuddeen, Mohamed. 2007. *Precedent in the World Court* (Hersch Lauterpacht Memorial Lecutres). Cambridge: Cambridge University Press.

Simmons, Beth A. 2009. *Mobilizing for Human Rights: International Law in Domestic Politics.* New York: Cambridge University Press.

Smith, James. 2000. "The Politics of Dispute Settlement Design: Explaining Legalism in Regional Trade Pacts." *International Organization* 54 (1): 137–80.

Staton, Jeffrey. 2010. *Judicial Power and Strategic Communication in Mexico.* Cambridge: Cambridge University Press.

Staton, Jeffrey K. 2006. "Constitutional Review and the Selective Promotion of Case Results." *American Journal of Political Science* 50 (1): 98–112.

Sverdrup, Ulf. 2004. "Compliance and Conflict Management in the European Union: Nordic Exceptionalism." *Scandinavian Political Studies* 27 (1): 23–44.

Stone Sweet, Alec, and Thomas L. Brunell. 1998. "Constructing a Supranational Constitution: Dispute Resolution and Governance in the European Community." *American Political Science Review* 92 (1): 63–81.

Thomson, Robert, Javier Arregui, Dirk Leuffen, Rory Costello, James Cross, Robin Hertz, and Thomas Jensen. 2012. A New Dataset on Decision-Making in the European Union before and after the 2004 and 2007 Enlargements (DEUII). *Journal of European Public Policy* 19 (4): 604–22.

Vanberg, Georg. 2001. "Legislative-Judicial Relations: A Game-Theoretic Approach to Constitutional Review." *American Journal of Political Science* 45 (2): 346–61.

Vanberg, Georg. 2005. *The Politics of Constitutional Review in Germany*. New York: Cambridge University Press.

Voeten, Erik. 2007. "The Politics of International Judicial Appointments: Evidence from the European Court of Human Rights." *International Organization* 61 (4): 669–701.

Voeten, Erik. 2008. "The Impartiality of International Judges: Evidence from the European Court of Human Rights." *The American Political Science Review* 102 (4): 417–33.

Voeten, Erik. 2010. "Borrowing and Nonborrowing among International Courts." *The Journal of Legal Studies* 39 (2): 547–76.

Volkens, Andrea, Pola Lehmann, Theres Matthieß, Nicolas Merz, Sven Regel, and Bernhard Weßels. 2017. The Manifesto Data Collection. Manifesto Project (MRG/CMP/MARPOR). Version 2017b. Berlin: *Wissenschaftszentrum Berlin für Sozialforschung (WZB)*.

Wood, B. Dan, and Richard W. Waterman. 1991. "The Dynamics of Political Control of the Bureaucracy." *American Political Science Review* 85 (3): 801–28.

Constitutional Courts in Europe

Quantitative Approaches

TANYA BAGASHKA AND NUNO GAROUPA

T HE TRADITIONAL critique that there are few empirical studies about constitutional courts (and other top courts and institutions) in Europe is now clearly outdated (Garoupa 2019; Krehbiel and Bilsback 2019). Though perhaps not extensive or exhaustive, there is a solid foundation of empirical literature on civil law European constitutional courts. A broad overview of the empirical literature confirms that concerns about local dynamics in specific Western European countries, rather than general comparative assessments, are the driving force of the literature. There are very few quantitative studies using data from multiple countries and looking for possible causal patterns. On the whole, the quantitative literature focuses on identifying the role of ideology or politics in the context of specific courts or assessing the specificities of certain judicial actors (for example, confirming the veto player role of constitutional courts in Western Europe or the influence of post-Communist institutional design in Eastern Europe). The literature rarely uses institutional variance to test theories of judicial behavior or court rulings.

Most earlier studies, from the 1990s and early 2000s, were largely "empirical analys[e]s of dissents" or identifiers of determinants of per curiam rulings. More recently, we see two methodological lines expanding in the literature. First, estimation of judicial ideal points (reflecting updated empirical techniques that acknowledge dissent suppression in light of Martin-Quinn scores and Fischman's work [Martin and Quinn 2002 and Fischman 2011]) and second, measurement approaches to explore how potentially different procedural questions impact court outcomes.

With few exceptions, we do not have a good understanding of how to compare constitutional courts empirically in Europe (Hönnige 2011). There are a few small-N studies concerning specific questions. Empirical work addressing the prevailing ideas based on comparative constitutional law is scarce. Thus, most scholarship is still fundamentally normative and driven by a few salient or landmark cases (Kelemen 2013) rather than systematic empirical knowledge. A small but growing literature investigates the effects of constitutional courts' independence on policy outcomes. For example, based on a cross-sectional analysis covering forty-two countries from both Eastern and Western Europe, Vaubel (2009) finds that the independence of constitutional judges is associated with fiscal centralization due to vested interests in centralization and self-selection effects.

Surprisingly, it is still common to read law review articles positing that European constitutional courts are less much politicized than American courts (see discussion by Ferejohn and Pasquino 2004, and Ferreras Comella 2004), an observation that goes back to the seminal work by Dawson (1968). That narrative echoes old myths about civil law versus US common law and legal fictions promoted by doctrinalism on both sides of the Atlantic. Notably, however, there is little empirical work to support such claims.

The authors organize this essay as follows. We start by summarizing the state of the art of empirical literature on Western Europe. The following section provides the same approach to Eastern Europe. In a later section, we address the main challenges and possible developments. The last section concludes the essay with final remarks.

SUMMARY OF THE EMPIRICAL LITERATURE ON WESTERN EUROPE

Three distinct lines of research summarize the broad range of European quantitative studies on constitutional and supreme courts. The first line comprises articles exploring dissent variations to identify potential political alignments and dynamics. These studies are common for jurisdictions where dissents are allowed (Germany, Spain, Portugal, for example). They tend to show that constitutional judges are not immune to the political environment, and ideology (measured by appointee or another variable) does matter. The degree to which politics is relevant varies across jurisdictions and requires a deep understanding of contextual determinants.

The second includes the many quantitative studies analyzing per curiam decisions, an approach dominant for countries that do not allow dissents (France, Italy, Belgium, for example). Since individual judicial behavior is unobservable, most empirical studies rely on panel composition to highlight the relevant political dimensions. Recent methodological advancements (on panel composition variance, for example, Fischman 2011) have enormously benefited the empirical literature about these countries.

Finally, a few comparative studies exist, based on either geographical and cultural proximities (such as Spain and Portugal) or availability of data (dissents or petitioners' identity). They highlight how a particular difference, being merely procedural or contextual, explains specific features. The quality of the data prompts a common critique of these articles. Most of these studies use either salient cases or semi-comparable decisions and thus raise questions of statistical sampling.

At the same time, across the distinct lines of research, there is a topic that emerges more often than any other theme in the Western European empirical literature—constitutional litigation of federalism or quasi-federalism (a relevant area of constitutional law in Germany, Italy, Spain, and Belgium, for example). Not surprisingly, the general results document a significant politicization of constitutional review when challenges to the allocation of powers between a central government and regional entities arise. The patterns of politicization vary considerably across countries and time, but they do not confirm the classic theory of Shapiro (2003) that centralized constitutional courts tend to side with the central government against regional interests.

Garoupa (2020) summarizes the set of courts and institutions that have been the subject of quantitative work in Western Europe in the field of constitutional review. It is a considerably long list of specialized (and usually centralized) constitutional courts plus the Nordic model of supreme courts. The article considers other courts and institutions that are important in adjudicating cases that can be incidental to constitutional review.

The long list of country studies in English as well as in other native European languages is presented by Garoupa (2020). Two important observations emerge after reviewing the literature. One observation is an inclination for two clusters of literature—Political Science (PS) journals on the one side, and Law and Economics or Law-related journals (LE) on the other side—as clearly identified by the author (a point also reflected in the analytical survey of comparative judicial politics by Krehbiel and

Bilsback 2019). For a while, these disparate literatures tended not to cite each other and seem to have developed entirely independently, though generally, the results of PS and LE approaches are not entirely inconsistent. Only more recently do we see cross-discipline citation as more common practice. A clear dialog has emerged at this point. The dialog across disciplines is not yet strong enough to facilitate productive communication of the results from quantitative research, but the trend is noticeable and should be welcome.

Another observation from Garoupa (2020) is that we currently cannot find studies in English for numerous civil law countries in Western Europe: Austria (where dissents are not allowed); Greece; most Nordic countries, including Finland, Iceland, and Sweden (apart from a comparative piece with Denmark on preliminary ruling procedure); the Netherlands (although the Dutch case is very particular due to the absence of formal constitutional review); and some of the smaller countries. We can never exclude the existence of empirical work in the native languages, but a limited number of European countries drive the overall empirical picture of constitutional review. The traditional comparative constitutional law analysis concentrates on the same comparator jurisdictions, which are the few remarkable and influential civil law jurisdictions such as Germany, France, Italy, and so on (see the critique by Albert 2017). This myopic focus in the literature is self-perpetuating and results in almost inexistent studies of too many Western European countries.

SUMMARY OF THE EMPIRICAL LITERATURE ON EASTERN EUROPE

A significant portion of the earlier studies of constitutional courts about the former Communist countries focuses on the origins of different institutional designs. Most of these are descriptive single-country studies (for example, Melone 1996 and 1997; Sabaliunas 1996; Ovsepian 1996; Trochev 2004). Exceptions are Magalhães (1999) and Smithey and Ishiyama (2000). Adopting a qualitative approach, Magalhães (1999) investigates institutional design in three Eastern European democracies—Bulgaria, Hungary, and Poland.[1] Smithey and Ishiyama (2000) reach similar conclusions in a study of the constitutional courts in the former Soviet Union, Mongolia, and Eastern Europe.[2] Based on the analysis of constitutional drafts, constitutional court decisions, and interviews, Trochev (2008) tests the strategic approach, linking electoral uncertainty with judicial empowerment in the context of the Russian Constitutional Court.[3]

Several studies investigate the Communist legacy broadly defined, which is expected to negatively affect judicial independence in the post-Communist period. A socialist judge's main function was to "facilitate the political agenda of those in power" (Hendley 1996, 117). Different studies focus on different aspects of the Communist legacy. Utter and Lungsgaard (1993) emphasize the variation in the empowerment of the courts under Communism. For instance, Romania and Hungary partially adopted the principle of judicial review by establishing special "legislative committees" to review the constitutionality of all statutes, decrees, and ordinances (Ludwikowski 1988). Magalhães also highlights the importance of judicial pluralism under Communism but finds that it has little explanatory power. Similarly, Smithey and Ihiyama (2000) fail to find evidence of the effect of judicial empowerment under Communism in their study of twenty post-Communist countries. They focus on another legacy factor, also highlighted in works on Russian politics: the emphasis on statist culture. This reliance on state-centered solutions, regardless of partisanship (Tolz 1992; Orttung 1992; Carter 1995), is expected to contribute to the emergence of a strong executive, unconstrained by a strong judiciary or other institutions. Generally, evidence of such effects is still lacking (see Smithey and Ishiyama 2000).

Many works focus on the consequences of institutions. Similar to the literature on institutional origins, most of these are descriptive single-country studies, and the "many variables, small N problem" plagues many of them. Within the literature on the consequences of different institutional designs, the most prominent approach is the formal institutionalist one. According to this approach, rules that encourage judicial independence can reduce corruption and strengthen the rule of law. Strong evidence that such rules have produced the intended outcomes in the post-Communist world is still lacking. In a study of seven post-Communist countries, Herron and Randazzo (2003) find that formal judicial powers (measured by Smithey and Ishiyama's 2000 index) do not significantly affect the probability that constitutional justices will overturn legislation partially or completely. By contrast, exogenous factors, particularly economic conditions, executive power, the identity of the litigants, and subject matter, significantly affect the likelihood that courts will nullify laws. The authors caution that formal guarantees of judicial independence are only a part of the story. A variety of factors intermediates the impact of formal rules, including informal norms and rules.

Similar to Herron and Randazzo (2003), other studies find that the effects of formal institutions are conditional on informal rules and norms.

Drawing on original surveys of justices (including some constitutional justices) conducted in Romania and the Czech Republic, Beers (2010) investigates judicial culture focusing on de facto judicial autonomy and the quality of justice. Beers (2010) identifies a significant attitudinal distinction between Romanian and Czech judges. In Romania, where there was elite resistance and buck-passing, judges feel less autonomous and are more tolerant of corruption. Conversely, in the Czech Republic, where elites demonstrated a strong commitment to judicial governing institutions and judicial reform, judges trusted judicial institutions and were less tolerant of corruption. Thus, the credibility of elite commitment was much more important for judicial autonomy and the quality of justice than the formal rules of the game.

More recent studies of institutional effects identify the expected positive consequences of institutions. Bumin (2017) investigates the effects of formal institutions and institutional reform on the willingness of constitutional courts in nineteen post-Communist countries, from 1992 to 2006, to engage in constitutional review. Bumin (2017) finds that higher levels of institutionalization, namely, formal provisions that improve the court's autonomy, its durability, and its ability to respond to the priorities of the political branches, increase the activism of the constitutional court. Similarly, presidentialism, economic performance, and legislative fragmentation positively affect constitutional court activism. Bumin's work highlights the broader methodological challenge of measuring judicial activism. Typically, measures are based on the probability that the court engages in a constitutional review of policies. However, this rate of invalidation is not very informative in hybrid regimes and young democracies because presidents and legislatures can use constitutional courts to legitimize themselves by creating the façade of democratic competition. Such dynamics explain the high rate of invalidation in Azerbaijan or Belarus, for example.

Other works focus on behavioral outcomes. Kantorowicz and Garoupa (2016) investigate whether justices on the Polish Constitutional Tribunal are ideologically biased, either by strategic incentives or sincere ideological preference. According to the results, judges are guided mostly by ideology and not by the law, especially judges appointed by left or extreme right parties. Institutional incentives such as peer pressure (unanimity) or particular functions of the judges in the adjudicating bench also play a role. Brown and Wise (2004) investigate whether the court is partial to a particular branch of government and how this affects the perceived importance and legitimacy of the Ukrainian Constitutional

Court. Based on the examination of separation of powers cases from 1997 to 2000, Brown and Wise (2004) find that instead of consistently favoring the president or the parliament, the Ukrainian Constitutional Court was relatively balanced. This balance contributed to greater perceived legitimacy and importance of the court by members of parliament and presidential representatives to the court. Schwartz and Murchison (2016) investigate what guides judicial decision-making on the Constitutional Court of Bosnia-Herzegovina. Based on the statistical analysis of an original data set, Schwartz and Murchinson (2016) find that ethnic affiliation is the best predictor of judicial behavior, an effect not mitigated by long-term judicial tenure. The results show that a judge is significantly more likely to find a violation when a petitioner is of the same ethnicity, even when controlling for the influence of party-political appointments. Bagashka and Tiede (2017) investigate the determinants of dissent on the Bulgarian Constitutional Court, which occurs frequently and is high by comparative standards. Based on the statistical analysis of all decisions of the Bulgarian Constitutional Court between 1992 and 2012, they find judges' prior political backgrounds or party alignments with the governing coalition drive dissent. Dissent is more likely for decisions on separation of powers, those with unconstitutional outcomes, or decisions made when the opposition has strong legislative support.

EMPIRICAL STRATEGIES AND CHALLENGES

In most existing quantitative studies, the authors have collected individual and country-specific data sets. Therefore, a few systematic problems arise. First and immediately, replication is not easy (in fact, none have been replicated so far). Also, comparability is almost impossible since, even within the same country and same period, classification and coding vary considerably. The published literature uses sophisticated econometric methods. At this stage, descriptive statistical analyses do not seem to be enough for publication in prestigious academic journals. Unfortunately, for many European courts, it is hard to go beyond basic descriptive analysis due to the quality of the current data.

There are three kinds of challenges to developing further quantitative studies on European constitutional courts. One is the inevitable issue of data availability. Gathering and coding data is a very cumbersome part of any empirical project on European constitutional courts. A second problem relates to the reception of this line of work in the community of constitutional law scholars (see evidence presented by van Dijck, Sverdlov, and Buck 2018, on the development of empirical legal studies in European law reviews). Although things have improved considerably, the community of constitutional law scholars in Europe is still very wary of quantitative methods at two levels—they tend to dislike empirical work, and more importantly, they largely ignore empirical research in their work (see discussions by Dyevre 2010; and Jakab, Dyevre, and Itzcovich 2017). Therefore, the current empirical literature has had little impact so far on the debates on constitutional law in Europe. A third concern is that empirical projects are not popular with European constitutional courts. Probably due to their training, constitutional judges handle dogmatic or doctrinal assessments much better than empirical analyses. In particular, they are very unhappy about the role of a field such as law or politics, empirically or conceptually. The consequence of this specific distaste is that most national constitutional courts do not have mechanisms to facilitate data gathering, much less any form of comparative empirical analysis. They also do not promote empirical scholarship in their intellectual discussions.

Sadly, the European judicial authorities have so far made no effort to promote consistent data analysis in this field. The European Commission for the Efficiency of Justice (CEPEJ) sponsors the only systematic and coherent effort but mostly on non-constitutional matters and with significant methodological drawbacks (see general discussion by Voigt 2016; also more specifically on European jurisdictions, see Melcarne and Ramello 2015; Bielen et al. 2018).[4] For example, Roussey and Deffains (2012) use CEPEJ data (for 2004, 2006, and 2008) to study trust in judicial institutions in Europe from an empirical perspective. Cross and Donelson (2010), in an alternative line of research, explore CEPEJ data (2008) to examine the quality of civil courts. Regrettably, none of these studies have a significant direct relationship to constitutional review in Europe.

There are, of course, deeper methodological concerns as already voiced by Spamann (2015) in the larger context of empirical comparative law. Causal inference from comparative data on constitutional courts is problematic due to extensive endogeneity problems. The appropriate use of instrumental variables is challenging in the context of constitutional review in Europe. However, within Western Europe, it could be easier to overcome some of these complicated issues given the more limited sources of variance (for example, similarities of legal culture, membership of European Union, Council of Europe, or Organization for Economic Co-operation and Development, as well as advanced economic development).

FUTURE RESEARCH IN EUROPE

The priority for future research in Europe is to address data availability and publicity. On the collection of data, a comprehensive project similar to CEPEJ that "unifies" measurement across European constitutional courts systematically and comprehensively would be very positive. Ideally, such a project would be able to gather standard data, including "housekeeping" variables (backlogs, length of sentences, costs, etc.), political variables, judicial styles, but also textual analysis (there is very little to no empirical work on this matter so far in Western Europe).

Conceptually, comparative constitutional law should evolve toward generating testable hypotheses for large-N studies (see discussion by Hönnige 2011; Krehbiel and Bilsback 2019). Particularly, from the viewpoint of law and politics, we should be able to hypothesize how different party dynamics and varying appointment mechanisms shape judicial performance and outcomes. Studies have not yet addressed general questions such as how different party systems impact court dynamics.

At this stage, realistically, we cannot answer questions like "Is the German Constitutional Court more activist than the Italian Constitutional Court?" (Garoupa 2016) or "Do different appointment mechanisms impact dissent suppression across European constitutional courts?" Sufficient data collection and appropriate comparative measurability should pave the way to empirical research that can truthfully answer these quiescent questions.

NOTES

1. Magalhães (1999) argues that the Communist legacy and "legal globalization" lack explanatory power. Institutional choices are instead the outcome of a bargaining process between self-interested domestic actors. In political contexts with high uncertainty such as Hungary, judicial insulation was combined with judicial responsiveness, not allowing the Communist Party to secure its hold on power. Conversely, where it was relatively certain that the Communist successor was facing bleak electoral prospects, the incumbent Bulgarian Socialist Party left an institutional legacy that insulated the judiciary from elected branches the party foresaw it could not control.

2. Their results are consistent with Magalhães's (1999) argument that a political bargaining approach has the greatest explanatory power. They find
that the post-Communist legacy and ethnic fragmentation do not significantly affect judicial power. By contrast, the political bargaining context,
captured by the effective number of legislative parties, has a significant
effect, and the identified dynamic is partially consistent with Magalhães's
(1999) argument. Whenever there was high uncertainty about the electoral fortunes of the incumbent, the incumbent (implicitly the Communist successor party) refrained from strengthening either the executive or
the judiciary as a hedging strategy.

3. Trochev (2008) argues that in the Yeltsin era, contrary to the predictions of the strategic approaches which link electoral uncertainty to judicial empowerment, diffused political power resulted in the collapse of
the constitutional order. Contrary to strategic explanations of judicial
politics, the changing preferences of politicians and the vagueness and
incoherence of the rules of the game made it impossible for judges to predict the responses of rulers to their judgments. Similarly, institutionalist
theories focusing on the judiciary's ability to resolve intragovernmental
conflicts and to monitor politicians and bureaucrats fail to explain why
the federal center was unable to enforce centralist decisions and to punish bureaucrats who ignored the decision of the Russian Constitutional
Court.

4. "European Commission for the Efficiency of Justice (CEPEJ)," Council
of Europe, accessed March 13, 2020, https://www.coe.int/en/web/cepej
/home.

References

Albert, Richard. 2017. "Introduction: The State of the Art in Constitutional
Amendment." In *The Foundations and Traditions of Constitutional Amend-
ment*, edited by Richard Albert, Xenophon Contiades and Alkemene
Fotiadou, 1–19. Oxford: Hart Studies in Comparative Law.

Bagashka, Tanya, and Lydia Tiede. 2017. "Explaining Dissensus on the Bulgarian Constitutional Court." *East European Politics* 34 (4): 418–39.

Beers, Daniel. 2010. "A Tale of Two Transitions: Exploring the Origins of
Post-Communist, Judicial Culture in Romania and the Czech Republic."
Demokratizatsiya 18 (1): 28–55.

Bielen, Samantha, Ludo Peeters, Wim Marneffe, and Lode Vereeck. 2018. "Backlogs and Litigation Rates: Testing Congestion Equilibrium across European
Judiciaries." *International Review of Law and Economics* 53: 9–22.

Brown, Trevor, and C. R. Wise. 2004. "Constitutional Courts and Legislative
Executive Relations: The Case of Ukraine." *Political Science Quarterly* 119 (1):
143–69.

Bumin, Kirill. 2017. "Judicial Institutionalization and Judicial Activism of the Post-Communist Constitutional Courts." *Journal of Politics and Law* 10 (2): 54–72.

Carter, Stephen. 1995. "The CIS and After: The Impact of Russian Nationalism." In *The Far Right in Western and Eastern Europe*, edited by L. Cheles, R. Ferguson, and M. Vaughan, 2nd ed., 174–97. New York: Longman.

Cross, Frank B., and Dain C. Donelson. 2010. "Creating Quality Courts." *Journal of Empirical Legal Studies* 7 (3): 490–510.

Dawson, John P. 1968. *The Oracles of the Law*. Ann Arbor: University of Michigan Law School.

van Djick, Gijs, Shahar Sverdlov, and Gabriela Buck. 2018. "Empirical Legal Research in Europe: Prevalence, Obstacles, and Interventions." *Erasmus Law Review* 11 (2): 105–19.

Dyevre, Arthur. 2010. "Unifying the Field of Comparative Judicial Politics: Towards a General Theory of Judicial Behaviour." *European Political Science Review* 2 (2): 297–327.

Ferejohn, John, and Pasquale Pasquino. 2004. "Constitutional Adjudication: Lessons from Europe." *Texas Law Review* 82 (7): 1671–704.

Ferreras Comella, Victor. 2004. "The Consequences of Centralizing Constitutional Review in a Special Court: Some Thoughts on Judicial Activism." *Texas Law Review* 82 (7): 1706–36.

Fischman, Joshua B. 2011. "Estimating Preferences of Circuit Judges: A Model of Consensus Voting." *Journal of Law and Economics* 54 (4): 781–809.

Garoupa, Nuno. 2016. "Comparing Judicial Activism—Can We Say that the US Supreme Court is more Activist than the German Constitutional Court?" *Revista Portuguesa de Filosofia* 72 (4): 1089–106.

Garoupa, Nuno. 2019. "Constitutional Review." In *Oxford Handbook of Public Choice*, edited by Roger D. Congleton, Bernard Grofman, and Stefan Voigt, 134–55. Oxford: Oxford University Press.

Garoupa, Nuno. 2020. "Constitutional Courts in Civil-Law Western Europe: Quantitative Approaches." *George Mason Law & Economics Research Paper* No. 20-05. https://papers.ssrn.com/sol3/papers.cfm?abstract_id=3537747.

Hendley, Kathryn. 1996. *Trying to Make Law Matter: Legal Reform and Labor Law in the Soviet Union*. Ann Arbor: University of Michigan Press.

Herron, Erik, and Kirk Randazzo. 2003. "The Relationship Between Independence and Judicial Review in Post-Communist Courts." *Journal of Politics* 65 (2): 422–38.

Hönnige, Christoph. 2011. "Beyond Judicialization: Why we Need More Comparative Research about Constitutional Courts." *European Political Science* 10: 346–58.

Jakab, Andras, Arthur Dyevre, and Giulio Itzcovich. 2017. "Comparative Constitutional Reasoning with Quantitative and Qualitative Methods: Introduction." In *Comparative Constitutional Reasoning*, edited by Andras Jakab,

Arthur Dyevre and Giulio Itzcovich, 1–35. Cambridge: Cambridge University Press.

Kantorowicz, Jaroslaw, and Nuno Garoupa. 2016. "An Empirical Analysis of Constitutional Review Voting in the Polish Constitutional Tribunal, 2003–2014." *Constitutional Political Economy* 27: 66–92.

Kelemen, Katalin. 2013. "Dissenting Opinions in Constitutional Courts." *German Law Review* 14: 1345–72.

Krehbiel, Jay N., and William Bradley Bilsback. 2019. "A Survey of Comparative Judicial Politics Literature: What Have We Learned in the Past Twenty Years." Unpublished manuscript on file with authors.

Ludwikowski, Rett. 1988. "Judicial Review in the Socialist Legal System: Current Developments." *International and Comparative Law Quarterly* 37: 89–100.

Magalhães, Pedro C. 1999. "The Politics of Judicial Reform in Eastern Europe." *Comparative Politics*, 32: 43–62.

Martin, Andrew D., and Kevin M. Quinn. 2002. "Dynamic Ideal Point Estimation via Markov Chain Monte Carlo for the U.S. Supreme Court, 1953–1999." *Political Analysis* 10 (2): 134–53.

Melcarne, Alessandro, and Giovanni Ramello. 2015. "Judicial Independence, Judges' Incentive and Efficiency." *Review of Law and Economics* 11 (2): 149–69.

Melone, Albert. 1996. "The Struggle for Judicial Independence and the Transition Towards Democracy in Bulgaria." *Communist and Post-Communist Studies* 29: 231–43.

Melone, Albert. 1997. "Judicial Independence and Constitutional Politics in Bulgaria." *Judicature* 80: 280–85.

Orttung, Robert. 1992. "The Russian Right and the Dilemmas of Party Organization." *Soviet Studies* 44: 445–78.

Ovsepian, Z. I. 1996. "Sudebnyi konstitutionyi kontrol' v RF: Problemy depolitizatsii (Sravnitel'nyi analiz)." *Gosudarstvo i pravo* 34: 32–42.

Roussey, Ludivine, and Bruno Deffains. 2012. "Confidence in Judicial Institutions: An Empirical Approach." *Journal of Institutional Economics* 8 (3): 351–69.

Sabaliunas, Leonas. 1996. "Comparative Perspectives on Judicial Review in Lithuania." *Europe-Asia Studies* 48: 783–95.

Schwartz, Alex, and Melanie Murchison. 2016. "Judicial Impartiality and Independence in Divided Societies: An Empirical Analysis of the Constitutional Court of Bosnia-Herzegovina." *Law & Society Review* 50 (4): 821–55.

Shapiro, Martin. 2003. "Judicial Review in Developed Democracies." *Democratization* 10 (4): 7–26.

Smithey, Shannon Ishiyama, and John Ishiyama. 2000. "Judicious Choices: Designing Courts in Post-Communist Politics." *Communist and Post-Communist Studies* 33: 163–82.

Spamann, Holger. 2015. "Empirical Comparative Law." *Annual Review of Law and Social Science* 11: 131–53.

Tolz, Vera. 1992. "Russia: Westernizers Continue to Challenge National Patriots." *RFE/RL Research Report* 1 (49): 1–9.

Trochev, Alexei. 2004. "Less Democracy, More Courts: A Puzzle of Judicial Review In Russia." *Law & Society Review* 38 (3): 513–48.

Trochev, Alexei. 2008. *Judging Russia: The Role of the Constitutional Court in Russian Politics 1990–2006*. New York: Cambridge University Press.

Utter, Robert F., and David C. Lundsgaard. 1993. "Judicial Review in the New Nations of Central and Eastern Europe: Some Thoughts from a Comparative Perspective." *Ohio State Law Journal* 54: 559–606.

Vaubel, Roland. 2009. "Constitutional Courts as Promoters of Political Centralization: Lessons for the European Court of Justice." *European Journal of Law and Economics* 28: 203–22.

Voigt, Stefan. 2016. "Determinants of Judicial Efficiency: A Survey." *European Journal of Law and Economics* 42 (2): 183–208.

Empirical Studies of the Behavior of Justices and High Courts in Latin America

An Overview

DIANA KAPISZEWSKI AND LYDIA B. TIEDE

OVER THE last three decades, high courts in many Latin American countries have become more involved in politics and policy-making. In parallel, scholarship on the region's high courts has grown by leaps and bounds, including seminal contributions from scholars located in Latin America and the United States. Indeed, comparing the essays in this volume with each other reveals that more scholarly attention has been paid to Latin American high courts than to courts in any other developing region. A number of causes might contribute to attention from US scholars. For instance, Latin America's presidential systems may make the region's courts an easier fit for the "separation of powers" framework that such scholars are used to deploying. Alternatively, our Cold War and continuing preoccupation—and familiarity—with politics in the region may play a part. More broadly, the focus likely results from a desire on the part of scholars across the Americas to understand why the rule of law continues to be weak even during the region's longest democratic moment and how courts can contribute to recapturing rights and the consolidation of democracy more generally.

This essay provides an overview of the breadth and scope of scholarly work on high courts in Latin America. We identify the main trends and substantive gaps in the literature, highlight the central challenges that analyzing these institutions poses, and offer some potential solutions.

We focus on empirical scholarship that addresses high court behavior, and high court interactions with other justice-sector and political actors, as these hold the potential to influence judicial decision-making. We consider work written in English, Spanish, or Portuguese by researchers in Latin America and the United States over roughly the last decade. By empirical, we mean studies that are based on the analysis of quantitative or qualitative data generated through observation or experiments rather than more abstract studies based on normative concerns. High courts, for us, include both constitutional and supreme courts, as well as the highest level of regional or state courts. We conclude by briefly considering the promise of, and challenges posed by, cross-regional analysis.

The review is based on three sources: 1) a database of literature including 204 articles and books on judicial behavior in Latin America penned by legal scholars and political scientists in Latin America and in the United States;[1] 2) an informal survey of political scientists and legal scholars selected as respondents due to their expertise on Latin American courts, conducted in April 2018;[2] and 3) our own knowledge of the scholarship. Our sources, and thus the conclusions we draw from them about work on the region's high courts, likely overrepresent scholarship produced in the United States. This artifact of our research strategy in no way suggests an under-appreciation of the empirical and theoretical innovation that marks work produced by scholars in the region; indeed, the work of Latin American scholars has made particularly significant contributions to our understanding of the more informal and less concrete aspects of the region's legal systems and of emerging high court practices. We include in our discussion below references to work by scholars in Latin America whenever we are aware of it.

SUBSTANTIVE FOCI OF THE LITERATURE ON HIGH COURTS IN LATIN AMERICA

There is a sense among scholars of the judicialization of politics in Latin America that the literature continues to focus disproportionately on the courts that sit at the very top of judicial hierarchies—supreme courts and constitutional courts—and continues to pay insufficient attention to the multiple layers of courts that operate beneath them.[3] However, a review of our database suggests that only about half of the literature (100 of the 204 articles and books in our database) focuses on high courts, with the rest examining "courts," "the judiciary," or "judges" in the region. While some portion of the latter scholarship likely analyzes high courts, it does seem that increasing attention is being paid to other judicial institutions, perhaps by Latin American authors to whom they may be more easily accessible for study.

For instance, more work is beginning to emerge on the "pillars" of specialized courts found in some Latin American judicial systems, in particular electoral courts, and on regional courts such as the Inter-American Court of Human Rights (IACtHR, e.g., García-Sayán 2010), the Caribbean Court of Justice (e.g., Alter, Helfer, and Saldias 2012), and the Andean Tribunal of Justice (e.g., Saldias 2014). The focus of our piece and the larger project notwithstanding, we find this increasing study encouraging: we strongly believe the literature should pay even greater attention to these other judicial institutions, the interactions among them, and the interactions between them and apex courts (see Ingram and Kapiszewski 2019). Collaboration among scholars located at US and Latin American institutions could help to broaden our empirical focus.

With regard to the particular aspects of high court politics that are studied, there is both continuity and change over the last decade. A previous review (Kapiszewski and Taylor 2008) found that the main areas of inquiry were 1) courts' interactions with other branches of government; 2) courts as policy makers; and 3) the rules regulating courts' composition and their powers (743).[4] Our analysis of the literature on Latin American high courts, which mainly addresses work published since this previous review, likewise suggests a predominant focus on individual judges' and courts' decisions, i.e., on judicial *behavior*, which is implicit in interbranch relations as well as in judicial policy-making.[5] Yet we also find an increasing focus on several dynamics and phenomena that derive from or influence how high courts rule, in particular how they interact with other actors and institutions *in addition to* through their decision-making. This increasing focus suggests that scholars understand high courts to form part of the broader legal and political systems in Latin American countries. We believe these additional foci merit more study, and we consider them briefly in this section.

Interactions between High Courts and Political Leaders

Scholars have begun to pay more attention to how high courts interact with the other branches of government, including and in addition to the "dialogical" (Gargarella 2014) processes that may be associated with their rulings. One emerging emphasis is judicial empowerment. For instance, Barros (2002) and Finkel (2004) advance a form of "insurance theory" to explain the delegation of power to courts; Schor (2009) examines the "constitutional transformations" Colombia and Mexico pursued in the 1990s in an effort to empower their high courts; and Nunes (2010b) offers a "governance" theory of judicial empowerment. The opposite dynamic—judicial manipulation and disempowerment and its consequences—are touched on in many studies of courts in the region (e.g., Pérez-Liñán and Castagnola 2009, 2016). Studying more systematically how political leaders delegate power to, and sap power from, high courts—both through formal reform processes, and in ad hoc, less institutionalized, more subtle ways—could contribute importantly to understanding cross-national variation in judicial behavior (see again Pérez-Liñán and Castagnola 2009). Of course, the idea that *judges* consider these dynamics is implicit in the literature that adopts a strategic approach to explain judicial decision-making.

Court empowerment and court curbing, as well as compliance with high court rulings, can significantly affect judicial independence. Encouragingly, increasing numbers of scholars have sought to conceptualize (e.g., Bowen 2013) and measure de jure (e.g., Castagnola 2010) and de facto (e.g., Taylor 2014) judicial independence. Systematic intra-regional comparisons that catalog and describe institutional rules, and reveal overall trends across time, are also emerging. For instance, Moreno, Crisp, and Shugart (2003), Hammergren (2007), Ríos-Figueroa (2011), and Brinks and Blass (2017) use constitutional rules and reforms related to a variety of judicial attributes to create indices to measure de jure judicial power and de jure independence (or autonomy). Other scholars have analyzed the relationship between democracy and judicial independence (Helmke and Rosenbluth 2009; Smith and Farrales 2010), and still others have considered how factors such as pluralism and institutional design (Dargent 2009), the introduction of judicial councils (Chavez 2007; Roth 2007), political competition (Leiras, Tuñón, and Giraudy 2015), and "strategic self-restraint" (Ruibal 2009) affect judicial independence. The increasingly sophisticated measures of de jure independence that have been created, and our growing understanding of the informal and ad hoc ways in which political leaders manipulate and disempower high courts, should help us to address the legendary challenge of measuring de facto judicial independence.

Another area to which more attention could be paid is Latin American high courts' effect on the legislative process, especially when they review law in areas in which law must undergo a priori review. Anticipation of negative decisions from courts has been shown to affect policy makers in the implementation or timing of legislation in France (Stone Sweet

1992), the United States (Shipan 1997), Germany (Vanberg 2001), and the American states (Rogers and Vanberg 2002). We still know little, however, about how anticipated court rulings shape policy and influence the strategy of policy makers in Latin America.

High Courts' Interactions with Other Justice-Sector Actors

Encouragingly, the literature has also begun to examine how high courts interact *with each other*. Supreme courts and constitutional courts in the same country interact in both productive and antagonistic ways, and scholars have begun to analyze that behavior (see, e.g., Scribner 2010 on Chile, and Rueda [n.d.] on Colombia). More attention could be paid to these dynamics, as well as to how high courts interact with lower courts whose judges they may be charged with disciplining and promoting (see Hilbink 2007; Bowen 2017). These latter interactions hold the potential to significantly constrain lower court decision-making should lower court judges fear being "punished" by higher courts, thereby affecting the types of cases and questions that ultimately appear before high courts. There is likewise little study of the interaction between high courts and other justice-sector actors such as prosecutors general or ombudspersons. Inattention to these interactions is related to our overall neglect of these other justice-sector actors (with important exceptions, e.g., McAllister 2008). Yet how high courts interact with these other justice-sector actors may significantly influence the roles that both they and high courts play in politics. Finally, more attention could be paid to the diffusion or transplantation of legal decisions or practices across high courts in different polities, as well as to the interactions between judges on domestic and international courts (see, e.g., Huneeus 2017, 2018), and in transnational communities of law.

Litigation at High Courts

Another way to examine high courts' interactions with other actors is by studying litigation at high courts. Under what conditions are these mainly passive institutions triggered through litigation? We might consider two important categories of litigation. First, in many countries, citizens and civil society groups can directly activate high courts to question political leaders' transgression of constitutional boundaries and to achieve societal objectives, such as protecting rights. Scholars of Latin American high courts have begun to explore such litigation and its influence on high court behavior (see, e.g., Iaryczower, Spiller, and Tommasi 2006; Wilson and Rodríguez Cordero 2006; and Ruibal 2015; as well as Skaar 2013; González Ocantos 2016). Additional attention should be paid to the causes and consequences of these forms of legal mobilization, to high courts' broader interactions with society, and to public opinion about high courts more generally. Second, scholars have also begun to consider when and why politicians and other political actors litigate at high courts (e.g., Taylor 2008; Taylor and Da Ros 2008; and Helmke 2010). However, we need to know much more about how, when, and why politicians and political parties use courts to achieve political objectives or resolve intractable political conflicts. Better understanding of all of these forms of litigation would allow us to more effectively address related questions, such as whether high courts react in the same ways to cases brought by different types of citizens, or by different government officials, and how those reactions compare to their responses to cases they receive through other means, such as obligatory review.

Compliance with and Broader Impact of High Court Rulings

Given that the judiciary is the weakest branch of government and lacks a means of enforcing its rulings, what effect judicial decisions have depends on how political leaders, administrative agencies, lower courts, and subnational governments react to them. Encouragingly, scholars have begun to lay the groundwork for studying compliance with Latin American high courts' rulings, the impact of those rulings more broadly, and what drives variation in each. For instance, Staton and Vanberg's (2008) work on the "value of vagueness," Staton's (2010) study of the Mexican Supreme Court, Kapiszewski's (2012) comparative analysis of interbranch interactions around cases concerning economic governance in Argentina and Brazil, and Gauri, Staton, and Cullell's (2015) study of orders issued by the Costa Rican Supreme Court, are all important examples of work on compliance. An important underlying belief of much of this literature is that courts themselves can influence—or at least seek to influence—whether their rulings are obeyed.

This important work notwithstanding, paying more scholarly attention to compliance with high court rulings is crucial. Doing so will both help us to understand what difference high courts *actually* make and will allow us to assess some of our tacit understandings of compliance. For instance, we often assume that political leaders are less likely to obey challenging high court rulings in less-democratic or semi-authoritarian polities (compared with more democratic settings). However, work such as that by Barros (2008) shows that compliance with court decisions in authoritarian contexts varies and may depend largely on the type and degree of political repression used by the regime over time. Likewise, compliance with high court rulings in democratic contexts may have quite practical and pragmatic bases: it may vary with the type of court power invoked or the financial costs of compliance. In short, a more nuanced understanding of the foundations of compliance with high court rulings is much needed.

Of course, we recognize that studying compliance involves significant analytic challenges. Collecting data to measure compliance can be difficult if political actors seek to obfuscate how they reacted to court rulings. Also, certain tendencies in Latin America's civil law systems (e.g., lack of stare decisis and the possibility of filing individual complaints against government officials in the form of *amparos*) result in the region's courts deciding a huge volume of cases, thus making compliance difficult to track. Establishing causality between judicial rulings and the behavior of political actors can also be challenging, particularly as more time passes between the ruling and the behavior posited as compliance. In addition, the causes of short-term compliance with rulings that affect only a limited number of individuals likely differ from the causes of compliance with rulings that call for broad change affecting a larger population. Further, the reasons why political actors comply with high court dictates likely differ from those that explain why lower courts do so (in particular in Latin America's civil law systems in which lower court obedience is not consistently required, and lower courts do sometimes "go rogue").

In sum, a variety of issues related to, and with a likely impact on, high court behavior are ripe for further analysis. We need to better comprehend judiciaries as a *system*, and gain clarity on the multiple ways in which high courts interact with other courts, as well as with political actors more generally. Until we accomplish these goals, we will continue to have an incomplete grasp on judicial power, and know less than we think we know about what difference courts make to politics, economics, and society in the region. Having highlighted these lacunae, the rest of this essay focuses on the literature on high court behavior specifically.

CORE THEORETICAL APPROACHES TO STUDYING THE BEHAVIOR OF LATIN AMERICAN HIGH COURTS

As in the canonical literature in US public law, scholars of Latin American high courts often assert that judges' behavior is driven by strategic motivations and individual attitudes and preferences. Analysts also examine how laws and facts constrain judicial behavior, and adopt more institutional approaches that explore how the "rules of the game" shape, structure, and constrain judges' behavior.[6] We review these theoretical approaches here, identify some of the analytic challenges that adopting them poses, and suggest some directions scholarship on high courts in the region might take in the future.

Strategic Explanations

Our research reveals that the strategic model of judicial decision-making—which argues that judges or courts alter their decisions in cases involving the government based on how they anticipate the political branches will react to challenging rulings—is prevalent in the study of Latin American courts. Given the relative precarity of courts in democracies with weak institutions, it is perhaps logical that they act strategically. According to some scholars, judges' calculations are based on the unity or fragmentation of the elected branches in Latin America's presidential systems, understood as a proxy for those branches' potential to coordinate on institutional retaliation (see Iaryczower, Spiller, and Tommasi 2002 on the Argentine Supreme Court; Chavez 2004 on Argentine provincial courts; Ríos-Figueroa 2007 on the Mexican Supreme Court; Scribner 2011 on the Chilean and Argentine Supreme Courts; and Tiede and Ponce 2014 on the Peruvian Constitutional Tribunal; Barros [2002] argues something similar regarding Chile's Constitutional Tribunal under the military junta). A variant of this argument focuses on how judges increasingly vote against political incumbents as incumbents' power weakens (Helmke 2002; Scribner 2004; Helmke and Sanders 2006; Rodríguez-Raga 2011; Basabe-Serrano 2012).[7]

Strategic accounts that imply that courts' and judges' decision-making is driven by their fear of an attack by the political branches raise several questions, however. For instance, in contexts where political leaders derive some value from judicial independence, judges should actually have considerable decision-making latitude (Vanberg 2015, 180). Kapiszewski (2012) argues that courts' "character" conditions their strategic behavior (30). Strategic approaches also confront methodological challenges. For example, measuring political fragmentation in multiparty systems, and in contexts where politicians often switch parties, is difficult. As Fischman (this volume, p. 48) reminds us, evidence of strategic behavior is "only as credible as the ideology variables on which it relies." Questions of how the broader political and historical context affects strategic interactions, and how to model strategies that change over time, are also ripe for additional thought and work.

Encouragingly, scholars of high court behavior in Latin America have begun to advance strategic explanations that further problematize, and extend beyond, judges' consideration of possible retaliation by the other branches of government. For instance, another strand of the strategic literature focuses on how courts' expectations of societal support for their rulings—e.g., from non-governmental organizations or civil society actors—affect their decision-making (see Brinks 2008; Bowen 2017).[8] Of course, to the degree that such work argues that judges' beliefs about societal support are important because that support affects political leaders' propensity to obey their dictates, it merges with the work discussed just above. Other scholars of Latin American courts have considered how judges' strategic interactions with other actors (e.g., prosecutors [Conaghan 2012], and state and local governments [do Vale 2013]) influence their decision-making. Given the multiple audiences to which judges speak (Baum 2006), and the many actors with whom they interact, further study of their decisional calculations is warranted.

Attitudinal Explanations

The attitudinal model, which has deep roots in the study of US high courts (Segal and Spaeth 2002; Martin and Quinn 2002), is also alive and well in scholarship on Latin American high courts. Scholars have demonstrated how judges vote their political (often partisan) preferences on Argentina's Supreme Court (González Bertomeu, Dalla Pellegrina, and Garoupa 2017); the Brazilian Supreme Court (Oliveira 2008; Ferreira and Mueller 2014; Desposato, Ingam, and Lannes 2015; Arlota and Garoupa 2016); the Ecuadorian Constitutional Court (Basabe-Serrano 2008, 2009); Chile's Constitutional Tribunal (Tiede 2016); the Mexican Supreme Court (Sánchez, Magaloni, and Magar 2011); and the Supreme Court of Uruguay (Skaar 2013). However, judges' political attitudes may not be as important to their decision-making in Latin America as they are in the United States (see Arlota and Garoupa 2014; Tiede and Ponce 2014). As Kornhauser (this volume) suggests more generally, scholars of Latin American high courts should consider how weaker party identification in the region, reforms to de-politicize the process of appointing judges, and supermajority voting rules on courts (which may preclude disagreement) interact with judges' political attitudes in driving their rulings.

As noted by Fischman (this volume), accurately measuring and coding judges' ideology and understanding its dimensionality represent a significant challenge to evaluating how judges' preferences affect their rulings. Judges' political attitudes are normally coded with proxies that are unsatisfactory, particularly in contexts of weak party identification (e.g., the political party of a judge's appointer). More troubling from a methodological standpoint, judges' attitudes are sometimes measured by their stances on controversial issues (e.g., a judge is coded liberal if he decides abortion should be legalized), which entails using the same measure to code both the independent and dependent variables. Other potential indicators, such as their own political party affiliation, may not capture gradations in judges' political attitudes. Further, justices' political preferences may evolve when they serve for long periods on high courts, yet coding schemes do not always take this into account (see, e.g., Martin and Quinn 2002; Smirnov and Smith 2013). Finally, even when judges have clear political preferences, it is difficult to determine whether and how they actually influence their decisions.

Institutional Explanations

A smaller number of scholars of Latin American high courts suggest that institutions (and thus institutional reform) affect judicial independence and power. For instance, researchers have used variation in institutional rules (e.g., concerning court composition or the power afforded to courts) to account for the expansiveness of constitutional review, as well as judges' assertiveness and engagement in policy-making (e.g., González Ocantos 2016 on human rights' prosecutions). Hilbink (2007) explains how institutional rules allowing for the internal review and ranking of lower-level judges by justices on the Chilean Supreme Court substantially constrained judges' behavior, and Zamora and Cossío (2006) examine the effect of institutions on constitutional structure, including the role of the Supreme Court. Others examine the influence of informal institutions on the judiciary (e.g., Basabe-Serrano 2015 on Paraguay).

As the weaker emphasis on this approach suggests, there are significant challenges to studying how institutional rules affect the behavior of courts and judges. Comparing institutional effects across contexts entails understanding exactly how particular institutions and rules operate in different legal cultures and how they influence judges' calculations and actions. The great diversity with regard to the rules guiding how Latin American high courts conduct their business both helps analytically (providing variation on the independent variable) *and* poses challenges, requiring scholars to grasp nuanced differences across systems. For example, the role of *relatores*, clerks, and other court staff, as well as the mechanisms through which cases are distributed to individual judges or panels of judges, are greatly under-studied. Also, a richer understanding of informal practices, which could be achieved through partnerships with legal experts in the field, is greatly needed to truly understand institutional impact.

As scholars of the US Supreme Court (see, e.g., Feldman 2005; Baum 2006; Tamanaha 2009; and Geyh 2010) have long highlighted, these models of judicial behavior are intrinsically complementary rather than competing: multiple factors almost certainly influence the decision-making of any high court or any justice (see also Kapiszewski 2011a). Developing an account of that multiple conjunctural causation (Ragin 1987), that is, a theory of the conditions under which different factors—individually and in combination—affect high court rulings, should be a priority for the field.

EMPIRICAL STRATEGIES FOR STUDYING LATIN AMERICAN HIGH COURTS' BEHAVIOR

While the literature on Latin American high courts is quite diverse with regard to empirical substance and theoretical approach, there seems to be less heterogeneity in the analytic methods and data-collection techniques that scholars employ to study the region's apex courts. This section discusses the core techniques scholars use to collect and generate data, considers the main methods they use to analyze data, and highlights key methodological challenges the field faces. Throughout, we encourage scholars of high courts to avail themselves of a greater range of methods.

Mode of Analysis

Most political scientists who study high courts in Latin America would consider themselves to be "comparativists"—i.e., analysts of the internal political dynamics in one or more countries (that are not their own). Single-country case studies still dominate the literature, as they did a decade ago: the majority of the work in our database focuses on national judicial dynamics in just one country, with particular emphasis on Brazil (the subject of far and away the most scholarship) and Colombia, as well as Argentina, Chile, and Mexico.[9] Far less attention is paid to apex courts in other Latin American subregions, i.e., the Andes and Central America.[10] While some might argue that the weaker independence and power of high courts in these subregions (see, e.g., Bowen 2017) makes them less worthy of inquiry, studying them could elucidate the factors that prevent them from gaining autonomy, clearly a valuable endeavor.

This continued single-country emphasis notwithstanding, scholars now compare high courts in Latin America more often and in more ways than they did before. While some studies engage in a paired comparison of two countries (e.g., Ríos-Figueroa and Taylor 2006; Wilson 2009), more often scholars compare more than two countries (e.g., Basabe-Serrano 2014; Bowen 2017), or include the whole region in their work (e.g., Couso 2008; Sikkink 2008; Helmke and Rosenbluth 2009; Pérez-Liñán and Castagnola 2009, 2016; Carrasquero 2010). However, with important exceptions (e.g., Ríos-Figueroa 2011; Brinks and Blass 2017), little work engages in rigorous, *systematic* cross-national analysis. Other scholars compare Latin American high courts with high courts in other world regions (e.g., Smith and Farrales 2010), and compare *regional* high courts with those in other regions (e.g., Alter, Helfer, and Saldias 2012).

Encouragingly, scholars have also begun to look "down and out" (as Shapiro [1989] long ago encouraged), comparing the behavior of apex courts at lower levels of the judicial hierarchy, particularly in the region's federal systems. Some studies focus on one or more subnational units in a single country, which offers extraordinary inferential leverage given the factors that such inquiry holds constant; others compare units across countries (e.g., Chavez 2004; Filgueiras 2013; and Leiras, Tuñón, and Giraudy 2015). These important studies remind us of the critical work done by lower-level courts—those with which most citizens interact most of the time.

All scholars who engage in comparison face methodological challenges. For instance, comparing units of any type requires addressing knotty questions of case selection, with important implications for the validity and potential generalizability of findings. Indeed, the fewer cases one studies, the more important the justification for including each case. Thankfully, the literature to which scholars of Latin American high courts can turn for tips on case selection is growing (e.g., Seawright and Gerring 2008; Gerring and Cojocaru 2016; Nielsen 2016). Further, accessing needed data, particularly for scholars located in the United States studying lower-level Latin American courts, can also represent a challenge. Gaining access offers an excellent opportunity for research partnerships among scholars from North, Central, and South America (see Ingram and Kapiszewski 2019 for a broader discussion of these questions).

Data-Collection Techniques and Measurement Challenges

Empirical studies of judicial behavior are only as good as the data on which they are based. Those data, in turn, are only as good as the techniques that scholars use to collect or generate them and the methods they use to analyze them. A review of our literature database suggests that most scholarship on high court behavior in Latin America relies on the analysis of qualitative data. Our survey respondents, however, who may have had the literature produced by scholars in the United States more in mind, suggest that there is an equal emphasis on quantitative and qualitative scholarship in the field.

Scholars of Latin American high courts often generate their own data.[11] Some create original quantitative data sets, for instance, by coding case decisions. Our own observations, and the results of our expert survey, suggest that the main techniques scholars use to collect or create qualitative data include conducting interviews and surveys (see, e.g., Hilbink 2007; Lamprea 2010; Montoya 2013; and Bowen 2017) and studying textual sources (e.g., archival documents, newspaper articles, or constitutions and judicial decisions themselves).

We applaud these efforts at data collection and generation, and we encourage scholars to avail themselves of additional sources of data. For instance, scholars could interview litigants and clerks of sitting of former justices (who may have key insights on how decisions were made and may feel more at liberty than do justices to discuss them), in addition to speaking with judges and other relevant political actors. Focus groups are also an underutilized yet potentially fruitful form of data generation. With regard to textual data, most high courts in the region provide websites with their case decisions, judges' concurrences and dissents, and often background information about judges, all of which can be rich data sources. Moreover, regional institutions, e.g., the Centro de Estudios de Justicia de las Américas (CEJA) and other entities affiliated with the Organization of American States (OAS), may have useful yet underutilized data, as may scholars at local law schools and universities.

Two other strategies to expand the existing pool of data on high court behavior are collaborative data generation and sharing data among scholars, within and across regional boundaries. Scholars can work together to develop databases of institutional attributes using quantitative and qualitative data.[12] Likewise, they can share the textual sources they acquire (being careful to adhere to copyright law) and possibly the fruits of more interactive data generation (while attending to human participants' concerns). In short, we encourage scholars to think creatively about the many types of information that can compose "data."[13]

Scholars often use the data they collect or generate to measure or evaluate the key variables in their analysis. As in many types of social science analysis, measurement challenges abound when studying high courts. One source of these challenges is our continued lack of clear definitions for core concepts such as judicial "activism," "independence," "power," and "authority." Yet measurement is difficult even for concepts on which there is some definitional consensus. For instance, evaluating judicial assertiveness by determining to what degree a particular set of decisions endorses or challenges elected leaders requires carefully considering the context in which the laws or actions under question were passed or engaged in, understanding the context in which the decisions were made, and doing painstaking content analysis of the decisions themselves. Identifying and assessing judges' attitudes or the foundations for their strategic behavior is equally difficult. The nature of coding data for statistical analysis can raise particularly tough questions of construct validity. While these challenges have no easy solutions, scholars being transparent about how they scored and coded their variables allows other scholars to evaluate their techniques and for all scholars to learn from each other.

Analytic Methods and Inferential Challenges

Given that scholars of the behavior of Latin American high courts employ both quantitative and qualitative data in their work, they also use both quantitative and qualitative methodologies to analyze those data. With regard to quantitative analysis, regression features prominently in the literature. Straightforward regression models are used more often than multilevel models, matching, or other more advanced techniques, potentially due to data limitations. It is more difficult to identify the particular qualitative methods that scholars employ, although they often use thick description (which facilitates descriptive inference, a prerequisite for effective explanatory analysis) and assert the use of process tracing.

We believe scholars can improve their use of both quantitative and qualitative tools in ways that would benefit the scholarship on the behavior of Latin American high courts. One concern is with what we see as a gap between theory and empirics (a common problem across multiple areas of social science inquiry). While our studies are often theory-driven, they do not always effectively test hypotheses derived from those theories[14] or persuasively demonstrate a causal connection between posited independent variables and high court behavior. Scholars who use quantitative analysis may come closer to making that connection, but cannot truly establish causation unless they carry out carefully designed randomized studies or quasi-experiments with observational data. Scholars might consider various ways to work randomization into their research designs, for example, by taking advantage of the random assignment of cases to panels or specific judges that occurs in some Latin American countries (see Kastellec 2007); of course, conditions for verifying true randomization may not exist (see Hanretty, this volume, on this point in the context of the United Kingdom). With regard to qualitative methods, while *rigorous* process tracing—the deployment of strong evidence marking the posited causal pathway—is rare in our field (as it is in other areas of political science), the accelerating development of literature on the epistemological underpinnings and practical requirements of process tracing (e.g., Collier 2011; Mahoney 2012; Bennett and Checkel 2015; Humphreys and Jacobs 2015; Fairfield and Charman 2017) should prove helpful.

A related challenge concerns generalizability. All scholars—regardless of whether they are using quantitative or qualitative techniques, or studying a single context or engaging in cross-national analysis—face the challenge of identifying the scope conditions for the inferences and conclusions they draw from their analysis. Of course, generalizability is not always our goal: understanding high court dynamics in a single country with precision is difficult and immensely valuable. When generalizability is an objective, however, thinking hard about to what empirical phenomena and contexts our conclusions generalize facilitates continued comparative analysis and the accumulation of knowledge.

Further, we would encourage scholars to employ a broader range of analytic methods in their studies of Latin American high courts. Given that our inquiries often rely on text as data, different forms of textual analysis (e.g., content analysis and discourse analysis, manual and automated) are promising techniques. Further, and in line with the importance of studying high courts as part of larger judicial *systems*, network analysis could be deployed in the field to a much greater extent (see, e.g., Ingram 2019). Another little-used method with great potential is Qualitative Comparative Analysis (QCA). Given the generalizability challenges that attend small-N analysis and the data and measurement challenges that attend large-N analysis, medium-N analysis may be the ideal approach for our area of study, and QCA is well suited to studying a medium-N number of cases. Ethnographies of high courts that delve into the details of judicial practice and how judges think about their work would likewise be fascinating.

The strategic interaction between judges and other political actors that many scholars posit occurs suggests that our work is ripe for the use of game theory (e.g., Staton 2010; Iaryczower, Spiller, and Tommasi 2002; Helmke 2002). In addition, more experimental work could be carried out, within practical and ethical limits: scholars should stay alert for opportunities to exploit natural experiments (see Dunning 2012) or to conduct field or lab experiments. The successful application of these methodologies in other sensitive areas of political science suggests their potential utility to the study of high courts. Finally, scholars might pair quantitative and qualitative analysis, for instance, using process tracing to examine a subset of a large-N set of cases to probe whether the relationship suggested by a correlation discovered through regression analysis actually has causal underpinnings.

Substantive Gaps and Unresolved Theoretical Puzzles

Despite the richness of the scholarship on Latin American high courts, many empirical puzzles remain unsolved. In this section we highlight some of the main substantive gaps we see in the literature. We discuss particular aspects of high court behavior that we believe are understudied or problematic, and we offer alternative explanations for high court behavior that we believe might feature more prominently in future work.

Under-Studied and Problematic Aspects of High Court Behavior

We believe more attention could be paid to several aspects of the decision-making and decisions of Latin American high courts. To begin, social scientists who analyze the decision-making of high courts in Latin America (and elsewhere) tend to focus almost exclusively on judges' votes and case outcomes rather than the reasoning articulated in high court rulings. This may be because scholars find it difficult to understand legal reasons and thus to code them for inclusion in statistical analysis. Alternatively, scholars may doubt that the reasoning in judicial rulings faithfully reflects why judges rule as they do, believing instead that judges rule strategically (without referencing the political foundations of their decisions in their opinions). No matter the reason, as Friedman (2006) observes, studying law "in a meaningful way" requires looking at the reasons and justifications that judges give for their decisions, in particular in common law systems with the doctrine of stare decisis.

We believe that studying the legal reasoning offered by high courts in Latin America's civil law systems is equally important (as also noted by Hanretty, this volume). Latin American justices often write lengthy opinions and indicate specific reasons and justifications for their concurrences and dissents, in part due to the broad tendency to adopt legal practices from, and create practices resembling those in, common law systems. Likewise, precedent *does exist* (albeit to varying degrees, and often informally) in Latin American legal systems.[15] The closer a particular Latin American legal system has moved toward common law practices, the greater the value of studying the legal reasoning of its courts.

With regard to judges' votes and case outcomes, more attention could be paid to variation in the form and function of judicial decisions, both of which depend on a country's legal rules. For example, there may be significant variation in how courts justify finding a case inadmissible (thus avoiding evaluating it on its substantive merits). Courts also vary as to the type of rulings they can issue. Courts that engage in judicial review, for instance, can often both strike down laws *and* rule that laws are conditionally constitutional (e.g., only constitutional if the legislature adopts the court's interpretation of the laws). Further, voting options on some courts extend beyond the three standard choices (majority, concurring, or dissenting). Faithfully reflecting these legal nuances is important and requires a high level of coding precision; misunderstandings can multiply when case outcomes are compared across high courts.

In addition, the type of constitutional review invoked, and the type of norm questioned, in particular cases, almost certainly affect judicial decision-making. For instance, Shapiro (2004) has noted that judges' behavior may change depending on whether they are engaging in concrete or abstract review. Drawing conclusions about judicial behavior based on studying only one type of case (i.e., all concrete review or all abstract review) can thus be misleading. Scholars of the Brazilian high court, for instance, generally focus on a particular type of abstract review case (*Acoes Diretas de Inconstitucionalidad,* ADIns) despite these cases composing a tiny subset of the court's docket. Likewise, the type of law or action that judges are evaluating probably also affects their rulings; accordingly, making claims about judicial behavior based solely on studying judicial review of legislation or of executive decrees could also be misleading.

Large-N studies could expand to include examination of how courts handle *amparos, tutelas,* and petitions for writs of habeas corpus and habeas data.

Scholars would also do well to integrate into their studies variables related to high courts' internal operations and procedures, both formal and informal. For example, scholars of Latin American high courts acknowledge that mandatory dockets and legal actions unique to the region (e.g., *amparos, tutelas,* etc.) overload under-resourced courts and judges. Nonetheless, there is little systematic research on the strategies and informal practices that justices and other court personnel develop to address that challenge or on how high courts' caseloads affect their decision-making (but see Buscaglia and Ulen 1997). Scholarship on US courts, by contrast, has examined how the work of law clerks and other personnel (Cohen 2002) can alleviate overburdened courts and judges; the effect of caseloads on courts (Hydebrand and Seron 1990; Epstein, Landes, and Posner 2013); and whether large caseloads encourage judges to take short cuts and depend on cues (Klein and Hume 2003). In short, more academic discussion of how Latin American high courts deal with heavy caseloads and the implications their coping mechanisms have for their decisions is warranted.

Another surprising omission in the literature on the behavior of Latin American high courts are panel effects, and collegiality or group dynamics among justices (although see Arlota and Garoupa 2016; Tiede 2020). It seems unquestionable that interactions among judges on collegial courts must affect their decision-making. Accordingly, scholarship on Latin American high courts could benefit from engaging with the rich literature on the effects of group characteristics and behavior on judicial decision-making (see, e.g., Epstein, Segal, and Spaeth 2001 on saving time, social pressure, and maintaining collegiality or consensus; Miles and Sunstein 2006 on group polarization; Kastellec 2007 on the threat of whistleblowing; and, Fischman 2015 on interaction among judges' vote choices).

Underutilized Approaches to Explanation

As noted previously, the three theoretical approaches most commonly adopted in the literature on high courts in Latin America are the strategic, attitudinal, and institutional approaches. At least among scholars at US institutions, the strategic approach clearly dominates. We believe that the attitudinal and institutional approaches could be further developed and that cultural and ideational approaches could receive more emphasis.

Some scholars have discounted the utility of the attitudinal approach for explaining high court behavior in legal systems based on civil law (like those in Latin America), in which judges are supposedly dispassionate *"bouches de la loi"* who generate decisions by applying law to facts with little latitude (or desire) for politically induced interpretation. Moreover, evidence of politically motivated decision-making on Latin American high courts is often ascribed to a lack of independence rather than a sincere expression of political preferences. Yet as studies that investigate justices' backgrounds have revealed (e.g., Pardow and Verdugo 2013), high court justices in some countries (e.g., Argentina and Brazil) have previous political careers, making it very likely that they have political preferences and leanings. While justices' political attitudes rarely *dictate* their rulings anywhere, it seems probable that they often influence those decisions, and we should learn under what circumstances, how, and how much they do so.

We also believe a greater emphasis on how institutions affect high court decision-making would benefit the literature. As mentioned previously, scholars have sought to identify, and sometimes aggregate into indices, the main "rules of the game" that regulate high court behavior. An important next step is to closely and systematically examine precisely how those rules affect judicial decision-making. Moreover, scholars should examine a broader range of rules (and how they affect decision-making), including rules guiding the resolution of different kinds of cases, rules regulating the effects of rulings (i.e., how broadly or narrowly they apply), as well as court-generated rules and *informal* institutions (e.g., concerning justices' conduct and interactions with each other and with other actors). Certainly identifying and understanding arcane legal rules is complicated. Yet even in weakly institutionalized contexts such as those of Latin American polities, institutions matter, and we should understand how.

It could also be beneficial for more scholars to adopt cultural and ideational approaches to explaining high court behavior. Legal culture and judicial culture—the values, attitudes, and beliefs shared by lawyers, judges, and other members of the legal profession—no doubt affect the way high court justices do their jobs (as Couso, Huneeus, and Sieder 2010 and others have argued). Likewise, judges' beliefs about the role courts should play in politics may affect their decisions, in particular when confronting other government actors (see, e.g., Hilbink 2007; Nunes 2010a; and Hilbink and Couso 2011), yet we know little about the effects of these beliefs. Developing and evaluating what Latin American scholars refer to as "ideational" explanations of judicial decision-making by identifying which philosophies or ideas motivate judicial behavior would also be beneficial. For example, Oliveira (2008) and Pardow and Verdugo (2013) show that judges' professions prior to serving on the Brazilian Supreme Court and Chilean Constitutional Tribunal, respectively, informed their preferences and ultimately their behavior (see also Sikkink 2008; Desposato, Ingram, and Lannes 2015).

The analytic challenges raised by adopting these latter theoretical approaches parallel those associated with the attitudinal model: it is difficult to test claims that judges' rulings are influenced by ideas, to identify which ideas matter and how much, and to code judges' views and ideas in a way that accommodates the possibility of—or captures—change over time. Nonetheless, scholars working in partnerships within and across borders can generate knowledge and develop solutions to address these challenges. The result will be a richer, better understanding of the decision-making of Latin American high courts.

Concluding Thoughts, and the Promise (and Challenges) of Cross-Regional Study

Latin America has undergone important political change since the turn of the twenty-first century. Democracy of varying degrees of quality has become increasingly rooted in the region. Politics took a "left turn" (Castañeda 2006), perhaps a right turn (Encarnación 2018), and was then thrown into chaos by the COVID-19 pandemic that emerged in 2020. The rule of law has grown arguably weaker in some countries (e.g., Venezuela), while in other polities anti-corruption efforts have proceeded farther and faster, if unevenly, than at any other time in the region's history (e.g., Brazil prior to 2019 and areas of Central America). Many countries entered, and exited, a commodities boom. Any of these dynamics might have affected the roles high courts play, and concomitantly the focus of those who study them. This essay has sought to track the empirical, theoretical, and methodological tendencies in, and challenges that complicate, scholarship on the region's high courts, and how they have evolved, over this time period (with a particular focus on the last decade). In this brief conclusion, we consider what our findings imply for future scholarship and for the potential, and perils, of cross-regional analysis.

As we have suggested, we believe that paying more attention to the behavior of high courts *beyond* their formulation of decisions will allow us to generate more holistic understandings of high courts and better comprehend the foundations of their rulings. Additional attention to the empowerment (and disempowerment) of high courts, litigation at high courts, and compliance with and the broader impact of judicial decisions, would certainly benefit the literature, as would greater consideration of the specifics of judicial reasoning, and norms of consensus and collegiality, on high courts. Scholars adopting underutilized theoretical approaches, such as cultural and ideational models, and availing themselves of more types of data, and a broader array of methods, would also enrich the scholarship, facilitating the drawing of both descriptive and causal inferences.

With regard to the broader preoccupation of this volume, we believe there are clear benefits to comparing high courts across world regions.[16] Doing so would allow scholars of courts in any particular world region to benefit from the knowledge of judicial politics held by scholars from other regions; formulate new and different questions; and adopt and adapt new theoretical approaches, data-collection techniques, and analytic methods. Considering the study of high courts to be a broader comparative enterprise could unite the field in extremely productive ways.

At the same time, engaging in cross-regional comparison would likely exacerbate some of the challenges that attend intra-regional analysis. A first challenge is determining what *general types* of questions can be most productively approached and answered by studying courts in more than one world region, and then what *specific* derivative questions should be asked in any particular context. Given that the latter is affected by politics, law, and institutions, another immediate challenge is keeping our field of inquiry coherent while simultaneously studying the most important dynamics in each context. In addition, many key terms (e.g., judicial "activism" and "liberal") mean different things in different contexts; cross-regional comparison would make conceptual coordination even more challenging. Likewise, context-specific indicators (Locke and Thelen 1995) would need to be developed to ensure that we are appropriately measuring important phenomena that likely manifest differently in diverse contexts. Knowledge-based challenges—e.g., operating (and understanding abstruse legal terminology) in multiple languages and comprehending diverse political and institutional contexts and legal systems—would also abound, although they could be partially addressed through cross-regional scholarly partnerships. Cross-regional study would also pose a series of methodological obstacles, such as effectively pooling rulings from different contexts for quantitative analysis.

These challenges aside, we applaud the focus of this volume. Given courts' potential to address, or at least highlight, the democratic backsliding and illiberal politics that are emerging and accelerating in more and more polities as the twenty-first century proceeds, comparative analysis of judicial institutions has never been more important. We believe that the study of Latin American high courts can be an anchor, and offer important lessons, for cross-regional inquiry. As we noted from the start, and as a perusal of this volume makes clear, more scholars have produced more work about Latin American high courts than about courts in any other developing region. Better understanding how high courts become involved in important political-legal dynamics in the Global South, what potential they have to contribute to the entrenchment of the rule of law and the quality of democracy, and under what conditions they realize that potential, are critical matters on which cross-regional comparison can shed considerable light. We hope the methodological and theoretical innovations in which scholars of Latin America have engaged can inform and facilitate that broader inquiry.

Methodological Note

The preceding essay draws on a literature database created for analysis in Kapiszewski and Newman (2021). This appendix discusses how the database was constructed and what adaptations were made to facilitate its use in the present paper.

The original database was constructed through a systematic search for literature that was published between 2007 and 2016 and that focused on the judicialization of politics in Latin America, Central and Eastern Europe, India, and South Africa. We searched for publication in English, Spanish, and Portuguese. English-language publications were identified through searching several online databases including JSTOR, Web of Science, IJCL and Google Scholar. We also searched the collections of several prominent US- and UK-based publishers, including Oxford, Cambridge, Harvard, Johns Hopkins, Notre Dame, Pittsburgh, Penn State, Stanford, Cornell, Lynne Rienner, Routledge, Palgrave, and Elsevier. Search terms included "judicialization of politics," "courts and politics," "courts political," "constitutional court," "judicial review," "judicial politics," and "judicial independence." These terms were paired with country names plus "Latin America." For literature in Spanish and

Portuguese, we searched using the previously mentioned terms in translation. This search occurred in JSTOR and Google Scholar and also in the collections of well-known publishers and presses in the region, including FGV (Brazil), CIDE (Mexico), UNAM (Mexico), Siglo XXI (Mexico), Fondo de Cultura Económica (Mexico), Dejusticia (Colombia), Universidad del Externado (Colombia), Universidad de los Andes (Colombia), and FLACSO (regional). Publishers were chosen based on recommendations from prominent scholars in the field.

Our searches returned 426 publications. For each, based on the abstract (for articles) or the table of contents and first few pages (for books), we noted the following characteristics: type (journal article, book), year of publication, author, publication title, abstract, institution of focus, outcome, approach, theoretical approach (if explanatory), geographic focus, time period of focus, analytic methods, argument, and themes. The database was then cleaned by removing publications that were reviews of other publications, were book sections (due to our concern that we had not systematically identified all relevant essays or chapters in edited volumes), did not focus on Latin America, or when reconsidered did not truly address the judicialization of politics; one article and one book were removed because we could not access the content. For the purposes of the current project, additional publications were removed, namely those that were purely conceptual or normative, were clearly concerned with institutions other than high courts (e.g., international or regional courts, electoral courts, judicial councils), or focused on an aspect of the judicialization of politics other than judicial behavior (e.g., appointments to or litigation at high courts). The resulting database contains 204 entries.

One caveat bears noting. For more than half of the publications in the resulting database (104 entries), the author(s) indicated that they were studying "the judiciary," "courts," or "judges" rather than high courts specifically. Given the tendency in the literature for scholars to indicate that they are studying "courts" when in fact their focus is high courts, and in order to be inclusive, we have retained these pieces in the database and the analysis. We are confident that much of this literature actually focuses on high courts, and we have no reason to believe that the analytic trends in the work that actually does not focus on high courts are dramatically different from those in the work that does.

Notes

1. The database is adapted from one created in association with Kapiszewski and Newman (2021); see appendix to this essay on the methodology.
2. Sixteen of thirty-five experts responded to the survey, a response rate of 46 percent.
3. In our survey, 88 percent of respondents expressed this belief.
4. This previous review examined the literature on judicial politics in Latin America more broadly (rather than being limited to high court politics) and only considered major articles and books written in English and published between 1980 and 2006.
5. Our expert survey indicated that judicial independence and judicial decision-making are the main areas of inquiry, followed by case interpretation, policy impacts of rulings, human rights, and democratization.
6. Survey respondents cited strategic, institutional, legal (jurisprudential), attitudinal, and ideational approaches most frequently, followed by cultural explanations.
7. Others remind us that judges also worry about how their rulings may affect the likelihood of compliance (Staton 2010), enhance their reputation or future job prospects (Garoupa and Ginsburg 2015), and promote the legitimacy of the court to other actors and to the public (Helmke and Staton 2011).
8. We still know little about public opinion of the region's high courts or how it might affect their legitimacy (or matter to their decision-making).
9. Surprisingly few *American* academics explore judicial politics in Brazil; given the interesting political roles its high court has played (see, e.g., Nunes 2010b; Brinks 2011; Kapiszewski 2011b), and variation in the court's ability to remain independent, it merits closer analysis by scholars located in the United States.
10. Important exceptions include Wilson (2007) on Costa Rica and Dargent (2009) on Peru.
11. Of course, some scholars reuse data collected or generated by other scholars, a practice we celebrate, as data should be used as much as possible within ethical and legal limits.
12. Two examples of databases that include (but are not limited to) Latin America are CompLaw (Comparative Law Project, http://complaw.wustl .edu) and the National High Courts Database (http://artsandsciences.sc .edu/poli/juri/highcts.htm). With regard to Latin American high courts specifically, Brinks and Blass (2017) and Ríos-Figueroa (2011) have each created a database of high court characteristics, and Susan Achury (University of Houston) assembled a database of fine-grained measures of judicial power (i.e., "micro" devices of judicial review).

13. The work included in Kapiszewski and Ingram (forthcoming) takes on these questions, considering the concepts, data, and methods used in the comparative study of law and politics.

14. As Jeff Staton has observed, the scholarship would benefit from more consistently allowing theory (and hypotheses derived therefrom), rather than data availability, to drive analysis.

15. While Latin American countries may not use precedent in the same way it is used in common law countries, high courts in the region do cite to other decisions in their rulings, use reasoning that depends on analogizing prior cases to an issue at hand, and declare that their decisions have precedential value (see, e.g., Cepeda and Landau 2017 on the Colombian Constitutional Court; and Case Rol #681 from the Chilean Constitutional Tribunal).

16. Encouragingly, scholars of high courts in Latin America have already begun to engage in such comparison (e.g., Smith and Farrales 2010, comparing Chile and the Philippines, and Llanos et al. 2016, comparing trios of countries in Latin America and Africa).

References

Alter, Karen J., Laurence R. Helfer, and Osvaldo Saldias. 2012. "Transplanting the European Court of Justice: The Experience of the Andean Tribunal of Justice." *The American Journal of Comparative Law* 60: 629–64.

Arlota, Carolina, and Nuno Garoupa. 2014. "Addressing Federal Conflicts: An Empirical Analysis of the Brazilian Supreme Court, 1988–2010." *Review of Law and Economics* 10 (2): 137–68.

———. 2016. "Do Specialized Courts Make a Difference? Evidence from Brazilian State Supreme Courts." *European Business Law Review* 27 (4): 487–500.

Barros, Robert. 2002. *Constitutionalism and Dictatorship: Pinochet, the Junta and the 1980 Constitution*. Cambridge: Cambridge University Press.

———. 2008. "Courts Out of Context Authoritarian Sources of Judicial Failure in Chile (1973–1990)." In *Rule by Law: The Politics of Courts in Authoritarian Regimes*, edited by Tom Ginsburg and Tamir Moustafa, 156–79. Cambridge: Cambridge University Press.

Basabe-Serrano, Santiago. 2008. "Preferencias Ideológicas y Políticas Judiciales: un Modelo Actitudinal sobre el Voto en el Tribunal Constitucional del Ecuador." *América Latina Hoy* 49: 157–77.

———. 2009. "Estabilidad Política y Jugadores de Veto Judicial: un Modelo Espacial Aplicado a Cortes Constitucionales" *Revista OPERA* 9: 121–34.

———. 2012. "Judges without Robes and Judicial Voting in Context of Institutional Instability: The Case of Ecuador's Constitutional Court." *Journal of Latin American Studies* 44 (1): 127–61.

————. 2014. "Some Determinants of Internal Judicial Independence: A Comparative Study of the Courts in Chile, Peru and Ecuador." *International Journal of Law, Crime, and Justice* 42 (20): 130–45.

————. 2015. "Institutions and Judicial Independence in Paraguay, 1954–2011." *Law & Policy* 37 (4): 350–78.

Baum, Lawrence. 2006. *Judges and Their Audiences: A Perspective on Judicial Behavior.* Princeton: Princeton University Press.

Bennett, Andrew, and Jeffrey T. Checkel, eds. 2015. *Process Tracing: From Metaphor to Analytic Tool.* Cambridge: Cambridge University Press.

Bertomeu, Juan González, Lucia Dalla Pellegrina, Nuno Garoupa. 2017. "Estimating Judicial Ideal Points in Latin America: The Case of Argentina." *Review of Law & Economics* 13 (1), available at https://www.degruyter.com /view/journals/rle/13/1/article-20150040.xml.

Bowen, Rachel E. 2013. "Judicial Autonomy in Central America: A Typological Approach." *Political Research Quarterly* 66 (4): 831–42.

————. 2017. *The Achilles Heel of Democracy: Judicial Autonomy and the Rule of Law in Central America.* New York: Cambridge University Press.

Brinks, Daniel M. 2008. *The Judicial Response to Police Killings in Latin America: Inequality and the Rule of Law.* Cambridge: Cambridge University Press.

————. 2011. "Faithful Servants of the Regime." In Gretchen Helmke and Julio Ríos-Figueroa, eds. *Courts in Latin America,* 128–53. New York: Cambridge University Press.

Brinks, Daniel M., and Abby Blass. 2017. "Rethinking Judicial Empowerment: The New Foundations of Constitutional Justice." *International Journal of Constitutional Law* 15 (2): 296–331.

Buscaglia, Eduardo, and Thomas Ulen. 1997. "A Quantitative Assessment of the Efficiency of the Judicial Sector in Latin America." *International Review of Law and Economics* 17 (2): 275–91.

Carrasquero, Guillermo Boscan. 2010. "Judicialización y Politización en América Latina: Una nueva estrategia para el estudio de la interacción entre los poderes públicos." *Revista de Ciencias Jurídicas* 4 (2): 50–83.

Castagnola, Andrea. 2010. "La diversidad institucional de los poderes judiciales provinciales en Argentina desde una perspectiva histórica." *POSTData: Revista de Reflexión y Análisis Político* 15 (2): 161–89.

Castañeda, Jorge. 2006. "Latin America's Left Turn." *Foreign Affairs* 85 (3): 28–43.

Cepeda Espinosa, Manuel José, and David Landau. 2017. *Colombian Constitutional Law Leading Cases.* Oxford: Oxford University Press.

Chavez, Rebecca Bill. 2004. *Rule of Law in Nascent Democracies: Judicial Politics in Argentina.* Stanford: Stanford University Press.

————. 2007. "The Appointment and Removal Process for Judges in Argentina: The Role of Judicial Councils and Impeachment Juries in Promoting Judicial Independence." *Latin American Politics and Society* 49 (2): 33–58.

Cohen, Jonathan. 2002. *Inside Appellate Courts: The Impact of Court Organization on Judicial Decision Making in the United States Courts of Appeals*. Ann Arbor: The University of Michigan Press.

Collier, David. 2011. "Understanding Process Tracing." *PS: Political Science and Politics* 44 (4): 823–30.

Conaghan, Catherine M. 2012. "Prosecuting Presidents: The Politics within Ecuador's Corruption Cases." *Journal of Latin American Studies* 44 (4): 649–78.

Couso, Javier A. 2008. "The Globalization of Latin American Constitutional Law. Verfassung und Recht in Übersee (Law and Politics in Africa, Asia and Latin America)." *Nomos Verlagsgesellschaft mbH* 41(1): 56–60.

Couso, Javier, Alexandra Huneeus, and Rachel Sieder, eds. 2010. *Cultures of Legality Judicialization and Political Activism in Latin America*. New York: Cambridge University Press.

Dargent, Eduardo. 2009. "Determinants of Judicial Independence: Lessons from Three 'Cases' of Constitutional Courts in Peru (1982–2007)." *Journal of Latin American Studies* 41 (2): 251–78.

Desposato, Scott, Matthew C. Ingram, and Osmar P. Lannes, Jr. 2015. "Power, Composition and Decision Making: The Behavioral Consequences of Institutional Reform on Brazil's Supremo Tribunal Federal." *Journal of Law, Economics, and Organization* 31 (3): 534–67.

do Vale, Helder Ferreira. 2013. "The Judicialization of Territorial Politics in Brazil, Colombia and Spain." *Brazilian Political Science Review* 7 (2): 88–113.

Dunning, Thad. 2012. *Natural Experiments in the Social Sciences: A Design-Based Approach*. Cambridge: Cambridge University Press.

Encarnación, Omar G. 2018. "The Rise and Fall of the Latin American Left." *The Nation*, May 9, 2018. https://www.thenation.com/article/archive/the-ebb-and-flow-of-latin-americas-pink-tide.

Epstein, Lee, William Landes, and Richard Posner. 2013. *The Behavior of Federal Judges, A Theoretical and Empirical Study of Rational Choice*. Cambridge: Harvard University.

Epstein, Lee, Jeffrey Segal, and Harold Spaeth. 2001. "The Norm of Consensus on the U.S. Supreme Court." *American Journal of Political Science* 45 (2): 362–77.

Fairfield, Tasha, and Andrew Charman. 2017. "Explicit Bayesian Analysis for Process Tracing: Guidelines, Opportunities, and Caveats." *Political Analysis* 25 (3): 363–80.

Feldman, Stephen. 2005. "The Rule of Law and Rule of Politics? Harmonizing the Internal and External Views of Supreme Court Decision-Making." *Law and Social Inquiry* 30: 89–135.

Ferreira, Pedro F. N., and Bernardo Mueller. 2014. "How Judges Think in the Brazilian Supreme Court: Estimating Ideal Points and Identifying Dimensions." *EconomiA* 15 (3): 275–93.

Filgueiras, Fernando. 2013. "Perceptions on Justice, the Judiciary, and Democracy." *Brazilian Political Science Review* 7 (2): 62–87.

Finkel, Jodi. 2004. "Judicial Reform in Argentina in the 1990s: How Electoral Incentives Shape Institutional Change." *Latin American Research Review* 39: 56–80.

Fischman, Joshua. 2015. "Interpreting Circuit Court Voting Patterns: A Social Interactions Framework." *The Journal of Law, Economics, and Organization* 31 (4): 808–41.

Friedman, Barry. 2006. "Taking Law Seriously." *Perspectives on Politics* 4 (2): 261–76.

García-Sayán, Diego. 2010. "The Inter-American Court and Constitutionalism in Latin America." *Texas Law Review* 89: 1835–62.

Gargarella, Roberto. 2014. *Por una justicia dialogica. El poder judicial como promotor de la liberacion democrática.* Buenos Aires: Siglo Veintiuno Editores.

Garoupa, Nuno, and Tom Ginsburg. 2015. *Judicial Reputation.* Chicago: University of Chicago Press.

Gauri, Varun, Jeffrey K. Staton, and Jorge Vargas Cullell. 2015. "The Costa Rican Supreme Court's Compliance Monitoring System." *The Journal of Politics* 77 (3): 774–86.

Gerring, John, and Lee Cojocaru. 2016. "Selecting Cases for Intensive Analysis: A Diversity of Goals and Methods." *Sociological Methods & Research* 45: 392–423.

Geyh, Charles Gardner. 2010. "Judicial Politics, the Rule of Law, and the Future of an Ermine Myth." Research Paper Number 165. Indiana University Maurer School of Law.

González Bertomeu, Juan, Lucia Dalla Pellegrina, and Nuno Garoupa. 2017. "Estimating Judicial Ideal Points in Latin America: The Case of Argentina" *Review of Law and Economics* 13 (1): 1–35.

González Ocantos, Ezequiel. 2016. *Shifting Legal Visions: Judicial Change and Human Rights Trials in Latin America.* Cambridge Studies in Law and Society. New York: Cambridge University Press.

Hammergren, Linn. 2007. *Envisioning Reform: Improving Judicial Performance in Latin America.* University Park: Pennsylvania State University Press.

Helmke, Gretchen. 2002. "The Logic of Strategic Defection: Court-Executive Relations in Argentina under Dictatorship and Democracy." *American Political Science Review* 96 (2): 291–303.

———. 2010. "The Origins of Institutional Crises in Latin America." *American Journal of Political Science* 54 (3): 737–50.

Helmke, Gretchen, and Frances Rosenbluth. 2009. "Regimes and the Rule of Law: Judicial Independence in Comparative Perspective." *Annual Review of Political Science* 12: 345–66.

Helmke, Gretchen, and Mitchell Sanders. 2006. "Modeling Motivations A Method for Inferring Judicial Goals from Behavior." *American Journal of Political Science* 68 (4): 867–78.

Helmke, Gretchen, and Jeff Staton. 2011. "The Puzzling Judicial Politics of Latin America: A Theory of Litigation, Judicial Decisions, and Interbranch

Conflict." In *Courts in Latin America*, edited by Gretchen Helmke and Julio Ríos-Figueroa, 306–31. New York: Cambridge University Press.

Hilbink, Lisa. 2007. *Judges Beyond Politics in Democracy and Dictatorship*. Cambridge: Cambridge University Press.

Hilbink, Lisa, and Javier Couso. 2011. "From Quietism to Incipient Activism: The Institutional and Ideological Roots of Rights Adjudication in Chile." In *Courts in Latin America*, edited by Gretchen Helmke and Julio Ríos-Figueroa, 99–127. Cambridge: Cambridge University Press.

Humphreys, Macartan, and Alan Jacobs. 2015. Mixing Methods: A Bayesian Approach. *American Political Science Review* 109 (4): 653–73.

Huneeus, Alexandra. 2017. "Pushing States to Prosecute: Positive Complementarity, the ICC and the Inter-American Court." In *New Legal Realism Studying the Law Globally, Volume II*, edited by Heinz Klug and Sally Engle Merry, 225–41. New York: Cambridge University Press.

———. 2018. "Legitimacy and Jurisdictional Overlap: The ICC and the Inter-American Court in Colombia." In *The Legitimacy of International Courts*, edited by Nienke Grossman, Harlan Grant Cohen, Andreas Follesdal, and Geir Ulfstein, 114–42. Cambridge: Cambridge University Press.

Hydebrand, Wolf, and Carroll Seron. 1990. *Rationalizing Justice: The Political Economy of Federal District Courts*. Albany: State University of New York Press.

Iaryczower, Matías, Pablo T. Spiller, and Mariano Tommasi. 2002. "Judicial Independence in Unstable Environments, Argentina 1935–1998." *American Journal of Political Science* 46 (4): 699–716.

———. 2006. "Judicial Lobbying: The Politics of Labor Law Constitutional Interpretation." *American Political Science Review* 100 (1): 85–97.

Ingram, Matthew C. 2019. "Judicial Councils in Mexico: Design, Roles, and Origins at the National and Subnational Levels." In *Beyond High Courts: The Justice Complex in Latin America*, edited by Matthew C. Ingram and Diana Kapiszewski. South Bend: University of Notre Dame Press.

Ingram, Matthew C., and Diana Kapiszewski. 2019. *Beyond High Courts: The Justice Complex in Latin America*. South Bend: University of Notre Dame Press.

Kapiszewski, Diana. 2011a. "Tactical Balancing: High Court Decision Making on Politically Crucial Cases." *Law & Society Review* 45 (2): 471–506.

———. 2011b. "Power Broker, Policy Maker, or Rights Protector?" In Gretchen Helmke and Julio Ríos-Figueroa, eds. *Courts in Latin America*. New York: Cambridge University Press, pp. 154–86.

———. 2012. *High Courts and Economic Governance in Argentina and Brazil*. New York: Cambridge University Press.

Kapiszewski, Diana, and Matthew C. Ingram, eds. Forthcoming. *Concepts, Data, and Methods in Comparative Law and Politics*. New York: Cambridge University Press.

Kapiszewski, Diana, and Katja Newman. 2021. "Judicialization of Politics." In *Oxford Handbook of Constitutional Law in Latin America*, edited by Conrado Hübner Mendes and Roberto Gargarella. New York: Oxford University Press.

Kapiszewski, Diana, and Matthew M. Taylor. 2008. "Doing Courts Justice? Studying Judicial Politics in Latin America." *Perspectives on Politics* 6 (4): 741–67.

Kastellec, Jonathan P. 2007. "Panel Composition and Judicial Compliance on the US Courts of Appeals." *Journal of Law, Economics, and Organization* 23: 421–41.

Klein, David E., and Robert J. Hume. 2003. "Fear of Reversal as an Explanation of Lower Court Compliance." *Law & Society Review* 37: 579–81.

Lamprea, Everaldo. 2010. "When Accountability Meets Judicial Independence A Case Study of the Colombian Constitutinal Court's Nominations." *Global Jurist* 10: 1–38.

Leiras, Marcelo, Guadalupe Tuñón, and Agustina Giraudy. 2015. "Who Wants an Independent Court? Political Competition and Supreme Court Autonomy in the Argentine Provinces (1984–2008)." *The Journal of Politics* 77 (1): 175–87.

Llanos, Mariana, Cordula Tibi Weber, Charlotte Heyl, and Alexander Stroh. 2016. "Informal Interference in the Judiciary in New Democracies: A Comparison of Six African and Latin American Cases." *Democratization* 23 (7): 1236–53.

Locke, Richard M., and Kathleen Thelen. 1995. "Apples and Oranges Revisited: Contextualized Comparisons and the Study of Comparative Labor Politics." *Politics and Society* 23 (3): 337–67.

Mahoney, James. 2012. "The Logic of Process Tracing Tests in the Social Sciences." *Sociological Methods & Research* 41 (4): 570–97.

Martin, Andrew, and Andrew Quinn. 2002. "Dynamic Ideal Point Estimation via Markov Chain Monte Carlo for the U.S. Supreme Court, 1953–1999." *Political Analysis* 10 (2): 134–53.

McAllister, Lesley. 2008. *Making Law Matter: Environmental Protection and Legal Institutions in Brazil*. Stanford: Stanford University Press.

Miles, Thomas J., and Cass R. Sunstein. 2006. "Do Judges Make Regulatory Policy? An Empirical Investigation of Chevron." *University of Chicago Law Review* 73: 823–82.

Montoya, Ana María. 2013. "'Si no vas al Senado, no te eligen magistrado': Instituciones informales y criterios de selección de los magistrados de la Corte Constitucional colombiana en el Senado (1992–2009)." *Colombia Internacional* 79: 155–90.

Moreno, Erica, Brian Crisp, and Matthew Shugart. 2003. "The Accountability Deficit in Latin America." In *Democratic Accountability in Latin America*, edited by Scott Mainwaring and Christopher Welna, 79–131. Cambridge: Cambridge University Press.

Nielsen, Richard A. 2016. "Case Selection via Matching." *Sociological Methods & Research* 45: 569–97.

Nunes, Rodrigo. 2010a. "Ideational Origins of Progressive Judicial Activism: The Colombian Constitutional Court and the Right to Health." *Latin American Politics and Society* 52 (3): 67–97.

———. 2010b. "Politics without Insurance: Democratic Competition and Judicial Reform in Brazil." *Journal of Comparative Politics* 42 (3): 313–31.

Oliveira, Fabiana Luci. 2008. "Justice, Professionalism, and Politics in the Exercise of Judicial Review by Brazil's Supreme Court." *Brazilian Political Science Review (online)* 2 (2).

Pardow, Diego, and Sergio Verdugo. 2013. "The Chilean Constitutional Court and the 2005 Reform A Casting between Career Judges and Academics." Working paper. University of California, Berkeley.

Pérez-Liñán, Aníbal, and Andrea Castagnola. 2009. "Presidential Control of High Courts in Latin America: A Long-term View." *Journal of Politics in Latin America* 1 (2): 87–114.

———. 2016. "Judicial Instability and Endogenous Constitutional Change: Lessons from Latin America." *British Journal of Political Science* 46 (2): 395–416.

Ragin, Charles. 1987. *The Comparative Method Moving Beyond Qualitative and Quantitative Strategies*. Berkeley: University of California Press.

Ríos-Figueroa, Julio. 2007. "Fragmentation of Power and the Emergence of an Effective Judiciary in Mexico, 1994–2002." *Latin American Politics and Society* 49 (1): 31–57.

———. 2011. "Institutions for Constitutional Justice in Latin America." In *Courts in Latin America*, edited by Gretchen Helmke and Julio Ríos-Figueroa, 27–54. New York: Cambridge University Press.

Ríos-Figueroa, Julio, and Matthew Taylor. 2006. "Institutional Determinants of the Judicialisation of Policy in Brazil and Mexico." *Journal of Latin American Studies* 38 (4): 739–66.

Rodríguez-Raga, Juan Carlos. 2011. "Strategic Deference in the Colombian Constitutional Court, 1992–2006." In *Courts in Latin America*, edited by Gretchen Helmke and Julio Ríos-Figueroa, 81–98. New York: Cambridge University Press.

Rogers, James R., and Georg Vanberg. 2002. "Judicial Advisory Opinions and Legislative Outcomes in Comparative Perspective." *American Journal of Political Science* 46 (2): 379–97.

Roth, Laura C. 2007. "Acerca de la independencia judicial en Argentina: la creación del Consejo de la Magistratura y su desempeño entre 1994 y 2006." *Desarrollo Económico* 47 (186): 285–318.

Rueda, Pablo. n.d. "Indigenous Cosmopolitans: Law, Oil, and Transnational Market Activism."

Ruibal, Alba M. 2009. "Self-Restraint in Search of Legitimacy: the Reform of the Argentine Supreme Court." *Latin American Politics and Society* 51 (3): 59–86.

Ruibal, Alba. 2015. "Movilización y contra-movilización legal: Propuesta para su análisis en América Latina." *Política y Gobierno* 22 (1): 175–98.

Saldias, Osvaldo. 2014. *The Judicial Politics of Economic Integration: The Andean Court as an Engine of Development.* New York: Routledge.

Sánchez, Arianna, Beatriz Magaloni, and Eric Magar. 2011. "Legalist vs. Interpretivist: The Supreme Court and the Democratic Transition in Mexico." In *Courts in Latin America,* edited by Gretchen Helmke and Julio Ríos-Figueroa, 187–218. New York: Cambridge University Press.

Schor, Miguel. 2009. "An Essay on the Emergence of Constitutional Courts: The Cases of Mexico and Colombia." *Indiana Journal of Global Legal Studies* 16 (1): 173–94.

Scribner, Druscilla L. 2004. "Limiting Presidential Power: Supreme Court— Executive Relations in Argentina and Chile." Ph.D. diss., University of California, San Diego.

———. 2010. "The Judicialization of (Separation of Powers) Politics: Lessons from Chile." *Journal of Politics in Latin America* 2 (3): 71–97.

———. 2011. "Courts, Power and Rights in Argentina and Chile." In *Courts in Latin America,* edited by Gretchen Helmke and Julio Ríos-Figueroa, 248–77. New York: Cambridge University Press.

Seawright, Jason, and John Gerring. 2008. "Case Selection Techniques in Case Study Research: A Menu of Qualitative and Quantitative Options." *Political Research Quarterly* 61 (2): 294–308.

Segal, Jeffrey, and Harold Spaeth. 2002. *The Supreme Court and the Attitudinal Model Revisited.* Cambridge: Cambridge University Press.

Shapiro, Martin. 1989. "Courts in Authoritarian Regimes." In *Rule by Law: The Politics of Courts in Authoritarian Regimes,* edited by Tom Ginsburg and Tamir Moustafa, 326–35. Cambridge: Cambridge University Press.

———. 2004. "Judicial Review in Developed Democracies." In *Democratization and the Judiciary The Accountability Function of Courts in New Democracies,* edited by Siri Gloppen, Roberto Gargarella, and Elin Skaar, 7–26. London: Frank Cass.

Shipan, Charles. 1997. *Designing Judicial Review: Interest Groups, Congress, and Communications Policy.* Ann Arbor: University of Michigan Press.

Sikkink, Katherine. 2008. "La cascada de justicia y el impacto de los juicios de derechos humanos en América Latina." *Cuadernos del CLAEH* 31 (96–97): 15–40.

Silveira e Silva, Rafael, and Álvaro P. S. Costa Júnior. 2011. "Judiciário e política regulatória: instituições e preferências sob a ótica dos custos de transação." *Brazilian Journal of Political Economy* 31 (4): 659–79.

Skaar, Elin. 2013. "Wavering Courts: From Impunity to Accountability in Uruguay." *Journal of Latin American Studies* 45 (3): 483–512.

Smirnov, Oleg, and Charles Anthony Smith. 2013. "Drift, Draft, or Drag How U.S. Supreme Court Justices React to New Members." *Justice System Journal* 34 (2): 228–45.

Smith, Anthony, and Mark Farrales. 2010. "Court Reform in Transitional States Chile and the Philippines." *Journal of International Relations and Development* 13 (2): 163–93.

Staton, Jeffrey K. 2010. *Judicial Power and Strategic Communication in Mexico.* Cambridge: Cambridge University Press.

Staton, Jeffrey K., and Georg Vanberg. 2008. "The Value of Vagueness Delegation, Defiance, and Judicial Opinions." *American Journal of Political Science* 52 (3): 504–19.

Stone Sweet, Alec. 1992. *The Birth of Judicial Politics in France: The Constitutional Council in Comparative Perspective.* Oxford: Oxford University Press.

Tamanaha, Brian. 2009. *Beyond the Formalist-Realist Divide: The Role of Politics in Judging.* Princeton: Princeton University Press.

Taylor, Matthew M. 2008. *Judging Policy Courts and Policy Reform in Democratic Brazil.* Stanford: Stanford University Press.

———. 2014. "The Limits of Judicial Independence: A Model with Illustration from Venezuela under Chavez." *Journal of Latin American Studies* 46 (2): 229–59.

Taylor, Matthew M., and Luciano Da Ros. 2008. "Political Parties in and out of Power in Brazil: Judicialization as a Contingent Result of Political Strategy." *Dados: Revista de Ciencias Sociais* 51 (4): 825–64.

Tiede, Lydia. 2016. "The Political Determinants of Judicial Dissent Evidence from the Chilean Constitutional Tribunal." *European Political Science Review* 8 (3): 377–403.

———. 2020. "Mixed Judicial Selection and Constitutional Review." *Comparative Political Studies* 53 (7): 1092–123.

Tiede, Lydia, and Aldo Ponce. 2014. "Evaluating Theories of Decision-making on the Peruvian Constitutional Tribunal." *Journal of Politics in Latin America* 6 (2): 134–64.

Vanberg, Georg. 2001. "Legislative-Judicial Relations: A Game-Theoretic Approach to Constitutional Review." *American Journal of Political Science* 45 (2): 346–61.

———. 2015. "Constitutional Courts in Comparative Perspective: A Theoretical Assessment." *Annual Review of Political Science* 18: 167–85.

Wilson, Bruce. 2007. "Claiming Individual Rights through a Constitutional Court: The Example of Gays in Costa Rica." *International Journal of Constitutional Law* 5 (2): 242–57.

———. 2009. "Institutional Reform and Rights Revolutions in Latin America: The Cases of Costa Rica and Colombia." *Journal of Politics in Latin America* 1 (2): 59–85.

Wilson, Bruce, and Juan C. Rodríguez Cordero. 2006. "Legal Opportunity Structures and Social Movements: The Effects of Institutional Change on Costa Rican Politics." *Comparative Political Studies* 39 (3): 325–51.

Zamora, Stephen and José Ramón Cossío. 2006. "Mexican Constitutionalism after Presidencialismo." *International Journal of Constitutional Law* 4 (2): 411–37.

Judicial Behavior Research in East Asia

CHIEN-CHIH LIN AND TOM GINSBURG

R ECENT DECADES have witnessed the emergence of a growing literature dealing with judicial behavior on high courts in East and Southeast Asia (Dressel 2012, 2014; Liu and Wang 2015; and Dressel, Sanchez-Urribarri, and Stroh 2017). This literature, however, is still incomplete, both in terms of breadth and depth. First, most contributions have focused on a small number of jurisdictions, in particular Japan, the Four Asian Tigers (South Korea, Taiwan, Hong Kong, and Singapore), and China. Other countries in the region, such as Mongolia, Indonesia, and Vietnam, to name just a few, have received only scant attention. This pattern is in part due to the fact that court data in developed countries is more accessible, but it also reflects scholarly attention. Of course, these two factors are interrelated. Second, much of the literature is descriptive, rather than empirical, in character. It is fair to say that empirical legal studies in this region are emerging but there is still much room for improvement.

Two major factors explain the dearth of empirical legal studies in this region. One is the lack of training of researchers. As mentioned above, data are more available in developed countries, such as Japan, Korea, and Taiwan. These are all civil law jurisdictions in which law professors generally lack statistical training and expertise. In other words, they are not able to conduct empirical legal studies independently, even if (and this is a big if) they are actually interested in the approach. This situation is gradually changing, and many law professors are collaborating with either social scientists or statisticians. At Institutum Iurisprudentiae, Academia Sinica in Taiwan (where one of the authors researches), for example, some faculty have started to work with statisticians and economists in other departments. And they are certainly not alone. This interdisciplinary collaboration may bring about more—and better—empirical legal studies in the near future. A related barrier, and it is a major one, is the methodological conservatism of many legal academies in the region, who suffer from the traditional civilian formalism and hostility to outside perspectives. If lack of attention is the first major barrier, the second is the availability of data, which is a general challenge not only in this region but also around the globe and will be discussed in detail below.

Our mandate in this essay is to examine, among other things, the gaps and challenges to empirical legal research in East and Southeast Asia, as well as unresolved theoretical puzzles and methodological issues. These questions are all intertwined and should be analyzed together. The most crucial methodological challenge for empirical legal studies in this area is quite obvious and can be summarized in one sentence: it's all about the data. Specifically, there are at least five reasons that contribute to data being unavailable or unusable in East and Southeast Asia. First, language matters. In countries where English is not the working language of the judiciary, the data are sometimes simply unavailable or incomplete. More often than not, only the constitutional courts, such as the Korean Constitutional Court and Taiwan Constitutional Court, which have lighter workloads, will translate their decisions into English. Even the Korean Constitutional Court, which has been a global leader in promoting dialog with other jurisdictions, translates it decisions only selectively, and frequently in abstract form only. This of course spawns selection problems when doing empirical legal research. The Taiwan Constitutional Court seems to be the only constitutional court in Asia that translates all of its decisions into English, but it has its own problem: on many issues, its rulings are too scarce to generate meaningful empirical findings. It only delivers fifteen decisions per year on average. Consequently, the result of empirical studies is usually unsatisfactory because the standard deviation is so large as to render questionable any findings or inferences. This happens not only in the study of Taiwan Constitutional Court but also in other apex courts that do not produce many decisions. By contrast, the supreme courts, such as the Japanese Supreme Court, which issues more than ten thousand decisions a year, do not translate their decisions into English. Therefore, no empirical legal studies can be done unless researchers speak Japanese. In short, there is a tradeoff here between data availability and scale of court activity.

Second, the institutional design of the judiciary in many Asian jurisdictions is different from that in the United States, which often makes the methodologies prevalent in US academia unreplicable or unsuitable in East and Southeast Asia. Specifically, many constitutional courts do not identify the votes of justices in each case, and the decisions are always signed by all sitting justices, even if some justices issue their dissenting opinions. This makes the Martin-Quinn score, to take one example of a mainstream approach in the United States, difficult to replicate in the Asian context. Moreover, judges are not allowed to have party membership in many countries, and the nominating mechanism does not usually follow the American model. These facts make studies on measuring judicial ideology difficult if not impossible. In East and Southeast Asia, moreover, no justice enjoys life tenure, as do the justices of the SCOTUS. As a corollary, it is not very meaningful to evaluate the ideological drift, if any, of each justice. In addition, the style of opinion writing is different from that in the United States. Judicial decisions, particularly majority opinions, usually have no citations and therefore do not explicitly cite foreign or transnational (case) laws. Hence, it is difficult for researchers to study whether and to what extent judicial dialog takes place in domestic courts. Finally, these institutional discrepancies have troubled empirical legal scholars in this region in another subtler sense. Specifically, because most empirical legal studies center in on the American judiciary, research design that is different from the American mainstream practice often requires additional justification. For example, to avoid the accusation of running kitchen-sink regressions, empirical legal scholars in Asia may need to do more to convince their American colleagues and reviewers that the independent variables they choose to control are indeed theory-driven and not the result of data-torturing, at least in local contexts. On the other hand, variables important or intriguing to Western scholars may not be equally consequential in Asia. Empirical legal scholars usually need more effort to justify their choices whether to include certain variables, and the debate can sometimes be an uphill struggle. These contextual nuances are more likely to be neglected in quantitative empirical legal studies, given their "more scientific" façade.

Third, media coverage of the judiciary, even the top courts, is not common in this region. This applies to both the court decisions and the judges, including the candidates of top courts. This leads to at least two problems: it is hard to measure the salience of court decisions because, be they important or not, they receive equally scant attention most of the time; it also makes the Segal-Cover score unlikely to be replicated in the Asian contexts because not many laypeople care about the candidates of top courts, even of the supreme courts. The situation is worse when it comes to lower courts. In the United States, many empirical studies focus on the circuit courts in addition to the Supreme Court. In Asia, it is simply unthinkable to measure the ideology of lower courts, partly because they are perceived as faceless judicial bureaucrats, and their decisions rarely attract media attention. Another related issue is that many Asian jurisdictions are either third-wave young democracies or semi-authoritarians regimes. That is, the freedom of expression should not be taken for granted and bans or limitations on newspapers or media have been commonplace in this region for decades. This makes information hard to come by and renders some empirical research methods unworkable, at least within a certain time span.

Fourth, and relatedly, the influence of legal family, or legal culture, increases the difficulty of empirical legal studies in Asia. Many countries here are civil law jurisdictions where the consensual norm still prevails. Therefore, it is thorny to evaluate how consensual or dissensual a constitutional court is because justices simply do not publish their separate opinions. Some countries prohibit them from doing so even if they want to. Furthermore, based on our discussions with some justices in Taiwan, they may label as concurring opinions some that are essentially dissenting because of norms of consensus, trying to maintain the façade of a cooperative and consensual court. Undoubtedly this not only skews the results of empirical research but makes empirical legal study as a research method less interesting in the eyes of domestic readers—the most important phenomenon are sometimes hard to observe. When it comes to supreme courts, the situation is worse because they are, in the region, usually seen as similar to bureaucrats. A related problem is that the region is very diverse in terms of legal heritage: there are former Dutch, French, British, Spanish, and Japanese colonies in the region, each with distinct legal histories that make it hard to conduct meaningful cross-country work of the type that might be possible in, say, Latin America.

Additionally, as alluded to above, legal culture also affects the training of legal scholars. Although the line is gradually becoming blurred, law professors in civil law jurisdictions tend to be more doctrinal and less interdisciplinary. Perhaps due to this, academic interests also differ. Empirical legal study is not as popular or even accepted as it is in Western academia. Empirical legal scholars in East Asia usually have to justify their methodologies to their domestic colleagues who doubt or do not appreciate empirical legal studies. This skepticism may be attributed to a plethora of subjective and objective reasons identified above, such as training, institutional differences, and data availability. Whatever the real reasons are, those who are more senior (i.e., more established and control more resources) tend to be less open-minded toward empirical legal studies. In East Asia, where seniority is a strongly felt norm, this can sometimes be very discouraging to young empirical legal scholars, particularly when they are pursuing grants, promotions, or other forms of recognition. It is also imaginable that even publication can sometimes be arduous simply because there is no qualified peer to do peer review. Ironically, lawyers outside academia, such as judges and advocates, may put more emphasis and pay closer attention to the empirical findings, which can be helpful to them during the decision-making process.

The final problem involves the empirical study in authoritarian regimes in general and in China in particular, since China has attracted so much scholarly attention. It is true that about half of judicial decisions in China are available online nowadays (in Chinese, of course, so the aforementioned language issue continues to be a problem), but the data in China are usually, if not always, selectively published by the government, which makes empirical legal studies on Chinese courts unreliable. As has sometimes been observed, "there are lies, damned lies, and Chinese statistics." To solve this issue, therefore, many empirical legal studies in China either rely on qualitative approaches, such as interviews, or leverage internal relationships or networks (*guanxi*) with the bureaucratic system (He and Ng 2017). That is, such research cannot be done by "outsiders" in whom the Chinese bureaucrats or politicians have no trust.

All the aforementioned difficulties force researchers either to find proxies for variables or to devise creative research designs. Some draw on mixed methods, combining interviews with statistical data; others rely on separate opinions as proxies for judicial votes to measure political ideology. Given that it is not realistic to expect that governments in this region will disclose more data in the near future, one practical way forward for researchers is to produce data themselves. Methods such as cross-national surveys would be feasible to produce useful data for national or comparative studies. For scholars acquainted with survey methods, designing questions applicable to different countries is difficult, though not impossible. The survey data could provide reasonable baselines for comparison across nations. Indeed, due to the diverse institutional contexts in this region, cross-national statistical comparison may be of little help for understanding judicial behavior in Asia. Nevertheless, Qualitative Comparative Analysis (QCA), Comparative Sequential Methods, and Process Tracing may solve the methodological predicament to some extent (Bennett and Checkel 2014; Ragin 2014; Thelen and Mahoney

2015). This is not to say qualitative methods are the only pertinent way to study judicial behavior in Asia. In fact, there are some quantitative empirical legal studies of high quality in this region (e.g. Chang et al. 2015), but many of them focus on lower courts and practitioners rather than apex courts, partly because of concerns about sample size.

Where We Are

Given the difficulties mentioned above, empirical studies on judicial behavior in Asia can be roughly divided into two categories with different emphases on theoretical traditions, research puzzles, and research methods: comparative politics and behaviorism. Roughly speaking, these two categories are correlated with the political system of the jurisdictions studied. Research on democratic countries tends to be done in a behaviorist fashion because data are relatively more available, while studies of authoritarian regimes tend to concentrate on paradigms from comparative law and politics. The comparative politics studies focus on the power relations between the judicial branch and other branches of the government, and they tend to study the court as a whole rather than individual judges. Most of the time, research questions can be stated as follows: "What is the role of court in the political process, such as democratization, recession of democracy or implementation of policies?" (Dressel 2014; Ginsburg 2003), or "Why would authoritarian regimes build somewhat independent courts, and to what extent the court can resist the pressure from authoritarian regimes?" (Ginsburg and Moustafa 2008).

These two categories have put emphases on divergent topics, though the line is sometimes blurred. Specifically, one of the major themes in comparative law and politics is the judicialization of politics. This might be attributed to the fact that regardless of regime type, courts are more involved in political cases nowadays than they were decades ago (Dressel 2012). Researchers under authoritarian regimes, by and large, rely on interview, survey, and archival data, that is to say, qualitative techniques to answer the research questions. The reason why most researchers rely on qualitative data can be attributed to the availability of data. In authoritarian regimes, data on judicial behavior of individual judges are few and far between and the decisions of the court are at best partially disclosed, as mentioned above. Given these inimical conditions, constructing and corroborating a behavioral model is not feasible under authoritarian regimes. This is not to say that all research in this school utilizes only qualitative methods; as we will discuss in the later sections, some meticulous quantitative research has been done. But, as alluded to in the label, "comparative politics approach," this approach stems from studies on democratization and authoritarian regimes and therefore focuses on the roles judges in the broader system. With so many hybrid regimes and new democracies in Asia, it is not unusual for the field of judicial politics is rooted in comparative politics.

While the comparative law and politics approach focuses on the court as an actor, judicial behaviorism centers on the strategic behavior of individual judges. Judicial behaviorism research tackles questions like "Does X factor have an impact on the decisions of judges?" This school relies heavily on quantitative methods, employing the cutting-edge statistical models and measurement techniques. And these studies have a tradition in law and economics, predicated on rational choice theory, namely, the assumption that judges have personal preferences (including ideological and others) and will act strategically to achieve their preferences. The past two decades have witnessed a surge in complicated modeling of judicial behavior thanks to the increasing computational capacity. Growing literatures have employed Item Response Theory to gauge the ideal point of judges all over the world (Martin and Quinn 2002) and Asian countries are no exceptions. For example, Dalla Pellegrina, Garoupa, and Lin (2012) and Dalla Pellegrina, Escresa, and Garoupa (2014) have used the technique to measure the ideological inclination of judges in Taiwan and the Philippines. No doubt there are other studies in the works using similar methods. Finally, with the increasing popularity of content analysis, students of judicial behavior have applied this method, trying to identify the confidential authors of majority opinions. Again, this question is meaningful outside the United States because the majority opinions in some Asian jurisdictions are signed by all participating justices, including those who dissent.

In the following paragraphs, we shall briefly introduce the developments of empirical legal studies in East Asia, with an eye to providing a broad overview rather than a detailed discussion.

East Asia, Excluding China

Since the late 1980s, many East Asian countries have undergone processes of democratization. Ginsburg (2003) traces the role of constitutional courts in the region's new democracies. Studying Taiwan, Mongolia, and South Korea, Ginsburg focuses on the political situation at the time of constitution-drafting as a key component of structuring judicial power. While the book's contribution is theoretical, he also uses a mixed-methods approach to understand constitutional courts in Northeast Asia. Other studies in this vein examine "the judicialization of politics." As Dressel (2012) and his contributors show in an edited volume, high courts and constitutional courts in Asia have engaged in high politics as well as daily policy-making. Additionally, Yap (2017) documents the court's intervention in election politics in different types of regimes and how party system constrains the court's capacity. All these studies attend to the relationship between judicial institutions and political actors.

A major line of work has come from the efforts of Ramseyer (sometimes with coauthors) on Japan. Ramseyer and Rasmusen (2010) focus on the influence of specific variables, such as anti-government judicial opinions or tacit political affiliation, on the career of judges in Japan. In this pioneering book on Japan's judicial politics, the authors find that political affiliation and judicial opinions do impact the career of judges. Those who write opinions against the Liberal Democratic Party or who affiliate with Communist Party tend to struggle on the career path. This result is not surprising for those who are familiar with Japan, where state corporatism still holds sway. After pointing out that politicians would meddle in the judiciary by rewarding judges who align with the government and punishing those who challenge the ruling party, the authors then propose a party alternation theory of judicial independence.

In another article, Ramseyer collects the opinions from two hundred murder cases, involving 440 judges. He finds out that, generally, collegiality does not influence the outcome of cases among all judges; however, judges who are alumni of elite schools, who pass the entrance exam within two years of graduation, and who start their careers at Tokyo District Court, are less likely to hand down the death penalty. The author contends that whether the panels include a majority of elite judges determines the probability of death penalty in Japanese court (Ramseyer 2012, 393–94).

Finally, Hatsuru Morita and Manabu Matsunaka have explored how the career judge system in Japan influences court decisions. Employing Fisher's exact test, they find that Japanese judges are biased toward case-handling efficiency because of the heavy workload (Morita and Matsunaka 2020, 157).

Garoupa, Grembi, and Lin (2011) also use a regression model to see whether the voting behavior of constitutional court justices in Taiwan is affected by their nominating presidents. In their data set, the authors coded the characteristics of ninety-seven important decisions from 1988 to 2008, using dissenting opinions and the outcome of the decisions as proxies for political ideology. However, the coefficient of the regression model seems to contradict the theoretical prediction. They contend that the impact of the presidents is statistically insignificant. As a result, the authors come to a conclusion that the attitudinal model is not strongly supported in the case of Taiwan. This article contends that during the transition period, the court was eager to build its reputation as independent and therefore chose to stand against the ruling KMT, despite the fact that most of the justices are appointed by KMT presidents.

Also focusing on Taiwan Constitutional Court, Dalla Pellegrina, Garoupa, and Lin (2012) examine 101 decisions from 1988 to 2009, utilizing item response theory to model the latent variable—namely, ideology of justices—and reporting the result of estimated ideal points. The method is exactly the same as Martin and Quinn (2002). When studying jurisdictions other than America, one serious methodological concern emerges for the use of Martin-Quinn scores: it relies on the observation of voting behavior of judges, which is not always available in other jurisdictions. Taiwan's constitutional court, for example, does not disclose the votes of individual justices; hence, the best data available to researchers is the presence of concurring and dissenting opinions. This data restriction renders the result vague at best, with the standard deviation so large that it makes most of the estimated ideal points among justices indistinguishable.

Chang (2013; see also Law and Chang 2011) takes on the question of citations in the constitutional court decisions. Through a plenary and encompassing survey of constitutional court decisions from 1948 to 2010, Chang reports that most direct citations of foreign legal sources are found in separate opinions but not in the holdings and reasoning. Employing multivariate logistic models, she argues that the background of judges (career judge or academia), the type of case (civil rights or separation of power cases), and the type of opinion (concurring or dissenting) can explain the variance of whether there is citation of foreign sources in an opinion. Not surprisingly, those who study in Germany are prone to cite German legal sources while those who study in the United States are more likely to cite American legal sources.

Yeh (2013) focuses on one specific category of constitutional decision in Taiwan: delayed declarations of invalidity. Employing descriptive statistical analysis, Yeh argues that the judicial practice of issuing deadline was originally to nudge the administrative and legislative branches to comply with the decisions. Later on, the judicial deadline served as a buffer between judicial power and legislative or executive power, relaxing the tension among these branches.

Taiwan Constitutional Court is one of the most studied top courts in this region. This may be attributed to the fact that it has translated all its decisions into English and that the appointment mechanism now follows the American model in which the president nominates and the congress approves the justices. Nevertheless, the small size of the court's docket and the non-disclosure of judicial votes continue to be obstacles for empirical legal studies. Fortunately, the Institutum Iurisprudentiae, Academia Sinica, has recently established a data set that includes more than 670 decisions (from Interpretation No. 80 to No. 750) and the characteristics of all the justices since the second term. Moreover, the judicial votes of the justices may no longer be secret after the revision of the Constitutional Interpretation Procedure Act in 2018. In the future, the author of the majority opinion will be identified and the quorum for passing a constitutional interpretation will be reduced from two-thirds of participating justices to a simple majority, with an eye to enhancing judicial transparency and efficiency. While the first reform may provide opportunities to enhance the study of judicial ideology for specific judges, the latter reform may be even more important for facilitating research on judicial behavior because, ceteris paribus, the Taiwan Constitutional Court will be more productive, which will directly increase the sample size.

China

As stated by Liu and Wang (2015), most empirical legal studies on China disproportionately center on the behavior of lawyers and layman. That is because few judicial opinions and records were available to the public in the past, and official data are only selectively provided by the government today. As a result, most researchers rely on archival methods, interviews, or ethnography to study the judicial system in China. He Xin, working alone and with Kwai Ng, is a leading figure here, as he has pursued careful interview-based studies that have illuminated the motives and orientation of Chinese judges (He and Ng 2017).

Despite methodological obstacles, most studies of the Chinese judiciary endeavor to explore one simple yet fundamental question: why, and to what extent, would the party-state build and tolerate judicial independence. Peerenboom (2002) argues that the judiciary as a whole in China serves as an institution for the central government to monitor the provincial governments, and the rule-of-law rhetoric has become the new source of legitimacy for Chinese Communist Party regime in addition to economic blossom. While Peerenboom (2002) provides an endogenous motivation for judicial reform in China, Wang (2014) provides a "demand-side theory," focusing on the demand of rule of law from foreign investment. Utilizing survey and panel data, he contends that because foreign companies are less likely to build crony relationships with local governments, competitive and efficient courts are built-in responses to the demand of foreign companies that will not invest unless the local governments provide a fair playing field. The author develops the argument step by step. First, he demonstrates that the foreign companies are not as good at building informal relationships with state officials as their Chinese counterparts; hence, there are incentives for foreign companies to demand competitive and fair courts to level the playing field. He then argues that the local government would invest in judicial quality and capacity in places where tax revenues from foreign direct investment constitute a substantial part of local incomes. Through a meticulously devised research design, Wang validates his demand-side theory of the authoritarian rule of law.

Another main theme of empirical legal studies in China is the entanglement of the CCP, the executive branch, and the judiciary (Liu and Halliday 2016; Wang 2014). From the standpoint of criminal defense lawyers, Liu and Halliday (2016) argue that the coordination among the "iron triangle"—police, prosecutors, and courts—makes it difficult if not impossible for lawyers to argue innocence. Hence only lawyers who have personal relationships with the iron triangle have a real chance to win. Ng and He (2017), on the other hand, contend from the perspective of courts that the judiciary is not only politically, but also economically and socially, embedded in the Chinese context. This means that judicial decision-making is determined not so much by the preferences of judges as by the political, economic, and social contexts in which they operate.

Despite the differences of methods and data, studies on courts in China by and large fall in what we have called the comparative law and politics camp. They seek to provide a comprehensive account of judicial landscape in China rather than approach a specific hypothesis with discrete data. Apparently, the prime impediment of studying China is the accessibility and availability of data. While most China studies scholars prefer qualitative data, such as interviews, to yearbook statistics, it is hard (and getting harder) to build rapport with state officials under the currently suffocating political atmosphere. As a result, empirical studies of Chinese courts may remain largely qualitative in nature for the immediate future. However, it is also the case that the courts are enhancing their capacity under the current regime, which means data quality may rise even if availability remains uncertain.

Southeast Asia

The main theme of studies on courts in Southeast Asia is similar to that in China, since most of the Southeast Asian countries are administered by hybrid or authoritarian regimes (Levitsky and Way 2010). The edited volume of Dressel (2012) provides an overview of judicial politics in Southeast Asia. In a later study, Dressel (2014) proposes that we can understand judicial politics in Asia as involving two dimensions: the degree of judicial involvement in politics and judicial independence. In Southeast Asian countries, where judicial independence is relatively low, it is not surprising that most studies are interested in discovering how the executive branch encroaches upon the judiciary. Through anecdotal and case studies, Dressel (2010) argues that the low judicial independence and high judicial intervention in Thailand have made it a case of politicization of the judiciary. Butt (2012) contends that the limited scope of constitutional review in Indonesia results in an active yet fragmented liberalism in the judiciary.

The bulk of studies in this subregion focus on the case of Singapore, which forms a kind of ideal type of an authoritarian regime with the rule of law. The low levels of judicial independence, low levels of judicial activism, and the repressiveness of the courts in this city-state, combined with high-quality dispute resolution in commercial matters, is characterized as "authoritarian rule of law" or "judicial muteness" (Dressel 2014; Rajah 2012). Rajah (2012) documents how the People's Action Party, the ruling party in Singapore for over fifty years, actively reconfigures the content of rule of law through the promise of economic prosperity and a rigorous observance of legal procedure. With descriptive statistics, Chua and Haynie (2016) argue that, at best, the Singaporean courts are guardians of the political status quo. They also show that the Singaporean courts are more willing to grant relief to cases involving economic interests and to dismiss cases of civil rights on procedural grounds. This evidence validates the claims by the authors and confirms the theory of authoritarian courts as offering credible commitments in the economic sphere (Moustafa 2014).

Yihan Goh and Paul Tan (2011) provide a wide and encompassing account of Singaporean law, focusing primarily on the citation of legal sources in the high court and court of appeal. Through descriptive statistics, the authors find that the citations of foreign as well as domestic cases have increased dramatically since the 1990s, and the ratio of domestic to foreign cases cited has also risen since then. The breakdown of the data suggests that criminal cases rely mostly on local sources while commercial cases preponderantly cite foreign cases. The authors then draw a conclusion that courts in Singapore have gradually gained independence (from the Commonwealth System) and have become localized in the last decades. Relatedly, Cheah Wei Ling and Yihan Goh (2017) evaluate the judicial citation of academic work in Singaporean Court of Appeal. Drawing on descriptive statistics, the authors demonstrate a substantial growth of average citation per decision since 2000. Further breaking down the data, the authors identify some trends in citation behavior: citations take place more frequently in emerging and developing subject areas (commerce law), textbooks among other types of sources are most cited, and judges' qualification does not affect the citation behavior.

In terms of judicial behavior of individual judges, there are relatively few studies. Escresa and Garoupa (2013) test the Helmke (2002) hypothesis of strategic defection, which states that judges become more likely to defect from the interest of their appointers as their term ends. Despite some anecdotal evidence during some periods, there is no robust evidence corroborating the model in the Philippine context. The follow-up study by Dalla Pellegrina, Escresa, and Garoupa (2014) utilizes item response theory to measure the ideological ideal points of Filipino judges on the bench and makes further inferences with estimated ideal points. Unsurprisingly, the authors found out that those who are appointed by the sitting president turn out to be more favorable to the current government. However, their estimation of ideal points is unsatisfactory: the standard deviation is so large that it renders further inferential statistics questionable. Similar to Dalla Pellegrina, Garoupa, and Lin's (2012) study on Taiwan Constitutional Court, other studies on the Philippines also suffer from the weakness of unsatisfactory standard deviations. Finally, Pruksacholavit and Garoupa (2016) focus on dissenting behavior in the Constitutional Court of Thailand. Relying on data comprised of decisions from 2008 to 2014, the authors contend that, while the legalist model would predict few dissenting votes cast under a civil law system, the result nevertheless suggests otherwise, with dissents in many cases. Pro-administration decisions under democratic government are more likely to elicit dissenting vote, and pro-constitutionality decisions are less likely to have dissenting opinions. This result is supportive of neither the legalist nor attitudinal model. Instead, the authors conclude, it indicates that the judges act strategically, observe the political climate, and act according to the political atmosphere.

Where to Go

As we can see from the previous sections, empirical studies are still an inchoate subfield within Asian law, with most of the studies published only in the past two decades. One of the promising areas for empirical legal studies in Asia is to find out whether, and to what extent, the results and methodologies developed in the American context can be applied in East Asia. We will first discuss this issue before suggesting further directions more grounded in local tradition.

One potentially inspiring subfield is the measurement of political ideology of the courts. As mentioned above, this topic has received scant scholarly attention, partly because of the difficulties just laid out, and partly because scholars lack the expertise to do empirical legal studies. It is certainly an under-studied approach in Asia and deserves more attention. To illustrate, one might expect that judges without life tenure would be more deferential to the executive branch. Are judges in East Asia less ideological, compared with their American counterparts, given that judges in East Asian countries generally have less power and job security?

Note that some scholars from the comparative politics tradition have argued that the attitudinal model, utilized by many researchers from the judicial behaviorism school, cannot explain informal institutions in the judiciary, especially the interwoven relationship between judges and the political institutions (Dressel, Sanchez-Urribarri, and Stroh 2017); hence, they provide a relational perspective and propose social network analysis as an alternative to regression models. Others go even further to accuse the attitudinal model of systematically neglecting the nuanced difference in political, historical, and social contexts, which will lead to different, sometimes opposite, results.

In the United States, political ideology is the critical independent variable that draws scholarly attention. In many Asian countries, professional background may be more important in studies of constitutional courts. Because of strong corporate identities in different branches of careerist legal systems, the prior occupations of constitutional judges may provide them with certain epistemic patterns as well as interests, and provide them with networks that can both advance careers and demand reciprocal action. For instance, a constitutional court justice who sat on the supreme court before appointment may be reluctant to offend former colleagues by striking down their decisions in concrete judicial review. Similarly, justices who are former scholars may pay more attention to the responses of academia to decisions, particularly when they have no life tenure. Geographic origins, too, might be an important determinant of behavior in some countries.

In addition, there are other theoretical and methodological challenges regarding empirical studies in this area. For example, studies have shown that notwithstanding the executive efforts to curb or co-opt the judiciary in authoritarian regimes, judges may still sometimes disobey the executive branch; yet the dynamics that produce such off-equilibrium outcomes remain unclear. Even in democratic countries, the institutional design of courts is different from that of the United States, where theories of judicial behavior have been built. Moreover, some crucial questions in this region, such as the conformity of the executive branch to judicial decisions, the impact of high courts on legal consciousness, and the influence of media on high court decision-making, remain unanswered. This makes Asia an ideal environment for the development of new approaches to extend our theories of judicial behavior.

Conclusion

In this essay, we have briefly introduced the current state of empirical legal studies in East and Southeast Asia and identified several difficulties scholars face in this region. On the one hand, empirical legal studies are certainly booming in this region; on the other, those institutional and cultural barriers that obstruct the blossoming of empirical legal studies are not likely to disappear in the near future. Given this environment, we suggest that empirical legal scholars in this region ought to consider asking different questions. To be more specific, instead of trying to replicate studies and ask the questions that have been formulated in the United States, empirical legal scholars in this region should formulate different questions, informed by the different institutional design of the judiciaries in their countries. To be sure, questions that have been asked in the United States may still be worthy of exploration, as results may differ across different jurisdictions. Nevertheless, given that institutional and informational hurdles are hard to overcome, and given the interesting dynamics that may result from different institutional design, asking new questions may further enrich our understanding of judicial behavior. For instance, whether justices' prior occupations affect judicial behavior is a question that is not frequently debated in contemporary American context because the SCOTUS is highly homogeneous in this regard (eight out of nine current justices were federal judges before appointment). It is plausible that justices who were advocates or law professors will bring with them to the bench different ideologies and legal philosophies. From this perspective, the different institutional design should be a boon to empirical legal scholars in this region, with implications beyond it.

References

Bennett, A., and J. T. Checkel. 2014. *Process Tracing: From Metaphor to Analytic Tool.* Cambridge: Cambridge University Press.

Butt, S. 2012. "Indonesia's Constitutional Court: Conservative Activist or Strategic Operator?" In *The Judicialization of Politics in Asia*, edited by B. Dressel, 98–116. London: Routledge.

Chang, W. 2013. "An Empirical Study on the Reference of Foreign Laws and Precedents by Constitutional Court Interpretations." In *Empirical Studies of Judicial Systems 2011*, edited by Yun-Chien Chang, 33–83. Taipei: Academia Sinica.

Chang, Y., T. Eisenberg, H. Ho, and M. T. Wells. 2015. "Pain and Suffering Damages in Wrongful Death Cases: An Empirical Study." *Journal of Empirical Legal Studies* 12 (1): 128–60.

Cheah, W. L., and Y. Goh. 2017. "An Empirical Study on the Singapore Court of Appeal's Citation of Academic Works: Reflections on the Relationship between Singapore's Judiciary and Academia." *Singapore Academy of Law Journal* 29: 75–125.

Chua, L. J., and S. L. Haynie. 2016. "Judicial Review of Executive Power in the Singaporean Context, 1965–2012." *Journal of Law and Courts* 4 (1): 43–64.

Dalla Pellegrina, L., L. Escresa, and N. Garoupa. 2014. "Measuring Judicial Ideal Points in New Democracies: The Case of the Philippines." *Asian Journal of Law and Society* 1 (1): 125–64.

Dalla Pellegrina, L., N. Garoupa, and S. C. Lin. 2012. "Judicial Ideal Points in New Democracies: The Case of Taiwan." *NTU L. Rev.* 7: 123–66.

Dressel, B. 2010. "Judicialization of Politics or Politicization of the Judiciary? Considerations from Recent Events in Thailand." *The Pacific Review* 23 (5): 671–91.

Dressel, B. 2012. *The Judicialization of Politics in Asia.* New York: Routledge.

Dressel, B. 2014. "Governance, Courts and Politics in Asia." *Journal of Contemporary Asia* 44 (2): 259–78.

Dressel, B., R. Sanchez-Urribarri, and A. Stroh. 2017. "The Informal Dimension of Judicial Politics: A Relational Perspective." *Annual Review of Law and Social Science* 13 (1): 413–30.

Escresa, L., and N. Garoupa. 2013. "Testing the Logic of Strategic Defection: The Case of the Philippine Supreme Court—An Empirical Analysis (1986–2010)." *Asian Journal of Political Science* 21 (2): 189–212.

Garoupa, N., V. Grembi, and S. C.-P. Lin. 2011. "Explaining Constitutional Review in New Democracies: The Case of Taiwan." *Pac. Rim L. & Pol'y J.* 20: 1–40.

Ginsburg, T. 2003. *Judicial Review in New Democracies: Constitutional Courts in Asian Cases.* Cambridge: Cambridge University Press.

Ginsburg, T., and T. Moustafa. 2008. *Rule by Law: The Politics of Courts in Authoritarian Regimes.* Cambridge: Cambridge University Press.

Goh, Y., and P. Tan. 2011. "An Empirical Study on Development of Singapore Law." *Singapore Academy of Law Journal* 23: 176.

He, X., and K. Ng. 2017. "'It Must Be Rock Strong!' Guanxi's Impact on Judicial Decision-Making in China." *American Journal of Comparative Law* 65 (4): 841–87.

Helmke, G. 2002. "The Logic of Strategic Defection: Court-Executive Relations in Argentina under Dictatorship and Democracy." *American Political Science Review* 96 (2): 291–303.

Law, D., and W. Chang. 2011. "The Limits of Global Judicial Dialogue." *Washington University Law Review* 86: 523–77.

Levitsky, S., and L. A. Way. 2010. *Competitive Authoritarianism: Hybrid Regimes after the Cold War.* Cambridge: Cambridge University Press.

Liu, S., and T. C. Halliday. 2016. *Criminal Defense in China: The Politics of Lawyers at Work.* Cambridge: Cambridge University Press.

Liu, S., and Z. Wang. 2015. "The Fall and Rise of Law and Social Science in China." *Annual Review of Law and Social Science* 11 (1): 373–94.

Martin, A. D., and K. M. Quinn. 2002. "Dynamic Ideal Point Estimation via Markov Chain Monte Carlo for the US Supreme Court, 1953–1999." *Political Analysis* 10 (2): 134–53.

Morita, H., and M. Matsunaka. 2020. "Career Judge System and Court Decision Biases." In *Selection and Decision in Judicial Process Around the World: Empirical Inquires,* edited by Yun-Chien Chang, 132–59. Cambridge: Cambridge University Press,

Moustafa, T. 2014. "Law and Courts in Authoritarian Regimes." *Annual Review of Law and Social Science* 10 (1): 281–99.

Ng, K. H., and X. He. 2017. *Embedded Courts: Judicial Decision-Making in China.* Cambridge: Cambridge University Press.

Peerenboom, R. 2002. *China's Long March Toward Rule of Law.* Cambridge: Cambridge University Press.

Pruksacholavit, P., and N. Garoupa. 2016. "Patterns of Judicial Behaviour in the Thai Constitutional Court, 2008–2014: An Empirical Approach." *Asia Pacific Law Review* 24 (1): 16–35.

Ragin, C. C. 2014. *The Comparative Method: Moving Beyond Qualitative and Quantitative Strategies*. Sacramento: University of California Press.

Rajah, J. 2012. *Authoritarian Rule of Law: Legislation, Discourse and Legitimacy in Singapore*. Cambridge: Cambridge University Press.

Ramseyer, J. M. 2012. "Who Hangs Whom For What? The Death Penalty in Japan." *Journal of Legal Analysis* 4: 365.

Ramseyer, J. M., and E. B. Rasmusen. 2010. *Measuring Judicial Independence: The Political Economy of Judging in Japan*. University of Chicago Press.

Thelen, K., and J. Mahoney. 2015. "Comparative-Historical Analysis in Contemporary Political Science." In *Advances in Comparative-Historical Analysis*, edited by James Mahoney and Kathleen Thelen, 3–36. Cambridge: Cambridge University Press.

Wang, Y. 2014. *Tying the Autocrat's Hands: The Rise of the Rule of Law in China*. Cambridge: Cambridge University Press.

Yap, P. J. 2017. *Courts and Democracies in Asia*. Cambridge: Cambridge University Press.

Yeh, J. 2013. "The Politics of Unconstitutionality: An Empirical Analysis of Judicial Deadlines and Political Compliance in Taiwan" In *Empirical Studies of Judicial Systems 2011*, edited by Yun-Chien Chang, 1–31. Taipei: Academia Sinica.

What Do We Know about the Middle Eastern Constitutional Courts?

AYLIN AYDIN-CAKIR

THE MIDDLE East is a region that refers to the lands around the southern and eastern side of the Mediterranean Sea and it includes several countries. Although there is not a clear demarcation line that can help us to determine the borders of this region, Turkey, Syria, Iraq, Iran, Lebanon, Israel, State of Palestine, Jordan, Saudi Arabia, the United Arab Emirates, Kuwait, Yemen, Oman, Bahrain, Qatar, and Egypt can be presented as the core Middle Eastern countries. The majority of these countries are Muslim and Arab, and most of them are ruled by authoritarian regimes. The common belief is that under the rule of authoritarian regimes the judiciary is not independent and cannot efficiently control and constrain the executive and ruling elite. In this regard, the constitutional courts are perceived as symbolic institutions. Although this assumption seems quite logical, it is very important to test it against empirical evidence and explain the decision-making processes of the Middle Eastern constitutional courts.

The objective of this essay is to critically review the existing literature on the Middle Eastern constitutional courts and look at the empirical strategies that are used to analyze their judicial behavior. Although the legal systems and structures of constitutional courts differ across the region, analyzing the empirical studies on the Middle Eastern constitutional courts provides a general framework to understand the main problems and opportunities in studying the judicial behavior in other countries with similar political regimes.

The literature review presented in this essay excludes the studies that use qualitative methods or the studies that evolve around theoretical and normative discussions. One should also note that this literature review extensively depends on the studies written in English. It has overlooked the studies written in Arabic and Hebrew, and this is an important limitation. For this reason, looking at this literature review one should not conclude that the constitutional courts in the Middle East are an understudied topic in the legal or political science field. In the Middle Eastern countries, many legal scholars study the structure, jurisdiction, and workings of the constitutional courts, but they do so from a theoretical and normative perspective and publish their studies mostly in their native language.

This essay reviews the empirical studies on the Middle Eastern constitutional courts. The first part presents and evaluates the breadth and scope of the literature from a theoretical and methodological perspective. It discusses the general gaps, unresolved theoretical puzzles, and methodological challenges. The second section of the essay presents possible future research topics. The final section includes a general overview of the literature and offers concluding remarks.

Empirical Explanations for the Judicial Behavior of the Middle Eastern Constitutional Courts

Explaining the judicial behavior of constitutional courts is of great importance not only in the field of legal studies but also in political science. Focusing especially on the behavior of the US Supreme Court, many scholars have tried to empirically explain the decision-making process in the Court. Since the 1990s an increasing number of scholars have tried to study this topic from a comparative perspective, and this has increased the number of empirical studies on Latin American and some European constitutional courts. Yet when it comes to understanding the judicial behavior of the constitutional courts in other parts of the world, we come across a very limited literature. When we focus specifically on the Middle Eastern constitutional courts, we see that only few studies have tried to empirically explain the behavior of these courts, and most of the studies look only at the Egyptian, Turkish, or Israeli constitutional courts.

The Supreme Constitutional Court of Egypt

Compared to the Turkish and Israeli cases, the number of the empirical studies on the Supreme Constitutional Court of Egypt is quite low.

Tamir Moustafa (2007), offers one instance of a quantitative study and uses simple descriptive statistics to explain the assertiveness of the court despite the rule of the authoritarian regime in the country. By looking at the Egyptian Supreme Constitutional Court decisions taken between the years 1980 and 2000, Moustafa (2007) argues that the ruling elite in Egypt has established an independent judiciary that is capable of protecting property rights in order to attract foreign direct investment. This study is very important in terms of challenging the assumption that judicial independence will not exist under authoritarian regimes. It overtly demonstrates the importance of studying judicial behavior in the context of authoritarian regimes. By looking at the percentages of the final decisions where the laws are found unconstitutional, Moustafa (2007) tries to show that despite the authoritarian government, the court has taken decisions against the ruling elite.

The Turkish Constitutional Court

When we look at the literature on the Turkish Constitutional Court (TCC), it is possible to say that until very recently the existing literature has been dominated by qualitative studies arguing that judicial bureaucrats are state-elites and the TCC defends the values and interests of the Kemalist state-elites (Koğacıoğlu 2003, 2004; Özbudun 2010; Shambayati and Kirdiş 2009; Tezcur 2009). Yet, this argument has not been tested with empirical evidence. Coding all TCC abstract review cases between 1984 and 2007, Hazama (2012) has tried to systematically examine whether constitutional review in Turkey is more likely to protect elite interests or to control and constrain the executive branch of government. In order to explain the decision-making process of the court, Hazama (2012) has looked at the identity of the litigants (state-elite versus non-state-elite opposition party) and referral reasons (based on secular-unitary state principles or horizontal accountability). Conducting binary logistic analysis, he has found that the TCC was no more likely to accept unconstitutionality claims by state-elite parties than by non-state-elite parties. Furthermore, he has found the court was more likely to accept unconstitutionality claims of executive wrongdoings than violations of the state-principle. As such, contrary to the assumptions of the previous literature, this empirical analysis showed that the TCC's preferences for horizontal accountability dominate over the desire for hegemonic preservation.

The majority of the existing studies on the TCC have either ignored or not taken into consideration the possible differences between the constitutional court judges. In other words, the scholars were arguing that all TCC judges share similar political preferences, but they had not empirically tested this hypothesis. Creating an original data set by coding all TCC decisions taken between 1984 and 2010, Aydin-Cakir (2018) has tried to empirically explain the judicial behavior of the TCC by considering the ideological preferences of the judges. Using the state-elite president versus non-state-elite president categorization of Hazama (2012), the political preferences of each judge was measured by looking at whether they were appointed by a state-elite president or non-state-elite president. Aydin-Cakir's study seeks to explain whether attitudinal or strategic models better explain the behavior of the TCC, and it finds that the impact of political fragmentation on the court's decisions changes across cases where different judicial preferences are at stake. The empirical results of the study show that the situational characteristics across cases can trigger judges' preferences so that the importance that a court places on a possible reaction from political branches will vary across different types of cases. In other words, Aydin-Cakir (2018) has found that the effect of political fragmentation on judicial behavior decreases when there is a weak political alignment between the court and the enacting government. On the other hand, when the TCC reviews a law that is argued to violate the individual rights principle, the court's tendency to annul such a law is significantly lower compared to those laws that were claimed to violate other constitutional principles. All these findings show that the judiciary will locate its decisions as closely as possible to its preferences but within the space defined by the preferences of the relevant outside actors. In countries where there is a strong external actor—the public or another institution, such as the military—who supports the judiciary, the judges will not fear political retaliation and will defy the incumbent government. Moreover, especially in developing democracies where the protection of individual rights and liberties are not internalized by the public and the political institutions, the political preferences of the courts may not show the considerable impact on the assertiveness of the judiciary.

Although Aydin-Cakir (2018) has tried to delineate the political preference of each judge in order to measure the political affinity between the TCC and the incumbent government at the time each decision was taken, the validity of this measure has certain weaknesses. First, categorizing Turkish presidents as state-elite versus non-state-elite is too simplistic because certain presidents have adopted state-elite orientation although they are categorized as non-state-elite by Hazama (2012).

Second, until the 2017 constitutional amendment, the Turkish Constitution had clearly stated that the president should be neutral and should have no affinity with any political party. Finally, the president has appointed TCC judges from a certain pool of candidates that are selected by lower courts or other institutions. As a result, one can argue that identity or ideology of the president would not be a good proxy to measure the political preferences of TCC judges.

Moral and Tokdemir (2017) solve this problem by measuring the political preferences of judges by looking at their opinions on party closure cases. By focusing on judge-level variation, Moral and Tokdemir (2017) attempt to explain whether and to what extent justices' ideological positions influence the party dissolution decisions of the TCC. In order to measure the justices' ideological positions, the authors use two measures. As the first measure, they use W-NOMINATE ideal point estimates. The W-NOMINATE estimates suggest that the Turkish political space, unlike the issue space of the US Supreme Court, is likely to be two-dimensional. Thus, the authors use two-dimensional W-NOMINATE estimates. The first dimension is the main ideological liberal-conservative dimension and the second one is the activist (anti–status quo)–restrainist (pro–status quo) dimension that explains whether justices, regardless of their political views, adopt an interventionist stance. For the measurement of the two-dimensional ideal point estimates of fifty-four judges who voted in the dissolution cases, Moral and Tokdemir (2017) use 726 judicial review decisions. As a result, the empirical analysis shows that communist, religious, and ethnic parties in Turkey with considerable public support are more likely to be dissolved by justices having an activist and pro–status quo ideological stance.

Although using a two-dimensional measure of the judges' preferences makes sense, the conceptualization of "activism" and "pro–status quo" is subjective and their operationalization is quite problematic because the status quo may change across different ruling governments. For instance, in Turkey what is referred to by the "status quo" has changed considerably in the last ten years. Before the rule of the Justice and Development Party (JDP) that came to power in 2002, status quo referred to the Kemalist and secularist values of the state. Hence, a conservative judge would have probably been against this notion of status quo. Yet under the rule of the JDP government, status quo has become linked with the values supported by the JDP and Recep Tayyip Erdoğan. As such, a conservative judge would most likely want to protect this status quo.

Moreover, although ideal point estimates provide valid measures of the judges' preferences, using the point estimates scores both as a measure of the dependent and independent variables can be problematic. In other words, trying to explain the decision for party closure with a decision in abstract review case might create theoretical and methodological problems. When deciding on any type of constitutional court case, the judges are not only affected by their political ideology but also by the political context or other external and internal (intra-court) factors. Thus, once you measure the independent and dependent variables by using the judges' decisions, you include the explanatory power of the same external and internal factors in both the dependent and independent variables. This may lead to the endogeneity problem in the model. Finally, the ideal point estimation model assumes that the judges' preferences are fixed and do not change over time, but this might not be true for the TCC judges.

Another empirical research study that focuses on the TCC judges' political preference is the article written by Yıldırım, Kutlar, and Gülener (2017). The authors try to empirically analyze the political attitudes of the TCC judges by using dynamic item response methodology (IRT) as a scaling method. The authors create an original database of the TCC decisions taken between 1962 and 1982 and code each judge's preference as liberalist or statist. The ideal point estimations show that for the given time period neither a liberalist nor a statist attitude was dominant for the majority of the TCC judges. In other words, contrary to the commonly held belief, scholars have found that the justices of the TCC did not adopt a strict statist attitude in the examined period. Yıldırım, Kutlar, and Gülener (2017) measure the ideal point estimates of the TCC judges on a single dimension that is liberalist or statist. Yet when we take into consideration the Turkish political space, categorizing the political preferences of the TCC judges on a single dimension would not provide a valid measure. The authors look at the decisions of sixty-seven judges, and that makes in total 5,768 observations that are coded as liberalist or statist. Yet the authors report that 38 percent of these observations are coded as neither statist nor liberalist. This condition reveals that the authors are excluding a considerable number of issues that might reflect an alternative dimension of the political preferences of the judges. Moreover, the scholars define "liberal" as an attitude to protect individual rights and freedoms and "statist" as an attitude to protect the state or public power as opposed to the protection of individual rights. Yet, these two concepts should not be taken as binary opposites. In other words, a person who is quite liberal in social issues might have a statist position in economic issues. Thus, the political preference of the judges might be affected by the issue of the law under review. If the authors had used a multidimensional scale the measurement would have been more precise.

Analyzing the impact of the constitutional reforms on judicial behavior is an important yet under-studied topic in the context of the TCC. Trying to fill this gap, Varol, Dalla Pellegrina, and Garoupa (2017) empirically show whether and to what extent the 2010 constitutional reforms that changed the structure, appointment, and removal processes of the TCC have changed the behavior of the court. They use an original data set of randomly chosen two hundred cases taken between 2007 and 2014. Half of these cases were decided before the reform and half of them were decided afterward. Using item response theory (IRT), the authors attempt to estimate the evolution of each judge's ideology. In order to empirically show whether the constitutional amendments have created a change in the ideological preferences of the judges, the authors use multivariate regression analysis. According to the ideal point estimation, they find a significant break in 2010 in the ideological position of the court and detect a conservative ideological shift following the reforms. Yet this shift does not appear to affect judicial outcomes in a statistically significant manner.

The impact of the judges' gender on their decisions appears as another issue that has been empirically studied in the context of the TCC. Yıldırım and Gülener (2017) analyze whether and to what extent the decisions of women judges differ from men judges. The research shows that there is not any specific gender effect and that women justices do not reveal specific judicial attitudes in their voting patterns. Although simple descriptive statistics show that women judges dissent more, the number of women judges in the TCC is too low to make a correct inference from these findings. In other words, since the establishment of the TCC, out of 127 judges, only 5 were female. This number is statistically insufficient to show the impact of gender on the decision-making process.

Israeli Supreme Court

When we look at the empirical studies on the Israeli Supreme Court (ISC) we see that they either try to explain the key determinants of judicial behavior or understand how the court behaves at times of crises. In this regard, one of the most important studies is the research conducted by Yoav Dotan (1999) where he focuses on the judicial behavior in national security cases and tries to explain whether and to what extent the ISC protects individual rights during episodes of national crisis. The previous qualitative literature has argued that during times of national crisis the court is not willing to intervene in the governmental policies that have violated the liberties of the Palestinian residents (Shamir 1990). Looking at the terror-related cases decided by the ISC between 1986 and 1995, Dotan (1999) compares the percentages of cases decided against the government before, during, and after the Intifada and finds that although during and after the Intifada the number of petitions from the Palestinians to the ISC increased, the rise in the number of cases was not followed by any corresponding decline in the settlement rate for Palestinian petitions. Although Dotan's (1999) study can be defined as an empirical study on the judicial behavior of the ISC, using only descriptive statistics to understand the key determinants of the judicial behavior in different settings weakens reliability of the results.

Another empirical study that aims to explain the judicial behavior of the higher courts at the times of warlike emergencies is the study of Hofnung and Weinshall-Margel (2010). Most of the studies on the Israeli Supreme Court argue that despite using the rhetoric of human rights, the ISC rarely intervenes in security-based decisions targeted to prevent terrorist activity. Accordingly, the authors try to find out whether the ISC will be reluctant to oppose restrictions on civil liberties while reviewing security-based cases. First, the authors categorize the court behavior into three groups: rejection of the petition, latent intervention, and overt intervention. Choosing two hundred terror-related cases decided by the ISC between 2000 and 2008 and looking at the individual opinions of judges for the cases, the authors find that the court makes assertive decisions regarding human rights violations by the state. But this intervention is usually subtle and not easily detected by the public. Going one step further, Hofnung and Weinshall-Margel (2010) try to empirically show whether and to what extent certain external and internal conditions—such as the identity of the litigant, political structure of the incumbent government, occurrence of deadly terror attacks when the decision was taken, and the personal inclination of each justice—affect justices' decisions. Conducting multinomial logistic regression, the authors find that the court's decisions in terror-related cases do take into consideration external political circumstances and that the influence of these factors is significant when deciding between rejection of a petition and overt intervention.

In the literature on the ISC we also see a few studies that focus on the explanatory power of the internal structure of the court. For instance, Sommer (2009) tries to explain the strategic behavior of the ISC at the level of the collegial game. Arguing that the judges' decisions, especially in controversial domains such as national security, state, and religion, might be highly influenced by the decisions of other justices in the court, Sommer (2009) develops a formal model that presents the judges' incentives to act strategically. In another article focusing only on national security cases, Sommer (2010) tests his theoretical framework with empirical analyses. Using an original data set that covers national security cases between 1997 and 2004 and conducting logistic regression, Sommer (2010) finds that the constitutional design, court leadership, ideology of the ruling coalition, litigation by interest groups, and the number of petitioners influence decisions of the ISC on national defense. As a result, the works of Sommer (2009, 2010) do not only enhance the understanding of the collegial game within the ISC but also put judicial decision-making in a context of institutional, ideological, and cultural constraints. In other words, he does not take the influence of internal and external institutions separately but asserts that the internal institutions of the court determine its ability to interact successfully with the other branches.

Another empirical study on the ISC is the study by Meydani (2011), which focuses on all cases that were brought to the ISC between 2000 and 2006. Looking at the percentage of cases decided against the government by the court across years, Meydani (2011) finds that despite the increase in petitions against the government, the ISC intervenes less frequently in the government's work. Although this research is quite interesting in its highlighting the activism level of the ISC, the study is based on descriptive statistics only and does not succeed in explaining the reasons of the decrease in judicial activism through the years. A similar descriptive analysis is found in the work of Dotan and Hofnung (2001). The authors look at the identity of the litigants and the final decisions of the cases between 1977 and 1995 in an attempt to explain whether and to what extent identity of the litigant affects the final decisions of the court. In their analysis, the authors show that there is a significant rise in the number of petitions issued by NGOs and a rise in the success rate of these groups. Although the authors find that the NGOs in general, and "repeat player" groups in particular, achieved a success rate significantly higher than other litigants, their analysis cannot empirically show the key explanatory factors of this situation.

Trying to compare the impact of attitudinal model and neo-institutionalist model in the context of the ISC, Weinshall-Margel (2011) tries to empirically show whether ideological positions or norms of the court as an institution affect the behavior of the court. The author uses an original database consisting of a sample of 260 judge-level decisions (seventy-eight court cases) between 1985 and 2008 in which freedom of religion clashed with some other rights or interests. In the model, the dependent variable is whether the final decision supports freedom of religion or not. The key independent variable is each judge's ideological religious attitude. The data that is used to measure the judges' attitudes are coming from the judges' biographies, and the measure is one-dimensional that ranges between religious and secular. The author finds that justices' attitudes in Israel have a very strong influence on their decisions. She finds that religious judges are significantly more likely to support freedom of religion than judges with low levels of religiosity. In order to test the impact of the legal norms, Weinshall-Margel (2011) tests the effect of constitutional change, and the author runs two different logistic regression analyses for cases decided before and cases decided after 1992, when the Knesset passed the first two Basic Laws that protect human rights and liberties. The empirical findings show that there is a significant difference in terms of making decisions in favor of religious freedom before and after the year 1992. More interestingly, the author finds that the change in the judicial behavior is different across religious and secular judges. While before the 1992 constitutional change, the probability of protecting religious freedom was 94 percent by a religious justice and 78 percent by a secular justice, after 1992, the probability of a religion-supporting vote in the same case is 64 percent by a religious justice and only 11 percent by a secular one (Weinshall-Margel 2011, 579). This shows that the constitutional revolution did not affect the behavior of the religious judges as much as it affected the rulings of the secular judges. Moreover, in her recent study comparing the dissenting opinions of the secular and religious judges, Weinshall (2016) finds that religious judges are more inclined to give dissenting opinions wherein they support religious interests.

Reviewing all these empirical studies on the Middle Eastern constitutional courts, we see that the majority of the studies try to explain the external and internal determinants of judicial behavior. In this regard, the political context, the issue under review, the identity of the litigant, the political preferences of the judges, and the internal structure and dynamics of the court appear as the most important determinants that are empirically shown to affect judicial behavior.

Unresolved Puzzles and Methodological Challenges

Looking at the empirical studies on the Middle Eastern constitutional courts, a few important methodological problems come to the fore. First, a substantial share of the studies uses only descriptive statistics. Although these types of studies can show certain patterns or changes in judicial behavior, they cannot successfully delineate the explanatory power of the political, attitudinal, or legal determinants of judges' decisions. Comparing the explanatory power of each of these determinants and providing information about the context under which these determinants have a greater impact on judicial behavior is still an unresolved puzzle in the literature. In order to compare the explanatory power of the strategic, attitudinal, and legal models in the context of Middle Eastern constitutional courts, scholars should focus on a larger number of cases and use regression and causal inference models.

Another methodological challenge in the field is measuring the political preferences of the constitutional court judges in the Middle East. Especially in countries where the political landscape is divided into different dimensions across different issues, measuring the political preferences of individual judges is quite difficult. The scholars who try to measure the judges' political preferences should take into consideration the fact that these issue dimensions can vary across each country. Thus, while calculating and measuring the judges' ideological preferences, using the traditional liberal-conservatism dimension may not be a proper choice. Moreover, instead of using judges' previous decisions to measure their political preferences, scholars should look for exogenous measures.

Another unresolved puzzle in the literature is an explanation for the impact of the collegial game on the judges' decisions in the context of authoritarian regimes in general and Middle Eastern countries in particular. Since we have only the studies of Sommer (2009, 2010) on Israel, we do not even know whether and to what extent the collegial game can explain the behavior of the constitutional courts in the authoritarian or hybrid regimes of the Middle East. Especially in the political environment where the government controls the judiciary, the strategic actions among the judges may not appear as an important determinant of judicial behavior. Analysis of whether and to what extent the collegial game and the internal structure of the court has an impact on the judges' decisions is of utmost importance in the context of the Middle Eastern countries. Another problem with this issue is measuring the collegial game itself. Focusing on the Israeli Supreme Court, Sommer (2010) has measured the impact of the collegial game by looking at the decision of the chief justice, but the decision of the chief justice is not the one and only indicator of the collegial game. Scholars should find other indicators that can measure the impact of the internal structure of the court. In this regard, the political fractionalization within the court might be used as an alternative indicator. Once scholars have good measures of judges' political preferences, measuring the political fractionalization within the court would not be problematic.

While most of the existing empirical studies on the Middle Eastern constitutional courts try to explain the political aspects affecting judicial decision-making processes, the impact of the constitutional reforms on judicial behavior remains as an under-studied topic. Especially in the context of authoritarian and hybrid regimes where the ruling elite is capable of creating a dependent judiciary through constitutional reforms, analyzing the impact of these reforms on judicial behavior is quite important. Yet in order to empirically show the impact of these reforms, scholars should have larger data sets that cover a large number of Middle Eastern countries and longer time periods.

Measuring the impact of the legal doctrines on judicial behavior might be another problematic issue in the context of Middle Eastern countries. In the Israeli case, for instance, Weinshall-Margel (2011) has taken the change in the Constitution and compared the period before and after the law was adopted. But in Middle Eastern countries, most of which have authoritarian regimes, constitutional changes may not depend on purely legal factors. In other words, constitutional change may include political maneuverings and reflect the government's desire to create a dependent judiciary. Therefore, instead of looking at the change in certain laws, comparing judicial behavior across certain legal issues might provide a better framework to visualize the impact of the legal aspects. But one should keep in mind that in different cases different political or social dynamics might be at work so that differentiating the impact of the legal aspects might still be problematic. As a result, measuring the impact of legal aspects on judicial behavior sets a methodological and theoretical challenge.

Finally, unavailability of data appears to be the most important problem for empirically studying the behavior of Middle Eastern courts. Searching for the availability of the constitutional courts' decisions, we have found that, with the exception of a few countries (e.g. Turkey, Iraq, Lebanon, Israel), in most of the Middle Eastern countries the constitutional court decisions are not published online. Moreover, when we look at the courts that have published their final decisions, we see that the cases are not published in English. Thus, the final decisions of the Middle Eastern constitutional courts appear not to be readily available (see table 1). If the constitutional court decisions are not publicly available, empirically analyzing judicial behavior will be impossible, and therefore, it would be very hard to provide a general explanation for the judicial behavior in the region.

Recently Weinshall, Epstein, and Worms (2018) developed the Israeli Supreme Court Dataset (ISCD) wherein different information on all final decisions of the ISC between 2010 and 2018 (16,109 cases and 48,634 opinions) is coded. The ISCD data include information on political parties, litigants and legal representation, the origin and history of appealed cases, proceedings and hearings in the ISC, case outcomes, and the opinions and background characteristics of the individual justices. Once similar data sets are developed for the other Middle Eastern constitutional courts, scholars would be able to systematically compare courts' behavior and explain the main aspects that affect their decisions. Moreover, these types of data sets would help scholars empirically evaluate the performance of each country's constitutional court and delineate the key factors that would increase judicial performance, public confidence in the judiciary, and judicial independence.

CONCLUSION: IDEAS FOR PROSPECTIVE RESEARCH

The literature review on the Middle Eastern constitutional courts reveals that few studies have tried to empirically explain the behavior of the courts in the region, and those studies are looking at the Egyptian, Turkish, or Israeli constitutional courts. In other words, only three out of fifteen Middle Eastern constitutional courts are studied empirically. Hence, one should approach the existing literature on Middle Eastern constitutional courts with caution. Egypt, Turkey, and Israel are very different from each other and very different from the rest of the Middle East. For this reason, the results of these studies cannot be generalized to the whole region.

In order to find out whether and to what extent the Middle Eastern courts share certain commonalities in terms of judicial behavior, scholars should conduct a systematic analysis of the Middle Eastern constitutional courts' decisions. Given the fact that the majority of the Middle Eastern countries have authoritarian regimes, studying these courts in a comparative setting would also help us to delineate the common determinants of

TABLE I. Data availability on the constitutional court decisions in the Middle East

Country	Name of the court	Establishment year	Website of the court	Court decisions online
Bahrain	Constitutional Court	2002	NA	NA
Egypt	Supreme Constitutional Court	1979	Available	Partially available
Iran	Supreme Court	1931	Available	NA
Iraq	Federal Supreme Court	2005	Available	Available (2006–2019)
Israel	Supreme Court	1948	Available	Available
Jordan	Constitutional Court	2012	Available	NA
Kuwait	Supreme Constitutional Court	1973	NA	NA
Lebanon	Constitutional Council	1993	Available	Available (1995–2014)
Oman	Supreme Court	1994	NA	NA
Qatar	Supreme Constitutional Court	2008	Available	NA
State of Palestine	Constitutional Court	2016	NA	NA
Saudi Arabia	Supreme Judicial Council	1973	Available	NA
Syria	Supreme Constitutional Court	1973	NA	NA
Turkey	Constitutional Court	1962	Available	Available (1960–2019)
United Arab Emirates	Federal Supreme Court	1973	Available	Partially available
Yemen	Supreme Court	1973	Available	NA

judicial behavior in the context of authoritarian regimes. Moreover, given that Sharia has an important role in the legal systems of the majority of the Middle Eastern countries, analyzing the use of religious sources by the constitutional court judges while they review the constitutionality of a law appears as another important question. Yet, the lack of cross-country data on the Middle Eastern constitutional court is the biggest challenge that should be tackled.

Most of the Middle Eastern countries are epitomized by protracted internal conflicts, terror attacks, or a civil war–like situations. As such, the Middle East provides a rich framework to understand the judicial behavior when these warlike situations are a factor. For this reason, using large data sets that cover long time periods and a large number of courts and that empirically explain the political, social, and legal determinants of judicial behavior in terror-related cases is of utmost importance. Since traditional conservative-liberal dimension may not be applicable in terror-related cases, analyzing the individual political preferences of the judges in these types of cases can be another interesting study. Focusing on a larger number of countries that experience civil wars, terror attacks, or emergency-like situations and explaining the behavior of their constitutional courts in a comparative setting would make an important contribution to the literature. Studying not only the determinants of judicial behavior but also studying the impact of the constitutional court decisions on the governments' policies or human rights violations would be of great importance as well.

Finally, in the context of authoritarian regimes' ability to influence the constitutional courts' decisions, the incumbent government can directly attack the judiciary and try to discredit it or threaten it. For this reason, studying the impact of these intervention mechanisms on Middle Eastern constitutional courts might be another interesting research topic. Moreover, when we look at the existing literature on the Middle Eastern courts, we see that the impact of public opinion on judicial behavior is overlooked. Media can be used by the government to discredit the authority and power of the court in the eyes of the public. In the context of authoritarian or hybrid regimes, the common belief is that the public would not be able to act as an efficient control and constraint mechanism. Yet this assumption needs to be empirically tested. For this reason, studying citizens' attitudes and perceptions toward the judiciary and analyzing whether the public opinion affects judicial behavior would be another important future study in the context of the Middle Eastern countries.

References

Aydin-Cakir, Aylin. 2018. "The Impact of Judicial Preferences and Political Context on Constitutional Court Decisions: Evidence from Turkey." *International Journal of Constitutional Law* 16 (4): 1101–20.

Dotan, Yoav. 1999. "Judicial Rhetoric, Government Lawyers, and Human Rights: The Case of the Israeli High Court of Justice during the Intifada." *Law & Society Review* 33 (2): 319–63.

Dotan, Yoav, and Menachem Hofnung. 2001. "Interest Groups in the Israeli High Court of Justice: Measuring Success in Litigation an in Out-of-Court Settlements." *Law & Policy* 23 (1): 1–27.

Hazama, Yasushi. 2012. "Hegemonic Preservation or Horizontal Accountability: Constitutional Review in Turkey." *International Political Science Review* 33 (4): 421–40.

Hofnung, Menachem, and Keren Weinshall-Margel. 2010. "Judicial Setbacks, Material Gains: Terror Litigation at the Israeli High Court of Justice." *Journal of Empirical Legal Studies* 7 (4): 664–92.

Koğacıoğlu, Dicle. 2003. "Dissolution of Political Parties by the Constitutional Court in Turkey: Judicial Delimitation of the Political Domain." *International Sociology* 18 (1): 258–76.

Koğacıoğlu, Dicle. 2004. "Progress, Unity and Democracy: Dissolving Political Parties in Turkey." *Law & Society Review* 38 (3): 433–62.

Meydani, Assaf. 2011. "The Intervention of the Israeli High Court of Justice in Government Decisions: An Empirical, Quantitative Perspective." *Israel Studies* 16 (3): 174–90.

Moral, Mert, and Efe Tokdemir. 2017. "Justices 'En Garde': Ideological Determinants of the Dissolution of Anti-Establishment Parties." *International Political Science Review* 38 (3): 264–80.

Moustafa, Tamir. 2007. *The Struggle for Constitutional Power: Law, Politics and Economic Development in Egypt.* Cambridge: Cambridge University Press.

Özbudun, Ergun. 2010. "Party Prohibition Cases: Different Approaches by the Turkish Constitutional Court and the European Court of Human Rights." *Democratization* 17 (1): 125–42.

Shambayati, Hootan, and Esen Kirdiş. 2009. "In Pursuit of 'Contemporary Civilization': Judicial Empowerment in Turkey." *Political Research Quarterly* 62 (4): 767–80.

Shamir, Ronen. 1990. "'Landmark Cases' and the Reproduction of Legitimacy: The Case of Israel's High Court of Justice." *Law & Society Review* 24 (3): 781–805.

Sommer, Udi. 2009. "Crusades against Corruption and Institutionally-Induced Strategies in the Israeli Supreme Court." *Israel Affairs* 15 (3): 279–95.

Sommer, Udi. 2010. "A Strategic Court and National Security: Comparative Lessons from the Israeli Case." *Israel Studies Forum* 25 (2): 54–80.

Tezcur, Güneş Murat. 2009. "Judicial Activism in Perilous Times: The Turkish Case." *Law & Society Review* 43 (2): 305–36.

Weinshall, Keren. 2016. *Law and Ideology in Supreme Court Decision-Making: A Comparative and Quantitative Analysis.* Hebrew University Press.

Weinshall, Keren, Lee Epstein, and Andy Worms. 2018. *The Israeli Supreme Court Database.* http://iscdbstaging.wustl.edu.

Weinshall-Margel, Keren. 2011. "Attitudinal and Neo-Institutional Models of Supreme Court Decision Making: An Empirical and Comparative Perspective from Israel." *Journal of Empirical Legal Studies* 8 (3): 556–86.

Yıldırım, Engin, and Serdar Gülener. 2017. "Kadın Üyelerinin Yargısal Tutumları: Ampirik Bir Araştırma." ("Judicial Attitudes of Female Justices of the Constitutional Court: An Empirical Analysis"). *Anayasa Hukuku Dergisi* 6 (11): 51–84.

Yıldırım, Engin, Aziz Kutlar, and Serdar Gülener. 2017. "1962–1982 Dönemi Anayasa Mahkemesi Üyelerinin Yargısal İdeal Noktalarının Belirlenmesi." *Amme İdaresi Dergisi* 50 (4): 1–31.

Varol, Ozan O., Lucia Dalla Pellegrina, and Nuno Garoupa. 2017. "An Empirical Analysis of Judicial Transformation in Turkey." *The American Journal of Comparative Law* 65 (1): 187–216.

Empirical Studies of African High Courts

An Overview

DOMINIQUE H. LEWIS

T HE EXISTING work on constitutional courts from a cross-national perspective covers a myriad of topics, debates, and regions, but it is clear that this does not apply to the study of the high courts across the African continent. The majority of the existing literature focuses on specific features of the courts themselves or features that are products of the judicial systems in place. Research typically concerns one or two countries (most notably, South Africa), while multi-national coverage is less common. Many of the studies themselves are qualitative in nature, relying on descriptive case studies and comparisons.

To begin, I summarize the current literature on African national courts. I conclude with suggestions for future empirical strategies and a discussion of interesting and useful lines of inquiry for which these strategies would be most useful.

BREADTH AND SCOPE

As mentioned above, cross-national perspectives on national courts are uncommon and efforts to measure specific institutional features of the courts have been relatively sparse in the African context. To the extent that formal legal institutions have been studied in-depth, much of that work is largely based on case studies and description. Scholars in the legal academy have focused primarily on constitutions and other written laws (e.g., Klug 2010) or on close comparisons of such formal instruments (e.g., Kende 2010) to the exclusion of the operation of (and influences on) legal institutions. What has been done often takes a political economy perspective, examining the role that courts and other legal institutions play in economic development (e.g. Widner 1999). That being said, the research that covers African high courts typically falls into one of two categories. First, there is considerable attention paid to the independence and autonomy of the courts with respect to executive influence and control. Second, there are various studies that examine the courts' role in countries experiencing or having previously experienced regime change or in post-conflict states; this includes attempts to measure and assess the legitimacy of the courts.

JUDICIAL INDEPENDENCE

A large proportion of the research in this area focuses on the independence of the courts, and in particular, the extent to which the legal system is characterized by executive control. Ellett (2012) elaborates on the somewhat unique institutional features that characterize many African court systems, namely the gap that exists between the formal and informal. This institutional dichotomy often involves a mix of neopatrimonial practices inherent in predatory states along with more formal institutional characteristics commonly associated with developmental states. For Ellett (2012), this mix is largely due to the legacy of colonialism and the imposition of the colonial power's legal system. More specifically, in Tanzania, Uganda, and Malawi, the imposition of the British legal system resulted in judicial power that was granted to individual judges whose "judicial decision-making reflected the role of judges as representatives of the government and not the people" (Ellett 2012, 347). The British adherence to "legal conservatism" did not become more formalized until much later. Because of this, the courts did not function as checks on governmental power and, in fact, were often used to repress the public and strengthen and protect the colonial governments. This original framework made it especially difficult to establish legitimately independent courts post–colonial rule.

Most models of judicial independence generally argue that the independence of the courts is related to the degree to which the court is able to make decisions in political matters important to those in power. For example, "thin strategic models" emphasize electoral security and the level of centralization of power within the party system. More specifically, judicial independence is more likely under electoral uncertainty and multiparty rule. VanDoepp and Ellett (2011) analyze judicial independence cross-nationally to expand on the argument that in many African cases the independence of the judiciary is highly dependent on the threat it poses to the executive. In their study, they find little support for the thin strategic models but find that judicial independence is largely determined by the degree to which the courts represent a direct threat to a leader's survival in office.

Under authoritarian regimes, the level of judicial independence varies and is highly dependent on the role it serves in strengthening and furthering the goals of the executive. In some occasions, the courts are afforded more autonomy, for instance, when the courts are deemed more effective in the control of corruption. This is particularly the case when the concern involves lower levels of administrative corruption in government. They can also help to bolster the country's reputation internationally as the institution most effective at establishing the "rule of law" and therefore may be afforded more independence when it serves the interests of those in power. Conversely, the courts can hinder the executive, especially during an election when contestation is at its highest. Widner and Scher (2008) argue that courts are more likely to remain independent in authoritarian regimes when political competition is low, when it is necessary to conform to international norms, or when public opinion considerably demands reform in the area of "rule of law."

VanDoepp and Ellett (2011) develop a categorical measure of governmental interference in judicial matters, that accounts for the different ways the government may undermine or suppress judicial autonomy. For instance, one of the more common instances of interference is a product of patronage systems whereby patron-client relationships undermine the normal functions of the courts. Another example is the use of "court packing" to manipulate the courts and ultimately undermine their autonomy by stacking the courts with political allies loyal to the executive. Overall, the measures focus on direct (and in many instances extralegal) "government behaviors" rather than actions related to the normal legal functions of other governmental entities and branches.

West African courts are the subject of Stroh and Heyl's (2015) research; the authors offer an explanation for the spread of constitutional review across West African countries starting with the third wave of democratization. They focus on institutional diffusion and the fact that many Western African countries chose to mimic Francophone models of constitutional courts. Furthermore, they contend that deviations from this baseline can be explained by domestic factors, most notably the level of political competition (insurance theory). They form an empirical measure of Formal Independence of the courts based on five dimensions that "refer to well-established categories in judicial politics research" (Stroh and Heyl 2015, 175). These include measures of accessibility of the court, powers of the court, autonomy of the court, job security, and legal reach. They use this index to compare each West African country's constitutional courts and the degree to which they deviate from the Gallic model; they conclude that political competition accounts for observed deviations, particularly in Benin, Burkina Faso, Niger, Guinea, Mauritania, and Senegal. The choice to adopt stronger and more independent courts is a strategic one best explained by insurance theory: the more competitive the system, the more likely incumbents will support stronger courts with higher levels of de jure independence (and therefore, the more they will deviate from the "baseline" French model).

INSTITUTIONAL LEGITIMACY

Other scholars focus on the legitimacy of the court and its ability to strengthen other institutional features and even regimes. Gibson (2016) and Gibson and Caldeira (2003) assess the popular legitimacy of the South African court, with an emphasis on the societal divisions within the country and their effect on the perceived legitimacy of the court. With the use of surveys, public perception of the South African Constitutional Court is assessed and the authors find that the public's trust and confidence in the courts has increased substantially over time. The authors note that this confidence is not necessarily a measure of legitimacy per se, but that the two are often related and correlated, and it may be demonstrative of the legitimacy of the Constitutional Court in South Africa in the future.

Widner (2001) examines the courts' potential to promote public trust and consequently their role in sustaining democratic transitions in post-conflict states. Through a cross-national comparison,[1] she stresses the mediating role of the courts and its impact on democratic stability. Although her focus is not limited to national courts, she argues that the courts can act in ways that decrease a resumption of armed conflict, namely in "disagreements about the rightful heirs to positions as chief or king, the legitimacy of elections, and contending claims to land" (70). The courts are also instrumental in reducing ethnic conflict through increased mediation in specific types of disputes involving vigilantism, witchcraft cases, and neighborhood disputes.

Ellett (2013) focuses on the courts in Uganda, Tanzania, and Malawi, all considered "hybrid" regime types, in order to examine the relationship between judicial power and the consolidation of democracy. The author points out that each country is shaped by its colonial past in distinct ways and the courts have struggled to assert their power without interference. Paradoxically, as the countries have moved toward more democratic institutions, namely multiparty elections, the weaker the judiciary and its legitimacy.[2] Combining this with Widner's observations above suggests that there is a need to focus on the courts in fragile African states, and this line of study would be strengthened by cross-country comparisons.

General Gaps in the Literature

As I noted at the outset, to date there has been relatively little comparative, cross-national empirical research on the high courts in Africa. I believe that this dearth of work is in part driven by data limitations; my own experience examining high courts in Africa suggests that in many developing countries, obtaining even basic information about formal procedures and processes in national constitutional courts can be difficult. Facts such as the manner in which justices are appointed and reappointed, the length of their terms, and the possibility of reappointment are often fugitive.

One consequence is that judicial institutions in the developing world are often relatively under-studied, with the result that our understanding of institutions in those contexts is underdeveloped. Therefore, future research in this area should focus heavily on the development and availability of consistent, flexible, high-quality data. One such development should be a data-based typology of national high courts in Africa. Second, in-depth qualitative studies of single decisions, institutions, or areas of the law are indeed invaluable but make cross-national comparison difficult. An ideal solution would bring together decisions and opinions from multiple courts across a range of countries and would do so in a way that allowed for both in-depth analyses and cross-institutional and cross-national comparisons. This database would be textual in nature and should be integrated with public data from other sources such as the *Afrobarometer*. The integration of data from other sources will allow for the examination of a host of hypotheses about the organization, operation, decision-making, and impact of their high courts.

To be sure, the development of this type of database is not an easy task; this is particularly the case in the African context, where judicial institutions are often underfunded, records are inconsistent, and technology is lagging. These challenges are outlined at great length by Ryan (2013) in the three-year quest to retrieve and research high court opinions across four African countries (Botswana, Kenya, Namibia, and South Africa) for the time period 1990–2010:

> [I]f my goal was to access a large percentage of high court cases from recent years, I could enlist only SAFLII.[3] Given the cost of print reporters, the free SAFLII site would be the go-to resource for most researchers. However, for researchers desiring exhaustive searches, or exploring lower courts or older case law, a combined print and electronic search is optimal. Of course, without triangulating search results with some other indicator of the number of opinions rendered (e.g., court press release), it is unwise to conclude that one has fully retrieved all of the cases for a given year. Thus, a perfect search requires use of print and online reporters, as well as corroborating evidence of the court's activity (300).

Despite these difficulties, databases such as the ones I suggested would allow researchers to explore aspects of African constitutional courts that, to date, have seen relatively little analysis. A key source of publicly available data is the Southern African Legal Information Institute (SAFLII 2018) databases of high court opinions for twelve sub-Saharan African countries.[4] The extent of data for each country varies widely. Altogether, the SAFLII databases currently contain a total of 8,594 decisions from twelve high courts in sub-Saharan Africa. Coverage generally encompasses the post-2000 era, with data availability for nearly every country through 2018 and some starting as early as the 1970s.

SUGGESTIONS FOR FUTURE RESEARCH

While one might consider a host of future research areas, two come immediately to mind. First, I believe that existing work on the protection of individual rights (including property and other economic rights) and the rule of law would be strengthened by the introduction of more nuanced understandings about the operation of African constitutional courts. To date, such work has relied on relatively simple characterizations of courts (e.g., their age and degree of formal independence). By developing a more nuanced measure of such courts' institutional characteristics, the hope is to better understand how those traits contribute to a country's protection of such rights.

A second area of inquiry is into the decision-making of such courts. Studies of courts in the US context have consistently revealed that institutional characteristics—especially those related to the selection, retention, and tenure of justices—play a crucial role in the decision-making of those courts. Collecting data and developing valid cross-national measures of such institutional traits would allow us to assess whether these empirical findings hold up in other settings.

NOTES

1. Botswana, Cameroon, Nigeria, Rwanda, Somalia, South Africa, Tanzania, Uganda, Zimbabwe.
2. This conclusion is quite different from the conclusions reached by Stroh and Heyl (2015) in their analysis of West African high courts.
3. Southern African Legal Information Institute.
4. Botswana, Lesotho, Madagascar, Malawi, Namibia, the Seychelles, South Africa, Swaziland, Tanzania, Uganda, Zambia, and Zimbabwe.

REFERENCES

Ellett, Rachel. 2012. "Courts and the Emergence of Statehood in post-Colonial Africa." *Northern Ireland Legal Quarterly* 63 (3): 343–63.

Ellett, Rachel. 2013. *Pathways to Judicial Power in Transitional States*. New York: Routledge.

Gibson, James L. 2016. "Reassessing the Institutional Legitimacy of the South African Constitutional Court: New Evidence, Revised Theory." *Politikon* 43 (1): 53–77.

Gibson, James L., and Gregory A. Caldeira. 2003. "Defenders of Democracy? Legitimacy, Popular Acceptance, and the South African Constitutional Court." *The Journal of Politics* 65 (1): 1–30.

Kende, Mark. 2010. *Constitutional Rights in Two Worlds: South Africa and the United States*. New York: Cambridge University Press.

Klug, Heinz. 2010. *The Constitution of South Africa: A Contextual Analysis*. Oxford: Hart Publishing.

Ryan, Sarah E. 2013. "The Challenges of Researching African High Court Opinions: Ten Lessons Learned from a Four-Country Retrievability Survey." *Legal References Services Quarterly* 32 (4): 294–306.

Stroh, Alexander, and Charlotte Heyl. 2015. "Institutional Diffusion, Strategic Insurance, and the Creation of West African Constitutional Courts." *Comparative Politics* 47 (2): 169–87.

VonDoepp, Peter, and Rachel Ellett. 2011. "Reworking Strategic Models of Executive-Judicial Relations: Insights from New African Democracies." *Comparative Politics* 43 (2): 147–65.

Widner, Jennifer. 1999. "The Courts as a Restraint: The Experience of Tanzania, Uganda, and Botswana." In *Investment and Risk in Africa*, edited by Paul Collier, 219–45. London: Macmillan.

Widner, Jennifer. 2001. "Courts and Democracy in Postconflict Transitions: A Social Scientist's Perspective on the African Case." *The American Journal of International Law* 95 (1): 64–75.

Widner, Jennifer, and Daniel Scher. 2008. "Building Judicial Independence in Semi Democracies: Uganda and Zimbabwe." In *Rule by Law: The Politics of Courts in Authoritarian Regimes*, edited by Tom Ginsberg and Tamir Moustafa, 235–60. Cambridge: Cambridge University Press.

Comparative Studies of Judicial Behavior

AMANDA DRISCOLL

THE PURPOSE of this essay is to review empirical research on judicial behavior that is explicitly comparative in nature. I define *empirical* as the systematic collection and analysis of data relating to judicial behavior in service of a research question (Cane and Kritzer 2010, 4). The particulars of this process may vary widely as a function of the research question, including the sort of data analysts consider (judges' votes, written opinions, dissents or concurrences, judicial procedures, case outcomes, survey results, etc.), the manner of analytic techniques applied (statistical analyses, process tracing, case study comparisons, etc.), and the sorts of interpretations or inferences which are feasible based on a given research design.[1] This definition sets aside research that is strictly normative or legalistic in nature, which have their own methodologies and norms of analysis.[2]

By *comparative*, I focus my attention on research that includes the analysis of more than one court, leveraging differences across contexts, time, institutional design, or court composition to generalize our theoretical knowledge. A far more common definition of comparative judicial politics would include "any research on judges or court behavior in systems outside of the United States" (Clark, Golder, and Golder 2018). Although some of the research reviewed below fits the latter criteria,[3] some of the most vibrant trends in cross-sectional research in this field has occurred where national contexts are held constant, leveraging differences across levels of judicial hierarchy, subnational actors, or across panels of judges to illuminate the various motives, constraints and determinants of judicial behavior.

Breadth and Scope of Comparative Judicial Scholarship

Comparative judicial politics has long been recognized as a subfield with enormous potential and possibility. Explicitly comparative research has been regarded by entrepreneurs in the judicial politics subfield as an exciting opportunity to advance our knowledge of court and judicial behavior beyond the US borders, both to test hypotheses and to generalize our conceptual and theoretical constructs (Tate 1983, 1989; Tate and Haynie 1994; Epstein 1999; Kawar and Massoud 2012; Walker 2012). The study of courts and judicial behavior outside the United States has inspired researchers from diverse methodological backgrounds, from the disciplines of law, political science, economics, and many others. Accordingly, the community of comparative judicial scholars is truly interdisciplinary and reflects the contributions of scholars from many different approaches. At the same time, many recognize the non-trivial barriers to conducting high-quality research in terms of requisite expertise (language, political, legal, etc.) and resources (financial, human, time, etc.).

A cursory glance at the essays in this volume suggests that the comparative analysis of judicial behavior is the exception rather than the rule. In their reviews of their respective countries or geographic regions, authors Bagashka and Garoupa (Europe), Hanretty (UK), Aydin-Cakir (Middle East), Lin and Ginsberg (Asia), and Lewis (Africa) report virtually no cross-national comparative research in their review of the literatures. Research on judges and courts in Latin America has made more progress in this regard, with roughly one-third of all research designs involving some comparative design component (Kapiszewski and Taylor 2008; Kapiszewski and Tiede, this volume). The exceptions to this rule are found in the study of the subnational courts of the United States (Hall, this volume; Fischman, this volume), and the small body of research using a similar design in the federal courts of Australia (Smyth, this volume).

I summarize here seven lines of inquiry in the area of comparative empirical research on courts and judicial behavior that embody the "comparative advantage" of comparative research (Epstein 1999). I have identified these research agendas for their explicitly cross-sectional research designs and for their distinction in having garnered contributions from scholars across the methodological spectrum and from many different disciplines. These are research agendas in which meaningful scholarly "cumulation" has occurred, in the sense that theoretical puzzles inform research design for empirical studies, the results of which inform and modify subsequent theoretical extensions.

I acknowledge that my review of these bodies of scholarship is not exhaustive; there are lines of inquiry I have no doubt missed. This summary is meant to point interested readers in the direction of research that exemplifies an ongoing stream of scholarly engagement, a trend which will no doubt continue. For more comprehensive reviews of empirical judicial behavior research in the United States, please see Hall (this volume), Fischman (this volume), and Kornhauser (this volume); for additional reviews on cross-national judicial research and judicial independence, please see Vanberg (2008, 2015), Helmke and Rosenbluth (2009), and Hirschl (2005, 2014).

Core Substantive Areas of Inquiry and Methodological Approaches

Leveraging Institutional Variance across the United States

Three of the most fruitful research agendas of comparative judicial politics have been in the realm of judicial politics within the United States. Brace and Hall (1995, 1997) sought to diversify the study of judicial politics beyond the subfield's narrow focus on the Supreme Court of the United States (SCOTUS), shifting the focus instead to the cross-sectional diversity of institutions found across the supreme courts of the states. Leveraging institutional variation in rules and nomination procedures across state supreme courts, this research demonstrates the myriad ways in which various features of judicial process—including case details, litigant resources or judicial appointments—are conditional on the institutional context in which the courts operate. The variance in judicial selection procedures across the US states has proven an especially fruitful line of inquiry, making clear how the electoral institutions and environments shape incentives for judges to appear "tough on crime," to stake out extreme positions on publicly divisive topics, or shape judicial opinion content in controversial decisions (Hall 1992, 2001; Hall and Bonneau 2006; Bonneau and Hall 2009; cf. Driscoll and Nelson 2013, 2014, 2015). These sorts of findings have been shown to have considerable downstream effects for the public's support for and relationship to judicial institutions (Bonneau and Hall 2009; Kritzer 2011; Nelson 2014; Canes-Wrone, Clark, and Kelly 2014).

Judicial Behavior within the US Judicial Hierarchy

A second US-centric literature concerns judicial behavior within a judicial hierarchy, leveraging variation in institutional constraints and professional incentives to explain collegial decision-making, majority opinion content, and evolution of the law. Pivoting away from the artificial distinctions between the canonical models of judicial behavior (i.e. the jurisprudential, attitudinal or strategic models), this literature makes clear how limited said models of judicial motives are in explaining the behavior of most judges in the world who do not sit on pinnacle courts. Instead, scholars in this vein point out that many aspects of judicial decision-making are constrained by concerns of collegiality (one sort of horizontal constraint) (Kornhauser 1992a, 1992b), as well as legal doctrine and professional incentives within the judicial hierarchy (vertical constraints). Some of the most important empirical insights from this body of research are how attitudinal and strategic considerations are both consistent with, but also conditional upon, the legal environment in which decisions are made (Lax 2011).[4] As one example, Hinkle (2015) models judges' citations as a function of the justiciability of precedent within and across appellate circuits, exploiting the fact that precedent is legally binding within circuits, but merely "persuasive" across them. Although stare decisis appears to shape judges' citations when precedent is binding, Hinkle demonstrates that judges appear ideologically motivated when citing non-binding precedent, empirically identifying the oft-cited notion of "legal constraint," as one of several central determinants of judicial behavior. Smyth, Hanretty, and Parikh (all this volume) all suggest that similar studies of lower court judges in countries outside the United States are a noted opportunity to expand our knowledge well beyond the US system.

Judicial Behavior on the US Supreme Court across Jurisprudential Regimes

A third US-centric line of research considers the existence and influence of distinct jurisprudential regimes on the United States Supreme Court (Pritchett 1948; Kornhauser 1992b; Kritzer and Richards 2003; Lax and Rader 2010; Scott 2006; Pang et al. 2012; Bartels and O'Geen 2015). While the analysis of cross-temporal data is the norm in most of the studies of the Supreme Court, the jurisprudential regimes literature conceives norms of jurisprudence—commonly agreed upon legal facts or evidentiary standards—to exert an independent and constraining effect on judicial decision-making, akin to a formal institutional rule. Acknowledging the ways in which these jurisprudential norms can change over time, proponents of this approach identify key judicial decisions or precedent that serve to crystalize justices' decisions and interpretations in future legal decisions. Although the empirical evidence of this is contested (Kritzer and Richards 2003; Lax and Rader 2010; Scott 2006; Pang et al. 2012), the cross-temporal structural break across jurisprudential regimes implies that while the empirical focus concerns nine justices on a single Court, we can nevertheless treat the cross-regime comparisons as if to analyze institutionally distinct courts.[5]

Generalizing beyond the US Context

One stated objective of comparative research is to test the conventional wisdom of what has been shown to explain a given context. In the domain of comparative judicial politics, cross-national research has aimed to delineate the extent to which conclusions drawn in the United States can be generalized to other contexts. Resource capability theory, for example, has been used to theorize the extent to which resource-rich litigants fare better in judicial hierarchies in courts around the world. Haynie and Sill's (2007) analysis of case outcomes in the South African appellate system underscores the value of experienced attorneys, a finding which is consistent with Sheehan and Randazzo's (2012) analysis of the judicial hierarchy of Australia. In a more stark departure from the logic of the US context, Haynie (1994, 1995) reports that litigants with fewer resources actually fare *better* when taking their cases to the Supreme Court of the Philippines, a fact which she contends is as a legitimacy-building mechanism whereby justices might seek to bolster institutional support by an otherwise untrusting public constituency.

Also considering litigant status, Epp's *Rights Revolution* (1998) explains the exponential expansion of judicially protected civil rights in the United States, emphasizing the central role that civil society, activist lawyers, and other "support structure" actors played in creating conditions for a "rights revolution" to occur. Comparing the varied trajectories of rights expansions in India, Britain, and Canada, Epp's comparative case study analysis underscores the need for vibrant civil society engagement to sustain rights-related litigation; judicial activism in the area of rights promotion may be a necessary condition but is by no means sufficient. Extending Epp's analysis, Sanchez-Urribarri et al. (2011) analyze judicial dispositions of civil rights cases in six pinnacle courts, providing a direct cross-national test of Epp's *Rights Revolutions* expectations regarding rights advocacy and legal support structures (cf. Wilson 2009; Couso 2005). The authors find little support for Epp's support structure hypothesis, arguing instead that ideological predictors are more strongly correlated with high courts' attention to civil rights. Taken together, this is but one example of comparative research designs being used to both generate theory—using Mill's comparative method to identify necessary and sufficient causes (Epp)—and to systematically test hypotheses using quantitative analysis of comparative data (Sanchez-Urribarri et al.).

The Separation of Powers Model and Political Fragmentation Outside the United States

A fifth body of scholarship extends the theoretical models developed to explain judicial decision-making in the United States to elucidate the role of courts and behavior of courts and judges in other systems around the world. One approach is exemplified by extensions of the formal theoretical models of the separation of powers in the United States, deriving equilibrium expectations for judicial behavior under variable institutional or contextual arrangements. This research is explicitly comparative in its orientation; hypotheses are derived and evidence analyzed regarding the extent to which the outcomes or observed behaviors are consistent with equilibrium expectations in a given context or condition (cf. Vanberg 2000, 2001). Cross-sectional comparisons are therefore made at the conceptual step of the analytical process; not all equilibrium behaviors or outcomes are equally scrutinized (or even empirically observable).

By way of example, Helmke (2002) extends the standard separation of powers model to contexts with marginally independent high courts, suggesting judges' future ambitions lead government-aligned judges to "strategically defect" in advance of incumbent losses, ruling against the outgoing government so as to curry favor with ascendant political coalitions. Considering the voting behavior of judges in the Argentine Supreme Court, Helmke shows that judges more often vote against the incumbent government during the last months of the incumbent's tenure and on cases that are of particular interest to the incoming political coalition. Likewise, economists Iaryczower, Spiller, and Tommasi (2002) consider the independence of the Argentine Supreme Court, noting that despite existing in a federal, separation of powers system that encourages political fragmentation, the Argentine Supreme Court is widely perceived to be lacking in judicial independence (cf. Chavez 2004). The authors reconcile these disparate facts in their analysis of judicial votes over most of the twentieth century, suggesting that judges appear more deferential as executive influence over the legislature expands.

Most separation of powers models based on the US case take the origins of judicial independence for granted, wherein an independent court is assumed to exist and its political origins are never scrutinized or overtly considered. The extension of separation of powers models to other contexts illuminates the requisite facilitating conditions for high courts to exert an independence influence on policy, far beyond the formal constitutional separation of powers. Where electoral rules incentivize high party discipline and legislative subservience to a powerful executive (Iaryczower, Spiller, and Tommasi 2002), or where presidents enjoy a supermajority control of legislative seats, incumbents' threats to undermine high courts is imminently credible, in spite of the constitutional separation of powers. Alternatively, the theoretical predictions for separation of powers models also shifts under different assumptions regarding judges' careers and professional aspirations: where judges perceive their future career to hinge on pleasing political incumbents, behavioral independence will be hard to come by, even in systems with formally independent courts (Helmke 2002, 2005; Hilbink 2007; Kapiszewski 2012).

Comparative Judicial Independence

A sixth literature central to comparative judicial politics theorizes the conditions that facilitate judicial independence, a question which is perhaps the longest standing in the field.[6] Existing theoretical accounts can be differentiated in the extent to which they theorize the *benefits* independent judicial review may yield to incumbent governments as opposed to the *costs* of undermining independent high courts (cf. Vanberg 2008; Stephenson 2003). First, I consider theoretical accounts that theorize ways that the existence of independent judicial review actually *serves* the interests of political incumbents, despite the possible constraints independent judicial review may impose.

One class of models is the "insurance model" of judicial independence, wherein incumbents might empower an independent court when faced with future electoral replacement (Landes and Posner 1975; North and Weingast 1989; Ramseyer 1994; Ferejohn 1999; Stephenson 2003; Ginsburg 2003; Finkel 2008). While different versions of the insurance model make varying assumptions regarding the motives and preferences of both incumbents and judges,[7] they share a common underlying logic:

incumbents will accept constraints on their power today so as to ensure support and protection from the court (or certain judges) in the future. The insurance model of judicial independence situates both the establishment and maintenance of judicial independence in the purview of incumbents' interest when faced with sufficiently long time horizons and meaningful electoral vulnerability (cf. Stephenson 2003).

The empirical consequences of the insurance model have inspired analysts from a diverse cross-section of academic disciplines, encompassing a wide variety of research designs and methodologies. Ramseyer (1994) used this logic to explain the relative independence of the modern US Supreme Court to that of the Japanese Supreme Court, arguing that regime stability and electoral competition induced incumbent respect for independent judicial review in the United States (Ramseyer and Rasumssen 1997). Hanssen's (2004) quantitative analysis of judicial appointment reforms across the US states documents that states shift to more independence-promoting appointment rules when political competition is high and the electoral future of key incumbents is uncertain. Similar arguments have been used to describe constitution-writing processes (Hirschl 2000, 2001; Moustafa 2007; North and Weingast 1989), the consequences for judicial reform implementation (Finkel 2005, 2008), and interbranch relations (Ginsburg 2003; Stephenson 2003; Chavez 2004). In a more recent take, Epperly (2013) scrutinizes the assumption that courts provide incumbents with "insurance" after leaving office and shows that leaders' exit from office are more likely to be "unpunished" when transfer of powers occurs in systems with independent courts. Other comparative research identifies the limits of this logic: Randazzo, Gibler, and Reid (2016) observe that the extent to which an independent court is useful to incumbents in the future is strongly conditioned by regime type; others suggest the relationship between competition and preferences for judicial independence is curvilinear (cf. Popova 2010; Stephenson 2003).

Yet the insurance model remains one of the most hotly contested models in comparative judicial politics. A central deficiency to all variants is the question of time inconsistency: although electoral insecurity might induce a short-term interest in judicial independence, there is no mechanism to preserve said judicial independence into the future (Finkel 2008). Finally, the two main variants of the insurance model are each premised to a greater or lesser degree on dubious assumptions regarding judicial behavior (Boudreaux and Pritchard 1994). Judges are not neutral arbiters, nor is it patently obvious that courts work to protect those not in power. Absent are intuitive rationales for how or why judges prioritize the preferences of the enacting legislative coalition, without any other considerations that have been shown to influence judicial decision-making, such as partisanship (Segal and Spaeth 2002), litigant status (Haynie 1994, 1995; Herron and Randazzo 2003), other judges (Maltzman, Spriggs, and Wahlbeck 2000), strategic professional calculations (Epstein and Knight 1997; Ramseyer and Rasmusen 1997; Helmke 2002; Kapiszewski 2012), or ideational considerations (Woods and Hilbink 2009; Hilbink 2012).

As to the potential *costs* to incumbents for undermining judicial independence, institutional or political fragmentation is theorized to frustrate incumbents' attempts to undermine high courts where multiple veto players' assent is required to threaten or change the institutional integrity of judicial institutions. More generally, fragmentation in the policy-making process, owing to the formal separation of the legislature and executive, coalition governments, or the devolution of policy-making power to subnational entities, opens the door for judicial influence. Cooter and Ginsburg (1996) draw on the classic spatial model of politics to theorize the cross-sectional variance in judicial assertiveness, anticipating that where many veto players (either constitutional or partisan) exist, courts will be more apt to behave in a manner that might invite legislative overrides. Hilbink (2012), by contrast, compares the behavioral independence of judges in six different regimes and argues that political fragmentation or competition is neither necessary nor sufficient for judicial independence to emerge. The other noted cost to undermining judicial independence is the potential for public backlash, a topic to which I now turn.

The Problem of Compliance and Public Support for Judicial Institutions

That courts and judges may concern themselves with public support and institutional legitimacy constitutes a seventh and final research agenda in the area of comparative judicial politics. The point of departure for much of this research is the observation that judicial institutions are unique for lacking both the "purse" and the "sword," rendering them unable to compel or incentivize acceptance of their decisions. Legitimacy theory—which assumes that given sufficiently broad levels of intrinsic support for judicial institutions, the public will be unwilling to tolerate abuse or dismissal of popular courts—posits that public support for courts is a central determinant of judicial power and influence of courts across time and space. Accordingly, understanding if, how, and why the public may confer legitimacy to unelected judicial institutions has a long-standing tradition in judicial politics more broadly and in the comparative arena in particular.

Gibson, Caldeira, and Baird (1998) were some of the first to extend the largely US-centric literature documenting public support for a national judiciary to the study of courts outside of the United States. Again seeking to evaluate the predictive relevance of legitimacy theory, Gibson, Caldeira, and Baird's analysis centers on a well-vetted battery of survey questions regarding the public's willingness to tolerate fundamental changes to national courts, with an unwillingness to do so interpreted as profound institutional fealty (Caldeira and Gibson 1992). Including this battery of questions on nationally representative surveys throughout Western Europe and Canada, the authors find that Europeans' support for national courts hinges on their awareness of high courts, a finding that corroborated decades of US-centric research into the correlates of the high court and of public support for the high court (Murphy and Tanenhaus 1968; Tanenhaus and Murphy 1981). At the same time, their cross-sectional research makes evident that widespread public support for the US Supreme Court was an anomalous feature of the North American case, as Europeans were generally much more skeptical, on average, of their national judicial institutions (Caldeira and Gibson 1995; Gibson and Caldeira 1995; Gibson, Caldeira, and Baird 1998; cf. Driscoll and Nelson 2018). This research highlights a previously unappreciated scope condition to earlier US-centric research.

Vanberg's (2000, 2001) work reorients focus on public awareness of courts as an individual-level predictor of institutional support to a structural precondition to explaining judicial power and influence. In yet another formal extension of the US separation of powers models, Vanberg (2000) asserts that neither the institutional fragmentation of powers nor the public's support for the judiciary are necessary conditions to maintain high court independence. Considering the behavior of the high court of Germany to substantiate the empirical outcomes his model implies, Vanberg identifies the conditions under which public support can effectively compel incumbent compliance with judicial decisions, underscoring the role of transparency as a facilitating informational condition (2005). Subsequent formal theoretic work since endogenized the transparency of the political arena, situating the informational environment as a focal object of strategic judicial behavior; judges may take actions to strategically publicize (or obfuscate) their decisions so as to cultivate their broader institutional legitimacy among the public (Staton 2006; Staton and Vanberg 2008; Krehbiel 2016).[8]

The study of public support for judicial institutions has experienced a renaissance of late, with the pendulum swinging again to emphasize empirical comparisons and cross-sectional analysis. The incorporation of survey experiments has revitalized the study of the correlates of public support for courts in the United States, wherein respondents are randomly exposed to varying portraits of judicial behavior, procedure, or case content, and then queried regarding the extent to which they approve of the court, judge, or judicial outcome. This scholarship has illustrated the extent to which public support for judiciaries is rooted in—rather than at odds with—their support for political incumbents and instrumental interests (Bartels and Johnston 2013; Gibson and Nelson 2015; Driscoll and Nelson 2019). Cross-nationally, new calls for expanded data-collection efforts highlight the dearth of comparative data that reliably measures the quantities of most interest to judicial scholars and the pressing need for new sources of cross-national data (Driscoll and Nelson 2018, 2019). The frontier of this research agenda probes deeply into the calculus of the public support for courts to identify when and why the public would prioritize the institutional integrity of a court over the possible policy outcomes courts may provide. Also, not yet well understood is how and why the public would come to prioritize the protection of an unelected court, a question of considerable import for future research.

This cursory review of these literatures reveals three general facts about the state of the research on comparative judicial behavior. The first is that some of the most successful instances of comparative research into *judges'* behaviors are those that focus on a single-country case, leveraging variance in subnational institutions, contexts, or judicial incentives within a hierarchy. Second, the comparative research that is explicitly cross-national in its research design and considers courts outside of the United States take one of two approaches. The first tends to be more explicitly comparative in its empirical analysis, using comparisons to evaluate the predictive accuracy of theoretical models generated in the US case, to test the extent to which the same logic generalizes in other cases. A second approach, one which generally is more formally theoretic in nature, makes comparisons at the conceptual step in the identification of equilibrium behaviors, subject to explicitly stated assumptions and limited scope conditions. In most cases, the empirical analysis that accompanies these formal theoretic models includes analysis of judicial behavior in a single-country case in order to evaluate the extent to which judges' behavior is consistent with equilibrium expectations. Finally, most empirical research on judicial behavior that is cross-national in orientation considers not the comparative behavior of judges but of *courts*.[9] As I discuss in more detail below, the reason for this shift in the unit of analysis can be explained not only by lack of "ready-to-go" data sources but also the difficulties of creating truly comparable data sets in the first place.

PUBLICATION TRENDS AND DATA AVAILABILITY IN COMPARATIVE JUDICIAL POLITICS

I now shift focus to explore publication trends and data availability in comparative judicial politics between 2000 and 2018.[10] In table 1, I report aggregate totals, (the original data is available upon request).[11] There are a few trends in this data that are of immediate interest based on the nearly three hundred articles and books the coding effort classified.

First, it is no longer the case that the study of the United States Supreme Court dominates the literature on empirical judicial behavior. Of 290 total articles and manuscripts coded, only 39 percent were focused exclusively on the US Supreme Court, a figure that constitutes a plurality of the publications but far from an absolute majority. Publications that attend to one or more courts outside of the United States account for a sizable proportion of the total, approximately 29 percent, suggesting that the plea to orient our study of courts beyond US borders appears to have been heeded (Tate 1989; Tate and Vallinder 1995; Epstein 1999; Gibson, Caldeira, and Baird 1998). Furthermore, if we take the work that is truly comparative in the sense of considering more than one country or court, we see that a full 40 percent of publications in the sample employ a comparative research design. Compare this to Epstein's (1999) figures in a similar state of the subfield analysis, wherein a meager 21 percent of articles published in top outlets addressed a court other than SCOTUS. We can conclude our subfield has made appreciable progress.[12]

This laudable progress aside, there are considerable differences between Americanist and comparativist research with respect to publishing outlets in political science. An absolute majority of judicial research that considered SCOTUS or other subnational courts appeared in the "top-three" journal outlets, while only a one-fifth of articles that were non-US courts related were published in these venues. Instead, most comparative judicial research was published in book format. Moreover, ten out of the twenty-five books (40 percent) were explicitly

TABLE I. Topic and publication outlet in judicial politics research, 2000–2018 count (percentage)

	United States		Non-US cases			
	Supreme Court	Comparative (subnational)	High Court	Comparative (subnational or cross-sectional)	Formal theoretic (no-empirical)	Total
"Top 3"	59 (52)	44 (57)	13 (30)	3 (7)	16 (100)	135 (47)
"Top 3" subfield	15 (13)	13 (17)	13 (30)	10 (25)	0 (0)	51 (18)
Book	39 (35)	20 (26)	18 (40)	27 (68)	0 (0)	104 (36)
Total	113 (100)	77 (100)	44 (100)	39 (100)	16 (100)	290 (100)

Source: Original compilation by the author, for additional information on sampling strategy and data collection, please see Methodological Appendix at the end of the essay.

cross-national comparative edited volumes, implying collaborative effort by many contributors.[13] If we assume that each edited volume includes somewhere between six and twelve contributed chapters or essays, then we might infer that a considerable bulk of recent work on comparative judicial behavior or politics appears in edited volumes, rather than in top peer-reviewed political science journals.[14]

These divergent patterns between US scholars and scholars of courts outside the United States have a number of downstream effects that impact the development of the subdiscipline of comparative judicial politics. One central disparity to this publication trend is one of access. The journal-publishing economy has adapted much more readily to the advent and expansion of the internet, which allows for enhanced capabilities to search and locate research of interest and offers enhanced opportunities for scholars to advertise and readily disseminate their work. Journal publishers have stepped up to this opportunity, allowing "Early View" access to the public without paywall or subscription requirements, advertising published work via social media and subscribers email lists, and joining with mainstream news media to disseminate academic scholarship to a broad, non-specialist audience (e.g. *The Conversation, The Monkey Cage*).

Academic book publishing has been slower to adapt to changes in the technological landscape. Though textbooks and e-books are increasingly published in digital format, libraries, Google Books, or related technologies cannot fill this tremendous lacunae, much less on a global scale. Individual book chapters are not as often assigned an individual DOI (digital object identifier) that would facilitate the discovery and indexing of digital content as discrete and discoverable. This trend is compacted by the very audiences of interest in comparative judicial work: international scholars, or country experts whose interest might be piqued by judicial scholarship owing to an interest in a given political system, stand a far better chance of accessing an online journal article than a book (much less a book chapter). All told, the downstream effects in terms of broader awareness of scholarship, possible impact, and citations for comparative judicial research is substantial.

Data Availability and Repositories

Turning now to the question of data availability, two major data-collection projects make available coded data of judicial decisions from more than one pinnacle court around the world. The first is the High Courts Judicial Database (HCJD), which provides coded information on decisions rendered by eleven pinnacle courts around the world (Tate et al. 1999; Haynie et al. 2007). The co-PIs selected countries based on their shared common law system, and they endeavored to collect data from as many years as possible for each country in their study—the time series in several countries span multiple decades; in others only a handful. The entire universe of cases were collected and coded where feasible, when high court dockets contained thousands of cases the investigators took a simple random sample of one hundred cases per year.[15]

The second major data-collection effort in this regard is the Comparative Law Project, formerly hosted at the Center for Empirical Research in the Law at Washington University in St. Louis.[16] The research team aimed to collect and code judicial decisions for as many countries as possible in the span of a single year (2010). The information the co-PIs aimed to code was akin to that in the HCJD, coded at the level of the legal controversy. Beyond the provision of data on judicial decision-making for a large number of countries, a major (and heretofore under-appreciated) contribution of the Comparative Law Project was the online database infrastructure, which allows for the collection and coding of cases from a large number of countries, with research teams working remotely.[17] This infrastructure would—in theory—be available for any interested researcher to remotely add and code cases of interest, as a sort of crowdsourcing data collection.

A second sort of data project hinges not on the coding and public provision of a large quantity of judicial decisions but instead on providing an outlet to disseminate and archive data and empirical research on high courts around the world. The public distribution of published data and replication files is now commonplace in political science, with many quantitative researchers archiving their replication materials in repositories like the Inter-university Consortium for Political and Social Research (ICPSR) and Harvard's Dataverse. For more qualitatively oriented researchers, the Qualitative Data Repository has a noted advantage of chronicling and archiving materials that are more qualitative in nature, such as interview transcripts, archival materials, or field research notes (Elman, Kapiszewski, and Lupia 2018; Elman and Kapiszewski 2014). Each submission is provided with not only a formal citation but a DOI for ease of citation and public dissemination.

More sources of data exist if we shift the unit of analysis from judges to courts, with rapid advances having occurred over the past decade. The Comparative Constitutions Project (CCP) codifies and classifies the institutional features of all constitutions from 1789 to the present (Elkins, Ginsburg, and Melton 2014). This effort includes many features of constitutions thought to ensure de jure independence, such as judge tenure, characteristics of the nomination process, stipulations for judge advancement or removal, and the like. The CCP also catalogs many constitutional characteristics thought to enhance judicial authority and power, such as standing, docket control, and de jure powers of review (e.g. abstract or concrete, constitutional or statutory powers of review).

As to de facto facets of judicial politics, the Variety of Democracies (VDEM) data set uses expert surveys to explore various metrics of judicial decision-making and interbranch conflict, spanning more than two hundred countries over the past two hundred years (Coppedge et al. 2019). Beyond descriptive characteristics of judicial systems and institutions, the data set also codes for concepts such as judicial independence, government compliance, the frequency of interbranch attacks or judicial purges, among others. Last but not least, Linzer and Staton's (2015) measure of latent judicial independence (LJI) deploys a measurement model to summarize and synthesize various measures of judicial independence, accounting for uncertainty, missingness, and possible boundedness or truncation of the various underlying measures. The authors provide data on more than two hundred countries in the postwar period, representing one of the most comprehensive measures of the concept to date.

Challenges and Opportunities to Comparative Judicial Research

I now turn to the question of challenges and opportunities in comparative judicial research. I have described various ways in which the field has improved in the past two decades—no longer are we a subfield only concerned with a single pinnacle court in a single country (i.e., SCOTUS), and comparative research designs are now common, some of which are published in general interest political science journals. The comparative study of law and courts has inspired researchers from economics, law, political science, history, and area studies, meaning it is a veritable enclave of interdisciplinary work. New sources of data provide systematic comparisons of high court behavior and interbranch relations for a large number of countries over time, the scope of which will no doubt only increase. These are reasons to be encouraged.

Yet notable deficiencies and obstacles persist. Non-US comparative research is less frequently published in general interest political science journals (Krehbiel and Bilsback 2019) and most often appears in books. These facts may have deleterious consequences in terms of public dissemination, as well as the eventual disciplinary impact of the research. Only two data sets exist that collect and code the decisional outcomes of judges in different countries; most non-US comparative analyses are based on single-country case studies of individual countries (cf. this volume). What explains the lack of progress? Why is progress such a slow-moving train?

At the turn of the twenty-first century, comparative judicial politics was a tiny enclave of researchers, owing in part to a lack of available data: we simply did not have access to judges' votes, their decisions, courts' dockets or opinions, such that a systematic evaluation of judicial behavior outside the United States—much less across more than one country—might be undertaken. A mere decade later, this was no longer true; as the "big data" revolution had witnessed dozens of high courts readily make their decisions, deliberations, dockets, opinions, and votes accessible on the internet for public consumption. We now have far more data than we know what to do with.

What to do with all of this information? What should be collected, and what is the relevant unit of analysis? What to code, and how to code it, what are the relevant informational parameters of highest analytical priority?[18] Once those decisions are made, to what universe can we generalize (cf. Hirschl 2005, 2014)? Are the countries or courts that self-select into transparent judicial proceedings representative of a population?[19] If so, which one? *None of these questions can be answered in a vacuum; none of these issues resolved without reference to theory.* It is theory that guides us to research questions, research design, and all the downstream analytical decisions empirical analysis may entail. *We do not lack for comparative data, but we are lacking in comparative theory.*

To then extend one's analysis to more than one court, second-order concerns quickly compound.[20] Are the data generated by one high court directly comparable to the data generated by a similarly situated pinnacle court?[21] Are the dockets comparable? Are panel assignments similarly composed? Are there any internal norms to judge deliberation or voting, such as the seniority norm of the US Supreme Court? Lacking cross-unit homogeneity, we put the validity of our comparisons at risk. Ultimately, the degree to which any comparisons can or should be made depends to a very large extent on the research questions one seeks to ask, which again, raise fundamental questions of theory, research design, and case selection.

This is one reason why the study of comparative *courts* as opposed to comparative *judicial behavior* has produced a comparatively robust and vibrant stream of research: making valid comparisons across courts is more straightforward than comparing judges' behavior across contexts. This is also why (among other reasons) formal theoretic models have been such a powerful tool in the field of comparative judicial politics. Formalizing theory requires abstracting away—making a clear statement of assumptions and scope conditions that guide one's analysis, and the universe of cases to which one's theory may apply. Simplifying assumptions and scope conditions are what make formal models tractable, abstracting away from all the heterogeneity and nuance that permeates (but also colors) the empirical world. The mathematic derivation of equilibrium behaviors makes explicit how expected behaviors vary across institutional or structural conditions; formal theorists are assured their theory is internally consistent when they can derive a closed form solution. Armed with this tool, their theory makes clear predictions for empirical scrutiny and testing.

The scholarly accumulation that has occurred in the area of American judicial politics, and then generalized in the US comparative scholarship, has been quick to advance due to a shared and common theory of the judicial adjudication process—a common theoretical model that lays out plainly the problems judges face in adjudication; delineates with great specificity judges' incentives, preferences, and priorities; and then derives mathematically equilibrium expectations from that model. Yet the sort of parsimonious and simplified model exemplified by Kornhauser's essay (this volume) is in fact a highly stylized, highly nuanced model of the world and judicial adjudication in that context, based in great part on the many idiosyncrasies of the US judicial system. Said parsimony requires idiosyncrasy.[22]

Americanist scholars are aided not only by theoretical consensus but also by context: the US political system is the most studied system by American political scientists, economists, legal scholars, and pundits. This allows judicial researchers to situate behavior of courts and judges with great specificity, to interpret judicial actions and behaviors in the broader political context.[23] This also implies a built-in constituency for US-focused judicial research, with a broad base of readers who might readily contextualize the political implications said judicial research may reveal. Take for example the quantitative scaling of judicial votes so as to map Supreme Court justices on a common ideological scale, not only with each other (Martin and Quinn 2002) but with other actors in the political system (Epstein et al. 2007; Shor and McCarty 2011). Armed with this sort of information, analysts can describe and analyze the causes and consequences of ideological composition on the Court and how the Court's policies have shaped American politics.

Yet the output from these item response models are not imbued with intrinsic meaning; it is a way of summarizing data based on correspondence analysis of judicial agreements and dissents. Despite being a primarily quantitative data-reduction technique, the resulting statistics are fundamentally qualitative in nature: for these statistics to be meaningful requires description and interpretation. It requires context. It requires a substantive knowledge and definition of what it means to be "conservative" or "liberal" in a given system, to a priori identify the major dimensions of political conflict that sort and divide actors in a given system.[24] An enterprising comparativist, eager to deploy neat statistical tools to enhance our understanding of judicial politics in other countries, would likely face questions in the peer review process that are largely taken for granted in the American context. "What does it mean for a judge to be on the left or the right?" "What does this tell us about politics in country X?" And if said comparativist happens to study a country that is not well known to the American academy, she may even encounter a more flippant "So what?" or "Who cares?"

Professional Incentives in an Interdisciplinary Field

To this end, it would seem there exist meaningful opportunities for straight (not mere) description in the area of comparative judicial politics.[25] An encyclopedic accounting of the mechanics of the data-generating process of judicial decisions across a large set of countries would constitute a meaningful contribution to the study of comparative judicial politics, as a first step in starting to answer some of the questions outlined above. This might help researchers in the field identify the contours of our collective knowledge, to start to collectively "know what we don't know." But the shortcomings to this suggestion are readily apparent. As soon as the data are compiled, history renders it obsolete. Second, and more importantly, professional incentives to publish this sort of basic research in mainstream political science are scant.[26]

To accurately characterize incentives, we must consider both necessary investments, and the (probabilistically weighted) eventual gains. Some of the requisite investments to good comparative political science research are well known and widely acknowledged: it usually requires expertise in the politics of more than one country and may require proficiency in a foreign language. Add to that, as in the case of judicial politics, sufficient expertise in the law or legal profession, as defined in both law and in practice. Many graduate programs now train doctoral students in the requisite skills to automate data-collection tasks to quickly harvest the data from the internet, as well as in the arts of quantitative data analysis to interpret statistical models. These skills can facilitate the collection and analysis of quantitative data, provided said data and analysis is appropriate for the research question and theory. And of course it is theory that guides the question and research design, so ideally our hypothetical researcher has already identified a theoretical puzzle of broad interest. If they are able to formalize the theoretical model, so much the better.[27]

Setting eventual payoffs aside, the scenario I just described sets a very high barrier to entry. Identify a theoretical question of broad general interest and craft a research design to appropriately test hypotheses. Gain regional (and possibly language) expertise. Also legal expertise. Training in quantitative methods and automated data collection. Training in formal theory a plus. Most graduate students struggle to accomplish even the first goal (theory and research question), much less all the rest. There are very few faculty or graduate institutions that can train students to do all of these things well. This may be an insurmountable bar for any one person to clear.

Or perhaps this is not for a single person to solve. I have stated from the outset that comparative judicial politics is a topic that brings together a strikingly diverse cross-section of scholars. Economists, legal scholars, political scientists, some with legal or country expertise, have all contributed to the field of comparative judicial politics, using varied methodologies to shine a light on a previously unappreciated aspect of judicial (or court) behavior. Said interdisciplinary diversity implies that members of the community will hold meaningful and legitimate differences of opinions about what questions we should be asking and how to best go about answering them. We must not let these differences stymie a shared path forward.

For the subfield to advance requires members of the community to value and openly celebrate this diversity as a noted subfield strength. This requires peer reviewers being open-minded to research that deploys methodologies that are divergent from their own. We must continue to organize panels and conferences that explicitly promote and publicize our comparative research, to build out and expand our network of scholars. This requires gatekeepers, when tasked with evaluating the materials for tenure and promotion, not to stigmatize or diminish research resulting from coauthorship and collaborative projects. This requires educating our peers and our colleagues about the peer-reviewed outlets that are most respected to our subfield, as they may not "fit" the traditional disciplinary molds. We must continue to engage related subfields, convincing other comparativists of the political import of judicial actors and educating our respective disciplines about the challenges and virtues of the "comparative advantage."

Methodological Note: Overview of Publications Trends Data

To examine publication trends between 2000 and 2018 as found in table 1, two research assistants were tasked with recording the title, author, and authors' institution and faculty ranking for all publications relating to the empirical study of judicial behavior in peer-reviewed journals that are considered to be the "top three" political science journals based on reputation and impact factor (the *American Political Science Review*, the *American Journal of Political Science*, and *The Journal of Politics*). Next, we turned to record this information in the two highest impact factor comparative subfield journals (*British Journal of Political Science* and *Comparative Political Studies*) and the flagship journal of the Law & Courts Section of the American Political Science Association, *The Journal of Law and Courts*.[28] To account for publications in books, we collected information on all published books on judicial politics as advertised in the *Law & Courts Newsletter*, a publication of the Law & Courts Organized Section of the American Political Science Association. With this information compiled, we coded each of the manuscripts based on their empirical foci (US Supreme Court only, US comparative, other national court, or other cross-sectional).

Notes

1. Though the term "empirical legal studies" (ELS) is often used to refer to research that is quantitative in nature, I am agnostic on this point. The systematic analysis of qualitative data and the accumulation of in-depth knowledge of particular cases in service of a research question is just not only acceptable in my working definition but also a necessary precursor for many quantitative studies.

2. My review will emphasize research published in mainstream political science, and in so doing will no doubt miss innumerable contributions of scholars in other fields. The interdisciplinary nature of the subfield of comparative judicial politics is a theme to which I return.

3. The extent to which any research is comparative in the first sense depends on the theory, the research question, and research design, which of course varies widely in application.

4. A related literature considers judicial voting and case outcomes throughout the US judicial hierarchy (Songer and Haire 1992; Songer and Sheehan 1992; Songer, Segal, and Cameron 1994). Although these pathbreaking studies represented a first move to study judicial decision-making outside of SCOTUS, cross-sectional or institutional variation are infrequently central explanatory factors.

5. For a non-US example of this approach, Smyth (this volume) suggests a similar approach has been used to understand dissent rates of judges on the Supreme Court of Australia (Smyth and Narayan 2004, cf. Sheehan and Randazzo 2012).

6. Despite its conceptual centrality, judicial independence is often conflated with related concepts, including judicial authority, autonomy, judge impartiality and judicial power, to name a few. For excellent overviews, see Kapiszewski and Taylor 2008; and Hilbink 2012.

7. While some researchers assume independent judicial review serves to constrain the majority, in a less benevolent interpretation (Hamilton, Madison,

Jay 2005; Shapiro and Stone Sweet 2002), incumbents regard judges as powerful policy makers whose tenure will outlast their own. In this "deck-stacking" vision, incumbents empower a court so as to institutionalize their preferences into the future (Landes and Posner 1975; McNollgast 1987). A related model construes the establishment of an independent court as a credible commitment to a particular policy, either to signal an incumbent's priorities (Hirschl 2005) or to monitor compliance to a predetermined set of principles (North and Weingast 1989; Stephenson 2003; Carrubba 2009). The credible commitment model does not hinge on assumptions regarding electoral competition or incumbent vulnerability but does explain the establishment of an independent high court as intentional based on the hope for future gain.

8. As is common with other formal theoretic literature, comparisons are often conceptual in nature, and empirical analyses tend to focus on whether the behavior of jurists or courts in a small number of countries is consistent with equilibrium expectations. These dynamics have been explored though quantitative analysis and qualitative case studies of judicial behavior in Mexico (Staton 2006) and Germany (Krehbiel 2016).

9. It bears noting that much of the literature that considers public support for courts does not empirically evaluate judicial behavior at all but rather considers public opinion.

10. For additional information on sampling strategy and data collection, please see the methodological note at the end of this essay.

11. I acknowledge the limitation to my empirical approach in that I cannot speak to the research published in economics journals, empirical legal studies outlets, or in law reviews. Indeed, of the comparative judicial literature summarized in the previous section, more than a third (37 percent) was published in non-political science peer-reviewed outlets. Of the 110 publications cited in the previous section of this essay, 50 percent (55) appeared in peer-reviewed journals outside of the general audience journals or the top subfield venues. Regarding the publication of the rest, 30 percent (33) appeared in general audience journals, 17 percent (19) in books, and 2.7 percent (3) in main subfield journals.

12. A related study by Krehbiel and Bilsback (2019) found that most cross-national judicial politics articles were published in specialized law and courts subfield journals, such as *Law & Society Review* and *Journal of Empirical Legal Studies*, a trend that has increased over time. The authors report far fewer examples of comparative judicial research being published in general interest journals, suggesting the field has a presence, albeit limited, in top political science outlets. This is additional evidence of the interdisciplinary nature of the subfield of comparative judicial politics.

13. One noted exception deserves mention because it relates to the publishing of judicial politics research into top peer-reviewed outlets. Our

coding process distinguished a class of articles that present original formal theories of judicial behavior or decision-making but that contained no empirical analysis. We include these in our study despite the lack of empirical analysis, as many are explicitly comparative in their theoretical contribution by virtue of their consideration of comparative statics equilibrium outcomes. Our research identified sixteen publications of this kind, all of which were published in the general interest peer-reviewed political science journals.

14. No decisive inferences can be drawn from these data alone. We have no information on impact factor, nor is this a metric of the quality of scholarship. Furthermore, we lack information on the supply side of journal submissions and have no sense of how this work was received by journal editors or blind peer-reviews. There are also subfield norms at play: the professional expectations in the broader field of comparative politics still often favors book publishing, while journal article publications are now the norm in American politics.

15. The coded information contains information on the history of the case throughout the judicial hierarchy, litigant characteristics and the identification of other interested parties, the treatment in the decision, and the number of dissenting and majority votes. Each case is coded for substantive issues as well as the directionality of the decision on that issue and whether the written opinion makes reference to one of a wide variety of legal standards.

16. This project identified more than eighty pinnacle courts (i.e., constitutional courts, tribunals, and supreme courts) around the world who publish their decisions or votes online.

17. Notably, both projects were funded by grants from the National Science Foundation. The successful acquisition of external funding would seem to imply that this sort of research and data collection efforts are appreciated by a broad cross-section of scholars, such that these proposals would have successfully passed a rigorous peer-review process.

18. As one case in point, the reason judicial decisions are coded at the level of the legal dispute is rooted in the adjudication model outlined in Kornhauser (1992b; this volume). Constructing an appropriate test of said theory requires information regarding judges' dispositions coded at the level of the legal dispute.

19. Indeed, much of what we claim to know about judicial politics of any sort is based in large part on the study of courts in the United States. We lack sufficient comparative information to evaluate the extent to which the US judicial system is typical in any sense of the word, but suffice it to say the US court system is probably highly idiosyncratic.

20. It is hard to overstate the human resources that are required to conduct this sort of research into more than one country. Beyond knowledge

of particular cases, researchers must have not only language expertise, but legal expertise to parse the nuance of judicial language and argumentation. Legal expertise in one country does not necessarily "translate" to another; legal terms in two countries may have two different legal meanings and implications, even when they share a common mother tongue.

21. Bevan (2019) provides a candid and illuminating discussion of the challenges of creating and sustaining a common codebook for the Comparative Agendas Project. Despite the research team's best efforts, multiple interpretations of codes as well as the proliferation of subcodes to accommodate the nuance of particular countries made the process unwieldy. Ultimately, Walgrave and Boydstun (2019) report that for the wealth of comparative data the Comparative Agendas Project contains, only rarely are the data used for inter-country comparisons.

22. Tweaking parameters in said model to accommodate alternative realities is no easy feat. Pull the wrong string and the whole sweater may well unravel—a closed-form solution is no longer tractable. Adding additional nuance may threaten internal coherency. Further, it is also not always obvious the appropriate place of departure. Which theoretical assumption deserves reconsideration? Would altering assumptions about judges' preferences be fruitful, or would it be better to tweak an assumption about judges' constraints? The extent to which models based on US adjudication credibly inform the study of judicial politics in other contexts is an open question, and one which deserves explicit justification for any scholars who seek to take a "have theory, will travel" approach.

23. Notice that the two essays in this volume on the US federal courts and the US state supreme courts dive deep into the particulars of their respective research areas. This is because of their general consensus about the data generating process of the US case: though Kornhauser (this volume) lays out in detail the theoretical and conceptual model of what is it that judges and courts *do* and *why they do it*, the theoretical model of judges' incentives is based in large part on the empirical realities of judging in the US system.

24. See Hanretty's (2013) discussion of the scaled voting records of the UK Supreme Court justices. The author finds the IRT estimates to measure no more than justices' propensity to dissent and not meaningfully differentiate judges on a left-right political continuum (cf. Varol, Dalla Pellegrina, and Garoupa 2017).

25. An excellent essay on case selection and comparative inference by Hirschl (2005) suggests that the comparative public law literature suffers not from a lack of description but from a lack of thoughtful comparisons and careful case selection, which again can only be remedied with reference to theory.

26. This confluence of factors poses a distinct challenge for the next generation of would-be comparative judicial scholars, as well as the advisors who

seek to guide them. At a conference held at Texas A&M Law School in the spring of 2018, a group of scholars convened to discuss the state of the subdiscipline of comparative judicial politics, with the hope of identifying a set of questions or research agendas to carry the field forward. To the question of whether they would advise graduate students or untenured faculty members to build a dissertation based exclusively on the publication of a new data set, the consensus from senior faculty in the room was a resounding "No." Lacking a clear theory, or better still a clear theoretical contribution, a data-driven approach forward is not a credible path to professional security.

27. There are larger discipline-wide trends that further shape graduate training and professional incentives. One ascendant intellectual trend is the "causal" revolution, which prioritizes clear identification of the effects of causes, often using tools based on random assignment or quasi-random analytical approaches (cf. Hanretty, this volume). The emphasis on causal identification is reflected in publication trends (Clark and Golder 2015) and in PhD curriculum at research universities, where causal inference is now considered a core methodological skill. Though a clear opportunity for future research, experimentation poses distinct challenges to scholars interested in intrinsically endogenous structures, such as markets and institutions, as experimental manipulation is infeasible at best, and unethical at worst.

28. The flagship journal for the Law and Courts section only began publishing in 2013 and so is underrepresented in comparison to the other journals considered here. Second, the journal selection here is biased toward comparative and cross-national research, as the "subfield" journals selected tend to be more comparative in orientation, thus likely precluding comparative judicial manuscripts published in more "mainstream" or US politics–oriented subfield journals.

References

Bartels, Brandon L., and Andrew J. O'Geen. 2015. "The Nature of Legal Change on the US Supreme Court: Jurisprudential Regimes Theory and Its Alternatives." *American Journal of Political Science* 59 (4): 880–95.

Bartels, Brandon L., and Christopher D. Johnston. 2013. "On the Ideological Foundations of Supreme Court Legitimacy in the American Public." *American Journal of Political Science* 57: 711–81.

Bevan, Shaun. 2019. "Gone Fishing: The Creation of the Comparative Agendas Project Master Codebook." In *Comparative Policy Agendas: Theory, Tools, Data*, edited by Frank R. Baumgartner, Christian Breunig, and Emiliano Grossman, 219–42. London: Oxford University Press.

Bonneau, Chris W., and Melinda Gann Hall. 2009. *In Defense of Judicial Elections*. New York: Routledge.

Boudreaux, D. J., and A. C. Pritchard. 1994. "Reassessing the Role of the Independent Judiciary in Enforcing Interest-Group Bargains." *Constitutional Political Economy* 5 (1): 1–21.

Brace, Paul, and Melinda Gann Hall. 1995. "Studying Courts Comparatively: The View from the American States." *Political Research Quarterly* 48 (1): 5–29.

Brace, Paul, and Melinda Gann Hall. 1997. "The Interplay of Preferences, Case Facts, Context and Structure in the Politics of Judicial Choice." *The Journal of Politics* 59 (4): 1206–31.

Caldeira, G. A., and J. L. Gibson. 1992. "The Etiology of Public Support for the Supreme Court." *American Journal of Political Science* 36 (3): 635–64.

Caldeira, G. A., and J. L. Gibson. 1995. "The Legitimacy of the Court of Justice in the European Union: Models of Institutional Support." *The American Political Science Review* 89 (2): 356–76.

Cane, Peter, and Herbert Kritzer. 2010. *The Oxford Handbook of Empirical Legal Research*. London: Oxford University Press.

Canes-Wrone, Brandice, Tom S. Clark, and Jason P. Kelly. 2014. "Judicial Selection and Death Penalty Decisions." *American Political Science Review* 108 (1): 23–39.

Carrubba, Clifford James. 2009. "A Model of the Endogenous Development of Judicial Institutions in Federal and International Systems." *The Journal of Politics* 71 (1): 55–69.

Chavez, Rebecca Bill. 2004. *The Rule of Law in Nascent Democracies: Judicial Politics in Argentina*. Stanford: Stanford University Press.

Clark, William Roberts, and Matt Golder. 2015. "Big Data, Causal Inference, and Formal Theory: Contradictory Trends in Political Science? Introduction." *PS: Political Science & Politics* 48 (1): 65–70.

Clark, William Roberts, Matt Golder, and Sona Nadenichek Golder. 2018. *Principles of Comparative Politics*. New York: CQ Press.

Cooter, Robert D., and Tom Ginsburg. 1996. "Comparative Judicial Discretion: An Empirical Test of Economic Models." *International Review of Law and Economics* 16: 295–313.

Coppedge, Michael, John Gerring, Carl Henrik Knutsen, Staffan I. Lindberg, Jan Teorell, David Altman, Michael Bernhard, et al. 2019. "V-Dem Dataset v9." https://doi.org/10.23696/vdemcy19.

Couso, Javier A. 2005. "The Judicialization of Chilean Politics: The Rights Revolution that Never Was." In *The Judicialization of Politics in Latin America*, edited by Rachel Seider, Line Schjolden, and Alan Angell, 105–29. Palgrave McMillian, New York, NY.

Driscoll, Amanda, and Michael J. Nelson. 2013. "The Political Origins of Judicial Elections: Evidence from the United States and Bolivia." *Judicature* 96 (4): 1–13.

Driscoll, Amanda, and Michael J. Nelson. 2014. "Ignorance or Opposition?: Blank and Spoiled Votes in Low-Information, Highly Politicized Environments." *Political Research Quarterly* 67 (3): 547–61.

Driscoll, Amanda, and Michael J. Nelson, 2015. "Judicial Selection and the Democratization of Justice: Lessons from the Bolivian Judicial Elections." *Journal of Law & Courts* 3 (1): 115–48.

Driscoll, Amanda, and Michael J. Nelson. 2018. "There is No Legitimacy Crisis: Support for Judicial Institutions in Modern Latin America." *Revista de la Sociedad Argentina de Análisis Político* 12 (2): 361–77.

Driscoll, Amanda, and Michael J. Nelson. 2019. "Collaborative Research: Judicial Legitimacy in Comparative Perspective." National Science Foundation Grants SES-1920997 and SES-1920915.

Elkins, Zachary, Tom Ginsburg, and James Melton. 2014. The Comparative Constitutions Project. Technical report. http://comparativeconstitutions project.org.

Elman, Colin, and Diana Kapiszewski. 2014. "Data Access and Research Transparency in the Qualitative Tradition." *PS: Political Science Politics* 7 (1): 43–47.

Elman, Colin, Diana Kapiszewski, and Arthur Lupia. 2018. "Transparent Social Inquiry: Implications for Political Science." *Annual Review of Political Science* 21 (1): 29–47.

Epp, Charles R. 1998. *The Rights Revolution: Lawyers, Activists, and Supreme Courts in Comparative Perspective.* Chicago: University of Chicago Press.

Epperly, Brad. 2013. "The Provision of Insurance? Judicial Independence and Post-Tenure Fate of Leaders." *Journal of Law and Courts* 1 (2): 247–87.

Epstein, Lee. 1999. "The Comparative Advantage." *Law & Courts Newsletter* 9 (3): 1–6.

Epstein, Lee, Andrew D. Martin, Jeffrey A. Segal, and Chad Westerland. 2007. "The Judicial Common Space." *The Journal of Law, Economics, and Organization* 23 (2): 303–25.

Epstein, Lee, and Jack Knight. 1997. *The Choices Judges Make.* New York: CQ Press.

Ferejohn, John. 1999. "Independent Judges, Dependent Judiciary: Explaining Judicial Independence." *Southern California Law Review* 72 (2–3): 353–84.

Finkel, Jodi S. 2005. "Judicial Reform as Insurance Policy: Mexico in the 1990s." *Latin American Politics & Society* 47 (1): 87–113.

Finkel, Jodi S. 2008. *Judicial Reform as Political Insurance: Argentina, Peru, and Mexico in the 1990s.* South Bend: University of Notre Dame Press.

Gibson, James L., and Gregory A. Caldeira. 1995. "The Legitimacy of Transnational Legal Institutions: Compliance, Support and the European Court of Justice." *American Journal of Political Science* 39: 459–89.

Gibson, James L., Gregory A. Caldeira, and Vanessa Baird. 1998. "On the Legitimacy of National High Courts." *American Political Science Review* 92 (2): 343–58.

Gibson, James L., and Michael J. Nelson. 2015. "Can the U.S. Supreme Court Have Too Much Legitimacy?" In *Making Law and Courts Research Relevant:*

The Normative Implications of Empirical Research, edited by Brandon L. Bartels and Chris W. Bonneau, 169–79. New York: Routledge.

Ginsburg, Thomas. 2003. *Judicial Review in New Democracies: Constitutional Courts in East Asia.* New York: Cambridge University Press.

Hall, Melinda Gann. 1992. "Electoral Politics and Strategic Voting in State Supreme Courts." *Journal of Politics* 54: 427–46.

Hall, Melinda Gann. 2001. "State Supreme Courts in American Democracy: Probing the Myths of Judicial Reform." *American Political Science Review* 95: 315–30.

Hall, Melinda Gann, and Chris W. Bonneau. 2006. "Does Quality Matter? Challengers in State Supreme Court Elections." *American Journal of Political Science* 50: 20–33.

Hamilton, Alexander, James Madison, and John Jay. 2005. *The Federalist Papers.* Hackett Publishing Company Incorporated. Indianapolis, IN.

Hanretty, Chris. 2013. "The Decisions and Ideal Points of British Law Lords." *British Journal of Political Science* 43 (3): 703–16.

Hanssen, F. Andrew. 2004. "Is There a Politically Optimal Level of Judicial Independence?" *American Economic Review* 94 (3): 712–29.

Haynie, Stacia L. 1994. "Resource Inequalities and Litigation Outcomes in the Philippine Supreme Court." *The Journal of Politics* 56 (3): 752–72.

Haynie, Stacia L. 1995. "Resource Inequalities and Regional Variation in Litigation Outcomes in the Philippine Supreme Court, 1961–1986." *Political Research Quarterly* 48 (2): 371–80.

Haynie, Stacia L., Reginald S. Sheehan, Donald R. Songer, and C. Neal Tate. 2007. "High Courts Judicial Database." Judicial Research Initiative, University of South Carolina. http://www.cas.sc.edu/poli/juri.

Haynie, Stacia L., and Kaitlyn L. Sill. 2007. "Experienced Advocates and Litigation Outcomes: Repeat Players in the South African Supreme Court of Appeal." *Political Research Quarterly* 60 (3): 443–53.

Helmke, Gretchen. 2002. "The Logic of Strategic Defection: Court-Executive Relations in Argentina Under Dictatorship and Democracy." *American Political Science Review* 96 (2): 291–303.

Helmke, Gretchen. 2005. *Courts under Constraints: Judges, Generals and Presidents.* New York: Cambridge University Press.

Helmke, Gretchen, and Frances Rosenbluth. 2009. "Regimes and the Rule of Law: Judicial Independence in Comparative Perspective." *Annual Review of Political Science* 12: 345–66.

Herron, Erik S., and Kirk A. Randazzo. 2003. "The Relationship Between Independence and Judicial Review in Post-Communist Courts." *Journal of Politics* 65 (2): 422–38.

Hilbink, L. 2007. *Judges beyond Politics in Democracy and Dictatorship: Lessons from Chile.* New York: Cambridge University Press.

Hilbink, Lisa. 2012. "The Origins of Positive Judicial Independence." *World Politics* 64 (4): 587–621.

Hinkle, Rachael K. 2015. "Legal Constraint in the US Courts of Appeals." *The Journal of Politics* 77 (3): 721–35.

Hirschl, Ran. 2000. "The Political Origins of Judicial Empowerment through Constitutionalization: Lessons from Four Constitutional Revolutions." *Law & Social Inquiry* 25 (1): 91–149.

Hirschl, Ran. 2001. "The Political Origins of Judicial Empowerment through Constitutionalization: Lessons from Israel's Constitutional Revolution." *Comparative Politics* 315–35.

Hirschl, Ran. 2005. "The Question of Case Selection in Comparative Constitutional Law." *American Journal of Comparative Law* 53 (1): 125–55.

Hirschl, Ran. 2014 *Comparative Matters: The Renaissance of Comparative Constitutional Law.* New York: Oxford University Press.

Iaryczower, Matías, Pablo T. Spiller, and Mariano Tommasi. 2002. "Judicial Independence in Unstable Environments, Argentina 1935–1998." *American Journal of Political Science* 699–716.

Kapiszewski, Diana. 2012. *High Courts and Economic Governance in Argentina and Brazil.* New York: Cambridge University Press.

Kapiszewski, Diana, and Matthew M. Taylor. 2008. "Doing Courts Justice? Studying Judicial Politics in Latin America." *Perspectives on Politics* 6 (4): 741–67.

Kawar, Leila, and Mark Fathi Massoud. 2012. "New Directions in Comparative Public Law." *Law & Courts Newsletter* 22 (3): 32–36.

Kornhauser, Lewis. 1992a. "Modeling Collegial Courts II: Legal Doctrine." *Journal of Law, Economics & Organization* 8 (3): 441–70.

Kornhauser, Lewis A. 1992b. "Modeling Collegial Courts I: Path Dependence." *International Review of Law and Economics* (12): 169–85.

Krehbiel, Jay N. 2016. "The Politics of Judicial Procedures: The Role of Public Oral Hearings in the German Constitutional Court." *American Journal of Political Science* 60 (4): 900–1005.

Krehbiel, Jay, and William Bradley Bilsback. 2019. "A Survey of the Comparative Judicial Politics Literature: What Have We Learned in the Past Twenty Years?" Paper presented at the 2019 Midwest Political Science Association Annual Meeting, April 5, 2019, Chicago, IL.

Kritzer, Herbert. 2011. "Competitiveness in State Supreme Court Elections, 1946–2009." *Journal of Empirical Legal Studies* 8: 237–59.

Kritzer, Herbert M., and Mark J. Richards. 2003. "Jurisprudential Regimes and Supreme Court Decisionmaking: The Lemon Regime and Establishment Clause Cases." *Law & Society Review* 37 (4): 827–40.

Landes, W. M., and R. A. Posner. 1975. "The Independent Judiciary in an Interest-Group Perspective." *Journal of Law and Economics* 18 (3): 875–901.

Lax, Jeffrey R. 2011. "The New Judicial Politics of Legal Doctrine." *Annual Review of Political Science* 14 (1): 131–57.

Lax, Jeffrey R., and Kelly T. Rader. 2010. "Legal Constraints on Supreme Court Decision Making: Do Jurisprudential Regimes Exist?" *The Journal of Politics* 72 (2): 273–84.

Linzer, Drew A., and Jeffery K. Staton. 2015. "A Global Measure of Judicial Independence, 1948–2012." *Journal of Law and Courts* (Fall 2015): 223–56.

Maltzman, F., J. F. Spriggs, and P. J. Wahlbeck. 2000. *Crafting Law on the Supreme Court: The Collegial Game.* New York: Cambridge University Press.

Martin, Andrew D., and Kevin M. Quinn. 2002. "Dynamic Ideal Point Estimation via Markov Chain Monte Carlo for the US Supreme Court, 1953–1999." *Political Analysis* 10 (2): 134–53.

McNollgast. 1987. "Administrative Procedures as Instruments of Political Control." *Journal of Law, Economics and Organization* 3 (2): 243–77.

Moustafa, Tamir. 2007. *The Struggle for Constitutional Power: Law, Politics, and Economic Development in Egypt.* New York: Cambridge University Press.

Murphy, Walter F., and Joseph Tanenhaus. 1968. "Public Opinion and the United States Supreme Court: Mapping of Some Prerequisites for Court Legitimation of Regime Changes." *Law & Society Review* 2 (3): 357–84.

Nelson, Michael J. 2014. "Responsive Justice? Retention Elections, Prosecutors and Public Opinion." *Journal of Law and Courts* 2 (1): 117–52.

North, Douglas, and Barry Weingast. 1989. "Constitutions and Commitment: The Evolution of Institutions Governing Public Choice in Seventeenth-Century England." *The Journal of Economic History* 49 (4): 803–32.

Pang, Xun, Barry Friedman, Andrew D. Martin, and Kevin M. Quinn. 2012. "Endogenous Jurisprudential Regimes." *Political Analysis* 20 (4): 417–36.

Popova, Maria. 2010. "Political Competition as an Obstacle to Judicial Independence: Evidence from Russia and the Ukraine." *Comparative Political Studies* 43 (10): 1202–29.

Pritchett, C. Herman. 1948. *The Roosevelt Court: A Study of Judicial Politics and Values 1937–1947.* New Orleans: Quid Pro Books.

Ramseyer, J. M. 1994. "The Puzzling (In)Dependence of Courts: A Comparative Approach." *The Journal of Legal Studies* 23 (2): 721–47.

Ramseyer, J. M., and E. B. Rasmusen. 1997. "Judicial Independence in a Civil Law Regime: The Evidence from Japan." *Journal of Law, Economics, & Organization* 13 (2): 259–86.

Randazzo, Kirk A., Douglas M. Gibler, and Rebecca Reid. 2016. "Examining the Development of Judicial Independence." *Political Research Quarterly* 69 (3): 583–93.

Sanchez-Urribarri, Raul A., Susanne Schorpp, Krik A. Randazzo, and Donald R. Songer. 2011. "Explaining Changes to Rights Litigation: Testing a

Multivariate Model in a Comparative Framework." *The Journal of Politics* 73 (2): 391–405.

Scott, Kevin M. 2006. "Reconsidering the Impact of Jurisprudential Regimes." *Social Science Quarterly* 87 (2): 380–94.

Segal, J. A., and H. J. Spaeth. 2002. *The Supreme Court and the Attitudinal Model Revisited.* New York: Cambridge University Press.

Shapiro, Martin, and Alec Stone Sweet. 2002. *On Law, Politics and Judicialization.* London: Oxford University Press.

Sheehan, Reginald S., and Kirk A. Randazzo. 2012. "Explaining Litigant Success in the High Court of Australia." *Australian Journal of Political Science* 47 (2): 239–55.

Shor, Boris, and Nolan McCarty. 2011. "The Ideological Mapping of American Legislatures." *American Political Science Review* 105 (3): 530–51.

Smyth, R., and P. K. Narayan. 2004. "Hail to the Chief! Leadership and Structural Change in the Level of Consensus on the High Court of Australia." *Journal of Empirical Legal Studies* 1 (2): 399–427.

Songer, Donald R., and Susan Haire. 1992. "Integrating Alternative Approaches to the Study of Judicial Voting: Obscenity Cases in the US Courts of Appeals." *American Journal of Political Science* 36 (4): 963–82.

Songer, Donald R., Jeffrey A. Segal, and Charles M. Cameron. 1994. "The Hierarchy of Justice: Testing a Principal-Agent model of Supreme Court-Circuit Court." *American Journal of Political Science* 38 (3): 673–96.

Songer, Donald R., and Reginald S. Sheehan. 1992. "Who Wins on Appeal? Upperdogs and Underdogs in the United States Courts of Appeals." *American Journal of Political Science* 36 (1): 235–58.

Staton, Jeffery K. 2006. "Constitutional Review and the Selective Promotion of Case Results." *American Journal of Political Science* 50 (1): 98–112.

Staton, Jeffery K., and Georg Vanberg. 2008. "The Value of Vagueness: Delegation, Defiance, and Judicial Opinions." *American Journal of Political Science* 52 (3): 504–19.

Stephenson, Matthew C. 2003. "'When the Devil Turns . . .': The Political Foundations of Independent Judicial Review." *The Journal of Legal Studies* 32 (1): 59–89.

Tanenhaus, Joseph, and Walter F. Murphy. 1981. "Patterns of Public Support for the Supreme Court: A Panel Study." *Journal of Politics* 43 (1): 24–39.

Tate, C. Neal. 1983. "The Methodology of Judicial Behavior Research: A Review and Critique." *Political Behavior* 5 (1): 51–82.

Tate, C. Neal. 1989. "Scientific Comparative Judicial Politics." *Law & Courts Newsletter* 7 (1): 1–7.

Tate, C. Neal, and Stacia L. Haynie. 1994. "Building a Scientific Comparative Judicial Politics and Arousing the Dragons of Antiscientism." *Law & Society Review* 28 (2): 377–94.

Tate, C. Neal, Stacia L. Haynie, Reginald S. Sheehan, and Donald R. Songer. 1999. "Collaborative Research: Fitting More Pieces into the Puzzle of Judicial Behavior: A Multi-Country Data Base and Program of Research." National Science Foundation Grant (SES-9975237). http://artsandsciences.sc.edu /poli/juri/highcts.htm.

Tate, C. Neal, and Torbjorn Vallinder. 1995. *The Global Expansion of Judicial Power*. New York: NYU Press.

Vanberg, Georg. 2000. "Establishing Judicial Independence in Western Europe: The Impact of Opinion Leadership and the Separation of Powers." *Comparative Politics* 32 (3): 333–53.

Vanberg, Georg. 2001. "Legislative-Judicial Relations: A Game-Theoretic Approach to Constitutional Review." *American Journal of Political Science* 45 (2): 346–61.

Vanberg, Georg. 2005. *The Politics of Constitutional Review in Germany*. New York: Cambridge University Press.

Vanberg, Georg. 2008. "Establishing and Maintaining Judicial Independence." In *Oxford Handbook of Law and Politics*, edited by Gregory A. Caldeira, R. Daniel Kelemen, and Keith E. Whittington, 99–118. New York: Oxford University Press.

Vanberg, Georg. 2015. "Constitutional Courts in Comparative Perspective: A Theoretical Assessment." *Annual Review of Political Science* 18: 167–85.

Varol, Ozan O., Lucia Dalla Pellegrina, and Nuno Garoupa. 2017. "An Empirical Analysis of Judicial Transformation in Turkey." *American Journal of Comparative Law* 5 (1): 187–216.

Walgrave, Stefaan, and Amber E. Boydstun. 2019. "The Comparative Agendas Project: The Evolving Research Interests and Designs of the CAP Scholarly Community." In *Comparative Policy Agendas: Comparative Policy Agendas: Theory, Tools, Data*, 35–48. Oxford: Oxford University Press.

Walker, Lee D. 2012. "Public Law, Comparative Public Law, and Comparative Politics." *Law & Courts Newsletter* 22 (3): 45–48.

Wilson, Bruce M. 2009. "Institutional Reform and Rights Revolutions in Latin America: The Cases of Costa Rica and Colombia." *Journal of Politics in Latin America* 1 (2): 59–85.

Woods, Patricia J., and Lisa Hilbink. 2009. "Comparative Sources of Judicial Empowerment: Ideas and Interests." *Political Research Quarterly* 62 (4): 745–52.

Overcoming the Barriers to Comparative Judicial Behavior Research

REBECCA GILL AND CHRISTOPHER ZORN

E MPIRICAL RESEARCH on judicial behavior has changed a lot in the past quarter century. It was nearly that long ago when Epstein and Goldman felt it necessary to explain what a Uniform Resource Locator (URL) was in the *Law & Courts Newsletter* (Epstein and Goldman 1996). In that same article, they try to convince scholars that "the Web" could be useful for researching courts. Compare this to a recent issue of the same newsletter, where Hazleton and her colleagues include several URLs in their discussion of how to use new technology to wade through the seemingly endless supply of primary data sources available online (Hazelton et al. 2018). At this writing, scholars of courts in the United States routinely rely on sources, tools, and data resources that were either unthinkable or considered pipe dreams a mere two or three decades ago.

In contrast, less has changed in the field of comparative judicial behavior research. On the one hand, it is true that we have made significant progress on some fundamental debates. For example, in the mid-1990s, Tate and Haynie (1994) were still defending the basic idea that it is a good thing to develop empirical theories about courts that could apply across national boundaries; Gillman (1994), though welcoming "narrative accounts" (356) of other courts, called such the quest for generalizable empirical theories "unreasonable" (359). Now, as the country- and region-specific essays of this volume demonstrate, most scholars have at least agreed to the premise that such a path is worthwhile to travel.

In other ways, however, not as much has changed. In the late 1980s, Tate called for the construction of multi-country databases of judicial decisions in order to reinvigorate such research (Tate 1989). Thirty years on, as the essays in this volume make clear, this key barrier to comparative empirical research on courts and judges has yet to be remedied satisfactorily. The frustration is palpable. Still, the contributors to this volume remain committed to the development of broader, cross-national studies of judicial behavior.

In this essay, we try to do three things. First, we bring together and integrate some of the challenges faced by researchers—including those in this volume—who study courts cross- and internationally. Second, we offer some suggestions for addressing and overcoming those challenges. Finally, where possible, we indicate some new directions for both substantive and methodological research that could appreciably benefit scholars of comparative judicial institutions. We believe the key barriers to this line of research fall into three broad categories: challenges regarding *data* from and about judicial institutions; challenges to *measurement*, including its validity, reliability, and comparability across national boundaries; and *institutional* challenges, relating both to the institutions themselves and to the context in which judicial politics research takes place in countries around the world. While the number and range of challenges facing such research is large, we are nonetheless optimistic about the future of that research.

DATA AVAILABILITY

An ongoing refrain in this volume is that a lack of access to reliable data is a key barrier to empirical judicial behavior research across countries. This "lack of appropriate, accessible data to support more rigorous analyses" (Tate 1992, 141) has long stymied this area of research, and the lack of progress on this problem is cited by authors throughout this volume as a lingering impediment to broad empirical research. Of course, the nature of the problem varies across the regions summarized here. A number of problems emerge in the preceding essays. Here, we focus on two of these. First, there are wide swaths of the world where primary source information is not available at all as a result of poor record-keeping, confidentiality rules, and/or the sequestering of this information into expensive proprietary databases. Second, where primary source data is available, much of it remains unsynthesized because of the practical difficulties associated with turning primary data into data sets that are appropriate for empirical analysis.

As Fischman points out in his essay, the status of empirical research on the behavior of US Supreme Court justices serves as an example of what can happen when you have strong data availability (see Fischman, this volume). Indeed, this work continues to dominate the top political science journals relative to studies of other federal courts and courts outside of the United States (see Driscoll, this volume). Primary data, including the full text of judicial opinions, biographical information about the justices, and other important institutional information, are publicly available and span the Court's entire history.[1] One of the key sources of this information is the Supreme Court Database (Spaeth et al. 2018). The creation and maintenance of this database required countless person-hours of attention from experts, who painstakingly read the opinions and translated them into database form using a comprehensive set of coding rules. The Supreme Court Database website calls it "an *invention* that has substantially advanced a large area of study."[2] The wealth of data available in analysis-ready format "has facilitated numerous empirical studies of the Court" (see Fischman, this volume, p. 55), encouraging other researchers to invest the time and resources necessary to collect even more data about the Court. Examples include data about interest groups that have participated as amici in Supreme Court cases (Box-Steffensmeier and Christenson 2012), data about citation patterns in Supreme Court opinions (Fowler and Jeon 2008), data about Supreme Court confirmation hearings (Collins and Ringhand 2013), and various estimates of judicial ideology (e.g., Bailey 2013; Epstein et al. 2017; Martin and Quinn 2017).

Aside from the US Supreme Court, however, user-friendly data sets are hard to come by. In many places, the root cause is the inaccessibility of primary source data about courts, judges, and judicial decisions. In the Middle East, for example, most of the national high courts are unstudied because primary source data is almost completely unavailable. As Aydin-Cakir points out in her essay, this is sometimes because the judicial opinions are not made public at all or because they are not available online or in digital format (Aydin-Cakir, this volume). Lin and Ginsburg observe a similar problem in their essay on studies of high courts in East Asia. Where we do have primary data in these regions, it is often not translated into English, which makes translating the cases into usable data far more difficult (Lin and Ginsburg, this volume). This latter problem is also at work in many Western European countries (Bagashka and Ga-roupa, this volume).

Even where primary source data are available, ready-to-use data sets about even the most well-studied courts have important limitations. In the United States, judicial opinions are generally accessible, but much of this primary data has yet to be assembled into data sets for studying the lower federal courts (Fischman, this volume) or state courts (Hall, this volume). The same problem can be found in the European Union (see Carrubba and Fjelstul, this volume), its member states (Bagashka and Garoupa, this volume), and the United Kingdom (Hanretty, this volume). The reasons for this are varied, and they tend to encompass a number of the barriers we address later in this essay. However, one of the overarching barriers to turning primary data into analyzable data sets has to do with the costly and time-consuming methods by which we have traditionally undertaken this task.

Traditional methods for coding cases are expensive and time-consuming. Many of the existing databases draw upon the methodology used by Spaeth and his team in the creation of the Supreme Court Database (Spaeth et al. 2018). This strategy requires researchers to read cases and code them "by hand" according to a rubric. This has proven to be a significant obstacle for the study of lower federal courts (Fischman, this volume); the most comprehensive data sets of US Courts of Appeals cases to date include only a random sample of published cases (Kuersten and Haire 2011; Songer 2006) or the subset of cases subsequently appealed to the US Supreme Court (Songer 2008) because hand-coding the full universe of cases was simply not possible. The authors in this volume identify similar problems with the collection of data in other institutions, including in US state supreme courts (Hall, this volume), the Supreme Court of Canada (Hausegger, this volume), the High Court of Australia (Smyth, this volume), and the European Union's highest tribunals (Carrubba and Fjelstul, this volume). This is especially problematic for studies of the Supreme Court of India (Parikh, this volume), as it comprises dozens of judges and issues roughly one thousand opinions each year (Chandra, Hubbard, and Kalantry 2017). As Driscoll notes, this is a key reason why comparative judicial behavior research is dwarfed by research on comparing court-level outcomes across countries: it is far less time-consuming and expensive to code annual country-level data than it is to code data at the judge- or case-level (Driscoll, this volume).

In addition, the availability of full-text judicial opinion data is only part of what we need in order to create useful data sets. The authors in this volume also note that it can be difficult to find and collect information about the judges—including how they are selected and retained—as well as other institutional characteristics. In Canada, a somewhat archaic system of record-keeping makes it time-consuming and expensive to gather this information where it exists, and some of the information is not archived properly at all (Hausegger, this volume). Similar obstacles are at work in comparative research among US state supreme courts (Hall, this volume). Western European courts often lack mechanisms for communicating this information publicly (Bagashka and Garoupa, this volume). In India, the judicial selection process is opaque, making it difficult to fill in the judge-level information necessary for many studies of judicial behavior (Parikh, this volume).

Among the types of challenges faced by students of comparative judicial politics, those associated with data offer both the least and the most cause for optimism. If courts, litigants, and other judicial actors simply refuse to make themselves and their actions available (or do so in only a carefully selected or curated fashion), then this problem will be nearly impossible to overcome. If this continues to be the case, data on these actors and institutions will remain either nonexistent or so plagued with selection bias as to make drawing inferences deeply suspect. In such cases, there is often little researchers can do to overcome that refusal. In countries with open-records laws, researchers could pursue requests for access to or the release of these documents. Existing research in the United States suggests that the likelihood and extent of institutional responsiveness to such requests can be an (inverse) function of the level of politicization of the institution (Wood and Lewis 2017). This presents researchers with something of a paradox because it suggests that the situations in which they are most likely to be interested in obtaining data on courts—those where courts are most active in and important to policy outcomes—are also likely to be the most difficult from which to obtain data.

However, once we gain access to primary source data, many of the remaining data challenges described above are especially amenable to technical solutions. Here, researchers can benefit from the introduction and use of tools developed in a host of other fields, including computer and information science, mathematics, and linguistics. Consider, as one example, case outcomes. In circumstances where judicial opinions are available online, a host of tools exists to facilitate their collection, coding, and analysis. In such cases, those files can be collected from online sources rapidly and efficiently using modern web-scraping tools.

Advances in optical character recognition (OCR) mean that researchers can work with files that are not provided in machine-readable formats. These technologies can also convert images and other non-text inputs into text quickly and with a high degree of reliability. Machine translation algorithms are also quite accurate, and they can translate to and from most widely used modern languages. Once data are collected and translated, modern methods of text analysis drawn from machine learning and computational linguistics can speed the coding of those decisions while retaining a high degree of reliability and validity. We discuss those tools at greater length in the sections below.

All of these advances mean that, in instances where data can be accessed at all, there is good reason to be optimistic that the pace of advancement will pick up. The potential to clean and translate full-text primary data is greater than it has ever been. One example is the recent paper by Fariss et al. (2015), which outlines the automated creation of "a large corpus of digitized primary source human rights documents from monitoring agencies that include Amnesty International, Human Rights Watch, the Lawyers Committee for Human Rights, and the United States Department of State" (2015). Fariss and his coauthors begin with over 14,000 detailed country-level human rights reports from four different organizations from 1974 to 2014. Noting that "reading each published report, even for a single country, requires a tremendous investment in time," they instead convert the scanned reports into a machine-readable format via character recognition methods. This allows them to apply other automated methods (here, topic models, which we discuss further below) to a body of documents that would otherwise require hundreds of person-hours to analyze and code. This is an important model for overcoming the resource barriers associated with synthesizing primary data into data sets. Of course, these methods necessarily require that the primary source documents be available, and no technological solution can overcome the unwillingness of government actors to provide these documents to researchers. This strategy also requires that researchers possess or acquire the necessary skills to use them. We address this second matter at some length below.

Measurement

At the heart of every scientific enterprise is measurement. Even assuming that the data challenges discussed above can be met, the cross-national study of judicial institutions and behavior raises an especially thorny set of issues around questions of measurement. As we discuss further below, many of these challenges are conceptual rather than technical in nature; these require a deep understanding of local and national processes and practices to overcome. At the same time, however, technical and methodological advances can offer new ways of thinking about those challenges. This is an important way to strengthen scholarship in the area.

Many central concepts in the field are not directly observable nor do they have "natural" observable forms. This is the problem of latency, and it complicates measurement of many of the key concepts related to the study of judicial institutions. At the level of an individual case, for example, we often need to characterize the *outcome* of a case. This means, at the most basic level, that we want to know who won and lost. Typically, we also need a way to describe the decision's potential implications for other cases and the law more broadly. Other key concepts that help us describe judicial behavior also require creative measurement techniques. These might include individual judges' political ideologies, role conceptions, and linguistic tendencies. At the institutional level, notions such as judicial independence, the role and importance of precedent, and institutional legitimacy are of central theoretical and empirical importance. In these examples and many others, the phenomena of interest lack valid, reliable, transparent indicators. This requires analysts to create and validate measures that capture these concepts of interest as accurately as possible.

Case outcomes are often a key component of empirical research on judicial behavior. The case outcome is a natural dependent variable, in that it can be "caused" by a number of characteristics of the case, the judge, the institution, and the broader sociopolitical context. At the level of individual decisions, case outcomes present what at first appears to be a relatively straightforward task. In nearly every case—particularly at the appellate level—there is a clear "winner" and "loser," suggesting that measurement of the outcome is simple.

That apparent simplicity, however, belies a host of complications. As Carrubba and Fjelstul note in their discussion of European courts, there is little agreement about how to characterize case outcomes. At various times, scholars have thought about case results in terms of ideological valence, the social or economic identity of the winning party, and the potential policy implications of the rulings. Driscoll expands on this theme, noting that, to date, comparative work on case outcomes has tended to reflect the substantive interests and theoretical perspective of the researchers (Driscoll, this volume). Such work includes studies of whether the more "advantaged" litigant wins (resource capability theory), of pro-rights outcomes in cases involving civil rights, and of pro-regime decisions (e.g., regime politics theory and studies of judicial independence). Driscoll also notes the extensive number of studies involving outcomes that are not directly case outcomes, such as changes in institutional rules (e.g., judicial selection processes) and public opinion related to the courts (legitimacy theory).

What makes this problem even more complicated is the lack of commensurability: the case outcomes we observe often mean different things in different contexts. Consider an example involving labor disputes. A ruling in favor of an employees' union and against a corporation in a labor dispute will have divergent legal and political implications depending on a number of factors: whether the union operates in an open or closed shop; whether the corporation is privately held, publicly traded, or nationalized; whether the decision itself sets a binding precedent for future cases; whether that decision is subject to legislative or executive review or response; and whether the court in question can expect the decision to be enforced in the current political and legal climate. Coding conventions in one context may not translate well into other contexts.

Perhaps predictably, measuring judicial ideology is still more fraught. After decades of work on measuring judicial ideology in the United States, active debates about the influence of political preferences on judges' decisions have largely subsided. However, there remain important disagreements about precisely how to define and measure judicial ideology in the US context (see, e.g., Harvey and Woodruff 2013). Outside of the United States, measures of judicial ideology tend to be underdeveloped for a host of reasons (see for example Smyth's essay and Hanretty's essay, this volume). Judicial ideology measures typically rely upon the assumption that judges have expressed their true preferences in ways that researchers can observe (Kornhauser, this volume). But courts in newly established democracies might not demonstrate political preferences at all (Ayden-Cakir, this volume). Where judicial independence is limited, as in post-Communist countries in Eastern Europe, the expression of political preferences can be muted by institutional constraints (Bagashka and Garoupa, this volume). This problem may be especially acute in many civil law countries, where judges are seen as "faceless judicial bureaucrats" (Lin and Ginsburg, this volume).

In his essay, Fischman organizes measures of judicial ideology into categories based on whether they are indirect proxy measures or are derived from observed judicial behavior (Fischman, this volume). But while the difficulties of building observable measures are notable, finding proxy measures that make sense can also be challenging. One of the key proxy measures for federal judges in the United States is the political affiliation of their appointing president. Such a measure is only valid, of course, when we know the president's party identification *and* when that affiliation has meaningful consequences for predicting judges' political ideology. This is often not the case outside of the United States. For example, since Turkish presidents are nonpartisan, it is very difficult to know the ideology of the appointing president (Ayden-Cakir, this volume). Similar problems can arise where selection processes are opaque, leaving few clear clues about the ideological positions of the judges (Lin and Ginsburg, this volume, and Parikh, this volume).

Segal and Cover (1989) developed an alternative proxy measure that relies upon content analysis of media coverage about judicial nominees before they ascend to the bench. Their idea was that news coverage will hint at whether the judge is seen as liberal or conservative by reporters and the experts they consult. However, this measure is also difficult to implement in different institutional contexts. Some research on the High Court of Australia uses this type of measure (Smyth, this volume). Given that these judges are not subject to a public confirmation process, though, there is much less news coverage of these nominees prior to their nomination; the news coverage that does exist does not generally provide many significant clues about the ideological leanings of those nominees. The same is true in other systems where selection processes are opaque.

Developing behavior-based measures of judicial ideology can also be difficult. Such measures typically rely either on the observable behaviors of the judges prior to their ascending the bench or on their actions (typically their votes and opinions) while on the bench. Of course, it is difficult to derive individual-level judicial ideology measures from primary data sources that are not available at the individual judge level, as in (for example) the European Court of Justice (Carrubba and Fjelstul, this volume). In the absence of individual opinions or individual votes, it is difficult to attribute a particular behavior to a specific individual. Strong norms of consensus often contribute to the inability to distinguish group outcomes from their individual-level components. These norms are often strong in countries with civil law traditions; this can make attribution difficult, since the behavior expressed in the vote coalitions may be the result of social contexts and not underlying ideological difference (Lin and Ginsburg, this volume).

Where we can create measures based on observed behavior, we must also take care when assigning meaning to those measures. Driscoll points out that these behaviorally derived measures are essentially without meaning on their own; they require "a substantive knowledge and definition of what it means . . . in a given system" (Driscoll, this volume, p. 292). In the US case, researchers have typically been willing to map ideology measures to a single left-right dimension that broadly mirrors the liberal-conservative continuum in other national institutions and among the mass public. In other contexts, however, multiple dimensions of judicial ideology may be required, and neglecting to measure these additional dimensions may introduce bias into our models (Fischman, this volume). This seems to be the case in the United Kingdom, for instance, where single-dimensional models of judicial ideology yield very little variation among judges (Hanretty, this volume). Moreover, courts outside of the United States are not likely to mirror its key ideological divide(s); most will require different substantive dimensions in order to capture the important operative components of judicial ideology (Aydin-Cakir, this volume).

These challenges are significant, but it is important that we find ways to move beyond them. The development of workable measures of judicial ideology is critical to improving our understanding of the judicialization of politics globally. Ideally, our strategies would link concepts of interest across time and space. In the United States, scholars have developed "bridging" measures that allow researchers to compare ideology of actors across institutions (Fischman, this volume). Where there are enough primary data, behaviorally derived measures may also be able to accommodate ideological shifts over time; such responsiveness to temporal change is absent in most existing measures employed outside of the United States (Kapiszewski and Tiede, this volume; Parikh, this volume).

Of course, this discussion dances around the larger issue that is central to the theme of this volume. Comparing even the most basic concepts across countries is incredibly difficult given the wide variety of institutional and social contexts in which these courts operate. At present, the most successful lines of comparative judicial behavior research are single-country studies (Driscoll, this volume). The non-generalizability of our existing measures certainly stymies truly multi-country empirical work. This is especially problematic when we are attempting to understand the behavior of courts like Taiwan (Lin and Ginsburg, this volume) and many of the courts in Eastern European countries (Bagashka and Garoupa, this volume), where the small docket sizes mean that we have few usable observations and little statistical power to find patterns when we limit our data to a single country.

This is not a straightforward barrier to overcome. The large variety of institutional structures in multi-country studies makes it difficult to assign meaning to the measures we develop. In comparative courts research, studies across different legal systems can hinder the generalizability of the meaning of our measures (Lin and Ginsburg, this volume). Traditions of Communist law, for example, make it very difficult to find variables that explain judicial outcomes (Bagashka and Garoupa, this volume). This problem is evident in the few cross-national data sets that exist, and overcoming this issue is key to furthering cross-national empirical research.

The High Courts Judicial Database (Haynie et al. 2007) provides a striking illustration of these challenges. In March 2000, the principal investigators for this National Science Foundation–funded project held a conference to workshop their codebook. They brought together country experts to help ensure that their proposed measures would be valid and coherent across the range of countries included in the project. Despite this effort, the resulting database coding still struggles to consistently capture the key concepts of interest across countries (Hanretty, this volume; Smyth, this volume). This means that pooling cases across countries into a single model is problematic because things like case outcomes (Kapiszewski and Tiede, this volume), judicial ideology (Hausegger, this volume), and case characteristics (Hanretty, this volume) do not mean the same thing across countries. This problem can even manifest among regions within the same country, as is evident in places like the United States (Hall, this volume) and India (Parikh, this volume), and across ethnic groups in places with significant ethnic fragmentation (Bagashka and Garoupa, this volume).

A consequence of this is a lack of standardization in existing data sets and their measures. To conduct the kind of large-scale empirical research envisioned in this volume (see the introduction, this volume), we need effective, standardized measures of the key variables (Hall, this volume). Existing data sets are limited, hand-coded, and do not mesh together well (Bagashka and Garoupa, this volume; Carrubba and Fjelstul, this volume). Once again, however, recent developments in machine learning and related fields suggest some promising approaches for overcoming these issues. For example, *transfer learning* methods use the results from the application of machine-learning methods in one context or experiment as a basis for applications in other contexts. Human beings "recognize and apply relevant knowledge from previous learning experiences when we encounter new tasks. The more related a new task is to our previous experience, the more easily we can master it" (Torrey and Shavlik 2009, 242).

The notion of "borrowing strength" across multiple applications is generally focused on increasing the speed and accuracy of the task being undertaken, but it also offers important possible benefits for adapting automated text-analysis methods to varying contexts. For example, recent applications in the social sciences have focused on applications ranging from causal inference problems (e.g., Künzel et al. 2018), to scaling the text in open-ended survey questions (Hobbs 2018), to analyzing image data of living room interiors (Liu et al. 2019). In addition, some recent work has begun to leverage transfer methods to overcome language barriers in the analysis of political texts (e.g., Goist and Monroe 2018). In each of these applications, a key element of the challenge is the changing context in which the information in question is presented. Such adaptability will be central to developing methods that can automatically extract comparable information from different institutional contexts.

A related approach that offers the potential to overcome these measurement challenges is *meta-learning*, or "learning to learn." Meta-learning methods are particularly useful in circumstances where "concepts in the real world are not eternally fixed entities or structures, but can have a different appearance or definition or meaning in different contexts" (Widmer 1997). Many of the recent technical developments in this area have focused on "fast" adaptation of automated methods to varying contexts; that is, training classifiers and other machine learners to "recognize" context (and therefore perform accurately) using very little data (e.g., Zintgraf et al. 2019). Such methods might be leveraged to address two of the challenges posed above: the context-dependent nature of measurement in comparative judicial politics, and the paucity of data.

Institutional Issues

In the section above, we refer somewhat obliquely to the way that institutional variations can complicate our efforts to measure concepts of interest in ways that are generalizable across time and space. This happens often, although not always, because of the way these rules compromise the generalizability of our measures across countries. Here, we focus our attention specifically on those institutional characteristics that make large-N comparative studies of judicial behavior difficult. We divide the discussion into two parts. First, we discuss the internal institutional rules that make it difficult to measure and interpret patterns of judicial behavior. Next, we provide a brief account of some of the contextual factors that impact our ability to understand judicial behavior as part of a sociopolitical system.

National high courts vary significantly in terms of the rules and traditions they follow as they conduct their work. Often, seemingly small differences in internal rules can lead to very different expectations about how particular concepts of interest can be measured. An example of this is the use of subsets (or "panels") of judges to hear cases in certain jurisdictions. Judicial panels can make understanding judicial behavior significantly more complicated, though it can also provide opportunities for developing and testing institutional-level hypotheses.[3]

The use of panel systems can make it difficult to estimate ideal points as measures of ideology, particularly in settings where there is also a strong tradition of unanimity on the panels (Fischman, this volume). Often, our behaviorally derived measures of judicial ideology are interpretable only relative to the other decision makers reacting to the same set of case facts and circumstances. On courts where all of the judges usually decide all of the cases together, placing members of a court on a scale relative to their colleagues is relatively straightforward because each judge has made an observable decision relative to each of the unique sets of case facts. Where panels are used, however, a significant number of the judge-level responses to the stimuli are essentially missing data.

The degree to which the panel structure impacts our ability to understand individual judicial behavior can depend upon a number of characteristics of the panel system. Among them is the size of the panels, which varies significantly both between and within countries that employ panel systems. Two-judge panels are common in India (Parikh, this volume); panels of up to five are possible in Australia, while the European Court of Justice hears cases in panels of three, five, or fifteen judges. The circumstances in which panels are constituted also vary widely. In Australia, for example, panels are used at the discretion of the chief justice; less important cases may be heard by a subset of the bench, while important cases are assigned to the entire court. This means that the number of judges who hear any given case is not constant, nor is it random.

The membership of panels themselves may also be non-random. Evidence from Canada and South Africa (Hausegger and Haynie 2003) shows that the chief justices who assign judges to panels in important cases often choose individual judges on the basis of their expertise and policy preferences. Even if these panels are assigned randomly, though, the timing of the announcement of the panels may influence litigant choices. While panel assignments are announced just before arguments in Canada and South Africa (Hausegger and Haynie 2003), panel assignments are known to the litigants in advance in the United Kingdom (Hanretty, this volume).

This discussion is just one example of the way internal processes can impact our ability to study judicial behavior cross-nationally. Hall's essay in this volume provides a helpful list of some of the relevant features that we need to understand (and have access to data about) in order to conduct comparative research.[4] But even understanding these factors internal to court processes cannot tell us all we need to know about what is happening in the courts. Instead, in order to interpret the behavior we observe, we need to understand the key characteristics of the broader institutional context in each country. For example, we need to understand the form and nature of the court's power relative to other branches of government in order to understand which observed behaviors are indicative of strategic judicial decision-making (Lin and Ginsburg, this volume). In other words, the strategic landscape each national high court faces is heavily dependent upon the court's position vis-à-vis other government actors. To know an exercise of judicial power when we see it, we need to accommodate these contextual characteristics in our theories and models.

One of the key powers of the US Supreme Court is to declare laws and actions of other branches and levels of government invalid when they abridge the US Constitution. The analogous process looks different in systems derived from the civil law tradition,[5] as most of these systems have separate tribunals that hear both abstract and concrete challenges to government legislation or action (Lewis, this volume). However, some national high courts, like those in the United Kingdom (Hanretty, this volume) and the Netherlands (Bagashka and Garoupa, this volume), do not have the formal power to overturn legislation. In these countries, exercises of power by the court over the legislature would likely take the form of declarations that a statute is in violation of an international treaty. In a way, then, international law can be used as a way to supplement judicial power in countries with traditions of formal legislative supremacy (Poorter 2013).

Relatedly, in countries where courts do have significant power relative to the other branches, these courts may face significant counter-threats in the form of court curbing. Understanding this kind of behavior requires that we supplement our data sets with information about the behavior of other branches of government. Unfortunately, this only exacerbates existing problems of data availability and difficulty in getting different data sets to link together. This is probably why even well-studied courts like American state supreme courts (Hall, this volume) and the Supreme Court of Canada (Hausegger, this volume) have significant gaps in the research about external influences on judicial behavior. This kind of work is critically important, particularly in authoritarian countries where judicial behavior may be significantly controlled by threats or reprisals (Aydin-Cakir, this volume). Where national high courts must rely upon international law to strike down domestic legislation, it is critical that we be able to trace cases between member states and international courts; at present, however, our existing data sets largely ignore this inter-institutional information (Carrubba and Fjelstul, this volume).

The degree of autonomy judges will demonstrate may well hinge on the relative political power of the other branches. Kapiszewski and Tiede note in their essay that Latin American judges can be expected to demonstrate more autonomy during times of divided government (Kapiszewski and Tiede, this volume). Of course, the meaning of "divided government" varies significantly across countries as a result of different configurations of institutional design, party systems, and electoral rules. At present, we know little about how these institutional arrangements impact how we observe exercises of judicial power (Bagashka and Garoupa, this volume). Strategies designed to measure things like political fragmentation in the United States do not translate easily to multiparty systems, making it difficult to capture this key characteristic of the political landscape (Kapiszewski and Tiede, this volume).

We also have very limited information about the way public opinion shapes (and is shaped by) national high courts. There is a very strong literature on this in the context of the US Supreme Court (e.g., Hoekstra 2000; Epstein and Martin 2010; Gibson and Nelson 2015), and to some degree in the American states (Devins and Mansker 2010). However, even in the United States, it is difficult to obtain effective measures of public opinion of state courts that are comparable across institutions

(Hall, this volume). Comparative research on legitimacy, like that on judicial politics in general, suffers from a lack of data (Driscoll, this volume; Aydin-Cakir, this volume). Beyond the challenges noted above, questions around institutional legitimacy pose particular problems in the comparative context, where national-level public opinion surveys may be impossible, nonexistent, or plagued by bias due to desirability effects or fear of retaliation. Yet, such data are critical to understanding the external influences on the courts, as well as for understanding the impact of judicial decisions. At present, we generally have only simple, under-tested theoretical models linking judicial behavior to its potential impact on society (Kornhauser, this volume).

Importantly, most of the more technical solutions to these problems proposed above offer somewhat less additional purchase here. Detailed, reliable institutional knowledge is rarely easily available, especially among countries in the developing world. Developing this level of expertise usually requires in-person, in-depth research at the institutions themselves. One potentially useful approach is crowdsourcing expert opinions, a method that has already shown some promise in the measurement of judicial ideology (Wijtvliet and Dyevre 2019).

The picture is somewhat brighter in the area of mass influences on (and by) national high courts. Crowdsourcing approaches have already been successfully employed in panel studies of public opinion, including recent work on attitude change toward the US Supreme Court (Christenson and Glick 2019). Platforms such as Amazon's Mechanical Turk (MTurk) allow for fast, reliable, low-cost collection of data on mass opinion and implementation of opinion experiments. Such methods, however, are also not without their drawbacks. While research in the United States has shown that crowdsourced samples can be reasonably representative of the public at large (Berinsky et al. 2012), their value in a cross-national context is still largely unknown. Particularly in the developing world, where access to technology and communication varies widely by age, class, and education, the ability reliably to secure representative samples of respondents remains in doubt. In one recent study comparing experiences in the United States and India (Boas, Christenson, and Glick 2019), the authors note that in the latter location MTurk and similar crowdsourced convenience samples were "disproportionately young, wealthy, male, highly educated and upper-caste" (2).

Conclusion

We have focused thus far on the range of technical and logistic challenges to studying courts cross-nationally. But there remains one further set of challenges: those intrinsic to national judicial and disciplinary norms and cultures. As we emphasize above, a deep understanding of laws, rules, norms, and practices is essential to conducting such work. Yet it is often the case that members of our own intellectual communities, and of regional and national legal systems themselves, are at best indifferent and at worst actively hostile toward such research. In much of the world, lawyers and judges are deeply skeptical about the value of empirical, scientific work on judicial processes and antipathetic toward individuals attempting to undertake that work. Many of the authors in this volume note these dynamics (see the essays by Hausegger, Hanretty, and Bagashka and Garoupa), pointing out that judges in particular are often opposed to the entire idea of quantitative research and unwilling to cooperate with researchers. The damaging effect of this hostility on our ability to better theorize and understand courts comparatively cannot be understated.

In much of the world, a similar dynamic occurs among members of the political science and legal disciplines themselves. In those fields, broad-based antipathy toward scientific (and especially quantitative) methods still holds sway throughout much of the world, but it seems particularly acute among individuals focused on legal and judicial studies. Traditions of legal formalism, sometimes combined with pernicious myths about judges operating either as apolitical bureaucrats or Solomonic umpires, often make country specialists averse to empirical work and dubious about the value of cross-country comparisons. In his essay in this volume, Smyth provides an all-too-characteristic illustration of this dynamic. Referring to Australia and New Zealand, he notes that, while acceptance and use of quantitative methods is growing, much of the discipline of political science in those countries is largely uninterested in questions surrounding the legal system, essentially ceding that to researchers in law schools. Conversely, legal scholars are either unable or reluctant to adopt data-based approaches to understand courts and judicial behavior. The result is a persistent lacuna in the understanding of courts in those countries, as well as an institutionalized lack of incentives for young scholars to conduct such work.

Yet despite the (perhaps) gloomy picture we paint of the challenges surrounding cross-national research on judicial politics, now is arguably the best time ever to be conducting that research. As we discuss above, innovations in data acquisition, processing, and analysis offer the opportunity to address questions that had previously seemed intractable, and to do so in a wider range of contexts than has been possible before. Accomplishing these goals will require some fundamental shifts in three broad, interconnected aspects of our work.

The first of these goes to the heart of cross-national work on courts: the *questions we ask*. From bioassays to Facebook experiments, the range of tools available to social scientists has expanded rapidly in recent decades. Beyond their utility for informing (and sometimes resolving) perennial debates, those tools open up the possibility of studying new topics and asking fundamentally new questions. Note here that we are not suggesting "looking for nails" as an approach to defining one's research agenda. But all of our research is limited in practice by the possible; expanding what is possible necessarily expands the range of potential questions we might choose to address. It was, after all, in part the systematization and dissemination of court proceedings that made the study of judicial politics as we now know it possible. Further advances in the latter half of the twentieth century—from citation references to legal search tools to the web itself—dramatically increased the range of subjects political scientists studying law and courts were able to tackle. Understanding what is possible thus provides the basis for innovative theorizing about novel puzzles and phenomena.

Accordingly, the second necessary change is in *training*. As the legal analyst's possible toolkit expands, the need to be aware of what is methodologically possible becomes both more important and more difficult. While this is a concern to all scholars, it is of particular importance to those who train new PhDs and JDs. Venerable approaches to learning how to do research—including statistical and data analytic tools, but also qualitative methods and theory-building—will need to adapt both in their focus, content, and approach to methods. In particular, students need to be trained in how to be adaptable in their approaches. It is critical that they learn how to learn new approaches over the life of their careers because the landscape of analytical tools is changing at a rapid pace. Training, in other words, must become dynamic; in addition to factual knowledge and methods, students will increasingly need to understand how to evolve intellectually in an intentional way.

Finally, new work on comparative courts will depend critically on changes in *collaboration*, and specifically on when, how, and with whom we collaborate. There are some projects that may still be amenable to single-authorship. When it comes to the kind of cross-national empirical research discussed in this volume, however, it is probably fair to say that the days of the lone scholar, working in isolation on a single massive "project," are over. The breadth of substantive and methodological knowledge required to conduct compelling cross-national work is enormous. More than that, the speed at which that knowledge changes has grown exponentially in recent decades. The vast amount one would need to know in order to execute a comparative empirical study of judicial behavior already eclipses the abilities of all but the most brilliant and polyglot individuals. Collaboration is, accordingly, becoming the norm. In our view, this approach stands to improve the quality of work in the field.

Going forward, we see two key areas in which wider and deeper collaborations will be both necessary and especially fruitful. The first, unsurprisingly, is in methods. Novel cross-disciplinary connections strike us as particularly fruitful. Many of the approaches we describe above are native to fields that historically have rarely collaborated widely with political science: computational linguistics, information science, statistics, and computer science. As a result, few of us working on questions around comparative courts have "native" knowledge of the sorts of tools developed there. At the same time, scholars—particularly junior scholars—are often among those pushing the boundaries of these disciplines and are also often the most eager to collaborate on novel (to their disciplines) applications. Rather than having to "go it alone" and be all things to all people (political theorist, historian, anthropologist, statistician, and so on), collaboration of the sort described here takes the burden of acquiring in-depth methodological expertise off the shoulders of the researcher, while at the same time providing potentially immense benefits to those in other fields. All of this suggests that methodological specialization and collaboration, as is common in the physical, natural, and medical sciences, will increasingly become the norm.

The second (perhaps obvious) area where expansion of collaboration seems especially promising is cross-national work among judicial and legal scholars. As we note above, scholars with deep local knowledge of legal systems and processes often face institutional and disciplinary constraints on their ability to conduct cross-national work, particularly of an empirical or quantitative nature. This seems especially true in countries in the developing world, where systematic understanding of the legal system is both less widespread and often more critical to public policy outcomes. Cross-national collaboration offers the potential to integrate theoretical, methodological, and area knowledge in ways that will improve all three. And the very technology that powers many of the methodological innovations described above also makes such collaboration easier and more productive.

In our view, we have already begun some of this evolution. The essays in this volume identify a wide range of successful research projects that provide the jumping-off point for broader, large-N cross-national studies. Unfortunately, we have not yet reached the stage where the major barriers to comparative judicial behavior research have fallen away. Researchers still face data deserts, where the key inputs to our work are either completely absent or practically impossible to gather and organize. Where we do have data, we have not yet coalesced around a strategy for ensuring the equivalence of measures necessary to compare judicial behavior across countries in a meaningful way.

There is good reason to be optimistic that we are on the cusp of a major sea change in this line of scholarship. Here, we have outlined just a few ways that we can streamline the expensive and time-consuming task of building data sets from raw primary data. We have also discussed ways that we can use computers to summarize large swaths of primary data into measurements that can be represented numerically. These developments can help redirect the time and energy of researchers out of the mundane tasks of generating human-coded data sets. Instead, that effort can be put into the work that requires human expertise and creative insights, like mapping our concepts of interest onto these measures in ways that make sense across institutional and cultural contexts. We are optimistic that it will not be long before *Law & Courts Newsletter* is linking researchers to vast swaths of ready-to-analyze data about judicial behavior around the world.

NOTES

1. The Supreme Court's website features a list of resources where this kind of information can be obtained ("Supreme Court of the United States," https://www.supremecourt.gov/opinions/obtainopinions.aspx).
2. This quote comes from "The Collection" in the "About" section of the website, found here: http://scdb.wustl.edu/about.php (accessed June 14, 2019).
3. A useful example of this is the substantial body of work on the US Courts of Appeals, which typically decide cases in randomly selected three-judge panels. Those courts have been the subject of a long, rich tradition of work

in political science, including numerous studies that have leveraged the practice of random assignment to test theories of judicial behavior (e.g. Atkins and Zavonia 1974; Boyd, Epstein, and Martin 2010).

4. This list is so helpful, in fact, that we include it here in its entirety: (1) docket composition, (2) rules for granting discretionary review, (3) caseload management techniques, (4) opinion assignment practices and other internal operating procedures, (5) selection and reselection practices, (6) terms of office, (7) judicial salaries and other resources provided to the state judiciary, (8) rules governing the participation of non-party intervenors, and (9) biographical information about the justices.

5. Here, we mean this to refer to legal systems following the Romano-Germanic or continental law traditions.

REFERENCES

Atkins, Burton M., and William Zavoina. 1974. "Judicial Leadership on the Court of Appeals: A Probability Analysis of Panel Assignment in Race Relations Cases on the Fifth Circuit." *American Journal of Political Science* 18: 701–11.

Bailey, Michael A. 2013. Data Page for "Is Today's Court the Most Conservative in Sixty Years? Challenges and Opportunities in Measuring Judicial Preferences." *Journal of Politics* 75 (3). https://michaelbailey.georgetown.domains /data-page-jop-2013/.

Berinsky, Adam J., Gregory A. Huber, and Gabriel S. Lenz. 2012. "Evaluating Online Labor Markets for Experimental Research: Amazon.com's Mechanical Turk." *Political Analysis* 20: 351–68.

Boas, Taylor, Dino Christenson, and David M. Glick. 2020. "Recruiting Large Online Samples in the United States and India: Facebook, Mechanical Turk, and Qualtrics." *Political Science Research and Methods* 8 (2): 232–50.

Box-Steffensmeier, Janet, and Dino P. Christenson. 2012. Database on Supreme Court Amicus Curiae Briefs. Version 1.0: http://amicinetworks.com.

Boyd, Christina L., Lee Epstein, and Andrew D. Martin. 2010. "Untangling the Causal Effects of Sex on Judging." *American Journal of Political Science* 54 (2): 389–411.

Chandra, Aparna, William H. J. Hubbard, and Sital Kalantry. 2017. "The Supreme Court of India: A People's Court?" *Indian Law Review* 1 (2):145–81.

Christenson, Dino P., and David M. Glick. 2019. "Reassessing the Supreme Court: How Decisions and Negativity Bias Affect Legitimacy." *Political Research Quarterly* 72 (3): 637–52.

Collins, Paul M., Jr., and Lori A. Ringhand. 2013. The US Supreme Court Confirmation Hearing Database. http://www.psci.unt.edu/~pmcollins/data .htm.

Devins, Neal, and Nicole Mansker. 2010. "Public Opinion and State Supreme Courts." *U. Pa. J. Const. L.* 13: 455–509.

Epstein, Lee, and Jerry Goldman. 1996. "Web-Footed Academics Point You to the Future: 'Tis True; There's Magic in the Web of It.'" *Law & Courts Newsletter* 6 (2): 20–22.

Epstein, Lee, and Andrew D. Martin. 2010. "Does Public Opinion Influence the Supreme Court? Possibly Yes (But We're Not Sure Why)." *University of Pennsylvania Journal of Constitutional Law* 13: 263–81.

Epstein, Lee, Andrew D. Martin, Jeffrey A. Segal, and Chad Westerland. 2017. Judicial Common Space Scores 2017 Data Files. http://epstein.wustl.edu /research/JCS.html.

Fariss, Christopher J., Fridolin J. Linder, Zachary M. Jones, Charles D. Crabtree, Megan A. Biek, Ana-Sophia M. Ross, Taranamol Kaur, and Michael Tsai. 2015. "Human Rights Texts: Converting Human Rights Primary Source Documents into Data." *PLoS One* 10 (9): e0138935. https://doi.org/10.1371 /journal.pone.0138935.

Fowler, James H., and Sangick Jeon. 2008. Supreme Court Citation Network Data. http://jhfowler.ucsd.edu/judicial.htm.

Gibson, James L., and Michael J. Nelson. 2015. "Is the US Supreme Court's Legitimacy Grounded in Performance Satisfaction and Ideology?" *American Journal of Political Science* 59: 162–74.

Gillman, Howard. 1994. "On Constructing a Science of Comparative Judicial Politics: Tate and Haynie's Authoritarianism and the Functions of Courts." *Law & Society Review* 28: 355–76.

Goist, Mitchell, and Burt L. Monroe. 2018. "Analysis of Multilingual Political Text." Paper presented at the New Directions in Text as Data Conference. Seattle, WA.

Harvey, Anna, and Michael J. Woodruff. 2013. "Confirmation Bias in the United States Supreme Court Judicial Database." *Journal of Law, Economics, and Organization* 29: 414–60.

Hausegger, Lori, and Stacia Haynie. 2003. "Judicial Decisionmaking and the Use of Panels in the Canadian Supreme Court and the South African Appellate Division." *Law & Society Review* 37 (3): 635–58.

Haynie, Stacia L., Reginald S. Sheehan, Donald R. Songer, and C. Neal Tate. 2007. High Courts Judicial Database. Accessed at the University of South Carolina Judicial Research Initiative. www.cas.sc.edu/poli/juri.

Hazelton, Morgan, Rachael Hinkle, Michael Nelson, and Jim Gibson. 2018. "2018 SPSA Conference-Within-A-Conference Resources." *Law & Courts Newsletter* 1 (28): 7–11.

Hoekstra, Valerie. 2000. "The Supreme Court and Local Public Opinion." *American Political Science Review* 94: 89–100.

Hobbs, William R. 2018. "Text Scaling for Open-Ended Survey Responses and Social Media Posts." Working paper. Cornell University. https://papers.ssrn .com/sol3/papers.cfm?abstract_id=3044864.

Kuersten, Ashlyn K., and Susan B. Haire. 2011. Update to the Appeals Courts Database: 1997–2002. http://www.songerproject.org.

Künzel, Sören R., Bradly C. Stadie, Nikita Vemuri, Varsha Ramakrishnan, Jasjeet S. Sekhon, and Pieter Abbeel. 2018. "Transfer Learning for Estimating Causal Effects Using Neural Networks." Working paper. UC Berkeley. https://arxiv.org/pdf/1808.07804.pdf.

Liu, Xi, Clio Andris, Zixuan Huang, and Sohrab Rahimi. 2019. "Inside 50,000 Living Rooms: An Assessment of Global Residential Ornamentation Using Transfer Learning." *EPJ Data Science* 8 (1): 4.

Martin, Andrew D., and Kevin M. Quinn. 2017. Martin-Quinn Scores 2017 Data Files. https://mqscores.lsa.umich.edu.

Poorter, Jurgen C. A. de. 2013. "Constitutional Review in the Netherlands: A Joint Responsibility." *Utrecht Law Review* 9 (2): 89–105.

Segal, Jeffrey A., and Albert D. Cover. 1989. "Ideological Values and the Votes of US Supreme Court Justices." *American Political Science Review* 83: 557–65.

Spaeth, Harold J., Lee Epstein, Andrew D. Martin, Jeffrey A. Segal, Theodore J. Ruger, and Sara C. Benesh. 2018. Supreme Court Database v.2018 r.02. http://supremecourtdatabase.org.

Songer, Donald R. 2006. United States Courts of Appeals Database Phase 1, 1925–1988. http://www.songerproject.org.

Songer, Donald R. 2008. United States Courts of Appeals Database Phase 2, 1952–1996. http://www.songerproject.org.

Tate, C. Neal. 1989. "Scientific Comparative Judicial Politics: An Assessment and a Call to Action." *Law & Courts Newsletter* 7 (1): 1–8.

Tate, C. Neal. 1992. "The Development of Comparative Judicial Politics." *Perspectives on Political Science* 21 (3):138–45.

Tate, C. Neal, and Stacia L. Haynie. 1994. "Building a Scientific Comparative Judicial Politics and Arousing the Dragons of Antiscientism." *Law & Society Review* 28: 377–94.

Torrey, Lisa, and Jude Shavlik. 2009. "Transfer Learning." In the *Handbook of Research on Machine Learning Applications*, 242–64. Information Science Reference Press.

Widmer, Gerhard. 1997. "Tracking Context Changes Through Meta-Learning." *Machine Learning* 27: 259–86.

Wijtvliet, Wessel, and Arthur Dyevre. 2019. "Measuring Judicial Ideology in Economic Cases: An Expert Crowdsourcing Design." Working paper. KU Leuven Faculty of Law. https://papers.ssrn.com/sol3/papers.cfm?abstract_id=3332943.

Wood, Abby K., and David E. Lewis. 2017. "Agency Performance Challenges and Agency Politicization." *Journal of Public Administration Research and Theory* 27: 581–95.

Zintgraf, Luisa, Kyriacos Shiarlis, Vitaly Kurin, Katja Hofmann, and Shimon Whiteson. 2019. "Fast Context Adaptation Via Meta-Learning." *Proceedings of the 36th International Conference on Machine Learning.* PMLR 97. Long Beach, CA. http://www.cs.ox.ac.uk/people/shimon.whiteson/pubs/zintgraficml19 .pdf.

CONTRIBUTORS

Aylin Aydin-Cakir is Assistant Professor of Political Science and International Relations Program at Yeditepe University, Turkey. Her publications have appeared in academic journals such as *International Journal of Constitutional Law (ICON)*, *Law & Society Review*, *Political Research Quarterly*, *International Political Science Review*, *Democratization*, and *Turkish Studies*.

Tanya Bagashka is Associate Professor of Political Science at the University of Houston, USA. Her publications have appeared in academic journals such as *American Political Science Review*, *Electoral Studies*, *Legislative Studies Quarterly*, *International Studies Quarterly*, and *East European Politics and Societies*.

Clifford Carrubba is the Samuel Candler Dobbs Professor of Political Science and Quantitative Theory and Methods at Emory University, USA. He is the author of *Courts and Compliance in International Law: The Role of the European Court of Justice in European Integration* (2015, with Matthew Gabel).

Amanda Driscoll is Associate Professor of Political Science at Florida State University, USA. Her research has been funded by the *National Science Foundation* and published in the *American Journal of Political Science* and the *Journal of Law & Courts*, among others.

Joshua Fischman is Professor of Law at the University of Virginia, USA. His publications have appeared in academic journals such as *Journal of Law and Economics*, *Journal of Law, Economics, and Organization*, *Journal of Legal Studies*, *American Law and Economics Review*, *Journal of Empirical Legal Studies*, and *Cornell Law Review*.

Joshua Fjelstul is a Post-Doctoral Research Fellow at Washington University in St. Louis, USA. He has recently authored "The Evolution of European Union Law: A New Data Set on the Acquis Communautaire" in *European Union Politics* and "The Politics of International Oversight: Strategic Monitoring and Legal compliance in the European Union" (with Clifford J. Carrubba) in *American Political Science Review*.

NUNO GAROUPA is a Professor of Law and Associate Dean for Research and Faculty Development, George Mason University, USA. He is the author of *Judicial Reputation: A Comparative Theory* (with Tom Ginsburg, 2015).

REBECCA GILL is Associate Professor of Political Science, University of Nevada Las Vegas, USA. She is the recipient of multiple research grants from the National Science Foundation, and her recent work has appeared in scholarly journals including *Georgetown Law Journal, the Ohio State Law Journal, Law & Society Review, State Politics and Policy Quarterly,* and *Politics, Groups, and Identities.*

TOM GINSBURG is the Leo Spitz Professor of International Law, Ludwig and Hilde Wolf Research Scholar at University of Chicago, and Research Fellow, American Bar Foundation, USA. He is the author of *Democracies and International Law: The Trials of Liberalism* (forthcoming) and *How to Save a Constitutional Democracy* (with Aziz Huq, 2018).

MELINDA GANN HALL is a Professor of Political Science, Michigan State University, USA. She is the author of *Attacking Judges: How Campaign Advertising Influences State Supreme Court Elections* (2015) and *In Defense of Judicial Elections* (with Chris W. Bonneau, 2009).

CHRIS HANRETTY is Professor of Politics, Royal Holloway, University of London, UK. He is the author of *A Court of Specialists: Judicial Behavior on the UK Supreme Court* (2020).

LORI HAUSEGGER is Associate Professor of Political Science at Boise State University, USA. Her work has appeared in academic journals such as the *American Journal of Political Science, Law and Society Review,* and the *Canadian Journal of Political Science,* and she is the author of *Canadian Courts: Law, Politics, and Process* (with Matthew Hennigar and Troy Riddell, 2020, third edition).

DIANA KAPISZEWSKI is the Provost's Distinguished Associate Professor of Government at Georgetown University, USA. She has authored, coauthored, or coedited five books on legal institutions and qualitative methods; she also coedits the Cambridge University Press book series Method for Social Inquiry.

LEWIS A. KORNHAUSER is the Frank Henry Sommer Professor of Law at New York University, USA. He has recently authored "Discrete Rent-Seeking Games with an Application to Evidence Production" (with Giuseppe Dari-Mattiacci), to appear in *Supreme Court Economic Review,* and "Stare Decisis and Judicial Log-Rolls: A Gains-from-Trade Model" (with Charles Cameron and Giri Parameswaran) in *Rand Journal of Economics.*

DOMINIQUE H. LEWIS is a Lecturer in Political Science at Texas A&M University, USA.

CHIEN-CHIH LIN is an Associate Research Professor at Institutum Iurisprudentiae, Academia Sinica, Taiwan. His publications have appeared in academic journals such as *International Journal of Constitutional Law (ICON)* and *American Journal of Comparative Law*.

SUNITA PARIKH is an Associate Professor of Political Science and Lecturer in the Law School at Washington University in St. Louis, USA. She is the author of *The Politics of Preference: Democratic Institutions and Affirmative Action in the United States and India* (2010).

RUSSELL SMYTH is a Professor of Economics at Monash University, Australia. His publications on courts and judicial behavior have appeared in academic journals such as *Economic Journal, Journal of Empirical Legal Studies, Journal of Legal Studies* and *Law & Society Review*, among others.

LYDIA B. TIEDE is Associate Professor of Political Science at University of Houston, USA. Some of her work has appeared in *Comparative Political Studies, International Studies Quarterly, Journal of Empirical Legal Studies* and *World Development*.

CHRISTOPHER ZORN is a Liberal Arts Professor of Political Science at Pennsylvania State University, USA. He has recently authored "Corpus-Based Dictionaries for Sentiment Analysis of Specialized Vocabularies" (with Douglas R. Rice), to appear in *Political Science Research and Methods*, and "Troll-in-Chief? Affective Opinion Content and the Influence of the Chief Justice" (with Douglas R. Rice) in *The Chief Justice: Appointment and Influence* (edited by David Danelski and Artemus Ward, 2016).

INDEX

Page numbers with an appended italic f or t indicate a figure or table.